THE DAUGHTERS OF HENRY II
AND ELEANOR OF AQUITAINE

Histoires de famille. La parenté au Moyen Âge

Collection dirigée par Martin Aurell

16

THE DAUGHTERS OF HENRY II
AND ELEANOR OF AQUITAINE

Colette BOWIE

BREPOLS

D/2014/0095/19

ISBN 978-2-503-54971-2

Printed in the EU on acid-free paper.

Acknowledgements

This book could not have been written without the help and support of many people, to whom I owe my thanks. Firstly, thanks are due to Professor Martin Aurell, whose encouragement and support has made the publication of this work possible. Christophe Lebbe at Brepols has also been of invaluable help in guiding me through the editorial process of this publication. Thanks are also due to my thesis supervisor, Professor Matthew Strickland, whose help and advice throughout the duration of my doctoral study was inestimable, and whom I am honoured to call both mentor and friend. Dr Stephen Marritt, Dr Stuart Airlie and Professor Stephen Church have also all given me unfailing encouragement, for which I am truly grateful.

Professor Anne Duggan and Professor Graham Loud were both very kind in allowing me access to their pre-publication work, and I would also like to thank Jitske Jasperse for sharing with me some of her German source material on Matilda, and for providing me with a translation of her article on Matilda's patronage.

Special thanks go to Laura Crombie, Daniel Gerrard, and James Thomson, who have all helped me in innumerable ways, both academically and on a personal level, and their friendship and support have been, and are, beyond worth or words.

Finally, I could not have completed this work without the emotional and material support I have received from my family: many thanks, and much love, to my parents Tina, John, and Roy. Most importantly, I want to thank my daughter Molly, whose love and patience whilst I've been living in the twelfth century are proof that we can teach the Angevins a thing or two about intergenerational relationships. This book is dedicated to her, and to my late grandfather, Colin.

Table of Contents

Acknowledgements 5
Table of Contents 7
List of Maps, Tables and Illustrations 9
Introduction 13
PART I: *Carissima filia nostra*: Birth, Childhood and Formative Education 29
   Chapter 1. Birth and Childhood 33
      Formative Experiences and Emotional Ties 35
   Chapter 2. Medieval Emotions 43
      Eleanor of Aquitaine as Mother 50
   Chapter 3. Medieval Childhood 55
      An Angevin Education 57
PART II: *Satisfied as to her beauty*: Marriage Negotiations and Political
   Motivations 65
   Chapter 1. Matilda and Henry the Lion 69
   Chapter 2. Leonor and Alfonso VIII of Castile 71
   Chapter 3. Continuation of Angevin Marriage Policy:
      Richard and Berengaria of Navarre 77
   Chapter 4. Joanna and William II of Sicily 81
      Re-opening of Negotiations 89
      The Royal Ambassadors 91
   Chapter 5. Love and Marriage in the Twelfth Century 95
PART III: *Bodas muy grandes*: Marriage, Dowry and Dower Settlements 99
   Chapter 1. Matilda, Duchess of Saxony 103
   Chapter 2. Leonor, Queen of Castile 107
      The Marriages of Leonor's Daughters 112
      Leonor's Dowry 119
   Chapter 3. Competing Queens and Conflicting Claims 123
      Berengaria of Navarre 123
      Margaret of France 126
   Chapter 4. Joanna, Queen of Sicily 131
      Joanna's Dower Settlement 133
      The Crisis of 1189 and the Problem of Joanna's Dower 137
PART IV: *The sins of the father*: Endowment, Benefaction and the Dissemination
   of the Cult of Thomas Becket 141
   Chapter 1. From Denial to Appropriation 145
   Chapter 2. The Role of Henry's Daughters 151
      Joanna and Sicily 152
      Matilda and Saxony 157
      Leonor and Castile 165
      A Different Perspective: Margaret and Hungary 167
   Chapter 3. Royal Women and Saints' Cults 169

PART V: *For the health of our soul*: Dynastic Connections, Nomenclature and Commemoration.. 173

Chapter 1. Dynastic Nomenclature 177

Chapter 2. Fontevrault, Patronage and Family Ties 185

Chapter 3. Burial Patterns and Dynastic Mausolea 193

    Eleanor and Leonor, Fontevrault and Las Huelgas................... 194

Chapter 4. The Tombs at Fontevrault and Las Huelgas 201

    The Tombs at Fontevrault 201

    The Tombs at Las Huelgas... 204

Conclusion 209

Bibliography 213

Index of Names 237

Index of Places 245

List of Maps, Tables and Illustrations

Map of the Angevin 'Empire' 10
Genealogical Table.. 11
Eleanor's Journeys with Matilda, 1156-60.. 36
Eleanor's Journeys with Matilda and Leonor, 1160-65... 37
Eleanor's Journeys with Matilda, Leonor and Joanna, 1165-67.................................... 39
Eleanor's Journeys with Leonor and Joanna, 1167-74.. 40
'Dearest' Richard in Eleanor's Charters 45
'Dearest' Joanna in Eleanor's Charters 47
'Dearest' John in Eleanor's Charters 47
Genealogical Table Showing Claims to the County of Toulouse 72
Map of Leonor's Dowerlands 109
Map of Joanna's Dowerlands.. 135

London •

Dover •

Salisbury • • Winchester

Cherbourg •

Rouen •

Bayeux •

NORMANDY

Falaise •

Argentan •

Domfront •

ROYAL DOMAIN

BRITTANY

MAINE

• Le Mans

BLOIS

ANJOU

• Angers

Chinon

TOURAINE

Fontevrault +
Abbey

POITOU

Poitiers •

AQUITAINE

• Bordeaux

TOULOUSE

GASCONY

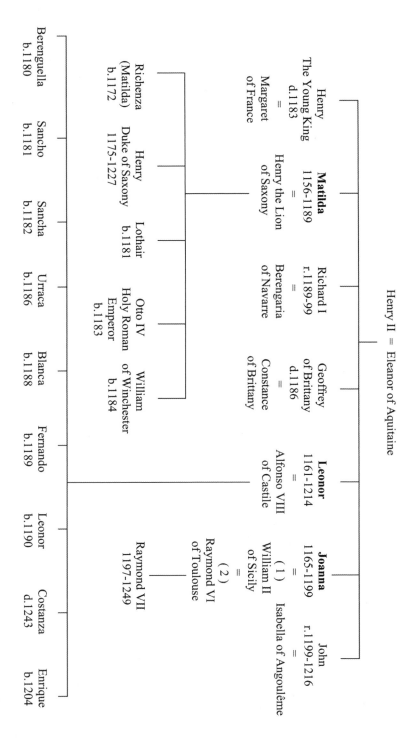

Introduction

'neglecting the queen often results in an incomplete picture of the court and the kingdom at large'.[1]

This study compares and contrasts the experiences of the three daughters of Henry II and Eleanor of Aquitaine. The exogamous marriages of Matilda, Leonor, and Joanna, which created dynastic links between the Angevin realm and Saxony, Castile, Sicily and Toulouse, served to further the political and diplomatic ambitions of their parents and spouses. It might be expected that their choices in religious patronage and dynastic commemoration would follow the customs and patterns of their marital families, yet the patronage and commemorative programmes of Matilda, Leonor, and Joanna provide evidence of possible influence from their natal family which suggests a coherent sense of family consciousness.

To discern why this might be the case, an examination of the childhoods of these women has been undertaken (Part I), to establish what emotional ties to their natal family may have been formed at this impressionable time. In Part II, the political motivations for their marriages are analysed, demonstrating the importance of these dynastic alliances, as well as highlighting cultural differences and similarities between the courts of Saxony, Castile, Sicily, and the Angevin realm. Dowry and dower portions (Part III) are important indicators of the power and strength of both their natal and marital families, and give an idea of the access to economic resources which could provide financial means for patronage. Having established possible emotional ties to their natal family, and the actual material resources at their disposal, the book moves on to an examination of the patronage and dynastic commemorations of Matilda, Leonor and Joanna (Parts IV-V), in order to discern patterns or parallels. Their possible involvement in the burgeoning cult of Thomas Becket, their patronage of Fontevrault Abbey, the names they gave to their children, and finally the ways in which they and their immediate families were buried, suggest that all three women were, to varying degrees, able to transplant Angevin family customs to their marital lands. The resulting study, the first of its kind to consider these women in an intergenerational dynastic context, advances the hypothesis that there may have been stronger emotional ties within the Angevin family than has previously been allowed for.

Historiographical Trends and Conceptual Themes

The study of queenship as an office first became a serious area of research for historians in the decades following the growth of feminism in the 1960s. The trend initially focused on individual case-studies of prominent women, rather than on the office of queenship itself. The growth of gender politics and gender studies in the 1970s led to a wider recognition of the place of women within historical narratives, although emphasis remained on prominent women in Western society.[2] Gradually, new interpretations of women's history emerged, and

---

[1] Lois Huneycutt, 'Images of Queenship in the High Middle Ages', *Haskins Society Journal*, 1 (1989), 61.

[2] For example, W.W. Kibler's edited volume *Eleanor of Aquitaine, Patron and Politician* (University of Texas Press, 1976). Amy Kelly's *Eleanor of Aquitaine and the Four Kings*, first published in 1952, was reissued in 1978 by Harvard University Press.

the traditional views of medieval women as little more than insignificant and submissive pawns in a male-oriented political structure began to be seriously challenged.[3] The study of women took a new direction in the 1980s, with a shift in focus from royal and aristocratic women to a more general, sociological approach, reflected in studies such as *Women in Frankish Society, The Fourth Estate*, and *Women in Medieval Life*.[4] The 1990s, however, saw a host of re-evaluations of the role of royal women in medieval society, with the appearance of edited volumes such as *Women and Sovereignty, Medieval Queenship*, and *Queens and Queenship in Medieval Europe*.[5] The articles in these volumes focus specifically on the roles and functions, ideologies and representations, and rituals of queenship, themes which will be addressed in more detail below.

Most recently, historiographical trends have seen the focus shift away from theoretical interpretations of queenship and back to individual case-studies, such as the recent biographies of Eleanor of Aquitaine by Jean Flori and Ralph Turner, and Lois Honeycutt's work on Matilda of Scotland.[6] Other recent research on medieval women has tended to focus on either one specific place – such as *Queenship and Political Power in Medieval and Early Modern Spain* – or on one specific theme, as with *Gender in the Early Medieval World*.[7] Stacy Klein's *Ruling Women* combines both specific theme and place, as does Erin Jordan's *Women, Power and Religious Patronage in the Middle Ages*, which focuses on the thirteenth-century countesses of Flanders and Hainault.[8]

Where my research differs from and adds to the current historiography on queenship is in its focus on intergenerational relationships, and how these could and did inform the choices made by the daughters of Henry II and Eleanor of Aquitaine in terms of patronage and dynastic commemoration. The traditional emphasis on life-cycles (a construct not applied to men), and the roles and functions of royal and aristocratic women is thereby supplemented and enhanced with a more nuanced methodology, which applies theories concerning the history of childhood and the history of *mentalités* to the actual experiences of Henry and Eleanor's daughters. The result is a more coherent picture of these women both as individuals in their own right, and as individuals within a family construct.

---

[3] Such as Pauline Stafford, *Queens, Concubines and Dowagers: The King's Wife in the Early Middle Ages* (Batsford, 1983; repr. Leicester University Press, 1998), which examines the many roles of queens from the sixth to eleventh centuries.

[4] Suzanne Fonay Wemple, *Women in Frankish Society: Marriage and the Cloister, 500-900* (University of Pennsylvania Press, 1981); Shulamith Shahar, *The Fourth Estate: A History of Women in the Middle Ages* (Methuen, London, 1983); Margaret Wade Labarge, *Women in Medieval Life* (Penguin, London, 1986). More recently, Lisa Bitel has taken a similar approach in her *Women in Early Medieval Europe, 400-1000* (CUP, 2002), which, despite a chapter devoted to 'famous women before and after 1000', is largely concerned with the history of women from the lower strata of society.

[5] Louise Fradenburg (ed.), *Women and Sovereignty* (Edinburgh University Press, 1992); John Carmi Parsons (ed.), *Medieval Queenship* (Sutton Publishing, Gloucs., 1993); Anne Duggan (ed.), *Queens and Queenship in Medieval Europe* (Boydell, Woodbridge, 1997).

[6] Jean Flori, *Eleanor of Aquitaine: Queen and Rebel*, trans. Olive Casse (Edinburgh University Press, 2007); Ralph Turner, *Eleanor of Aquitaine* (Yale University Press, 2009); Lois Huneycutt, *Matilda of Scotland: A Study in Medieval Queenship* (Boydell, Woodbridge, 2003).

[7] Theresa Earenfight (ed.), *Queenship and Political Power in Medieval and Early Modern Spain* (Ashgate, Aldershot, 2005); Leslie Brubaker and Julia M.H. Smith (eds.), *Gender in the Early Medieval World, East and West, 300-900* (CUP, 2005).

[8] Stacy Klein, *Ruling Women: Queenship and Gender in Anglo-Saxon Literature* (2006); Erin Jordan, *Women, Power and Religious Patronage in the Middle Ages* (Palgrave MacMillan, New York, 2006).

Whilst Eleanor of Aquitaine herself deservedly continues to be the subject of much scholarship, the role of her daughters not only in forging dynastic marriages, but as royal women and patrons in their own right has been until now comparatively neglected.[9] Matilda, the eldest daughter of Henry and Eleanor, has attracted the interest of German scholars, but has been largely overlooked by English historians.[10] Miriam Shadis and Rose Walker have contributed various recent articles about Henry and Eleanor's second daughter, Leonor, but these have focused largely on Leonor's foundation of the abbey of Las Huelgas, and on the patronage of Leonor's own daughters.[11] In contrast, the short entry in the *Dictionary of National Biography* remains the sole work specifically dedicated to the life of Henry and Eleanor's youngest daughter, Joanna.[12] None of these works, however, consider the importance of intergenerational relationships. This study demonstrates that the relationships these women forged with their natal family as children significantly impacted on their later choices as adults, particularly in terms of patronage and dynastic commemoration.

As the daughters of Henry II and Eleanor of Aquitaine married into the dynastic houses of Castile, Sicily, Saxony and Toulouse, this book has a broad geographical range, examining twelfth-century queenship in a variety of European contexts as well as considering the cross-cultural relationships that such dynastic alliances generated. In addition to the themes of patronage and commemoration, this study explores the multi-faceted roles of royal and aristocratic women alongside the network of relationships within the Angevin family, which casts important light on the wider subjects of the royal and aristocratic medieval family and the history of emotions.

Methodology and Sources

For the early years of Henry and Eleanor's daughters, the Pipe Rolls of Henry II proved to be an invaluable resource.[13] From these, I was able to piece together the time these women spent travelling with their parents during their early childhood, as well as to find details of Matilda's and Joanna's journeys to their new kingdoms, the personnel who accompanied them, and the material gifts they brought with them as dowry. There is no record in the Pipe Rolls of Leonor's journey to Castile, nor any reference to her dowry, because the Rolls refer only to

---

[9] Recent volumes on Eleanor include John Carmi Parsons and Bonnie Wheeler (eds.), *Eleanor of Aquitaine, Lord and Lady* (Palgrave MacMillan, Basingstoke, 2002); Martin Aurell (ed.), *Aliénor d'Aquitaine* (Nantes, 2004); Marcus Bull and Catherine Léglu (eds.), *The World of Eleanor of Aquitaine: Literature and Society in Southern France between the Eleventh and Thirteenth Centuries* (Boydell, Woodbridge, 2005).

[10] Matilda's husband, Henry the Lion, continues to attract German scholars, as a quick glance at recent contributions on Amazon booklists shows. Works on Matilda herself tend to focus on her patronage, such as Wilhelm Kellerman, 'Bertran de Born und Herzogin Mathilde von Sachsen', *Etudes de Civilisation Médiévale* (1974), 447-60, and more recently, Jitske Jasperse, 'Het Cultureele patronaat van Mathilde Plantagenet (1156-1189)', in *Millenium: Tijdschrift voor Middeleeuwse Studies*, 21:2 (2007), 89-103. My thanks to Jitske Jasperse for providing me with an English translation of this article.

[11] See for example Rose Walker, 'Leonor of England, Plantagenet Queen of King Alfonso VIII of Castile, and her Foundation of the Cistercian Abbey of Las Huelgas. In Imitation of Fontevrault?', *Journal of Medieval History*, 31:4 (2005), 346-68; Miriam Shadis, 'Piety, Politics, and Power: The Patronage of Leonor of England and her Daughters Berengaria of Leon and Blanche of Castile', in June Hall McCash (ed.), *The Cultural Patronage of Medieval Women* (University of Georgia Press, 1996), 202-27. For more on Leonor and Las Huelgas, see Part V.

[12] D.S.H. Abulafia, 'Joanna [Joan, Joanna of England], countess of Toulouse (1165-1199), queen of Sicily, consort of William II', *Oxford Dictionary of National Biography* (online resource; hereafter *DNB*).

[13] *The Pipe Rolls of Henry II* (38 Vols., Pipe Roll Society, 1884-1925; hereafter PR Hen II).

payments made to or by the English exchequer, and Leonor was resident at that time in France, travelling overland from Bordeaux to her new kingdom of Castile. The Rolls do, however, provide details of gifts subsequently sent to Leonor in Castile from her father's court, as well as supplying valuable information for the period which Matilda and Henry the Lion spent in exile in England.

Further information on these women is supplied by contemporary chronicles, although these provide variable amounts of detail. There are ample sources for the reign of Alfonso VIII of Castile. The most detailed, and perhaps the best known, is the *Primera Crónica General*.[14] Lucas de Tuy's *Crónica de España*, written at the request of Leonor's daughter Berenguella, and the anonymous *Crónica Latina* have also been utilised here.[15] In contrast, there are very few chronicles covering the reign of Henry the Lion in Saxony. Helmold of Bosau's *Cronica Slavorum* covers the early years of his rule until 1172;[16] the continuation by Arnold of Lübeck goes up to 1209.[17] Matilda, however, is barely mentioned in either of these works. Helmold refers to the expensive dowry Matilda brought to Henry the Lion at her marriage, but declines to mention her by name, and she does not appear anywhere else in his chronicle.[18] Arnold, on the other hand, stresses her piety, although this eulogistic description appears in the chronicle only after Matilda's death in 1189.[19]

Chronicles for the reign of William II of Sicily are similarly in short supply. Whilst there are a wealth of chronicles available for the reigns of his predecessors, such as Falcandus' *History of the Tyrants of Sicily*,[20] only one chronicle exists which relates to Sicily in the later twelfth century. Romuald of Salerno's chronicle is detailed and generally trustworthy, although he has little to say with regard to Joanna, and nothing at all beyond her marriage and coronation.[21] The majority of contemporary chronicle accounts utilised here have therefore come from the Angevin realm. Roger of Howden, ever the most detailed of the Angevin chroniclers, provides various details on the daughters of Henry and Eleanor, largely pertaining to their marriages, in his *Gesta* and later *Chronica*.[22] Robert of Torigni, abbot of Mont-Saint-Michel, who was a personal friend of the Angevin dynasty and who acted as sponsor at Leonor's baptism, offers supplementary information, often giving details of the date and place of birth

---

[14] *Primera Crónica de España*, ed. Ramón Menéndez Pidal (Nueva Biblioteca de Autores Españoles, Vol. 5, Madrid, 1906; hereafter *PCG*).

[15] Lucas de Tuy, *Crónica de España*, ed. Julio Puyol (Real Academia de la Historia, Madrid, 1926); *Crónica Latina de los Reyes de Castilla*, ed. Luis Charlo Brea (Madrid, 1999).

[16] Helmold of Bosau, *Cronica Slavorum*, ed. B. Schmeidler (*Monumenta Germaniae Historica SS rer. Germ*, 3rd edn., 1937; hereafter *MGH*); Eng. trans: *The Chronicle of the Slavs by Hermold, priest of Bosau*, ed. and trans. F.J. Tschan (New York, 1935).

[17] Arnold of Lübeck, *Cronica Slavorum*, ed. M. Lappenberg (*MGH SS rer. Germ.*, 1868).

[18] Helmold of Bosau, *Chronica Slavorum* (*MGH SS*, 32, Hanover, 1937), 209; see also Part II, Chapter 1.

[19] Arnold von Lübeck. *Chronica Slavorum* (*MGH SS*, 14, Hanover, 1868), 11-12; see also Part IV, Chapter 2.

[20] Hugo Falcandus, *The History of the Tyrants of Sicily*, ed. and trans. G.A. Loud and T. Wiedemann (Manchester University Press, 1998).

[21] Romuald of Salerno, *Chronicon*, ed. L.A. Muratori, in *Rerum Italicarum Scriptores, Raccolta degli Storici Italiani dal cinquecento al millecinquecento*, VII.1 (Città di Castello, 1725).

[22] Roger of Howden, *Gesta Regis Henrici Secundi Benedicti Abbatis. The Chronicle of the Reigns of Henry II & Richard I AD 1169-1192; Known Commonly Under the Name of Benedict of Peterborough*, ed. William Stubbs, 2 Vols., in *Chronicles and Memorials of Great Britain and Ireland During the Middle Ages* (Rolls Series, 49, London, 1867); *Chronica Magistri Rogeri de Houedene*, ed. William Stubbs, 4 Vols., in *Chronicles and Memorials of Great Britain and Ireland During the Middle Ages* (Rolls Series, 51, London, 1868-71).

of Henry and Eleanor's children.[23] In the main, however, collating information on these women has been a patchy process. It has been necessary to identify all references in chronicles pertaining to them, however brief, sparse, or incomplete, in order to piece them together to make as complete a picture as possible. At times, there was no extant primary source evidence to support my arguments, and this is reflected in footnotes which cite recent scholarship rather than chronicles, charters, and so forth.

No personal letters drafted by any of Henry and Eleanor's daughters survive, and the authorship and authenticity of those letters purporting to be written to Pope Celestine by Eleanor of Aquitaine have been questioned.[24] One letter which does survive, however, is that written to Blanca of France by her sister, Berenguella of León.[25] The chance survival of this letter suggests that there may have been other correspondence between the female descendants of the Angevin dynasty which have not survived the passage of time.

In terms of diplomatics, I have been fortunate in being able to access the edition of the charters of Alfonso VIII of Castile, published in 1960 by Julio González.[26] Statistical analysis of this body of diplomatic reveals that Leonor appears on approximately 88% of her husband's charters, suggesting that Castilian queens, in contrast to those of other western European kingdoms, routinely played a part in governmental affairs. By way of contrast, Matilda appears on only two charters issued by Henry the Lion of Saxony, which have been edited and published by Karl Jordan, and both of these concern donations to religious houses.[27] Unfortunately, the survival rate of diplomatics from twelfth-century Sicily is poor. Only a handful of William II's charters survive, the majority of which relate to the abbey-church of Monreale.[28] Whilst it is difficult to attempt statistical analyses on the basis of such a small sample, it is safe to assume that, as Joanna appears on none of William's extant charters, Sicilian queens, unlike their counterparts in Castile, did not routinely appear on official royal documents.

Ideology and Representation

Issues such as succession politics, dynasticism, perceived gender limitations, clerical misogyny, and the influence of the cult of the Virgin appear frequently in works on medieval royal and aristocratic women. These common themes can be categorised into three main sections: ideologies and representations of queenship in different eras and in different genres; the roles and functions expected of and available to queens and other royal women and how these might be manipulated; and the ritual elements of queenship, from marriage and coronation to burial and *memoria*. The following discussion will address each of these themes, in order to establish how and where they are applicable to Henry and Eleanor's daughters.

---

[23] Robert of Torigni, *Chronica de Robertus de Torigneio: The Chronicle of Robert of Torigny, Abbot of the Monastery of St. Michael-in-peril-of-the-sea*, in *Chronicles of the Reigns of Stephen, Henry II, and Richard I*, ed. Richard Howlett, 4 Vols., in *Chronicles and Memorials of Great Britain and Ireland During the Middle Ages* (Rolls Series, 82.4, London, 1889).

[24] See Part I, Chapter 3.

[25] See Part III, Chapter 2.

[26] Julio González, *El Reino de Castilla en la Epoca de Alfonso VIII* (3 Vols., Madrid, 1960). I have used this edition of Alfonso's charters in preference to José Manuel Lizoain Garrido's edition contained in *Documentacion del Monasterio de Las Huelgas de Burgos* (Burgos, 1985).

[27] *Die Urkunden Heinrichs des Löwen, Herzogs von Sachsen und Bayern*, ed. K. Jordan (*MGH*, 1941-9; repr. 1957-60); see also Part IV, Chapter 2.

[28] See Millunzi, G., 'Il tesoro, la biblioteca ed il tabulario della Chiesa di Santa Maria Nuova in Monreale', in *Archivio Storico Siciliano*, 28 (1903), 249-459. I am grateful to Professor Graham Loud for allowing me to make use of his forthcoming *Calendar of Extant Charters of William II* prior to publication.

Ideologies and representations of queens changed and evolved over different eras and in different genres. Patristic writings, biblical precedents, liturgies, chronicles, charters, letters, commissioned works, *vitae*, female hagiography, Marian ideology, as well as the lives of previous queens, both fictional and historical – all offered models either to aspire to or avoid. The roles and functions of queens were thereby outlined and encoded. The different life stages of daughter, wife, mother and widow impacted on these roles and functions, leading to sub-categories of models and representations. Ideas about gender, stereotypes, and clerical misogyny all had some bearing on expectations of how queens should conduct themselves, and these ideas influenced not only those propounding them, but also women themselves.

Mary, the Virgin Mother of Christ, was by far the most popular and widely used model for queenship in the West from at least the twelfth century onwards.[29] Visual representations of the Virgin from this time always depicted her regally, whether or not she was crowned, and the emphasis was always on her position as the mother of a great king, thereby stressing the primary function of secular queens.[30] The ability of secular queens to produce a son and heir was paramount, and churchmen, such as Bernard of Clairvaux, repeatedly stressed that the Virgin's regality stemmed from her son.[31] As will be seen in Part III, Chapter 2, the fecundity of Leonor, which matched that of her mother Eleanor, cemented both her position and her posthumous reputation as queen of Castile, and provided her with the opportunity to play an instrumental role in dynastic politics through arranging the marriages of her daughters. Conversely, Joanna's failure to provide William of Sicily with an heir led to a succession crisis and civil unrest in the kingdom.

The Virgin is almost always depicted with the Christ-child, indicating that she owes her position as queen to him: the Virgin is thus queen only by virtue of her ultimate submission and obedience to a higher (male) power. Her intercessory role as *Mater Misericordiae* added symbolism and provided a further parallel to that of secular queens, as did her role as patron and *Mater Ecclesiae*, thereby firmly establishing the link between queenship and mercy, piety, and patronage.[32] As the devoutly pious ideal of bride, mother, queen and intercessor, the Virgin exemplified the ideal earthly queen, providing a model of impossible, unattainable perfection.[33]

---

[29] For Marian ideology and queenship, see Mary Stroll, 'Maria *Regina*: Papal Symbol', in *Queens and Queenship*, 173-203; Diana Webb, 'Queen and Patron', in *ibid.*, 205-21; Rosemary Muir Wright, 'The Virgin in the Sun and in the Tree', in *Women and Sovereignty*, 36-59. Devotion to the Virgin as an individual began in the fifth century, from which time churches dedicated to her, versions of her life, and interest in Marian relics first appear. She is first represented as a queen at this time, as evidenced in mosaic work at Santa Maria Maggiore in Rome, the first Roman church dedicated to the Virgin, where she appears in imperial Byzantine dress. For an illustration of this, see Stroll, 'Maria *Regina*', 190. Veneration of the Virgin had decreased in the Carolingian era, but the reform papacy of the twelfth century revived the model of the Virgin as "*imperatrix et regina, regina mundi, regina coeli et terra*", Stroll, 'Maria *Regina*', 177-8.

[30] For further images of the Virgin in art, see Stroll, 'Maria *Regina*', 191, 202.

[31] See Stroll, 'Maria *Regina*', 178-9, 219-20. In a letter to Queen Melisende of Jerusalem, Bernard pronounced that "It is not normal for a woman to wield *potestas*; if, by lineage...she is endowed with power, it falls to the man to whom she has been entrusted to exercise it", although he does concede the possibility of female rule in the absence of a suitable, legitimate male, Jordan, *Women, Power and Religious Patronage*, 33. For more on queenship in the Latin kingdom of Jerusalem, see Deborah Gerish, 'Holy War, Royal Wives, and Equivocation in Twelfth-Century Jerusalem', in Niall Christie & Maya Yazigi (eds.), *Noble Ideals and Bloody Realities: Warfare in the Middle Ages* (History of Warfare, 37, 2006), 119-44; Bernard Hamilton, 'Women in the Crusader States: the Queens of Jerusalem 1100-90', in Derek Baker (ed.), *Medieval Women* (Blackwell, Oxford, 1978), 143-74.

[32] Much as Christ's role as Judge paralleled the judicial function of secular kings.

[33] Anne Duggan has highlighted the ambiguous qualities of the Virgin, both regal and obedient, 'a sublime example of the paradox of Christian abnegation: 'he who humbles himself shall be exalted' (Lk 14:11)', 'Introduction', in *Queens*

It was not just churchmen, however, who were able to use and manipulate Marian ideology for their own purposes. Leonor's daughter, Blanca of Castile, was extolled as an excellent role model, most likely on account of her saintly son, Louis IX. A thirteenth-century French Bible miniature depicts Blanca in Marian attitude, enthroned and crowned at the side of her son, with her hands in the advocate position.[34] Miriam Shadis has suggested that both Leonor and her daughters appropriated the ideal of the Virgin for their own use, and in so doing, equated themselves with Mary as queen and mother, noting that the official names of Las Huelgas in Burgos and of Blanca's foundation of Maubisson (Santa Maria Regalis and Notre Dame la Royale respectively) both refer to the Virgin.[35] This assessment, however, fails to take into account that both of these houses belonged to the Cistercian order, which always dedicated its houses to the Virgin.

Whilst the cult of the Virgin presented both positive and negative images for queens, and indeed for all women, it was not the only available model of queenship. Secular literature, from *chansons de geste* to troubadour poetry and Arthurian romance, contains various images of women, including both fictional and historical queens,[36] and as Karen Pratt has noted, poetry and literature provide insights 'not only into contemporary reality but also into the ideologies of authors and their publics'.[37] Previous queens of both the ancient world and of more contemporary times were sometimes employed as models either to aspire to or avoid, and there are also a number of extant *vitae* of exemplary queens, although these are largely hagiographical, which were often commissioned either by the woman in question or by her biological or political successors.[38]

Similarly, *Lives* of female saints were often propounded as models of the excellence of female piety, although as Elisabeth van Houts has noted, the emphasis on suffering in accounts of female sanctity serve to underline 'the powerlessness of contemporary women in a male world of chivalry', and the 'absence of sexual violence in the lives of male saints of the same period

---

and Queenship, xvi. However, the very ambiguity of the Virgin's position makes it possible to concentrate on either the positive or the negative aspects, and Duggan rightly warns against concentrating on the negative aspects alone.

[34] For an image of this, see Stroll, 'Maria *Regina*', 203.

[35] Shadis, 'Piety, Politics, and Power', 214-5. See also Part V, Chapter 4.

[36] For more on this theme, see Karen Pratt, 'The Image of the Queen in Old French Literature', in *Queens and Queenship*, 235-59; Joan Ferrante, 'Public Postures and Private Maneuvers : Roles Medieval Women Play', in Mary Erler and Maryanne Kowaleski (eds.), *Women and Power in the Middle Ages* (University of Georgia Press, 1988), 213-29. The Provençal troubadour Marcabru, whilst not representative of all troubadour poets, described women as "impassioned whores" who "know how to cheat and lie", Carolly Erickson, *The Medieval Vision* (OUP, 1976), 200. Elisabeth van Houts has pointed out that women had no control over the content of chivalric literature and "courtly love" romances, which depict 'the male world of violence', even when the women were themselves the patrons of such works, 'The State of Research: Women in Medieval History and Literature', in E.M.C van Houts, *History and Family Traditions in England and the Continent, 1000-1200* (Ashgate Variorum, Aldershot, 1999; first published in *Journal of Medieval History*, 20 (1994).), 279-80. For more on the literary patronage of the Angevins, see Part I.

[37] Pratt, 'Image of the Queen', 235, although she notes that, like the qualities of the Virgin, literary representations of queens are frequently ambiguous. It is worth noting here Joanna and Leonor's contemporary Marie de France, whose *lais* present both positive and negative images of women, *French Medieval Romances from the Lays of Marie de France*, trans. Eugene Mason (J.M. Dent & Sons, London and Toronto, 1911; repr. 1932).

[38] For example, Henry I's queen Edith-Matilda commissioned the *vita* of her mother, St. Margaret, in c. 1104-7, although Lois Huneycutt believes this text to be 'too worldly and personal to be pure hagiography', viewing it as more of a "mirror" for Edith-Matilda, 'The Idea of a Perfect Princess: The *Life of St Margaret* in the Reign of Matilda II (1100-1118)', *Anglo-Norman Studies*, XII (1989), 81-97, at 88. Scott Waugh has argued that all courtly literature served as "mirrors" for both men and women, concluding that ultimately, the ideal king (or queen) should moderate and control their emotions, 'Histoire, hagiographie et le souverain idéal à la cour des Plantegenêts', in Martin Aurell and Noël-Yves Tonnerre (eds.), *Plantagenêts et Capetiens: Confrontations et Héritages* (Brepols, Belgium, 2006), 429-46.

[from the twelfth century onwards] underlines this point'.[39] Where these accounts are anonymous, however, the possibility exists that the author was female, especially when the text is connected to a particular convent, and this consequently affects the portrayal of the protagonist.[40] Biblical women, too, offered both positive and negative examples, with Leah, Rebecca, Rachel and Sarah held up as examples of fertility, and Esther and Judith as models of charity. These women were regularly referred to in the ritual formulae of queenly coronations, serving to emphasise what the expected primary functions of the queen were. Jezebel, 'that wickedest of Wicked Queens', is perhaps the most-cited biblical example of a bad woman, and was a name frequently applied to queens who overstepped socially constructed gender limitations.[41]

The image of the Virgin as the ideal model for all women, and especially for queens, was, however, most often presented as the stark contrast to its polar alternative – the temptress Eve, the first (female) sinner, and epitome of woman's weakness and capacity to inspire lust. As all women, 'even those destined eventually to be successful royal consorts' were "daughters of Eve", they needed to be constrained and restrained from being led by sexual impulses.[42] The Mary-Eve dichotomy was especially apparent in the writings of the early Church Fathers, whose opinions of women largely echoed the thoughts of Tertullian, and who heavily influenced later medieval clerical writings on women.[43] Eleanor of Aquitaine in particular, twice-married, heiress to a vast and extremely wealthy duchy, and highly politically active throughout her long life, was the subject of much salacious gossip and rumour in the works of contemporary clerics, although her daughters, in comparison, do not seem to have been deemed "guilty by association", and references to them in chronicle accounts range from neutral comments to effusive praise.[44]

Carolly Erickson is one of a number of historians who have emphasised the role of the early Christian Fathers in influencing medieval thoughts on women, although Elisabeth van Houts has noted that misogyny in medieval texts was not as widespread as is commonly supposed.[45] Nevertheless, misogynistic texts such as works by the early Church Fathers were the most copied throughout the Middle Ages, being thought, on the grounds of age and authorship, to be the most authoritative, leading to a self-perpetuating misogynistic tradition of clerical views on women.[46] Yet whilst it is without doubt true that women in general were

---

[39] Van Houts, 'State of Research', 281.

[40] *Ibid.*, 286; and for more on the theme of female authorship, van Houts, 'Women and the writing of history in the early Middle Ages: the case of Abbess Matilda of Essen and Aethelweard', in *History and Family Traditions* (first published in *Early Medieval Europe*, 1 (1992), 53-68, where she notes that the more space devoted to women in anonymous works, the greater the chance the author was female, 53.

[41] *Cf.* Janet Nelson, 'Queens as Jezebels: The Careers of Brunhild and Balthild in Merovingian History', in Lester K. Little and Barbara H. Rosenwein (eds), *Debating the Middle Ages: Issues and Readings* (Blackwell, Oxford, 1998), 219-53, with citation at 241; Nicholas Vincent, 'Isabella of Angoulême: John's Jezebel', in Stephen Church (ed.), *King John: New Interpretations* (Boydell, Woodbridge, 1999), 165-219.

[42] Pratt, 'Image of the Queen', 236. She notes further that female desire was viewed as 'far more politically and socially disruptive than male desire', 'Image of the Queen', 251.

[43] Walter Map, writing under the classically-inspired pseudonym Valerius, warned in the twelfth century that "no matter what they intend, with a woman the result is always the same. When she wants to do harm – and that is nearly always the case – she never fails. If by chance she should want to do good, she still succeeds in doing harm...Fear them all.", Erickson, *Medieval Vision*, 198-9.

[44] Even Richard of Devizes, whose chronicle is in the main laudatory of Eleanor, makes an oblique reference to her supposed affair with her uncle, Raymond of Antioch, *Gestis Ricardi*, 402.

[45] Van Houts, 'State of Research', 277-92.

[46] *Ibid.*, 282. For more on clerical misogyny, see the collected articles in Christiane Klapisch-Zuber (ed.), *A History of Women in the West: II. Silences of the Middle Ages* (Harvard University Press, 1992).

viewed as naturally inferior to men, the special status of a queen must fall beyond these paradigms. A queen's exaltation by virtue of the rituals of coronation and / or consecration placed her above ordinary women, and indeed, above ordinary men, yet she was still subject to her husband, the king. This subjection was on account of her biological sex, but how far can socially-constructed gender limitations be applied to queens?

Women may have been deemed to be suspect, or at any rate inferior, in the minds of most medieval clerics, but as Julia Smith reminds us, 'gender is in essence about power relationships and the language which legitimates or denies their existence'.[47] When medieval authors used gendered stereotypes, such texts were largely 'generated by those centres which had most at stake in the maintenance of hierarchies of power, whether sacred or secular'.[48] But how did perceived gender differences affect or influence politics, religion, culture and society in the twelfth and early thirteenth centuries? Where were gender differences most often applied? It should be noted that medieval views on gender, and especially on women, were neither uniform nor static. Nevertheless, gender constraints were in the main placed on positions of power within political and religious structures, and these limitations 'rested on the presumption that neither political nor sacred power was to be wielded by women'.[49] We should not over-rely on gendered clerical discourses for a general view of medieval thoughts on women. And yet, often these are all we have to go on, and some women, such as the highly educated Hildegard of Bingen, appear at least outwardly to have accepted and subscribed to their social subordination as the natural order of things.[50] A queen's elevated social position, however, enabled her to transcend these boundaries to a far greater degree than would have been possible for ordinary laywomen, indicating that status plays as important a role here as gender. Queens and other royal and aristocratic women are visibly active in politics, arts and culture, and their participation in patronage, in transmitting cultural values, and in dynastic commemoration – all spheres of activity that were both acceptable for and expected of queens, and in which Matilda, Leonor and Joanna all participated – granted them access to the so-called "public sphere".

Roles and Functions

The roles and functions of medieval queens were outlined in treatises and, by the ninth century, formally set down in liturgy, with ideological precedents taken from scripture and influenced by patristic writings.[51] A queen should be beautiful but modest, dignified but humble, faithful and chaste, prudent, charitable, pious, and above all, obedient. These qualities, which paralleled those of the Virgin, are frequently found as *topoi* in contemporary writings about queens, both fictional and historical, although as will be seen in Part III, Chapter 2,

---

[47] Smith, 'Introduction: gendering an early medieval world', in *Gender in the Early Medieval West*, 7.

[48] *Ibid.*, 18.

[49] *Ibid.*, 17.

[50] Hildegard, defining a woman's inferior role with her usual eloquence, wrote in the twelfth century that "woman is weak, and looks to man that she may gain strength from him, as the moon receives its strength from the sun; wherefore is she subject to the man, and ought always to be prepared to serve him", Erickson, *Medieval Vision*, 211. Ferrante, however, points out that female authors such as Hildegard manipulated perceived gender limitations in order to 'make it work for them', 'Public Postures', 227.

[51] In the ninth century, Adelard of Corbie, Hincmar of Reims and Sedulius Scottus all outlined the roles and functions of the ideal queen in treatises. See Janet Nelson, 'Early Medieval Rites of Queen-Making and the Shaping of Medieval Queenship', in *Queens and Queenship*, 304-5; Huneycutt, 'Images of Queenship', 69; Pratt, 'Image of the Queen', 240-1.

effusive praise of queens was not always mere *topoi*. A queen was also consort, mother, intercessor, and patron, and was viewed differently – and was expected to act accordingly – at
differing stages of her life: as daughter, wife, mother and widow. Yet political opportunities
were available to queens. In the first place, they were transmitters of culture, and of family
reputation. Their position within the family gave them an important dynastic role to play, in
their function of providing heirs, and as educators and marriage-brokers for their children.
Moreover, their roles as patrons and commemorators afforded them an avenue to potentially
great power and influence, and whilst intercession served to highlight the queen's inherently
subordinate role, it was an acceptable and very public means to power and influence that could
be – and often was – manipulated and exploited by a clever and ambitious queen.

The practice of royal exogamy has been the focus of much historiography on medieval
women. Whilst some historians have pointed to this practice as further evidence of the marginalisation of royal and noble women,[52] more recent scholarship has noted that it in fact
afforded women opportunities for their own advancement, as disseminators of culture and of
the traditions and reputation of their natal families.[53] As Anne Duggan points out, a "foreign
queen in a foreign land' may in some circumstances have suffered suspicion and isolation, but
by her very presence she attested the international standing of the family into which she
married'.[54] As will be demonstrated in Part II, the prestige of a woman's adopted family could
be further enhanced by association with her natal family, or vice versa. Evidence of continued
links to a royal woman's natal family is often found on their tombs, and on those of their
husbands and descendants, such as are found on the tombs of Eleanor of Castile and Raymond VII of Toulouse.[55] As will be shown in Part V, commissioning tombs was one way to
promote the dignity and prestige of their lineage; another was the commissioning of *vitae* and
chronicles, such as Queen Edith-Matilda's commissioning of the *Life of St Margaret* and William of Malmesbury's *Gesta Regum*, and Berenguela of Castile's commissioning of Lucas de
Tuy's *Crónica de España*.[56]

Whilst royal and aristocratic women had little or no say over their own matrimonial destinies, they were in the best position to determine matches for their own daughters, having
had personal experience in these matters. As demonstrated in Parts II and III, both Eleanor
of Aquitaine and her daughter Leonor were highly involved in negotiating the marriages of
their daughters. This leads to the theory that queens may have felt some kind of shared queenly
identity; it also raises the question of degrees of emotional attachment within medieval royal
and aristocratic families. Was there such a thing as a "group identity" amongst queens? Was

---

[52] Such as Georges Duby, *Love and Marriage in the Middle Ages*, trans. Jane Dunnett (Polity Press, Cambridge,
1994); *Medieval Marriage: Two Models from Twelfth-Century France*, trans. Elborg Forster (John Hopkins
University Press, Baltimore, 1978); David Herlihy, *Medieval Households* (Harvard University Press, 1985).

[53] See for example Janet Nelson, 'Women at the Court of Charlemagne: A Case of Monstrous Regiment?', in
Medieval Queenship, 43-61; John Carmi Parsons, 'Mothers, Daughters, Marriage, Power: Some Plantagenet
Evidence, 1100-1500', in *ibid.*, 63-78; John Gillingham, 'Love, Marriage and Politics in the Twelfth Century', in
Forum for Modern Language Studies, 25 (1989), 292-303. Walter Pohl has noted the possibility that early Lombard
queens were responsible for the Lombard origin myth, and suggests that the Lombard queen Theodelinda may have
commissioned the first known history of the Lombards, the now-lost *Historiola* of Secundus of Trento, 'Gender and
ethnicity in the early Middle Ages', in *Gender in the Early Medieval West*, 36-40.

[54] Duggan, 'Introduction', xix.

[55] For a full discussion of Eleanor's tomb, see John Carmi Parsons, 'Never was a body buried in England with such
solemnity and honour': The Burials and Posthumous Commemorations of English Queens to 1500', in *Queens and
Queenship*, 317-37. For the tomb of Raymond VII, see Part V, Chapters 3 and 4.

[56] For more on this, see Part III, Chapter 2.

queenly identity shaped by past queens, and if so, did mothers form part of this group? The argument advanced in this study is that the daughters of Henry II and Eleanor of Aquitaine did indeed feel some kind of shared queenly identity, and that this identity was in no small part formed through an emotional attachment to their mother. All queens had similar experiences which they held in common: most were crowned and some were anointed, and almost all were of the highest nobility, destined at birth for politically important marriages and educated accordingly to enable them to be both worthy of the dynastic role they were to play, and able to educate their own children in like manner.[57]

The role of consort and mother made female royalty very different from their male counterparts, whose duty was to rule directly. The traditional queenly role of continuator and promoter of the dynastic line, exemplified by the Virgin and expounded by critics and supporters alike, relegated women to a so-called "domestic sphere" and the begetting and raising of heirs, leading historians such as Georges Duby to conclude that the power and influence of medieval royal women was proscribed, marginal, and limited. Recent historiographical trends, however, have highlighted the very real opportunities to power and influence that could be available in such a "domestic sphere", or, as I prefer to term it, within domestic politics.[58] Their positions as wives and mothers *was* the source of their authority, as 'ruling the people, and ruling the children, were...two intimately linked spheres of queenly activity';[59] and as Duggan has pointed out, 'these activities were not only socially respected but dynastically and politically important'.[60] Motherhood was essential for the continuation of the dynastic line, and was both the primary reason for a queen's existence and the main source of her power. Bearing an heir usually – although not always – cemented a queen's position, and provided possible opportunities for real authority through exercising regency powers. Furthermore, a queen-regent or queen-dowager could, and sometimes did, exercise an enormous amount of independent power, influence and authority in the so-called "public sphere", and could often overshadow a queen-consort, as did Eleanor of Aquitaine with Richard's queen Berengaria of Navarre.[61]

As the milder arm of monarchy, petitions for intercession or patronage were frequently addressed to the queen rather than the king, and her role as patron, mediator and intercessor provided a significant means to contribute to and share in the formal power to rule invested in her husband.[62] Such acts of mercy or patronage were expected to be performed publicly, in order to encourage others to emulate her, although clerics frequently warned against the dan-

---

[57] Huneycutt has noted that the letters and patronage of Henry I's queen Edith-Matilda demonstrate the level of her literacy and education, 'Perfect Princess', 95. The levels of literacy and education of the Angevin family, and the education of royal daughters by their mothers is considered in Part I, Chapter 3.

[58] See for example, Jordan, *Women, Power and Religious Patronage*; Pauline Stafford, 'The Patronage of Royal Women in England, Mid-Tenth to Mid-Twelfth Centuries', in *Medieval Queenship*, 143-67; Armin Wolf, 'Reigning Queens in Medieval Europe: When, Where and Why', in *ibid.*, 169-88; Lois Huneycutt, 'Female Succession and the Language of Power in the Writings of Twelfth Century Churchmen', in *ibid.*, 189-201.

[59] Nelson, 'Queen-Making', 305.

[60] Duggan, 'Introduction', xvii, arguing further that 'to discount or de-value the roles of queens and empresses in the social, charitable and religious aspects of the life of their societies constitutes the real marginalisation of the feminine'.

[61] Queens-regnant, on the other hand, were a far more thorny political issue, as the case of the Empress Matilda amply demonstrates. The best work on the Empress remains Marjorie Chibnall's *The Empress Matilda, Queen Consort, Queen Mother and Lady of the English* (Blackwell, Oxford, 1991).

[62] For more on female patronage, see the articles in McCash (ed.), *Cultural Patronage*. For more on the patronage of Eleanor's daughters, see Part IV.

gers of prodigality and the sin of pride.[63] Intercession, too, could be a double-edged sword. It was the Marian ideal of queenship, but queens were expected to support their husbands publicly, even if they believed him to be in the wrong, and too much influence over the king was always viewed as dangerous.[64] The queen's inherently subservient role necessitated finding indirect ways of wielding power and influence. That medieval queens were able to find ways to manoeuvre within their proscribed roles and functions is evident from a glimpse at not a few notable case studies, and as shown in Part III, Chapter 2, Leonor in particular presents a prime example of a queen using her persuasive powers over the king to good effect.

Extant charters, documents and narratives from the tenth century onwards demonstrate that under specific circumstances, some queens were also highly politically active. As Lois Huneycutt notes, queens were often recognised by their contemporaries as 'an influential political force...[and] to overlook the high medieval queen is a mistake that would have been made by very few of her contemporaries'.[65] The realities of their power bases included a personal income, frequently in the form of dower lands and their associated revenues, and an independent household. The dower portions allocated to Henry and Eleanor's daughters, and their access to the revenues these supplied, are examined in Part III. Many queens also had their own seals, which were applied to official documents issued either in their own name or jointly with the king, their husband (or, in some cases, their son).[66] As with tomb effigies (discussed in Part V), seals could provide a medium in which queens could control the representation of their image.[67]

Ritual

The ritual elements of queenship demonstrate how ideology and roles and functions developed and became established. The first ritual involving a new queen was that of the marriage ceremony, at which she may or may not be crowned, and perhaps also consecrated, as queen.[68] Unlike kings, who were invested with formal authority over their subjects at their coronations, queens were elevated to their positions by virtue of marriage, but their coronations did not grant them any formally recognised authority. The new queen did not swear an oath at her coronation, and her power therefore remained undefined. The ritual element was nevertheless important and significant. As Janet Nelson has shown, without a coronation, the king's wife was not designated with the title of queen.[69] The ritual thus conferred on her a tangible and

---

[63] Huneycutt, 'Images of Queenship', 69.

[64] Karen Pratt's analogy of the medieval chessboard, with its 'vulnerable king' and 'more mobile queen', as exemplifying 'the real king's dependence on his consort's cooperation for effective rule' is aptly fitting here; 'Image of the Queen', 259.

[65] Huneycutt, 'Images of Queenship', 70-1.

[66] For more on women's seals, see Susan M. Johns, *Noblewomen, Aristocracy and Power in the Twelfth-Century Anglo-Norman Realm* (Manchester University Press, 2003); Brigitte Bedos Rezak, 'Women, Seals and Power in Medieval France, 1150-1350', in *Women and Power*, 61-82.

[67] Joanna's pointed oval silver comital seal-die is held at the British Museum, cat. no. P&E 1897,0508, 1&2 (Tonnochy cat. no. 5). A reproduction of Leonor's seal can be found in González, *Alfonso VIII*, I. Matilda's seal is no longer extant, though she presumably had one.

[68] For coronation rituals, see the collected articles in János M. Bak (ed.), *Coronations – Medieval and Early Modern Monarchic Ritual* (University of California Press, 1990); Paul Binski, *Westminster Abbey and the Plantagenets: Kingship and the Representation of Power, 1200-1400* (Yale University Press, New Haven & London, 1995), 128-39, 194-5.

[69] See Nelson, 'Queen-Making', 301-15, for a discussion of the earliest surviving coronation ordines from the

immediate change in status: only after the ceremony had been performed could she be proclaimed as queen. That this status was recognised by contemporaries as a highly significant indicator of power is evidenced by continual references to Joanna as *quondam regina siciliae* in chronicle accounts even after the premature death of William II and Joanna's remarriage to Count Raymond VI of Toulouse.[70] Joanna herself also continued to use the title on her seal as countess of Toulouse.[71]

The main difference between a king's coronation and that of a queen was that the king was crowned by clergy alone, whilst the queen was crowned by both clergy and the king, symbolically and visually demonstrating her inherent inferiority and subordination, and her position as consort rather than ruler. The formulae for the consecration of a queen were formally established by the mid-ninth to early tenth centuries, which led to a 'firmer delineation, or institutionalisation, of the queen's function'.[72] The rituals of coronation and consecration profoundly influenced the developing ideology of the office of queenship, which in turn shaped expectations of queens throughout the medieval period. From the ninth century onwards, the functions of the king were outlined in new liturgical tracts as protector of the church and dispenser of justice, and Nelson notes that it was 'hardly surprising that alongside this enhanced concern with the king's function went an increased interest in the queen's'.[73] The ritual of consecration set out in liturgy the qualities expected of queens, such as beauty, mercy, and above all chastity, whilst any claim to formal power was ambiguous at best. The queen was primarily the king's consort, his helpmate, the merciful arm of secular authority, and, most importantly, the mother of his future heirs.

The ritual elevation of both king and queen provided added legitimacy and significance to their heirs, as the sons, and daughters, of anointed rulers. Coronation ordines for queens explicitly stated their function as wife and mother, whilst at the same time stressing their subordination to the king. This is clearly evident in the charter of dower bestowed on Joanna at the time of her marriage to William II of Sicily, discussed in Part III, Chapter 4. Nevertheless, despite this emphasis on her role as genetrix, the sexual side of a queen's relationship with the king was always played down. The emphasis on submission and chastity, and, at the same time, fertility, in coronation ordines seemed to present no paradox to the composers of such texts.

Carolingian era. The earliest surviving coronation ordo for a queen is that for Judith, the daughter of Charles the Bald who married the Anglo-Saxon king Aethelwulf in 856. For the text of this ordo, Nelson, 'Queen-Making', 313-4. For the coronations of queens and empresses in the Holy Roman Empire from the tenth to fourteenth centuries, see Karl-Ulrich Jaschke, 'From Famous Empresses to Unspectacular Queens: The Romano-German Empire to Margaret of Brabant, Countess of Luxemburg and Queen of the Romans (d. 1311)', in *Queens and Queenship*, 75-108.

[70] For example, Howden notes that in 1196, 'the count of Saint Gilles...married Joanna, the sister of Richard, king of England, and *former queen of Sicily*', *Chronica*, IV, 13. My italics. Likewise, at her death in September 1199, 'Joanna, wife of Raymond, count of Saint Gilles, *former queen of Sicily*, and sister of John, king of England, died at Rouen in Normandy', *Chronica*, IV, 96. My italics.

[71] For Joanna's seal, see n .67 above. Marie de Montpellier, the queen of Pedro II of Aragón and mother of the future Jaime I, also refers to Joanna as 'queen' in the document expressing her grudging consent to the betrothal of her infant daughter Sancha to Joanna's son, the future Raymond VII, Elizabeth Haluska-Rausch, 'Unwilling Partners: Conflict and Ambition in the Marriage of Peter II of Aragon and Marie de Montpellier', in *Queenship and Political Power*, 11-12. As Sancha did not survive infancy, the marriage was never realised.

[72] Nelson, 'Queen-Making', 302.

[73] *Ibid.*, 304.

After the ceremonies of marriage, coronation, and consecration, the next major rituals in which a queen would be involved are those concerning *memoria* and dynastic commemoration. Queens were viewed as being responsible for the care of the souls of their husbands and families from at least as early as the Carolingian era, and women in general had a traditional and firmly established role as 'chief remembrancers of ancestral dead'.[74] The commissioning of tombs gave queens an important arena in which to exercise control over public memory of the deceased, and as will be seen in Part V, both Eleanor of Aquitaine and her daughter Leonor were ultimately responsible for creating dynastic mausolea for their families.

John Carmi Parsons' study of the burials of English queens up to 1500 deals largely with the burial of Eleanor of Castile; nevertheless, his work remains significant as one of the first studies to concentrate on queenly burials.[75] Previous historiographical trends in royal death, burial, and commemoration tended to focus on the king, as only the king's demise marked a tangible change in the transmission of power.[76] A queen's death was deemed to be less politically significant as (usually) it did not mean a change of ruler, although the issue of her dower could potentially be explosive, as is demonstrated in Part III. The rituals concerning burials of queens served to commemorate or even legitimise the ruling dynasty as well as to exalt the office of monarchy itself (rather than the queen as an individual), and may also have afforded 'Christological resonances to the birth of a king's son and heir' through the employment of Marian imagery.[77] Queens needed to be monumentalised as well as kings in order to emphasise the legitimate and noble ancestry of the ruling dynasty. Moreover, nobly commemorating a deceased queen ensured that future queens could, in theory, look forward to the same degree of respect, and would also be suitably commemorated and remembered after their own deaths.

Parsons suggests that, in death, the queen had "two bodies", one on display, and one hidden. The effigy displayed on her tomb reflected the ideal, especially important in terms of posthumous restoration of reputation when a queen had been less than ideal in her lifetime. Conversely, the hidden, actual body inside the tomb, 'like that of any woman', was 'impugned as a site of sin and pollution'.[78] A queen's tomb effigy therefore afforded opportunities to construct an idealised image of queenship, a sort of 'blank canvas' onto which 'an 'official' image could inscribe accepted gender-power relations', especially by employing Marian imagery.[79] As queens were frequently in control of planning their own commemorative monuments, one wonders how far such "official" images were manipulated by the women themselves. Therefore, an examination of the tombs of queens and how they are represented on their effigies suggests much about individual queens and the 'collective awareness of their office, or even of their self-image'.[80] As will be shown in Part V of this study, commissioning tombs could

---

[74] Parsons, 'Burials of Queens', 328. See also Jaschke, 'Famous Empresses', 81-5 for tenth-century examples from the Holy Roman Empire.

[75] Parsons, 'Burials of Queens', 317-37.

[76] Such as Elizabeth Hallam, 'Royal Burial and the Cult of Kingship in France and England, 1060-1330', *Journal of Medieval History*, 8:4 (1982), 359-81; see also Michael Evans, *The Death of Kings – Royal Deaths in Medieval England* (Hambledon & London, 2003). For women and *memoria*, see Elisabeth van Houts, *Memory and Gender in Medieval Europe, 900-1200* (MacMillan Press, London, 1999); Gerd Althoff, Johannes Fried and Patrick Geary (eds.), *Medieval Concepts of the Past: Ritual, Memory, Historiography* (CUP, 2002).

[77] Parsons, 'Burials of Queens', 326. He asserts that the 'innate tensions' of a queen's position were apparent on her tomb, which combined individuality with a 'submissive Marianising effigy', noting that 'it was easier (and safer) to exalt a deceased consort than to praise the king's living bedfellow', 'Burials of Queens', 336-7.

[78] Parsons, 'Burials of Queens', 333.

[79] *Ibid.*, 333.

[80] *Ibid.*, 326.

provide a visual medium for queens to acknowledge and glorify their own lineage and ancestry as well as that of their affinal family. The frequency with which tombs commissioned for and by queens emphasise the glory of their natal family serves to highlight the reality of emotional ties, and 'recalls the links of training and education, silent and often ignored, that evolved as queens raised their daughters as a new generation of diplomatic brides'.[81]

Themes and Approaches

This book has been divided thematically into five main sections, treating the childhood, marriages, dower portions, patronage, and dynastic commemorations of Henry and Eleanor's daughters. Throughout the discussion of these important issues, comparisons have been made, where relevant, with their sisters-in-law Margaret of France and Berengaria of Navarre. Part I explores the history of childhood and the history of *mentalités*, and applies this theoretical method to the actual childhood experiences of Matilda, Leonor and Joanna in order to discern what degree of emotional attachment these women may have had to their natal family. An extensive examination of the Pipe Rolls, the only extant fiscal records of Henry II's administration, along with contemporary chronicle material, reveals that all three sisters spent a considerable amount of their childhoods with their itinerant mother.[82] Charter material and extant letters, as well as the choices in patronage and commemoration that these women made as adults, suggest that keenly felt emotional ties may have been forged in their early childhoods, before their exogamous marriages.

Parts II and III examine theoretical, theological, and practical approaches to the marriages of royal women, which has necessitated both a consideration of the life-cycle of the medieval woman and the multi-faceted roles she might play within these cycles, as well as an examination of the importance – and complications – of dower and dowry settlements. The political motivations for the dynastic marriages arranged for each of Henry and Eleanor's three daughters is discussed, as are the negotiation processes and the envoys involved in these. I have also studied in detail the still-extant charters of dower settlements with which Joanna and Leonor were endowed, in order to map the extent of their dower lands and assess the extent of their possible independent revenues.[83] Finally, the roles and functions of queens – both theoretical and actual – have been examined in order to ascertain how well Matilda, Joanna and Leonor lived up to their expected roles as consorts, mothers and benefactresses, along with a consideration of other notable royal women who may have acted as role models for them. Arguably, the surest avenue to power and influence for a queen was through motherhood, and the relationships which mothers had with their own children. Progenitrixes they may primarily have been viewed as, both by contemporary society and by their natal and marital families; however, patronage and dynastic commemorations, which are both discussed in depth in Parts IV and V, could offer a route to power and influence which was clearly not peripheral but effective, affective, and pervasive.

---

[81] *Ibid.*, 328. By the fifteenth century, queens were being buried in the same formalised way as kings. Their bodies were anointed, before the period of lying-in-state, followed by a grand funeral procession to the place of interment. However, this formal, ritualised method of burying queens undoubtedly served to curtail the freedom which previous queens had been able to wield over their own burials and commemorations.

[82] The main source of expenditure for the king and his family was the itinerant Chamber, whose records do not survive, and hence the Pipe Roll evidence, whilst valuable, is incomplete as a record of expenditure.

[83] There is no extant record of Matilda's dower settlement.

Part IV treats the religious patronage of royal and aristocratic women, and in particular concentrates on the involvement of Matilda, Leonor, and Joanna in the dissemination of the cult of Thomas Becket. What religious institutions did they establish or endow? And to what extent were they responsible for the propagation of the cult of Becket in Saxony, Sicily and Castile? The role of royal women in the dissemination of saints' cults has been the subject of much historical study, although these studies largely concentrate on royal women who were considered to be saintly themselves, such as Huneycutt's work on Margaret of Scotland and her daughter Edith-Matilda.[84] This study focuses on the possible influence of Matilda, Leonor, and Joanna's natal family in informing their decisions to involve themselves in the cult of the newly-canonised martyr. It is arguable that their involvement in promoting this cult is evidential of patrilineal influence, and an attachment to their natal family which was forged in early childhood.

This is also the focus of Part V, which examines patterns in nomenclature and dynastic commemoration, although here the discernible influence from the natal family is matrilineal. The links between Fontevrault, which ultimately became the dynastic mausoleum of the Angevin dynasty, and the foundations of Brunswick Cathedral in Saxony, Monreale in Sicily, and Las Huelgas in Castile, have been explored, leading to the hypothesis that in terms of dynastic commemoration, there is some evidence that Eleanor may have been inspired and influenced by her daughters. My conclusions on this demonstrate that intergenerational influence was not always a linear, one-way exchange, but could be far more symbiotic. Dynastic nomenclature as a commemorative device has also been considered here, as it is clear that, in contrast to notions that the naming of children followed strictly agnatic and patrilineal lines, the daughters of Henry and Eleanor were able to transport new, specifically Angevin names, to the dynasties they married into. As it appears that the choices made by Matilda, Leonor and Joanna as adults seem to have been informed in several cases by an emotional attachment to their natal family, it is necessary to begin this study with an examination of their childhoods in order to discern the depth and extent of these possible emotional ties.

---

[84] See n. 6 above. See also Dagmar Ó Riain-Raedel, 'Edith, Judith, Matilda: The Role of Royal Ladies in the Propagation of the Continental Cult', in Clare Stancliffe and Eric Cambridge (eds.), *Oswald: Northumbrian King to European Saint* (Paul Watkins, Stamford, Lincolnshire, 1995), 210-29.

PART I

Carissima filia nostra:
Birth, Childhood and Formative Education

The majority of information for Matilda, Joanna and Leonor is only available in contemporary chronicles from the time of their proposed marriages to, respectively, Henry the Lion of Saxony, William II of Sicily and Alfonso VIII of Castile. Their births are on the whole either recorded in few words, sometimes without even giving their names, or attributing an erroneous date, or they are completely ignored. This compares unfavourably with references to the births of the male issue of Henry II and Eleanor of Aquitaine.[1]

Thenceforth, references to Matilda, Joanna and Leonor are largely concerned with their marriages, dower settlements, and the children (or lack of) whom they bore. The political context of their marriages must therefore be closely examined. Why were unions with Saxony, Sicily and Castile desirable, and why did the marriages occur when they did? These questions involve an examination of the links between Angevin England, Norman Sicily, Saxony and Castile, and of the personnel at the Sicilian, Saxon and Castilian courts who acted as envoys in the negotiation processes. Who was chosen, and why, for the task of conducting the royal women to their new homelands? These questions will be addressed in Part II. Part I focuses on what can be gleaned from documentary evidence of the childhoods of these royal women, what form of education or training they may have received, and what contact, both physical and emotional, they had with their parents and siblings. By studying the formative experiences of Matilda, Leonor and Joanna, it is then possible to determine the extent of the emotional ties to their natal family which were forged in their early childhoods.

---

[1] Gervase of Canterbury, for example, refers to the births of the Young King, Richard, John, and Geoffrey, but only mentions Henry's daughters when they are sent abroad for marriage. Diceto notes the births of all of Henry's children, including his daughters, whereas Ralph of Coggeshall notes only the births of Henry's sons. Howden, however, does not mention the births of either Henry's sons or his daughters, and neither do Devizes or Newburgh. Torigni's references seem arbitrary: he records the births of Leonor and Joanna, but not that of Matilda; and with regard to Henry's sons, the births of William, Richard, and John are noted, but not those of Henry or Geoffrey.

Chapter One
Birth and Childhood

The birth of Henry and Eleanor's eldest daughter Matilda in June 1156 is only recorded by Diceto and Wendover.[1] Named for her grandmother the Empress, Matilda was baptised by Theobald, Archbishop of Canterbury (d. 1161) at the church of Holy Trinity in Aldgate.[2] Her birth is not recorded by Torigni, although he does provide details of the German embassy which arrived at Henry's court in 1165 seeking a marriage between his eldest daughter and Henry the Lion, and another between his second daughter Leonor and a son of the emperor, Frederick I.[3] Torigni also refers to the three-year period of exile that Matilda and her husband subsequently spent at the court of Henry II, pointing out that they were maintained financially by Henry II, and that it was he who effected Henry the Lion's return to favour.[4] Howden does not mention Matilda at all in the *Gesta* until her arrival, with her husband and children, at Henry II's court in Normandy in 1182, where they celebrated Christmas at Caen with Henry II and his sons Richard and Geoffrey.[5] Matilda's marriage to Henry the Lion is referred to only briefly in the later *Chronica*, placed erroneously under the year 1164.[6] References to Matilda in Angevin chronicles therefore largely pertain to the period between 1182 and 1185 when she and her husband were exiles in the court of her parents.[7]

Joanna's birth at Angers in October 1165 is also largely overlooked in the Angevin sources, being noted solely by Robert of Torigni.[8] Like Joanna, Leonor appears only very occasionally in Angevin chronicles; less, indeed, as Leonor's life proved to be considerably less turbulent than that of her younger sister. Leonor's birth is recorded only by Torigni - Leonor's godfather - and by Diceto, who states merely that Leonor was born in Rouen in 1162.[9]

---

[1] Ralph of Diceto, *Ymagines Historiarum*, in *Radulfi Diceto Decani Lundoniensis Opera Historica: The Historical Works of Master Ralph de Diceto, Dean of London*, ed. William Stubbs, 2 vols. (Rolls Series, 68.1, London, 1876; hereafter Diceto, I), 302; Roger of Wendover, *Liber Qui Dicitur Flores Historiarum Ab Anno Domini MCLIV. Annoque Henrici Anglorum Regis Secundi Primo. The Flowers of History by Roger de Wendover: From the Year of Our Lord 1154, and the First Year of Henry the Second, King of the English*, ed. Henry G. Hewlett, 3 vols. (Rolls Series, 84, London, 1886-9), I, 13.

[2] Kate Norgate, 'Matilda, duchess of Saxony (1156-1189)', *DNB*.

[3] Torigni, 224. See also below and Part II, Chapter 2.

[4] Torigni, 303-4. See also Part III, Chapter 1.

[5] Howden, *Gesta*, I, 291, and 249-50 for Henry the Lion's dispossession by the Emperor Frederick I. See also Howden, *Chronica*, II, 273, and 269-70, 288-9 for Henry the Lion's conflict with the emperor. Their exile is also briefly referred to in the *Gesta*, II, 56, and by Diceto, *Decani Lundoniensis Opuscula*, in *Radulfi Diceto Decani Lundoniensis Opera Historica: The Historical Works of Master Ralph de Diceto, Dean of London*, ed. William Stubbs, 2 vols. (Rolls Series, 68.2, London, 1876; hereafter Diceto, II), 12-13, Wendover, I, 129, and Gervase, I, 310-11. For more on Matilda and Henry's exile, see Part III, Chapter 1.

[6] Howden, *Chronica*, I, 220.

[7] Even her death in July 1189 is treated in the briefest of terms, and then only by Howden, *Chronica*, III, 3; Diceto, II, 65; Wendover, I, 160; and the author of the *Gesta Ricardi*, 72.

[8] Torigni, 266. For the relationship between Torigni and the Angevin dynasty, see Elisabeth van Houts, 'Le roi et son historien: Henri II Plantagenêt et Robert de Torigni, abbé du Mont-Saint-Michel', *Cahiers de Civilisation Médiévale*, 37 (1994), 115-18.

[9] Diceto, I, 306. Diceto's error is surprising, as he made use of Torigni's chronicle for his work until 1171, or possibly as late as 1183; see Antonia Gransden, *Historical Writing in England, c.550-c.1307* (Routledge & Kegan Paul, Lon-

Torigni gives the more detailed, and more accurate, information that Leonor was born at Domfront in Normandy, in the autumn of 1161. She was baptised by the cardinal legate Henry of Pisa, and Torigni himself, along with Achard, bishop of Avranches, stood as sponsor to Leonor's baptism.[10]

Torigni, whose chronicle focuses in the main on Normandy and local affairs in the region of his abbey at Mont-Saint-Michel, appears to have been better informed about Iberian affairs than many of his contemporaries. He provides sporadic accounts of events in Spain (as well as other European kingdoms), such as the continual conflict with the Moors, notably the invasion from North Africa in early 1170.[11] Torigni also records the conquest of Lisbon, and the reclamation of Almeria by Emperor Alfonso VII of Castile- León,[12] as well as the conflicts caused by the division of Alfonso's "empire" after his death, and the problems which ensued when Alfonso VIII succeeded his father Sancho III at just three years of age.[13]

Leonor appears once more in Torigni's work, in a passage describing her as 'my most dear lady and god-daughter'.[14] His obvious affection towards Leonor - the only child of Henry II and Eleanor of Aquitaine whose baptism is recorded in his work - is apparent in his praise of her as the driving force behind the majority of Alfonso's noble deeds: according to Torigni, Leonor's 'good counsel and assistance brought much good fortune to her husband Alfonso', who captured various towns (Cuenca, Cordoba, Valencia and Murcia) from the Moors, and 'did many other good deeds'.[15] In other words, Torigni presents Leonor as a substantial force helping the Reconquista. However, whilst there is evidence that Leonor held some degree of influence over her husband, and that the marriage appears to have been a happy and mutually beneficial one, Torigni's affection for his god-daughter clearly led him to exaggerate the effect

---

don, 1974), 232. Joanna's and Leonor's births are also noted by Wendover, I, 20, 39. Whilst Wendover was neither an eye witness not a contemporary author, his inclusion of Joanna's birth suggests that he had access to Torigni's chronicle as well as that of Diceto. For the relationship between Wendover's text and that of Diceto, see Gransden, *Historical Writing*, 359.

[10] Torigni, 211; R.W. Eyton, *Court, Household, and Itinerary of King Henry II, Instancing also the Chief Agents and Adversaries of the King in his Government, Diplomacy, and Strategy* (James Foster, Cornhill, Dorchester, 1878), 54-5. Eyton wondered if the marriage negotiations for Leonor in 1165 led Diceto to erroneously place her birth in that year, *Itinerary*, 54n, although in fact Diceto places Leonor's birth in 1162, see n.9, above. Nicholas Vincent has noted various errors in Eyton's *Itinerary*. Pending Vincent's forthcoming publication of the *Acta* of Henry II, recourse to the *Itinerary* has been undertaken, but only where the information can be corroborated by other sources.

[11] Torigni, 249. This is also briefly related by Howden under the year 1171, *Chronica*, II, 33. Alfonso VIII's defeat at Alarcos in 1195, and his victory at Las Navas de Tolosa, also given as 1195, is recorded at *Chronica*, III, 302, 305, with the peace treaty concluded between the Spanish kings in 1200 at IV, 113. An account of the Moorish invasion of Spain in 1195 is also given by Newburgh, 445-7. As Torigni had died by 1186, these events do not appear in his chronicle.

[12] For Alfonso VII, see Joseph O'Callaghan, *A History of Medieval Spain* (Cornell University Press, London, 1975), 256. After the division of Alfonso's kingdom between his two sons, both his son Fernando II of León and later his grandson Alfonso VIII occasionally referred to themselves as '*rex Hispaniae*', but by the end of the twelfth century the peninsula was divided into the five distinct Christian kingdoms of Castile, Navarre, Aragón, León and Portugal, O'Callaghan, *Medieval Spain*, 256.

[13] Torigni, 193-5. He notes the threats Alfonso faced during his minority from Fernando 'of Galicia, patruus ejus', and Alfonso of Navarre, 'avunculus ejus', 247. Torigni was clearly confused here; Fernando II of León was Alfonso's paternal uncle, whereas the Navarrese king, who was Alfonso's maternal uncle, was Sancho VI. Richard Howlett pointed out that the threat to Alfonso's minority was only recorded in the *Gesta* after the event, under the year 1177, as 'Benedict' [*sic*] was at the time 'absorbed in Becket's affairs', Torigni, 247n.

[14] Torigni, 303: *carissimam dominam meam et filiolam in baptismate*.

[15] Ibid.: *Anforsus...duxit...in uxorem, Alienor...cujus consilio et auxilio multa bona ei acciderunt... et multa alia bona fecit.*

of Leonor's influence.[16] Indeed, as Elisabeth van Houts has pointed out, Torigni was a lifelong partisan of the Angevin dynasty, and his desire to retain their favour, coupled with his personal attachment to Leonor as her godfather, provides a plausible explanation for such exaggeration.[17] As the cartulary of Mont-Saint-Michel contains no documents dating to later than 1149,[18] however, there is no extant documentary evidence that might confirm a continued interest on Leonor's part for her godfather's abbey.[19]

Formative Experiences and Emotional Ties: The Childhood Journeys of Matilda, Leonor and Joanna

Little is known about the childhoods of Leonor and Joanna. Their absence from Angevin sources before their marriages – as opposed to their elder sister Matilda, who is frequently recorded travelling with her mother – might suggest that they spent their formative years in their parents' continental domains, with the abbey of Fontevrault being cited by some historians as their most likely residence. However, we have evidence of this only for Eleanor's two youngest children, Joanna and John, and it is far from clear how long they spent there.[20] What is clear, however, is that both Leonor and Joanna, like Matilda, spent much of their infancies and early childhoods with their itinerant mother. It is the contention here that these early childhood experiences had a strong influence on Eleanor's daughters, and that the emotional bond they formed with their mother at this time was both powerful and long lasting.

Matilda spent most of her infancy and early childhood years travelling with her mother (see Table 1). She made her first journey with Eleanor and her elder brother Henry to Normandy in July 1156, when she was just one month old. After joining Henry II in Rouen, Eleanor then travelled south to Aquitaine to receive homage from the Aquitanian nobles, and she remained in the south to celebrate Christmas at Bordeaux.[21] Eleanor then returned to Normandy with her children Matilda and Henry in January 1157, which suggests that they had accompanied their mother on her journey to the south.[22] The fact that Matilda had accompanied Eleanor from England to Northern France, and then south to Aquitaine, demonstrates that Eleanor kept her daughter close at hand during this crucial stage of her childhood. Clearly, Eleanor wished to have her infant daughter with her.

It is likely that Eleanor employed wetnurses for her children, as this was usual practice in royal and aristocratic families in the Middle Ages; but such practices do not imply that highborn ladies such as Eleanor simply passed off their childcare responsibilities onto others.[23]

---

[16] González, *Alfonso VIII*, I, 193, 193n. The *Crónica Latina* notes that Alfonso was still a minor (*Adolescente ya*) when he completed the conquest of Cuenca, 35. For more on Leonor and Alfonso's marriage, see Part III, Chapter 2.

[17] Van Houts, 'Le roi et son historien', 116-8.

[18] MS 210, Bibliotheque Municipale, Avranches; K.S.B. Keats-Rohan, *The Cartulary of the Abbey of Mont-Saint-Michel* (Shaun Tyas, Donington, 2006).

[19] For the relationship between Mont-Saint-Michel and the dukes of Normandy (and subsequently, the Norman kings of England), see Keats-Rohan, *Cartulary*, 14-25. A necrology for Mont-Saint-Michel is contained in MS Avranches 214.

[20] See below.

[21] PR 2 Hen II, 4-5; Eyton, *Itinerary*, 18; Flori, *Eleanor of Aquitaine*, 75-6; Turner, *Eleanor of Aquitaine*, 132, 151.

[22] Flori, *Eleanor of Aquitaine*, 75-6; Turner, *Eleanor of Aquitaine*, 132, 151.

[23] Indeed, it was commonly held that nursing might prevent further pregnancy, and wetnurses, who often acted as a sort of long-term nanny, were carefully selected from good families of the lesser gentry, and were frequently well rewarded for their services. For more on the practice of using wetnurses, see Part I, Chapter 3. For the possible use of wetnurses by Eleanor, see Turner, 'Eleanor of Aquitaine and her Children', 326, and *idem, Eleanor of Aquitaine*, 146.

Moreover, whilst infants may well have formed an emotional attachment to their wetnurses, this did not necessarily prevent them from forming affectionate bonds with their mothers as well, and as we shall see, if Eleanor did employ a wetnurse for Matilda – or indeed for any of her children – this certainly did not prevent a strong mother-daughter bond from forming.[24]

Table 1: Eleanor's journeys with Matilda, 1156-1160.

June 1156	Matilda born
July 1156	Matilda travels to Rouen with Eleanor & young Henry
	Eleanor & Henry II journey to Aquitaine (with Matilda & young Henry?)
Christmas 1156	Eleanor & Henry at Bordeaux (with Matilda & young Henry?)
January 1157	Eleanor returns to Normandy with Matilda & young Henry
February 1157	Matilda returns to England with Eleanor
Feb 1157 – Dec 1158	Matilda in England with Eleanor?
1157	Eleanor travels between Hampshire, Berkshire, Wiltshire & Devon
February 1158	Eleanor travels from Winchester to London
Aug – Sept 1158	Eleanor at Winchester
October 1158	Eleanor travels between Winchester, Oxford & London
November 1158	Eleanor at Salisbury
Christmas 1158	Eleanor joins Henry II at Cherbourg
Christmas 1159	Eleanor with Henry II at Falaise
December 1159	Eleanor returns to England
September 1160	Matilda travels to Rouen with Eleanor

When Eleanor returned to England in February 1157, she took Matilda with her.[25] From Pipe Roll evidence, Eleanor appears to have spent most of 1157 in Hampshire, Devon, Berkshire, and Wiltshire. In February 1158, she travelled from Winchester to London, and in October she travelled between Winchester, Oxford, and Woodstock. She was at Winchester from August to September, and in Salisbury by November.[26] Eleanor stayed in England until December 1158, when she joined Henry II for the Christmas court at Cherbourg, and she seems to have remained on the Continent throughout the following year, spending the Christmas court of 1159 with Henry II at Falaise before returning to England at the end of December.[27]

It is unclear whether or not Matilda was continually with her mother during this time, but it seems likely that she was, as we know that Matilda made several more cross-channel trips with her mother during her childhood years: most notably, in September 1160, when they

---

[24] Eleanor's daughter Leonor certainly employed wetnurses for her own children, and charter evidence demonstrates that these women were richly rewarded for their services. For more on this, see Part III, Chapter 2.

[25] PR 3 Hen II, 107; Eyton, *Itinerary*, 24.

[26] See PR 3 Hen II, 107, 171; PR 4 Hen II, 171, 175; PR 5 Hen II, 25; Eyton, *Itinerary*, 24, 31, 40-2.

[27] PR 5 Hen II, 41; PR 6 Hen II, 23; Torigni, 200, 206; Eyton, *Itinerary*, 43, 49.

journeyed together to Rouen, for the the marriage of Eleanor's eldest son Henry to Margaret of France.[28] Matilda was probably with both her parents for the Christmas court held at Le Mans that year, and she seems to have remained with her mother for the rest of Eleanor's stay in France.[29] Clearly, Eleanor was determined to keep her daughter with her as much as possible, and a sense of family unity can be discerned by the fact that the Angevin dynasty were together at important occasions such as Christmas and family weddings.

Eleanor was on the Continent from September 1160 until January 1163 (see Table 2), and she seems to have stayed in Normandy more or less permanently throughout 1161 and 1162.[30] This is likely because for much of this time she was pregnant with her second daughter Leonor, who was born at Domfront in September 1161.[31] Eleanor spent Christmas of that year with Henry II at Bayeux, and she probably had both of her daughters with her at this time, as she celebrated the following Christmas with Matilda, Leonor, and her husband Henry at Cherbourg.[32] Again, this provides evidence of the Angevin family spending time together for the greatest feast in the Christian calendar.

When Eleanor returned to England in January 1163, she took both Matilda and Leonor with her. She stayed mostly in the south and south-west of the country – she was in Hampshire until February, when she removed to Wiltshire; in the summer of 1164, she was in Wiltshire, Devon, and Hampshire; and from February to May 1165 she was in Hampshire, at Winchester and perhaps also on the Isle of Wight – and she seems to have kept her daughters with her throughout this time.[33] Matilda was certainly with her mother in Berkshire in April 1165, when the Archbishop of Cologne arrived in England to negotiate Matilda's marriage to Henry the Lion of Saxony.[34] Eleanor may well have been present at these negotiations, as she later was for the negotiations for Leonor's marriage to Alfonso of Castile.[35] It also seems likely that both Leonor and Eleanor's son Richard were with their mother at this time, because when Eleanor brought Matilda to Henry II in Rouen the following month, she took Richard and Leonor with her.[36]

Table 2: Eleanor's journeys with Matilda and Leonor, 1160-1165.

Sept 1160 – Jan 1163	Matilda in France (largely Normandy) with Eleanor
Christmas 1160	Eleanor & Henry II (with Matilda?) at Le Mans
September 1161	Leonor born at Domfront in Normandy
Christmas 1161	Eleanor & Henry II (with Matilda & Leonor?) at Bayeux
Christmas 1162	Eleanor, Henry II, Matilda & Leonor at Cherbourg

---

[28] PR 6 Hen II, 23, 47; Torigni, 207; Eyton, *Itinerary*, 50; Flori, *Eleanor of Aquitaine*, 78; Turner, *Eleanor of Aquitaine*, 138.

[29] For the Christmas court at Le Mans in 1160, see Torigni, 209; Eyton, *Itinerary*, 52.

[30] PR 9 Hen II, 54; Eyton, *Itinerary*, 58; Flori, *Eleanor of Aquitaine*, 80.

[31] Torigni, 211.

[32] Torigni, 211, 216; Eyton, *Itinerary*, 55, 58.

[33] See PR 9 Hen II, 45, 54, 56; PR 10 Hen II, 14, 19, 25; PR 11 Hen II, 40; Eyton, *Itinerary*, 58-9, 69, 85. Eyton, *Itinerary*, 85, assumes 'Ulferton' to be Wolverton, on the Isle of Wight. Winchester was 'a frequent residence for the queen and her younger children', Ralph V. Turner, 'Eleanor of Aquitaine and her Children: An Enquiry into Medieval Family Attachment', in *Journal of Medieval History*, 14. 4 (1988), 324.

[34] Diceto, I, 318; Eyton, *Itinerary*, 78n. Gervase of Canterbury erroneously places this embassy in 1167, I, 204-5.

[35] See below.

[36] PR 11 Hen II, 40; Torigni, 225; Eyton, *Itinerary*, 78.

January 1163	Matilda returns to England with Eleanor & Leonor
Jan 1163 – May 1165	Eleanor in England with Matilda and Leonor
February 1163	Eleanor travels from Hampshire to Wiltshire
Summer 1164	Eleanor travels between Wiltshire, Devon & Hampshire
Feb – May 1165	Eleanor, Matilda & Leonor largely in Hampshire
April 1165	Eleanor & Matilda (and Leonor?) in Berkshire
May 1165	Matilda, Leonor & Richard travel to Rouen with Eleanor

Henry II had sent for Eleanor, Richard and Matilda to join him in Rouen, following negotiations for the marriages of his two daughters.[37] Ambassadors of Emperor Frederick had reached Henry at Rouen in April 1165, to negotiate a marriage between Matilda and Henry the Lion, and between Leonor and a younger son of the Emperor.[38] Although no mention is made in the sources of Leonor travelling with Eleanor and Matilda at this time, it is apparent that she did, as her presence at Angers the following Michaelmas is noted.[39]

Eleanor spent over a year in Angers, acting as Henry's regent for Maine and Anjou (see Table 3).[40] In October 1165, Eleanor's youngest daughter, Joanna, was born at Angers, and Eleanor was still there with all of her children for both Easter and Michaelmas 1166,[41] with the exception of the young Henry, who had been established in his own household by this time.[42] Eleanor and her children remained on the Continent, mostly at Angers, until she returned to England with Matilda in October or November 1166.[43] Leonor and Joanna had clearly accompanied their mother and eldest sister to England, as they are seen to be travelling back to the Continent with Eleanor the following year.[44]

Eleanor remained in England until the eleven-year-old Matilda was taken to Saxony for her marriage to Henry the Lion in September 1167.[45] Eleanor may have spent some time preparing her daughter, both mentally and materially, for her impending wedding.[46] This would have been an important time for both mother and daughter, and Eleanor certainly had enough experience of her own to be able to advise her daughter about the vagaries and permutations of married life. Eleanor personally accompanied Matilda to Dover, before entrusting her to Henry the Lion's envoys for her onward journey.[47] The Pipe Rolls for 1167-68 list

---

[37] Torigni, 224-5.

[38] Torigni, 224, although Diceto, I, 318, places this meeting in Winchester. Eyton suggests that the Archbishop of Cologne travelled first to Rouen and thence to London, *Itinerary*, 78n. PR 11 Hen II, 108 records that he crossed to England at Henry's expense; his journey to Berkshire suggests that he had an audience with Eleanor, and perhaps also saw Matilda.

[39] Torigni, 225-6; Eyton, *Itinerary*, 78, 98; Flori, *Eleanor of Aquitaine*, 84-5; Turner, *Eleanor of Aquitaine*, 143.

[40] Eyton, *Itinerary*, 79, 86; Turner, *Eleanor of Aquitaine*, 141.

[41] Torigni, 225-6; Eyton, *Itinerary*, 98; Flori, *Eleanor of Aquitaine*, 84-5; Turner, *Eleanor of Aquitaine*, 143.

[42] Eyton, *Itinerary*, 86. The sons of Henry and Eleanor left the familial home in early adolescence in order to establish their own households. See Ralph V. Turner, 'The Households of the Sons of Henry II', in Martin Aurell (ed.), *La Cour Plantagenêt 1152-1204* (Poitiers, 2000), 49-62, which focuses on the households of the Young King and Richard.

[43] PR 12 Hen II, 93; Eyton, *Itinerary*, 108-9. See also Flori, *Eleanor of Aquitaine*, 81; Turner, *Eleanor of Aquitaine*, 141. Torigni, usually accurate in his chronology, places their return a year later, 233.

[44] PR 13 Hen II, 169; Eyton, *Itinerary*, 108-9; Flori, *Eleanor of Aquitaine*, 84-5; Turner, *Eleanor of Aquitaine*, 143.

[45] For more on Matilda's marriage to Henry the Lion, see Part II, Chapter 1.

[46] As Flori, *Eleanor of Aquitaine*, 85, and Turner, *Eleanor of Aquitaine*, 143, have both suggested.

[47] Flori, *Eleanor of Aquitaine*, 85; see also Turner, *Eleanor of Aquitaine*, 143; Eyton, *Itinerary*, 109. Gervase, I, 204,

the expenses for Matilda's crossing to Saxony, as well as the cost of the clothes and household goods, including seven scarlet-covered chairs, which had been provided for her by her parents for her use in her marital lands.[48] She was also provided with a palfrey and a courser, or swift horse, at Henry's own expense, for her use in Saxony.[49] These goods may have constituted all or part of Matilda's dowry. Nevertheless, it is clear that both Henry and Eleanor wished to see their eldest daughter leave the family home suitably prepared for her marriage.

Table 3: Eleanor's journeys with Matilda, Leonor and Joanna, 1165-1167.

May 1165 – Oct 1166	Matilda & Leonor in France (largely Angers) with Eleanor
Michaelmas 1165	Matilda & Leonor with Eleanor at Angers
October 1165	Joanna born at Angers
Easter 1166	Matilda, Leonor & Joanna with Eleanor at Angers
Michalemas 1166	Matilda, Leonor & Joanna with Eleanor at Angers
Oct / Nov 1166	Matilda, Leonor & Joanna return to England with Eleanor
December 1166	Eleanor at Oxford
September 1167	Matilda travels to Dover with Eleanor Matilda journeys to Saxony for marriage to Henry the Lion

After Matilda's departure, Eleanor remained in England until the end of the year (see Table 4). She was at Winchester from Michaelmas until December, when she crossed to Normandy with Richard, John, Leonor and Joanna to celebrate Christmas with Henry II at Argentan.[50] When Eleanor left Argentan for Poitou the following January, she took Richard, John, Leonor and Joanna with her, suggesting that they had been with her for the 1167 Christmas court.[51] Eleanor remained in Poitou more or less permanently from 1168 until she was taken captive by Henry II in 1173.[52] She was certainly there in April 1168,[53] although in May 1170 she was at Limoges with Richard, and in June she was at Caen.[54] She also spent

---

states that Matilda was accompanied from Dover to Saxony by the Elect of Cologne, and by her mother Eleanor. Eyton, however, doubts this, concluding that Eleanor travelled no further than Normandy and returned to England soon thereafter, *Itinerary*, 109. The 'elect of Cologne' must refer to Reginald of Cologne's successor, as Reginald himself died in 1167 and was thus unlikely to have travelled to England himself, Eyton, *Itinerary*, 109. Diceto, I, 330, names the earls of Arundel and Striguil as amongst those who accompanied her. Matilda's departure for Saxony in late September 1167 is also recorded by Torigni, 234. Howden places Matilda's marriage to Henry the Lion in 1164, *Chronica*, I, 220.

48   PR 13 Hen II, 193-4; PR 14 Hen II, 208; PR 13 Hen II, 2-3.
49   PR 13 Hen II, 2-3, 5; PR 14 Hen II, 15, 34, 50, 60-1, 100, 117, 139, 157, 174, 192, 208. The sheriff of Buckinghamshire & Bedfordshire paid double for two palfreys and two coursers, PR 14 Hen II, 7. As Eyton pointed out, this was not a feudal exaction of aid, which was calculated at 2 marks per knight's fee, but a gift from the king from his own revenues, *Itinerary*, 117, 117n. For more on Matilda's marriage, see Part II, Chapter 1.
50   PR 14 Hen II, 190; Eyton, *Itinerary*, 112-3; Turner, *Eleanor of Aquitaine*, 143.
51   Turner, *Eleanor of Aquitaine*, 144.
52   *Ibid.*, 144. Eleanor was resident in Aquitaine from the time of the Peace of Montmirail in 1169 until her imprisonment in 1173; thereafter Richard, who had been in Aquitaine with his mother during this period, took control of the duchy. See Jean Dunbabin, *France in the Making, 843-1180* (OUP, 1985; 2nd edn., 2000), 342.
53   Eyton, *Itinerary*, 113.
54   *Ibid.*, 137.

Christmas 1172 with Henry at Chinon, and attended the Council at Limoges the following February.[55]

Jean Flori has questioned whether Eleanor's younger children were with her during her lengthy stay in Poitou, and Ralph Turner has stated that whilst Richard was with her 'continuously', Geoffrey and the young Henry, if they were with her at all, were there only briefly.[56] Eleanor's two youngest children, Joanna and John, spent some time being educated at Fontevrault.[57] Her six-year-old daughter Leonor, however, seems to have stayed with her mother for the next two years, until in 1170 she also left her natal family for marriage to Alfonso VIII of Castile.[58] We can assume that Eleanor spent some of this time preparing Leonor for her marriage, as she must have done with Matilda in 1167. Similarly, Eleanor personally accompanied Leonor to Bordeaux where she was met by the Castilian envoys, and she also presided over the council which settled the terms of her daughter's marriage.[59] Clearly, Eleanor was determined to guarantee the best settlement for her daughter that she could broker.

Table 4: Eleanor's journeys with Leonor and Joanna, 1167-1174.

Sept – Dec 1167	Eleanor at Winchester (with Leonor & Joanna?)
Christmas 1167	Eleanor & Henry II at Argentan with Leonor, Joanna, Richard & John
February 1168	Leonor, Joanna, Richard & John travel to Poitou with Eleanor
Feb 1168 – July 1174	Eleanor in France (largely Poitou)
May 1170	Eleanor at Limoges with Richard
June 1170	Leonor travels to Bordeaux with Eleanor Leonor journeys to Castile for marriage to Alfonso VIII
June 1170	Eleanor at Caen
Christmas 1172	Eleanor & Henry II at Chinon
February 1173	Eleanor at Council of Limoges before returning to Poitou
July 1174	Joanna & John return to England with Eleanor (now captive)
July 1174 – Sept 1176	Eleanor at Salisbury (with Joanna?)
September 1176	Joanna at Winchester with Eleanor Joanna journeys to Sicily for marriage to William II

---

[55] Howden, *Gesta*, I, 35; Eyton, *Itinerary*, 170.

[56] Flori, *Eleanor of Aquitaine*, 88-9; Turner, *Eleanor of Aquitaine*, 193.

[57] See the epitaphs of John and Joanna, printed in Balthazar Pavillon, *La Vie du bienheureux Robert d'Arbrissel* (Paris-Saumur, 1666), 585, no. 90, and 588, no. 96. My thanks to Stephen Church for this reference. See also Alfred Richard, *Histoire des Comtes de Poitou, 778-1204* (2 Vols., Paris, 1903), II, 375; Flori, *Eleanor of Aquitaine*, 89; Turner, *Eleanor of Aquitaine*, 194-5; *idem.*, 'Eleanor of Aquitaine and her Children', 325.

[58] Turner, 'Eleanor of Aquitaine and her Children', 325, notes that Richard was also with his mother during this time. Turner has also suggested that Leonor 'may have spent some time at Fontevraud with her younger brother John and her sister Joann[a]', *Eleanor of Aquitaine*, 194, but he provides no primary source evidence for this, and the suggestion remains speculative.

[59] Turner, 'Eleanor of Aquitaine and her Children', 194. As Leonor's marriage was negotiated and financed in Henry's continental domains, there are no records in the Pipe Rolls relating to it.

It is far from clear how long Joanna spent at Fontevrault, although the evidence suggests that her time there was of short duration.[60] What is certain is that she travelled to England in July 1174, at the age of nine, with her father, younger brother John, sister-in-law Margaret, and her mother, who was at that time Henry's prisoner.[61] This is striking, as it implies that Margaret, the Young King's wife, was effectively Henry's hostage; moreover, Eleanor was not punished for her part in the rebellion by having her children removed from her care. A theme here can be discerned of an extra-vigilant watch on Henry's children in the years 1173-4, because of the desertion of all of his sons bar John. There was also a possible dynastic threat if Henry's remaining unmarried children were to fall under the control – including that of their matrimonial destinies – of Louis VII of France. It was therefore imperative for Henry to ensure that as many of his dependants as possible were securely guarded in England, safely close at hand as well as far from Louis' clutches. Eleanor was placed under house arrest at Salisbury, where she seems to have remained until at least Michaelmas 1176.[62]

It is unclear whether Joanna was resident with her mother during Eleanor's captivity, but it is certain that they saw each other at least once before Joanna's departure for marriage to William II of Sicily in September 1176. The Pipe Roll for this year records expenses for Eleanor at Winchester, where she had been residing since Easter, and where Joanna was also resident.[63] It is likely that Eleanor was involved in the preparations for Joanna's forthcoming marriage, much as she surely had been for her daughters Matilda and Leonor. After the arrival of William's ambassadors, Henry II also journeyed to Winchester before Joanna's departure, perhaps to see his daughter before she departed for Sicily.[64] He furnished Joanna with gold and silver plate and clothing for her journey, including robes – probably intended to be worn at her wedding in Palermo – which cost a staggering £114 5s 5d.[65] No one could accuse the Angevin rulers of providing poorly for their daughters, at least in terms of the material goods which they brought, possibly as dowries, to their husbands.

---

[60] Joanna's epitaph states merely that she was fostered there 'for a short time' (*quibuscum nutrita fuerat parvo tempore*), see Pavillon, *Vie du bienheureux Robert d'Arbrissel,* 588, no. 96.

[61] Eyton, *Itinerary,* 98, 179. Joanna's presence with her captive mother is noted by Diceto, I, 382. Howden makes no mention of either Joanna's or John's presence, noting merely that Eleanor, Margaret, and the counts of Leicester and Chester, both of whom were Henry's prisoners, crossed to England with Henry on 8 July, *Chronica,* II, 61. Turner and Eyton state that Alice of France and Constance of Brittany – the betrothed of, respectively, Richard and Geoffrey – were also brought to England at the July crossing, Turner, *Eleanor of Aquitaine,* 231; Eyton, *Itinerary,* 179. The fresco in the chapel of St Radegonde in Chinon of five mounted people, two of whom are crowned, has been viewed by some historians as a depiction of this event which may have been commissioned by Eleanor after Henry II's death. See Flori, *Eleanor of Aquitaine,* 115; Nurith Kenaan-Kedar, 'Aliénor d'Aquitaine et les arts visuals, de l'art dynastique à l'art courtois', in *Plantagenêts et Capétiens,* 85. If one of the figures depicts Joanna, as Flori suggests, it is one of the only extant representations of her, the other being that on her seal. It is debatable, however, how much of a true likeness either image represents.

[62] PR 20 Hen II, 29; PR 21 Hen II, 100; PR 21 Hen II, 171; Eyton, *Itinerary,* 197. Margaret, along with Henry's other captives, was lodged at Devizes in Gloucestershire, PR 20 Hen II, 21; Eyton, *Itinerary,* 180.

[63] PR 22 Hen II, 198; Eyton, *Itinerary,* 204. Flori proposes that Eleanor may at this time have 'helped in readying her daughter's trousseau and prepared her for life at the Sicilian royal court by recalling her own visit there [on return from crusade in 1149]', *Eleanor of Aquitaine,* 238.

[64] As evidenced from charters granted to St Albans monastery whilst Henry was at Winchester. See *Monasticon Anglicanum,* ed. William Dugdale (6 Vols., Vol. 2, London, 1819), nos. xiv & xv; Eyton, *Itinerary,* 199.

[65] PR 22 Hen II, 12-3. For Joanna's crossing, and the expenses incurred for this, PR 22 Hen II, 199.

Frequent entries in the Pipe Rolls from 1155, when her first child was born, until 1173, when she was captured for her part in her sons' rebellion, demonstrate that Eleanor was financially responsible for the care of her children during this time; or at least, she was responsible for authorising the payments for this, including the cost of providing their clothes. These provisions, often authorised by Eleanor's own writ, provide further evidence that until her enforced captivity began in 1173, Eleanor maintained close contact with her children.[66] They demonstrate, when considered beside the frequent contact that Eleanor had with her children, especially her daughters, when they were young, that Eleanor was neither an absent nor a neglectful mother.

It is the contention here that these early childhood experiences had a strong influence on Eleanor's daughters, as well as on her sons, and that the emotional bond they formed with their mother at this time was both powerful and long-lasting. As will be seen in Parts IV and V, further evidence of emotional ties is suggested by the choices Matilda, Leonor, and Joanna later made with regard to patronage and dynastic commemoration. There is also evidence that Eleanor maintained a degree of contact with all three of her daughters after they had left the family home for marriage, and as will be seen, both Joanna and Matilda turned to their mother as adults when they were facing situations of great personal crisis. As Turner has pointed out, contact between mothers and their daughters, who were married off abroad, were 'seldom entirely severed, and Eleanor doubtless corresponded with her daughters, although no copies of her letters survive'.[67] But how did Eleanor interact with her daughters, and what can one say about the nature of emotions and emotional relationships in the twelfth century?

---

[66] See for example PR 4 Hen II, 175; PR 5 Hen II, 1.

[67] Turner, *Eleanor of Aquitaine*, 149. He states that Matilda, Leonor, and Joanna, 'married to princes who were conspicuous as cultural patrons, were almost certainly literate', although he believes that because of the ages at which they left their natal home, the 'major portion of their education would have taken place at the courts of their in-laws', *Eleanor of Aquitaine*, 149. For more on the education of the Angevin children, see Part I, Chapter 3.

Chapter Two
Medieval Emotions

How did Eleanor, Matilda, Leonor and Joanna interact in a mother-daughter relationship? How did aristocratic families in general function in the twelfth century? Were they unloving, cold and unsentimental prior to the age of Enlightenment, as Philippe Ariès and Lloyd de Mause suggested?[1] Historians have long debated the inner emotional world of our medieval forebears, since the debate was opened by Lucien Febvre in 1941.[2] The progressivist view held that, until the advent of societal control over emotions in the modern era, medieval displays of emotion were "childlike" – primitive, violent, destructive, and irrational – and this view remained unchallenged until the 1960s, with the advent first of cognitive psychology and then, in the 1970s, of social constructionism. It was not until the 1980s, however, that the idea of a "childlike" Middle Ages was radically revised, with historians such as Gerd Altoff,[3] Barbara Rosenwein[4] and, most recently, Hanna Vollrath,[5] making important contributions to the field. Indeed, until the 1980s, the history of emotions remained relatively little studied, being largely viewed as tangential to political history.

Whilst the ephemeral nature of emotions makes them difficult either to study or define, medieval emotions clearly were felt, expressed, and manipulated just as they are today. The problem, according to Rosenwein, is not what medieval men and women felt, but how historians have treated medieval displays of emotion.[6] She dismisses the "emotionology" theory created in the 1980s by Peter and Carol Stearns, which suggests that societal control over emotions is inapplicable to history before the early modern "advice manuals", and thus echoes the theory of a childlike Middle Ages. Similarly, Rosenwein rejects over-reliance on the idea of human passivity to control by social institutions which forms the basis of French studies of the history of *mentalités*.[7] She agrees that the study of the history of emotions 'demands

---

[1] Ariès, *Centuries of Childhood*, trans. Robert Baldick (Pimlico, London, 1962; repr. 1996); de Mause, 'The Evolution of Childhood', in Lloyd de Mause (ed.), *The History of Childhood* (Jason Aronson Inc., New Jersey, 1974; repr. 1995). For more on the history of childhood, see Part I, Chapter 3.

[2] Lucien Febvre, 'La sensibilité et l'Histoire. Comment reconstituer la vie affective d'autrefois?', in *Annales d'Histoire Sociale*, 3 (Paris, 1941), 4-29; cited in Hanna Vollrath, 'Aliénor d'Aquitaine et ses enfants: une relation affective?', in *Plantagenêts et Capétiens*, 113-23. For further discussion of Febvre's works, see Barbara Rosenwein, 'Worrying about Emotions', *American Historical Review*, 107:3 (June 2002), 821-3.

[3] Altoff was one of the first historians to directly challenge Huizinga's view of a "childlike" Middle Ages, believing emotions served social functions which followed set rules and noting that displays of anger were predominantly political, as 'the medium through which power was expressed, understood, and manipulated', adding that 'Certain emotions were appropriate at certain times, in certain people who held certain statuses', cited in Rosenwein, 'Worrying about emotions', 841. Rosenwein, who reopened the debate at the turn of the century, views the contributions of Altoff and others as 'welcome and important correctives' to previously held views of a childlike Middle Ages, 'Worrying about emotions', 841, and 841n. for a bibliography of Altoff's works.

[4] Barbara Rosenwein, 'Worrying about emotions'; 'Writing Without Fear about Early Medieval Emotions', *Early Medieval Europe*, 10:2 (2001).

[5] Vollrath, 'Aliénor d'Aquitaine', 113-23.

[6] Rosenwein, 'Worrying about emotions', 841-2. A further problem lies in how sources, especially by clerical authors, were accustomed to treat (or not treat) issues of emotion. Conventions of form, style, and so on, all further disguise or distance the historian from what might be accurate reflections of emotions by contemporaries.

[7] For further discussion on French works on the history of *mentalités*, see Rosenwein, 'Worrying about emotions',

careful attention to linguistic, social, and political contexts', but reminds us that these should in any case be part of any historian's methodology.[8]

Rosenwein has proposed a new concept, which she terms "emotional communities", although perhaps a better term would be "emotional interaction".[9] In other words, we should focus on what people felt about the familial or social milieu they belonged to, and how they adjusted their behaviour according to the group or situation they were in. Rosenwein has pointed out that '*even within the same society* contradictory values and models...find their place',[10] a fact that is clearly as applicable to medieval times as it is to our own – compare, for example, how one behaves around one's family as opposed to how one acts amongst colleagues or friends.

Hanna Vollrath agrees with Rosenwein's conclusions, noting that although in the Middle Ages human actions were governed more by belief in the will of God, compared to the concept of free will in the modern era, mankind is, nevertheless, subject to strong universal emotions often beyond its control.[11] Vollrath asserts that free will and emotions are inseparable in human nature, and that it is impossible to make a distinction between emotions and the manifestation of emotions. To support her argument, Vollrath points to the letters exchanged between Abelard and Héloise as evidence of medieval emotions found in contemporary texts, reflective of the dominant perceptions of emotional thought in their time and influenced by contemporary theology, philosophy, psychology, and medicine.[12] In the absence of extant letters between Eleanor of Aquitaine and her daughters, it is impossible to ascertain their emotional content. Some have viewed the letters to Pope Celestine concerning the lack of papal action regarding Richard I's imprisonment by the German emperor, attributed to Eleanor but almost certainly drafted by Peter of Blois, as revelatory of the deep anguish of "a pitiable mother...[whose] grief cannot be comforted".[13] Anne Duggan, however, has recently argued convincingly that these letters are more likely to constitute an exercise in rhetoric, and may not even have been intended to be sent to the pope.[14]

Absence of evidence, however, is not evidence of absence, and the lack of documented letters between Leonor and her mother after her marriage to Alfonso VIII, for example, cannot be seriously interpreted as signifying a total breakdown in relations, as Rose Walker has suggested.[15] Only a handful of women's letters survive from this period, in contrast to the numerous extant letters of churchmen such as John of Salisbury and Peter of Blois, and in any

---

831-4, and for a bibliography, 832n.

[8] Rosenwein, 'Worrying about emotions', 839n.

[9] *Ibid.*, 842.

[10] *Ibid.*, 842-3.

[11] Vollrath, 'Aliénor d'Aquitaine', 113-23, although this generalisation overlooks changing attitudes within the Middle Ages.

[12] *Ibid.*, 115-7, although whilst these letters are important for the history of emotions, they might not be what they purport to be; see *The Letters of Abelard and Heloise*, trans. Betty Radice, rev. Michael Clanchy (Penguin, London, 1974; rev. 2003), esp. lxiii-lxxv.

[13] Anne Crawford, *Letters of the Queens of England, 1100-1547* (Stroud, 1994), 34-5. The Latin originals are preserved in *Foedera*, I, 72-6; see also Peter of Blois, *Epistola*, 2, *Patrologia Latina* 206, col. 1262-5; 3, *Patrologia Latina* 206, col. 1267-72. Crawford states that whilst the letters were 'certainly not' written by Eleanor personally, the emotions contained therein are 'all Eleanor's', *Letters*, 34-5.

[14] Duggan, 'On Finding the Voice of Eleanor of Aquitaine', in *Voix de femmes aux moyen âge. Actes du colloque du Centre d'Études Médiévales Anglaises de Paris-Sorbonne (26–27 mars 2010)*, ed. L. Carruthers, *Association des Médiévistes Anglicistes de l'Énseignement Supérieur*, 32 (Paris, 2011), 129–58. I am grateful to Professor Duggan for allowing me to read this article pre-publication.

[15] Walker, 'Leonor of England', 348.

case Eleanor of Aquitaine spent most of the early years of Leonor's marriage in Henry's custody.[16] Any personal correspondence that may have existed between mother and daughter is, therefore, obviously a matter of conjecture; however, one would expect some degree of communication if the relationship was good, and there is nothing to suggest that it was not.

As letters surviving from this period are concerned largely with statecraft (and almost exclusively written by men, to other men), it is hardly surprising that we have no documented letters between Eleanor and Leonor after 1170. We are, however, very fortunate to have a large number of surviving charters issued by Eleanor.[17] An analysis of these charters demonstrates that Eleanor frequently refers to her children, most notably Richard, John, and Joanna, as *dilectus*, or *carissimus*, meaning "most dear" (see Tables 5-7). It has been questioned as to whether or not this constitutes proof of Eleanor's maternal love for her children.[18] However, the key word here is frequently. The terms *dilectus* and *carissimus* do not appear consistently when Eleanor refers to her children in her charters, and neither are these terms applied only once her children have died. The term "dearest" is applied 15 times to Richard, at least three of which occur before his death in April 1199. Joanna and John are each referred to as "dearest" eight times.[19] The majority of these references to Joanna occur around the time she was with her mother shortly before her death in September 1199. John, however, outlived his mother, therefore all of the references to Eleanor's youngest son as "dearest" occur while he was still living. Such inconsistency in the application of these terms suggests that this was no mere convention of form, but a true expression of genuine emotion denoting a degree of maternal affection.

Table 5: 'Dearest' Richard in Eleanor's Charters – 15 instances

Terminology	Place & Date	Grant	Acta No.
karissimi filii nostri regis Richardi	Westminster [July 1189 X February 1190]	To Bury St Edmund's, restoration of gold cup	20

[16] See *Letters of John of Salisbury*, ed. W.J. Millor and C.N.L. Brooke, 2 vols. (Oxford, 1955-79); Peter of Blois, *Petri Blesensis Bathoniensis in Anglia Archidiaconi opera omnia*, in *Patrologia Latina*, 206 (1855).

[17] Eleanor's charters, as well as those issued by Henry II and his sons, are in the process of being edited by the Angevin Acta Project under the direction of Professor Nicholas Vincent, to whom I owe my thanks for being allowed access to the pre-publication findings.

[18] See Flori, *Eleanor of Aquitaine*, 137, although he has no doubt that Eleanor was devoted to her children, and that these feelings were reciprocated. It is perhaps significant that Berengaria of Navarre is never described with such affection on Eleanor's charters; see Ann Trindade, *Berengaria: In Search of Richard the Lionheart's Queen* (Four Courts Press, Dublin, 1999), 119. For discussions of Eleanor's charters, see H.G. Richardson, 'Letters and Charters of Eleanor of Aquitaine', in *English Historical Review*, 74 (1959), 193-213; and more recently, Marie Hivergneaux, 'Aliénor d'Aquitaine: Le pouvoir d'une femme à la lumière de ses chartes (1152-1204)', in Martin Aurell (ed.), *La Cour Plantagenêt 1152-1204* (Poitiers, 2000), 63-871; *idem.*, 'Autour d'Aliénor d'Aquitaine: Entourage et pouvoir au prisme des chartes (1137-1289)', in Martin Aurell & Noël-Yves Tonnerre (eds.), *Plantagenêts et Capétiens: Confrontations et Héritages* (Brepols, Belgium, 2006), 61-73; Nicholas Vincent, 'Patronage, Politics and Piety in the Charters of Eleanor of Aquitaine', in *ibid.*, 17-59.

[19] See the forthcoming *Acta*, nos. 2, 5, 13, 15, 20, 26, 33, 42, 42a, 59, 62, 72, 73, 74, 79, 80, 97, 101, 111, 115, 130, 135, 136, 142, 149. Eleanor's daughter Alix by her first husband Louis VII is also referred to as her "dearest daughter" on a charter from 1199, in which Eleanor grants her an annual £10 Poitevin, Jane Martindale, 'Eleanor of Aquitaine', in Janet Nelson (ed.), *Richard Coeur de Lion in History and Myth* (King's College, London, 1992), 18. The charter is preserved at Angers, Archives Départementales de Maine-et-Loire.

Terminology	Place & Date	Grant	Acta No.
karissimus filius noster rex Anglie Ricardus	London [1192 X 1193, ?1193]	To Christchurch, Canterbury, notification of Richard's captivity	26
dilecti filii nostri regis Ricardi	Perigueux [February 1190 X April 1199]	To Dalon Abbey, grant of protection and confirmation of grants	42
karissimus filius noster rex Ric(ardus)	Saumur [February 1194 X November 1199]	To Grandselve Abbey, confirmation of grant by Richard	74
karissimi filii nostri Ric(ardi)	Fontevraud, 21 April 1199	To Turpenay Abbey for Richard's funerary services	149
karissimi domini sui regis Richardi, filii nostri	Fontevraud, c.11 April 1199	To Fontevraud, confirmation of grant	59
carissimi filii nostri regis Richardi	Loudun, 29 April 1199	To Ralph de Mauléon, grant of castles in exchange for La Rochelle	97
karissimi filii nostri Richardi regis Anglie	[April 1199 X March 1200]	To Grace-Dieu Abbey, confirmation of grant	72
karissimi filii nostri Ricardi regis Anglorum	Poitiers, 4 May 1199	To Montierneuf, confirmation of rights and liberties	101
karissimo filio nostro R. rege Angl(orum)	Montreuil, 5 May 1199	To Abbey of Ste-Croix, Poitiers, restoration of lands	111
carissimus filius noster dominus Ricardus rex Anglie	Niort [May 1199 X March 1200]	To Grandmont, confirmation of grant	73
karissimi filii nostri Richardi regis Anglie	Bordeaux, 1 July 1199	To the men of Bordeaux, abolition of customs	15
karissimum filium nostrum Richardum	Fontevraud, 6 October 1200	To Abbey of St-Maixent, quittance from all dues and for masses for the Queen	135
carissimum filium nostrum Richardum	Fontevraud, 6 October [1200]	To Abbey of St-Maixent, quittance from all taille and customs	136
karissimus filius noster rex Ricard(us)	Fontevraud [1200 X March 1201]	To Adam the Cook, grant of lands	2

Table 6: 'Dearest' Joanna in Eleanor's Charters – 8 instances

Terminology	Place & Date	Grant	Acta No.
in presentia nostra et coram Iohanna dilecta filia nostra olim Sicilie regina	Fontevraud [May 1194 X March 1195]	To Fontevraud, grant of lands	62
Testibus karissima filia nostra regina Iohanna	Rouen, 1 August 1199	To Amesbury Priory, confirmation of grant	5
Hiis testibus: carissima filia nostra regina Iohanna	Rouen, 1 August 1199	To Abbey of Notre-Dame, Saintes, restoration of all rights and liberties	130
Hiis testibus: karissima filia mea regina Iohanna	[April 1199 X March 1200]	To Puyravault Priory, confirmation of rights and liberties	115
Testibus...carissima filia nostra domina Iohanna comitissa Tholose ducissa Narbon'	Niort [May 1199 X March 1200]	To Grandmont, confirmation of grant	73
T(estibus)...regina Ioanna k(arissi)ma filia nostra	St-Jean-d'Angely [1199 X 1204]	To Deuil Priory, grant of protection	42a
k(arissi)me filie nostre regine Ioh(ann)e	[1200 X 1204]	Notification of Joanna's will	142
Testibus regina Iohanna k(arissi)ma filia nostra	Fontevraud [????]	To Henry de Bernevalle, grant of vill of Biddestone	13

Table 7: 'Dearest' John in Eleanor's Charters – 8 instances

Terminology	Place & Date	Grant	Acta No.
karissimi filii mei Ioannis regis Anglie	Westminster [July 1189 X February 1190]	To Bury St Edmund's, restoration of gold cup	20
karissimum filium nostrum Iohannem regem Anglie	[Bordeaux], 1 July 1199	To the men of Bordeaux, abolition of customs	15
regis Iohannis karissimi filii nostri	Rouen, 1 August 1199	To Amesbury Priory, confirmation of grant	5

Terminology	Place & Date	Grant	Acta No.
karissimi filii nostri Iohannis regis Anglorum	Rouen, 1 August 1199	To Abbey of Notre-Dame, Saintes, restoration of all rights and liberties	130
karissimo filio nostro I(ohanni) Dei gratia illustri regi Anglorum	[May X December 1199]	To John, granting Poitou	79
carissimus filius noster Ioh(anne)s rex Angl(orum)	Le Vaudreuil [May 1199 X March 1200]	To Andrew de Chauvigny, grant of St-Sauveur	33
Karissimo filio suo etc I(ohanni) Dei gratia <regi Anglorum>	Fontevraud [c.1200]	Letter to John	80
dilecti filii nostri Iohannis	Fontevraud, 6 October [1200]	To Abbey of St-Maixent quittance from all taille and customs	136

Was the medieval nobleman or woman then really devoid of emotions? Can we make such generalisations? It is of course unwise to suggest that emotions are felt and expressed everywhere in the same manner: aside from the fact that emotions are always subjective, there are also different norms and expectations not just in different societies but within different strata of society. We may, however, admit certain similarities, such as, for example, the emotions that rise following a birth or the death of a loved one. For Vollrath, it is a universal truism that all women experience emotion at the death of one of their children, although the manifestation of this emotion will differ according to circumstance and cultural tradition. Shulamith Shahar has highlighted the lengths medieval parents went to to ensure the well-being of their children, such as recourse to physicians or visiting saints' shrines (as Louis VII did for his son Philip in 1179), as being indicative of deep-rooted emotional concerns for the welfare of their children, and Colin Heywood asserts that 'responses to infant deaths show the extent to which childhood was valued' – or, rather, the extent to which parents loved their children.[20]

Infant mortality, as well as death in childbirth, was so common in the Middle Ages that one might expect a certain degree of resignation to such events as inevitable occurrences.[21] The lack of record of parental grief over the loss of a child in many medieval texts seems to correspond to the lack of record of that child's death (or indeed birth) as a consequence

---

[20] Shulamith Shahar, *Childhood in the Middle Ages* (Routledge, London, 1990; repr. 1992), 145-62. She states that 'it cannot be said that the death of a child was an event lacking emotional import', 155. For Louis' visit to the shrine of Thomas Becket, see Part IV, Chapter 1. Colin Heywood, *A History of Childhood: Children and Childhood in the West from Medieval to Modern Times* (Polity Press, Cambridge, 2001), 60.

[21] Approximately 30% of children died before their first year, and only half of those who survived their first year reached the age of five, Shahar, *Childhood in the Middle Ages*, 149. I cannot agree with Heywood's assertion that 'the death of a newly born baby was always less distressing for parents than that of a child with whom they had experienced several years of bonding', *History of Childhood*, 59.

of the high rates of infant mortality.[22] Nevertheless, we should not expect that these losses were not frequently mourned. As Lorraine Attreed has rightly pointed out, evidence suggests that there was an emphasis on safeguarding children, and a 'preparedness for death does not mean that love was not risked or present'.[23] Biblical examples of parental grief at the loss of their children, often presented in Corpus Christi plays and other popular medieval dramas, 'would be incomprehensible to a society and an audience which did *not* care for its young and treasure their lives'.[24]

The late twelfth-century Winchester Bible contains a depiction of the grief of King David at the death of his son Absalom.[25] Does this image represent a "conventional" expression of grief? Does this even matter? Are not symbolic, ritual, or conventional expressions of emotion signifiers of real feelings? If not, would their expression be so powerful? Conventional depictions and ritual gestures can shape and enable the 'externalization of emotional experience in culturally familiar patterns', which make for the effective communication and conveyance of such emotion 'even when not 'authentic'".[26] Moreover, as Catherine Cubitt has noted, formulaic, ritual expressions and genuine feelings are not antithetical, and the former can be, and often was, used to demonstrate the latter.[27] Indeed, the Winchester image may be an allusion to Henry II's grief at the death of the Young King, who was also referred to as 'another Absalom'.[28] Rosenwein has argued that in the Middle Ages, as now, emotions may seem 'straightforward (but may not be); at other times they may be utterly repressed; and at all times they are shaped by *topoi* or conventions'.[29] As Mary Garrison has rightly pointed out, however, the use of *topoi* does not necessarily indicate artificial expressions, and such *topoi* may have been selected 'precisely because of their communicative power'.[30]

---

[22] Vollrath, 'Aliénor d'Aquitaine', 118.

[23] Lorraine C. Attreed, 'From *Pearl* Maiden to Tower Princes: Towards a new history of medieval childhood', *Journal of Medieval History*, 9 (1983), 46, although her examples are all from the later medieval period, with the earliest being the mid-fourteenth century *Pearl* narrative, which demonstrates the grief of a medieval father at the loss of his only child.

[24] Attreed, '*Pearl* Maiden', 50. Mary McLaughlin reached similar conclusions from the abundance of evidence pertaining to advice on "good milk" and other ways of caring for infants, 'Survivors and Surrogates: Children and Parents from the Ninth to the Thirteenth Centuries', in *The History of Childhood*, 132-4. McLaughlin also sees a symbiotic relationship between the rise in the eleventh and twelfth centuries of the cult of the infant Jesus and the Virgin as Mother, and that of the Massacre of the Innocents, and real parent-child relationships. David Herlihy sees a similar thread in the recurring familial references in saints' lives, as well as a comparability with devotion to the Virgin and that of real mothers, *Medieval Households*, 112-30. Female saints as "mothers" of their followers can equate to earthly mothers, who also gave their children religious instruction, *Medieval Households*, 122-4. Similarly, "the cult of the infant Jesus exploited real attitudes toward babies", *Medieval Households*, 126.

[25] See Rosenwein, 'Worrying about Emotions', 840, for this image. For more examples of ritual or symbolic displays of emotion, see Stuart Airlie, 'The History of Emotions and Emotional History', *Early Medieval Europe*, 10:2 (2001), 235-41.

[26] Mary Garrison, 'The study of emotions in early medieval history', *Early Medieval Europe*, 10.2 (2001), 244.

[27] Catherine Cubitt, 'The History of Emotions: a debate. Introduction', *Early Medieval Europe*, 10:2 (2001), 226. Similarly, bodily changes in texts, such as flushed faces, are often indicators of a physical manifestation of emotion, see Carolyne Larrington, 'The psychology of emotion and the study of the medieval period', *Early Medieval Europe*, 10.2 (2001), 253-4.

[28] Newburgh, I, 233. For Henry's agonised reaction to the Young King's death, Howden, *Gesta*, I, 301; *Chronica*, II, 279-80.

[29] Rosenwein, 'Writing Without Fear, 233. See also the collected articles in Rosenwein (ed.), *Anger's Past: The Social Uses of an Emotion in the Middle Ages* (Cornell University Press, 1998).

[30] Garrison, 'Study of emotions', 246. She wonders whether the trend for denying medieval expressions of grief might represent 'a scholarly version of the same awkwardness that makes many people unable to respond appropriately to the recently bereaved', *ibid.*, 249.

Both written and visual expressions of emotions abound in medieval texts – according to the *Crónica Latina*, Leonor was so distressed by the imminent death of her son Fernando that she entered his chamber, climbed into bed with him, and, taking hold of his hands, tried either to revive him with a kiss, or else to die with him.[31] The *Crónica* relates further that after the death of her husband Alfonso, Leonor, 'deprived of the solace of so great a man', died from grief and sadness.[32] From 1211 until the year of their deaths, Leonor and Alfonso issued a number of grants to Las Huelgas for the welfare of the soul of Fernando, '*carissimi primogeniti nostri*'.[33] Similarly, the death of Henry and Eleanor's first-born son William must, as Turner states, have been mourned by them, 'Like parents in any age', and the charter concerning the gift made to Reading Abbey for the welfare of his soul was given 'at the queen's request and with her assent'.[34] Eleanor's purported letters to Pope Celestine, discussed above, and her 1199 charter to Fontevrault, discussed in Part V, are also suggestive of the depths of her feelings for the children who predeceased her.[35]

Historians have debated both the maternal instincts of Eleanor of Aquitaine and the degree of her patronage, but as will be seen in Part V, it appears that she did have a degree of influence on the patronage patterns of her daughters, especially Leonor, in their choice of bolstering the prestige of their natal families through female religious institutions.[36] My approach to try and discern a strong emotional mother-daughter bond through acts of patronage and commemoration thereby considers the field of emotions in a different way from Rosenwein and Vollrath.[37]

Eleanor of Aquitaine as Mother

It is often taken for granted that Eleanor of Aquitaine was at best an absent mother, and at worst, a neglectful one. Some historians have even gone so far as to state that Eleanor only paid attention to her children when they were of useful political value. But is this an accurate

---

[31] *Crónica Latina*, 47-8. Similarly, in the first of two letters to Pope Celestine regarding Richard's captivity, purported to have been written by or for Eleanor, she expresses the wish to "die for you, my son...how could a mother forget the son of her very womb?...what I most want to see, the face of my son", Crawford, *Letters*, 36-43.

[32] *Crónica Latina*, 60.

[33] See González, *Alfonso VIII*, III, nos. 885-8, 917, 923.

[34] Turner, *Eleanor of Aquitaine*, 130. For the death and burial of William, see Torigni, 189. The choice of burial for William at the feet of his great-grandfather Henry I was no doubt a politically informed gesture; see Flori, *Eleanor of Aquitaine*, 69, 72.

[35] The second letter to Celestine laments that Eleanor has lived to see two of her sons dead and buried, and a third in captivity, *Foedera*, I, 74-6; Crawford, *Letters*, 36-43. Even if these letters are not attributable to Eleanor, they still indicate what her feelings were assumed to have been. Eleanor's grant to Fontevrault, given soon after Richard's death, refers to him as *potentis viri Regis Ricardi*, Martindale, 'Eleanor of Aquitaine', 18; see also Part V. The *Life* of Hugh of Lincoln records that the bishop paid a special visit to Berengaria of Navarre in April 1199 in order to console her for her loss, *Magna Vita Sancti Hugonis Episcopi Lincolniensis*, ed. James F. Dimock (RS, 37, London, 1864), 286.

[36] For positive views of Eleanor as patron, see June Hall McCash, 'Cultural Patronage', 6; Kathleen Nolan, 'The Queen's Choice: Eleanor of Aquitaine and the Tombs at Fontevraud', in *Eleanor of Aquitaine: Lord and Lady*, 377-406. For a less positive view of Eleanor's patronage and of her maternal role, Elizabeth Brown, 'Eleanor of Aquitaine: Parent, Queen, and Duchess', in *Eleanor of Aquitaine: Patron and Politician*, 9-34; Vincent, 'Patronage, Politics and Piety', 17-59.

[37] Studies on intergenerational relationships and the ties between brothers and sisters are now proving to be a serious and fruitful area of research for political historians. See for example the recent excellent study of familial relationships in medieval Germany by Jonathan R. Lyon, *Princely Brothers and Sisters: The Sibling Bond in German Politics, 1100-1250* (Cornell University Press, 2013).

representation of Eleanor's role as a mother? How invested was she really in her children's lives? I would argue that Eleanor was, in fact, a loving and caring mother, and there is evidence to support this, if we care to look. The sources we use as historians were produced by the agency of men, but what we are looking for is the agency of women. This means we must look carefully, to see beyond the actions of the man who produced a document, in order to find the agency of the woman behind it. The evidence from the Pipe Rolls, the fiscal and administrative records of Henry II's reign discussed in Chapter 1, demonstrates that all three of Eleanor of Aquitaine's daughters, and Leonor in particular, spent the majority of their formative years in the company of their mother. We can therefore prove that not only did Eleanor care for her daughters - and indeed her sons - but that she kept in close contact with them both during their infancies and early childhoods, and after they had left their home for marriage.

In his 1988 article on Eleanor's relationship with her children, for example, Ralph Turner did little to redress the often-cited argument that Eleanor was, at best, lax in her maternal duties.[38] Whilst acknowledging that the delegation of royal and aristocratic children to wet-nurses and tutors was usual practice in the Middle Ages, Turner reiterated the view that Eleanor was only interested in her children – by which he meant her sons – when they were politically useful.[39] However, he seems to have missed a vital point when listing the number of times Eleanor travelled with her children: that, for the most part, it was her daughters who accompanied her. Certainly there was a difference in the way aristocratic sons and daughters were raised, with sons commonly being sent to live and be educated in noble households from the age of about seven, as the Young King was to Becket's household, for martial and courtly training.[40] The fact that Eleanor would have been fully aware that her daughters would leave their natal land for marriage at an early age is perhaps one reason why she chose to travel with them so often.

More recently, Turner has noted that what he still views as Eleanor's limited contact with her children was due to custom and circumstance, rather than any 'lack of maternal feeling',[41] and whilst Jean Flori doubts that the "conventional" diplomatic terms *dilectus* and *carissimus*, used of her children in Eleanor's charters, can be taken as proofs of maternal love, he does not doubt that Eleanor was devoted to her children, and that these feelings were reciprocated.[42] The proof of her efforts as a mother are revealed in the loyalty and devotion shown to her by her sons and daughters as adults; the Young King certainly loved her, as his letter to Henry, written on his deathbed in 1183, requests first and foremost that Henry treat his captive mother with more indulgence.[43] Eleanor's maternal instincts were amply rewarded by Richard,

---

[38] Turner, 'Eleanor of Aquitaine and her Children', 321-35.

[39] *Ibid.*, 326.

[40] For more on the Young King's upbringing, see Matthew Strickland, 'On the Instruction of a Prince: The Upbringing of Henry the Young King', in C. Harper-Bell & N. Vincent (eds.), *Henry II: New Interpretations* (Woodbridge, 2007), 184-214.

[41] Turner, *Eleanor of Aquitaine*, 145, noting that it is '[un]necessary to conclude that Eleanor was indifferent to her young children nor that she made little 'psychological investment' in them. There is no evidence to show that she and Henry failed to cherish their children, to provide for their care, to place their hopes in their futures, or to experience grief at their deaths.'

[42] Flori, *Eleanor of Aquitaine*, 137. He believes that the vehement and grief stricken letters written to Pope Celestine imploring (or ordering) him to assist her in the matter of Richard's captivity are more instructive of Eleanor's feelings as a mother, *Eleanor of Aquitaine*, 164-6. See also above, notes 13-14, 31, 35, for the authorship of these letters.

[43] Vigeois, *Gaufredi prioris Vosiensis pars altera chronici lemovicensis*, in *Receuil des Historiens des Gaules et de la France*, 24 vols., ed. Martin Bouquet (Paris, 1869-1904 ; hereafter *RHGF*), XVIII, 220; Flori, *Eleanor of Aquitaine*, 126; Turner, *Eleanor of Aquitaine*, 244.

who, once king, immediately released Eleanor from captivity, restored all her rights and liberties and increased her income considerably, granted her regency powers before his departure for crusade, and afforded her precedence at court before his own queen Berengaria.[44] Later, King John undertook a speedy response to Eleanor's call for assistance at the siege of Mirebeau in 1202, when, in Turner's phrase, 'his strong feelings for his mother moved him to his most robust action in his largely listless defense of his Continental domains.'[45]

Turner's assertion that only chance and misfortune would reunite Eleanor with her daughters after their marriages holds true – Matilda rejoined her natal family during her years of exile from Saxony, spending the Christmas courts of 1182-4 with her parents and accompanying her mother to France in 1185.[46] We must assume that Matilda and her husband had been in contact with Henry and Eleanor prior to their arrival, in order for preparations to be made for their reception at the Angevin court. There are frequent references in the Pipe Rolls from 1175-89 relating to gifts from Henry II to Henry the Lion and vice versa,[47] as well as expenses for Henry the Lion, Matilda, and their children during their years in exile at Henry II's court.[48] Two of their children, William and Richenza, remained at the Angevin court long after Henry the Lion's restoration and return to Saxony.[49]

There is also evidence of continued contact with Leonor in Castile. In the year 1200, Eleanor spent some two months in Castile with Leonor and her family, where she had gone to collect Leonor's daughter Blanca for marriage to the heir to the French crown.[50] Nineteen years previously, in July 1181, Henry II had sent Leonor a gift of clothing and silver plate to mark the birth of her first child, Sancho.[51] The expenses for the purchase and conveyance of this gift are listed in the Pipe Rolls, and the fact that such a gift was sent suggests that either Leonor or her husband Alfonso had written to Henry and Eleanor to inform them of their happy news. Leonor had also sent her clerk, John, to be educated in the schools in Northamptonshire between the years 1175-81, an indication of the esteem she had for an Angevin education.[52]

[44] Flori, *Eleanor of Aquitaine*, 142.

[45] Turner, *Eleanor of Aquitaine*, 292; see also Flori, *Eleanor of Aquitaine*, 198-9. Richard and John in particular seem to have been emotionally attached to their mother, affording her precedence at court even over their own queens and allowing her to enjoy 'the perquisites of a queen-regnant', Turner, 'Eleanor of Aquitaine and her Children', 331.

[46] Turner, 'Eleanor of Aquitaine and her Children', 328. In 1184, Eleanor was temporarily granted more freedom, and was reunited with her eldest daughter Matilda and her exiled husband Henry the Lion at Winchester; on Henry II's orders, they joined him in Normandy after Easter 1185, at which time Richard was forced to return Poitou to Eleanor, and Eleanor was returned to Winchester, Flori, *Eleanor of Aquitaine*, 128-30. John had been kept in Henry II's household from the time of their forced return to England in 1174 until he was sent to the household of the justiciar, Ranulf de Glanvill, in 1181, Turner, *Eleanor of Aquitaine*, 240.

[47] Such as a gift of ten hauberks given to Henry the Lion, PR 25 Hen II, 94, and a gift of a falconer and twenty falcons given to Henry II, PR 26 Hen II, 150.

[48] PR 27 Hen II, 157; PR 29 Hen II, 161; PR 30 Hen II, 58, 120, 134-5, 137-8, 144-5, 150; PR 31 Hen II, 9, 21, 171-2, 206, 215, 218; PR 32 Hen II, 49, 168, 185.

[49] PR 33 Hen II, 40, 194, 203, 204, 212; PR 34 Hen II, 14, 18, 27, 171.

[50] Turner, *Eleanor of Aquitaine*, 289.

[51] PR 27 Hen II, 157. Sancho is the only child born to Leonor to be mentioned by Torigni, 295. For more on Leonor's children, see Part III, Chapter 2, and Part V, Chapter 1.

[52] PR 22 Hen II, 47; PR 23 Hen II, 89; PR 24 Hen II, 49; PR 25 Hen II, 61; PR 26 Hen II, 81; PR 27 Hen II, 67.

Joanna was also reunited with Eleanor: first, in 1191, when the dowager queen brought Berengaria of Navarre to Richard in Sicily, and apparently charged her youngest daughter with accompanying Berengaria on crusade to ensure that her marriage to Richard took place.[53] Some years later, in 1199, Joanna fled to her mother in Poitou after failing to withstand a siege in Toulouse: pregnant and sick, Joanna did not survive the ordeal of childbirth and died at Rouen, having been granted a pension of 100 marks by King John, "by counsel of our dearest mother", for the purpose of making testamentary benefactions.[54] Eleanor herself acted as executor of Joanna's will, travelling personally to Toulouse to ensure that Joanna's husband, Raymond VI, acted in accordance with her daughter's dying wishes.[55]

Both Matilda and Joanna thus fled to their mother in their times of deepest trouble, although their individual circumstances were very different. Possibly they felt they had nowhere else to turn; but the fact that they chose to return to their natal family, and that they were welcomed when they did so, suggests not just strong family ties, but also continued correspondence after their marriages. Matilda's exile from Saxony in 1182 and Joanna's flight to her mother's court in 1199 both suggest some degree of contact between Eleanor and her daughters, as it is highly unlikely that Matilda and Joanna would have arrived at the courts of their parents completely unannounced. That there was such correspondence after these sisters had left their natal lands is confirmed by the various entries in the Pipe Rolls noted above. Can it then seriously be argued that the Angevin family was merely 'an institution for the transmission of a name and an estate', with no evidence of affective bonds?[56] Were royal and aristocratic methods of childcare really 'aimed at placing children at a distance from their parents, both physically and emotionally'?[57] Or is this an anachronistic assumption based on our own modern standards of how best to raise children? How were medieval royal and aristocratic sons and daughters raised?

---

[53] Turner, 'Eleanor of Aquitaine and her Children', 329. Ivan Cloulas offers a highly emotive, if conjectural, description of Eleanor and Joanna's reunion in Sicily: Eleanor's eyes 'filled with tears' and she 'embraced her [Joanna] for a long time, like a child', 'Bérengère de Navarre raconte Aliénor d'Aquitaine', in *Aliénor d'Aquitaine*, 231-2.

[54] Turner, 'Eleanor of Aquitaine and her Children', 329. For the grant, which also describes Joanna as John's "dearest sister", see Thomas Duffy Hardy (ed.), *Rotuli Chartarum in Turreni Londiniensi Asservati* (Record Commission, London, 1831), I, 13. Joanna's maids had clearly fled with her to Fontevrault, as shortly after her death John granted two of them pensions for their maintenance there. The charter's first witness was Joanna's mother, Eleanor; see Turner, 'Eleanor of Aquitaine and her Children', 329; *Rotuli Chartarum*, I, 25; see also Part V.

[55] For more on Joanna's death and burial at Fontevrault, and the terms of her will, see Part V, Chapter 4.

[56] Turner, 'Eleanor of Aquitaine and her Children', 332.

[57] *Ibid.*, 325.

Chapter Three
Medieval Childhood

Medieval daughters have traditionally been viewed essentially as dynastic pawns, to be moved across the chessboard of Europe at their fathers' whim. But was that it? Was that the extent of medieval parents' involvement in their children's upbringing, to find them suitable marriage partners? Political historians have largely ignored childhood as a stage in medieval people's lives. This may be due to a lack of information – like some historians today, contemporary chroniclers were more concerned with medieval men and women once they grew up and actually *did* something. But people do not leap from their mother's wombs fully formed and ready to take on the destiny life has set out for them. Childhood is an absolutely crucial stage of human development, when formative experiences shape the person that the child will eventually become. Therefore, as historians, we should not seek to deny medieval men and women that stage in development between birth and adulthood, however difficult finding information for this key stage in medieval people's lives may be.

The state or concept of childhood over the centuries has proved to be a fruitful field for historians, since Philippe Ariès first opened the debate in the 1960s, when he proposed that childhood as a concept did not exist in medieval times. According to Ariès, until the fourteenth century, children passed from a stage of helpless infancy when they were wholly dependent on adults (mothers or nurses), directly into adult society at about the age of five or seven.[1] However, Ariès has little to say on childhood prior to the fourteenth century, when, according to Ariès, the first 'concept of childhood – characterized by 'coddling" appeared; the second, pioneered by moralists in the seventeenth century, sought to ensure discipline; with health and hygiene only becoming a real concern in the eighteenth century,[2] although he noted that this does not necessarily mean that parents did not have affection for their children.[3]

Ariès' progressivist approach, his conclusion that the concept of childhood was a seventeenth century invention, and that there was no medieval concept of a transitional stage between infancy and adulthood until the fourteenth century at the earliest, heavily influenced subsequent historians of medieval childhood; most notably, Lloyd de Mause, who believed that the farther back in history one looks, the worse parents treated their children. Although he argues against Ariès' "invention" of childhood, de Mause also has a progressivist, and very negative, outlook, viewing the eighteenth century as a positive turning point in parenting practices and identifying six progressive "ages" of childrearing, with corresponding general tendencies – the Middle Ages, according to de Mause, was the 'age of abandonment'.[4] The majority of his "evidence" is, however, eighteenth century or later, and he tends, on the whole, towards over-generalisations and an almost deliberate anachronism when dealing with the medieval period.[5]

---

[1] Ariès, *Centuries of Childhood*, 316, 395.
[2] *Ibid.*, 129.
[3] *Ibid.*, 125.
[4] De Mause, 'Evolution of Childhood', 51-4.
[5] For example, he seems almost deliberately to misunderstand the point of swaddling, equating the deed with a

More recently, the contentious theories of Ariès and de Mause have been criticised and challenged. Mary Martin McLaughlin notes the problems of the evidence for medieval childhood as being largely hagiographical, and written by, or about, people who by and large had never been parents themselves.[6] Pauline Stafford has pointed out that medieval people clearly conceived that there was a difference between childhood and adulthood,[7] and Shulamith Shahar and Colin Heywood have both noted the medieval awareness of the three Classical stages of childhood – *infantia*, *pueritia*, and *adolescentia*, which correspond to the modern psychological stages of infancy and early childhood (from birth to the age of seven), of middle childhood (from seven to twelve years for girls, and fourteen years for boys), and adolescence (from twelve or fourteen to around twenty years of age).[8] Shahar states that the early integration into adult life for medieval children should not be construed as being demonstrative of a lack of conception of childhood as a separate stage (or stages), and asserts that parents in the Middle Ages differed little in their attitudes toward children – in other words, there were as many affectionate or neglectful parents then as now, and medieval parents quite clearly 'invested both material and emotional resources in their offspring'.[9]

Lorraine Attreed reaches the same conclusion, asserting that 'medieval children were no more spoiled or neglected than children are today', and that medieval literature reflected the reality of home life where children – including royal children – were valued.[10] Heywood has cited Steven Ozment's compelling argument, that "surely the hubris of an age reaches a certain peak when it accuses another age of being incapable of loving its children properly".[11] Indeed, it seems unnecessary, even arrogant, to suggest that medieval parents were any more or less emotionally attached to their children than parents at any other time in history. As Turner has pointed out, Eleanor's 'involvement in her children's upbringing differs from the ideal of

---

belief that the child was evil, rather than being performed in the belief that it was safest for the child, 'Evolution of Childhood', 11, 37-8. He also deems the practices of fostering (sending children to other households at around age seven), using children as hostages or surety, and, especially, using wetnurses, as forms of 'institutionalised abandonment', 'Evolution of Childhood', 32-5.

[6] McLaughlin, 'Survivors and Surrogates', 110. Her assessment of medieval childhood is largely positive, although she does wonder if early separation led to a need to seek "surrogate" mothers, 'whether earthly or celestial' – i.e. in the form of religious or courtly devotion, 'Survivors and Surrogates', 135.

[7] Pauline Stafford, 'Parents and Children in the Early Middle Ages', *Early Medieval Europe*, 10.2 (2001), 257-71. She questions whether the concept of childhood was viewed as 'unitary', or whether it was thought to be comprised of 'cycles', in a similar way to the stages or life-cycles of a woman's life, and concludes that the separation of the sexes at around the age of seven suggests that there must have been some perception of different stages of childhood, 'Parents and Children', 261-2.

[8] See Shahar, *Childhood in the Middle Ages*, 23-31 for a fuller discussion of each of these stages. This difference in ages for boys and girls in the attainment of adulthood has led Stafford to describe it as both gendered and socially constructed, 'Parents and Children', 261. Heywood has argued that whilst there was a loosely defined medieval conception of childhood, it differed from modern conceptions, and sees a cyclical ebb and flow in interest in children rather than a definitive, linear 'discovery', *History of Childhood*, 12-20, 31. He has criticised de Mause for writing 'little more than a history of child abuse', *History of Childhood*, 41. Like de Mause, however, Heywood is also critical of the medieval practice of using wetnurses, noting that the nobility 'probably took for granted the privilege of handing over childcare responsibilities to someone else without much reflection', *History of Childhood*, 66. Shahar, on the other hand, points out that the fact that a wetnurse is employed does not prevent emotional ties being formed with the mother, see *Childhood in the Middle Ages*, 53-76, especially 64-5, 74-5.

[9] Shahar, *Childhood in the Middle Ages*, 1. This raises the key question of what adults *expected* of children in terms of conduct, engagement with political affairs, and so on, often when still very young.

[10] Attreed, '*Pearl* Maiden', 44, 45.

[11] Cited in Heywood, *History of Childhood*, 42.

parenting today, but it hardly differs from practises of royalty or the aristocracy *in any age*'.[12] The evidence for the Angevin family, and for Eleanor and her daughters in particular, suggests strong, lasting, emotional ties.[13] To suppose that there was no correspondence between mother and daughters on the grounds that there is no extant documentary evidence for such is, it seems, misguided, especially as contact prior to their marriages was so frequent.[14]

An Angevin Education

It has been suggested that Leonor, along with her younger sister Joanna and their brother John, was educated at Fontevrault as a child.[15] It is plausible that the placing of daughters and youngest sons under the care and instruction of this favoured community was an Angevin family custom. All of Henry and Eleanor's offspring are relatively absent from the sources in their early years, but if they spent any time at Fontevrault it is probable that they would have received some degree of religious and intellectual training there.[16] The evidence from the Pipe Rolls, however, which demonstrates that Eleanor of Aquitaine frequently had her children with her on her travels, would discount any notion of a prolonged stay at Fontevrault, and as Katy Dutton has demonstrated, the norm for Angevin children was to be kept at or very near to home.[17]

Ralph Turner has suggested that Eleanor's role in the education of any of her children was limited at best.[18] Whilst he asserts that Matilda, Leonor and Joanna were 'almost certainly literate', he believes that due to the young age at which they left their natal home, the majority of their education would have been undertaken in their adopted lands.[19] This seems an unlikely

---

[12] Turner, *Eleanor of Aquitaine*, 149. My italics. Both Turner and Flori agree that Eleanor's children felt more affection for her than they did for their father, which strongly suggests that at some point during their childhoods, Eleanor had 'cemented solid ties of affection with them', Turner, *Eleanor of Aquitaine*, 145; see also Flori, *Eleanor of Aquitaine*, 89.

[13] It is worth noting in brief here Eleanor's relations with her daughters Marie and Alix from her first marriage to Louis VII of France. According to medieval law and custom, children were the property of their father; therefore, when Eleanor's marriage to Louis was annulled, she had no choice but to leave Marie and Alix behind. As Flori noted, Louis would 'never have agreed to let his daughters go, even if Eleanor had expressed a wish to keep them with her: children 'belonged' to their father. It was in the King's political interest to have them in his charge so that he might marry them off as it suited him…[which] he very soon did', *Eleanor of Aquitaine*, 56. Turner comments that whilst Eleanor must have 'felt deep sorrow at parting from her children…she knew that losing them was inevitable… There was no possibility of her having custody of them or visiting them, and after the annulment it is doubtful that she ever saw them again', *Eleanor of Aquitaine*, 107.

[14] Unlike the daughters, the political divisions made by Henry II for his sons could cause tension and bitterness between them. The Young King and Richard, as Walter Map noted, hated each other. My thanks to Matthew Strickland for this reference.

[15] See Part I, Chapter 1. Amy Kelly suggests that their elder sister Matilda received some degree of instruction from her grandmother, the Empress Matilda, *Eleanor of Aquitaine*, 210. She is not, however, always accurate in her information – for example, she gives the year of Joanna's marriage to William of Sicily as 1174, *Eleanor of Aquitaine*, 259 – and overall tends to favour a rather romanticised approach.

[16] Shahar has pointed out that convents were viewed as suitable centres for the placing of daughters not just for educational purposes, but also because young girls would be better protected from men in such an institution, thereby safeguarding their honour – and their virginity, *Childhood in the Middle Ages*, 220.

[17] Kathryn Dutton, '*Ad erudiendum tradidit*: The Upbringing of Angevin Comital Children', *Anglo-Norman Studies*, 32 (2009), 24-39. She states that there is 'strong evidence that the Angevin counts had a good deal of contact with their children', 24n, noting that 'rulers did not always, or even frequently, send their children away', 39.

[18] Turner, 'Eleanor of Aquitaine and her Children', 326-7. He has little to say on the education of Eleanor's daughters, focusing rather on the intellectual and martial training of her sons.

[19] Turner, *Eleanor of Aquitaine*, 149.

proposition, as it is doubtful that Henry and Eleanor would have seen their daughters remain largely uneducated until the ages of ten or twelve. A brief consideration of the levels of learning and interest in education within the Angevin dynasty will serve to underline this point.

Eleanor's own education is undocumented, although a comment in Matthew Paris' *Chronica Majora* seems to suggest that she studied alongside boys.[20] She may have received some degree of intellectual training from the renowned scholar and archbishop Geoffrey of Bordeaux, who acted as her guardian for the brief period between her father's death until her marriage to Louis VII.[21] Geoffrey's position as Eleanor's guardian has led Flori to suggest that he may well also have been her tutor prior to this time.[22] Eleanor's grandfather, William IX, was clearly well educated, and saw to it that his son, Eleanor's father, was educated at the cathedral school at Poitiers.[23] Turner has no doubts that Eleanor 'received a sound grounding in letters', and that she 'almost certainly learned to read Latin, tutored by chaplains in the ducal household', with her education possibly being overseen by the archbishop of Bordeaux.[24] As well as this, religious instruction, including the reading of saints' lives and psalms, would have formed part of her education, as was the norm for medieval royal and aristocratic daughters.[25] There is also some evidence to suggest that Eleanor may have been responsible for sending a copy of the *Gynaecia Cleopatrae* to the Byzantine Emperor Manuel I Comnenus in c.1155-7, whose interest in all things medical may have been known to Eleanor from her time spent in Constantinople during the second crusade.[26]

Henry II's education, on the other hand, is much better documented.[27] The pursuit of learning had 'long been characteristic of the counts of Anjou', and Henry's parents ensured that he was tutored by 'the best teachers available'.[28] As a child, Henry was taught by the poet Peter of Saintes; aged ten, he attended the Bristol court of Robert of Gloucester, his uncle and guardian and a noted patron of art and literature, where he may have met Geoffrey of Mon-

---

[20] Matthew Paris records the gift to St Albans of a sapphire ring, presented by one Richard Animal, who had received the ring from Eleanor, to whom it had previously belonged, in remembrance of when they were schoolmates. See *Matthaei Parisiensis, Monachi Sancti Albani, Chronica Majora*, ed. Henry Richards Luard (Longman & Co., London, 1882), VI, 385. Martin Aurell has pointed out that co-ed schooling at this time seems 'implausible'; nonetheless, the passage in Matthew Paris provides tantalising evidence that Eleanor received some level of education. See Aurell, *Le Chevalier lettré : savoir et conduite de l'aristocratie aux XIIe et XIIIe siècles* (Fayard, Paris, 2011), 212-3.

[21] Turner, 'Eleanor of Aquitaine and her Children', 327-8. Peter Dronke noted that there is also some evidence to suggest that the poet Marie de France, celebrated for her epic *lais*, was in Eleanor's entourage in the period 1162-5, 'Peter of Blois and Poetry at the Court of Henry II', *Mediaeval Studies*, 38 (1976), 188. This raises the possibility that her eldest daughters, Matilda and Leonor, may have had some contact with this remarkably educated woman.

[22] Flori, *Eleanor of Aquitaine*, 281-2.

[23] Turner, *Eleanor of Aquitaine*, 20. Eleventh-century Poitiers was a noted centre of both learning and religion, see Turner, *Eleanor of Aquitaine*, 23-4, 33.

[24] *Ibid.*, 32.

[25] *Ibid.*, 33-4. Turner cites a thirteenth century guide for the education of young children of both sexes, which instructs that belief in God should be the first thing children learn *from their mothers*, 33-4.

[26] Elisabeth van Houts, 'Les femmes dans le royaume Plantagenêt: Gendre, Politique et Nature', in *Plantagenêts et Capetiens*, 98-102.

[27] Adelard of Bath had dedicated his treatise on the astrolabe to Henry when he was still a child, and Robert Cricklade compiled for Henry an epitome of natural history. Henry as king was the recipient of various chronicles, treatises, mirrors of princes, poetry and prose collections, and 'edifying hagiographical works', see Dronke, 'Peter of Blois', 186; van Houts, 'Gendre, Politique et Nature', 95-6. Henry's tutor, William of Conches, dedicated his *Dragmaticon* (c.1120) to Henry's father, Geoffrey of Anjou; see van Houts, 'Gendre, Politique et Nature', 95.

[28] Turner, 'Eleanor of Aquitaine and her Children', 327; see also Turner, *Eleanor of Aquitaine*, 102. Henry's mother, the Empress Matilda, certainly owned several books, as they were bequeathed to the abbey of Bec in 1134, although none survive; see van Houts, *Memory and Gender*, 117.

mouth. On his return to Normandy, his tutors included the philosopher and grammarian William of Conches, Adelard of Bath, and Master Matthew, the future bishop of Angers who had also served as tutor to Henry's paternal aunts, Sibylla and Matilda.[29]

This evidence for the education of girls within the Angevin family suggests that twelfth-century aristocratic children of both sexes in south-western France received an education, and that the education of both male and female children was an Angevin family custom. It is therefore highly improbable that Henry and Eleanor would have failed to supply the best of educations for their own children, daughters as well as sons, in order that they be fully prepared for the political roles destined for them. And it is surely unfeasible that Henry and Eleanor's children would have remained ignorant of the collections of vernacular works – especially those glorifying their ancestors – which their parents had accrued over the years, such as Wace's *Roman de Brut* and *Roman de Rou*,[30] and Benoît of Sainte-Maure's *Chronique des Ducs de Normandie*.[31]

Henry and Eleanor's sons, certainly, displayed in their later years evidence of an interest in literature and a sound knowledge of Latin grammar;[32] however, Turner's suggestion that due to the ages at which their daughters left the natal home, whatever schooling they received 'was largely gained abroad', must be revised.[33] Although they were all still young when they left for their marriages – between nine and eleven years of age – there is no reason to believe that Henry and Eleanor's daughters had remained without any form of schooling until this time. On the contrary, it is unthinkable that they would have left for married life wholly uninstructed on wifely duties and seemly pastimes, such as weaving and conversation, the management of a household and the rearing of their own children.

---

[29] Flori, *Eleanor of Aquitaine*, 59; Turner, *Eleanor of Aquitaine*, 102-3; van Houts, 'Gendre, Politique et Nature', 104; Dutton, 'Angevin Comital Children', 34. Sibylla and Matilda's mother, Eremburga, had a *magistra* called Beatrice, who appears as a witness on one of Eremburga's charters; see Dutton, 'Angevin Comital Children', 35.

[30] Wace's *Roman de Brut*, a vernacular version of Geoffrey of Monmouth's *Historia*, was dedicated to Eleanor in 1155; see Dronke, 'Peter of Blois', 186-7; Flori, *Eleanor of Aquitaine*, 214, 286-92. His later *Roman de Rou*, composed c.1160-74, was commissioned by Henry as a vernacular version of the *Gesta Normannorum Ducum* (hereafter *GND*), which details the lives of the dukes of Normandy up to the death of Henry's grandfather, Henry I; see Elisabeth van Houts, 'Local and Regional Chronicles', *Typologie des Sources du Moyen Âge Occidental*, 74 (Brepols, Belgium, 1995), 39; van Houts, 'The Adaptation of the *Gesta Normannorum Ducum* by Wace and Benoît', in van Houts, *History and Family Traditions*, 115-24; *The Gesta Normannorum Ducum of William of Jumièges, Orderic Vitalis, and Robert of Torigni*, ed. and trans. Elisabeth van Houts (Clarendon Press, Oxford, 1992). See also Peter Damien-Grint, 'Benoît de Sainte-Maure et l'idéologie des Plantagenêt', in *Plantagenêts et Capetiens*, 413-27.

[31] Benoît de Sainte-Maure's history of the Norman dukes, commissioned by Henry in 1174, was also a vernacular revision of the *GND*; see Dronke, 'Peter of Blois', 186-7; Flori, *Eleanor of Aquitaine*, 214, 286-92. The section on Henry I's reign was composed by Torigni at the behest of the Empress Matilda, and although the *GND* was not continued to include the reign of Henry II, there were plans for an 'Anjevin (*sic*) continuation', van Houts, 'Local and Regional Chronicles', 54. See also van Houts, 'Le roi et son historien', 116-7. Torigni had apparently planned to do so; and certainly Benoît stated in his *Chronique*, which ends, as does Torigni's section of the *GND*, with the death of Henry I, that it was his intention to undertake such an enterprise, *GND*, I, xcii-xciv; van Houts, 'Adaptation of the *GND*', 115. The fact that neither Torigni nor Benoît in fact completed such a work has not been satisfactorily explained, although van Houts has suggested that it may be due to the fact that Henry was as much, if not more, count of Anjou, duke of Aquitaine, and king of England, as well as duke of Normandy, *GND*, I, xciii. However, these very facts would surely have made Henry's inclusion in the *GND* all the more impressive. A further work by Benoît, the *Roman de Troie*, was 'probably written to please the Queen [Eleanor]', Flori, *Eleanor of Aquitaine*, 44.

[32] Turner, 'Eleanor of Aquitaine and her Children', 328, citing the examples of Richard's correction of Archbishop Hubert's grammar, and of John's extensive library; see also Turner, *Eleanor of Aquitaine,* 148.

[33] See Turner, *Eleanor of Aquitaine*, 148.

Children of both sexes learned the basics of Christianity, the three main prayers – the Credo, the Pater Noster, and the Ave Maria – as well as some psalms and how to make the sign of the cross, from their mother, nurse, or tutor.[34] Mothers were expected to raise their sons until they were sent to another household for education at around the age of seven,[35] but a mother's primary role was 'to raise her daughters – to furnish them with a religious education and to prepare them for their roles as mothers and housewives'.[36] Heywood states that it was further hoped that mothers would also pass on to their daughters 'those virtues of humility and submissiveness supposedly appropriate to their sex'.[37] Religious instruction was, however, the main focus of a girl's education – indeed, Shahar views religious and moral instruction as the goal of medieval education, with intellectual training viewed as secondary – with prayers, psalms, and scriptural and hagiographical extracts being learnt.[38] The medieval mother was thus 'the first inculcator of religious and cultural values'.[39]

As noted above, some noble daughters received instruction from a male or female tutor, although they were educated 'not in order to prepare them for an occupation or for office... but to train them for their roles as wives', as well as to 'instruct them in fitting conduct and certain pastime skills'.[40] Such skills would include reading, recitation, and sometimes writing, a degree of arithmetic, and rudimentary first aid skills. They would also learn arts such as etiquette and social graces, weaving and embroidery, storytelling, singing, dancing, musical composition and how to play stringed instruments, as well as riding, falconry, and how to play popular games such as chess.[41] Indeed, Shahar maintains that noble daughters received essentially similar educations to noble sons, and even that girls spent more time reading than boys did.[42] Mary McLaughlin agrees that literacy was 'probably higher among women of the nobility than it was among their husbands and brothers, unless these last were monks or clerics',[43]

---

[34] Shahar, *Childhood in the Middle Ages*, 210; Heywood, *History of Childhood*, 91-2. Shahar, 175 and 114, states that 'Mothers and nurses transmitted popular female culture to girls', as well as popular songs, stories, and other oral traditions, an argument that echoes David Herlihy's assertion that medieval mothers were 'repositories of sacred wisdom...channels through which a significant part of the cultural inheritance is passed from the old to the young', *Medieval Households*, 129.

[35] Shahar, *Childhood in the Middle Ages*, 113, 209; and 209-220 for more on the education of noble sons in other households.

[36] Shahar, *Childhood in the Middle Ages*, 174; see also Heywood, *History of Childhood*, 105. Georges Duby describes the familial home as 'the setting for female pastoral care', *Love and Marriage*, 99; see also Duby, *Medieval Marriage*, 3-4.

[37] Heywood, *History of Childhood*, 105, noting that it was often during the years of puberty and adolescence that strong emotional bonds were formed between mothers and daughters 'as they came to depend on them for help and advice'.

[38] Shahar, *Childhood in the Middle Ages*, 220; and for more on the goals of medieval education, see 166-72.

[39] *Ibid.*, 116.

[40] *Ibid.*, 221.

[41] *Ibid.*, 222. Both boys and girls from noble families learnt the game of chess as well as other pastimes, and young girls also seem to have played with dolls, Shahar, *Childhood in the Middle Ages*, 223. Other toys included rocking horses, balls, rattles, building blocks, drums, cymbals, spinning tops, see-saws, toy soldiers and animals, and wooden boats. See Shahar, *Childhood in the Middle Ages*, 104; Heywood, *History of Childhood*, 93.

[42] Shahar, *Childhood in the Middle Ages*, 222.

[43] McLaughlin, 'Survivors and Surrogates', 125. Shahar's and McLaughlin's arguments provide an important corrective to Ariès' assertion that, until the seventeenth century, daughters were given 'virtually no education [and]... were virtually illiterate', *Centuries of Childhood*, 319. Indeed, Ariès believed that there was no concept of education in medieval civilisation, and that what he viewed as the advent of education in the seventeenth century was the key for changes in the concept of childhood, see *Centuries of Childhood*, 395-8.

and Heywood suggests that noble children may have begun to learn to read and write from as early as around four years of age.[44]

Literacy seems to have been an important component of a royal and aristocratic girl's education. Jerome recommended that mothers teach their daughters to busy themselves in reading and writing to 'escape harmful thoughts and the pleasures and vanities of the flesh', and girls were taught to read at an early age in order to model themselves on biblical women, especially the Virgin Mary.[45] A vignette of two noble sisters chatting about a two-hundred-year-old love story, which appears in the anonymous *Le Conte de Floire et de Blancheflor*, composed c.1160, suggests that both education (if not literacy) and the oral transmission of history through storytelling (commemoration as well as interest in the past), were common features of a high born lady's life.[46] The many pictures of the Virgin from the eleventh century onwards which depict her engaged in reading further demonstrate that contemporary artists viewed this activity as both fitting and usual for women.[47]

If the eleventh century Bavarian noblewoman Beatrix was able to display not just rudimentary literacy but also knowledge of the Classics in her letter to her brother, Bishop Udo of Hildesheim, and if, by c.1300, most English countesses owned an alphabet book, how much more likely is it that women of higher status would have received similar, if not better, educations?[48] It is surely implausible to suggest that the daughters of royalty – and specifically, the daughters of Henry and Eleanor, who, as has been shown, were both educated and patrons of learning – remained illiterate. That Beatrix's letter (the only one of around one hundred letters surviving from the Hildesheim archives to be penned by a woman) survives is fortunate, as so many letters which must have been written by women have not. Not only does the letter demonstrate the high level of learning of one individual Bavarian noblewoman, it is also evidence of continuing familial links between sister and brother, even after the occasion of her marriage and indeed widowhood. Clearly, her brother, as bishop of Hildesheim, was an important man with some degree of power and influence, and therefore a good candidate for Beatrix to seek assistance from – how much more then, must this have been the case for the daughters of Henry and Eleanor, whose parents were without doubt the most powerful rulers in the Western world? When Joanna fled to her mother in 1199, is it conceivable that she did so without sending some form of notice first? Eleanor must surely have been appraised of her daughter's impending flight from danger and made arrangements for her reception at her court accordingly.

Elisabeth van Houts has pointed out that most noble families had 'at least one member who was particularly interested in preserving family history', and women in particular were involved in the transmission of family traditions, which was viewed as a traditionally female

---

[44] Heywood, *History of Childhood*, 92. Royal children are probably an exceptional case in this regard.

[45] Susan Groag Bell, 'Medieval Women Book Owners: Arbiters of Lay Piety and Ambassadors of Culture', in *Women and Power*, 162, 158.

[46] See van Houts, *Memory and Gender*, 76-7. Gaimar's *Estoire des Engles*, composed in the first half of the twelfth century, was also apparently commissioned by a noblewoman: Constance, wife of Ralph FitzGilbert. See *Lestoire des Engles, solum la translacion Maistre Geffrei Gaimar*, ed. Thomas Duffy and Charles Trice Martin (*RS*, 91, 2 Vols., London, 1888-9), ix.

[47] Bell, 'Women Book Owners', 163. She advances some interesting hypotheses, such as the theory that mothers commissioned Books of Hours for their daughters, particularly as wedding gifts, although the degree of influence over their content that Bell assumes they would have had is doubtful.

[48] Bell, 'Women Book Owners', 163; van Houts, *Memory and Gender*, 80-1, and Appendix 3, 154-5 for a translation of the letter in which Beatrix requests her brother's assistance in the matter of the marriage of her daughter to a man Beatrix considers to be of too low a social standing.

role.[49] For example, in a letter to Brian FitzCount, one of the Empress' supporters during the Anarchy, Gilbert Foliot relates the tale that Matilda, queen of William the Conqueror, bent over the crib of her god-daughter Edith-Matilda – the future queen of Henry I – and that the infant gripped her veil in her fist and pulled it over her head. The incident was interpreted as an omen that the baby would one day assume the office of queen herself. Edith-Matilda apparently related the tale to her own daughter, the future Empress, perhaps on the occasion of her departure for marriage to Henry V; its appearance in a letter to one of her supporters is highly suggestive of Matilda's views on her inheritance, as well as being evidence of the passing down through three generations of a sense of shared identity and the importance of the role of a queen.[50]

As well as being entrusted with the care of younger women who became wards of the family through marriage or otherwise, as both Joanna and Berengaria of Navarre were to do,[51] women were also charged with ensuring their sons were fully informed of the illustrious and exemplary deeds of their forebears.[52] Tenth century Ottonian royal women, such as Matilda I (d. 968) and her granddaughters, Abbess Matilda of Quedlinburg (d. 999) and Abbess Gerberga of Gandersheim (d. 1001), were the 'prime movers behind the surge in commemorative writing', especially in terms of necrologies and *vitae*.[53] Their cousin, Abbess Matilda of Essen (d.1011; granddaughter of Edith, first wife of Otto I) requested and received from her kinsman Aethelweard a Latin translation of the *Anglo-Saxon Chronicle*, which illustrated the ancestry of Edith, demonstrating the ancestral and dynastic links between Anglo-Saxon England and Ottonian Saxony.[54]

In England, Queen Edith had commissioned a *vita* of Edward the Confessor, the end result of which is substantially a history of her own Godwin family.[55] Henry I's queen Edith-Matilda commissioned William of Malmesbury to compose his *History*, and van Houts believes it possible that it was Edith-Matilda herself who 'helped to fill in gaps in the genealogical information'.[56] Edith-Matilda also commissioned Turgot of Durham to compose the *vita* of her mother, St Margaret of Scotland, which according to Elisabeth van Houts contains 'an exaltation of royal motherhood as well as an illuminating contribution to the historiography of queenship'.[57] Henry I's second wife Adela commissioned a now lost *vita* of Henry; his daughter the Empress Matilda commissioned Torigni to compose a life of her father, requesting further that he add *vitae* of her mother and her grandmother to the *Gesta Normannorum Ducum*.[58] The inclusion of Matilda's paternal and maternal ancestors would have served a

---

[49] Van Houts, 'Local and Regional Chronicles', 41, although her assertion that this was because women were likely to live longer than men due to their lack of participation in warfare seriously underestimates the equally perilous dangers women faced in childbirth. For more on commemoration as preservation of the past and women as 'transmitters of information' and 'carriers of tradition', see van Houts, 'Women and the Writing of History', 54.

[50] See van Houts, *Memory and Gender*, 73.

[51] See below.

[52] Van Houts, 'Local and Regional Chronicles', 42.

[53] Van Houts, *Memory and Gender*, 67-8.

[54] *Ibid.*, 69-70. For more on these dynastic links, see Part IV, Chapter 3.

[55] Van Houts, *Memory and Gender*, 72.

[56] *Ibid.*, 71.

[57] *Ibid.*, 74.

[58] *Ibid.*, 71. These *vitae*, if they were ever executed, do not survive. Matilda was also the dedicatee of the *History of the Recent Kings of France* by Hugh of Fleury, van Houts, *Memory and Gender*, 71.

legitimising function, as it highlighted the fact that her children, as 'future heirs to the English throne...combined Norman and Anglo-Saxon blood'.[59]

Commemorative prayers for ancestors, another task associated largely with women, served not just to ensure the salvation of departed souls but to set a precedent for their own descendants to perform the same acts for them.[60] Van Houts thus views women's role in the preservation and transmission of family histories and traditions as going some way to explaining the number of chronicles dedicated to women, such as Wace's *Roman de Brut*,[61] those patronised or commissioned by women, such as Lucas de Tuy's *Crónica de España*,[62] or even, in some cases, composed by women, such as the works of Hrotsvita of Gandersheim.[63]

Royal and aristocratic women were trained for marriage. Accordingly, some household management skills, conversational skills and some degree of intellectual instruction would have formed part of Leonor's, Joanna's and Matilda's education. Whilst a woman should never appear to be more educated than her husband it would presumably be desirable for them to be able to converse, which may have led to some degree of competency in various languages such as French or Latin. Many royal and aristocratic women would also have learned to read, and perhaps also to write, and considering the Angevin family interest in learning and education, it seems likely that the daughters of Henry and Eleanor were all literate. Religious education would have been high on the agenda, and skills such as weaving, embroidery, singing and perhaps acquiring an instrument were common learned arts amongst the high nobility. Leonor in particular appears to have been accomplished in weaving, as testified by the existence of several stoles woven by her which are now housed at San Isidoro in León.[64] Spanish sources consistently laud Leonor's education and learning, and while this may perhaps be mere literary *topos*, she was clearly educated enough to oversee the education of her own children, and, as will be seen, was deemed intelligent enough to play a considerable role in Castilian politics.[65] Similarly, Richard entrusted Joanna with the care of his betrothed Berengaria of Navarre upon her arrival in Sicily, and she had seemingly received instruction from her mother to accompany Berengaria to the Holy Land.[66] Finally, if the amount of contact Matilda, Leonor and Joanna had with their parents (especially their mother) during their early childhoods did in fact engender a strong emotional bond, is it possible to see evidence of this in their later lives? The subjects of their later patronage and commemoration will be discussed in Parts IV and V. It is with their marriages, however, that these women first become truly visible in the

---

[59] Van Houts, *Memory and Gender*, 74.

[60] Van Houts, 'Local and Regional Chronicles', 59. The subject of dynastic commemorations will be treated in depth in Part V.

[61] See above, n. 30.

[62] See Part III, Chapter 2.

[63] Van Houts, 'Local and Regional Chronicles', 59. For more on Hrotsvitha and other Saxon women involved in the composition of dynastic writings, see Part IV, Chapter 3; see also van Houts, 'Women and the Writing of History', 54-68; van Houts, *Memory and Gender*, 63-92.

[64] González, *Alfonso VIII*, I, 193, with one reproduction at 192.

[65] For references to Leonor's learning, see Part III, Chapter 2.

[66] Although they were to be constant companions for the next two years or so during their time in the Holy Land, Joanna and Berengaria do not appear to have maintained relations after their return to France, and Berengaria is not named as one of the many beneficiaries in Joanna's will, see Trindade, *Berengaria*, 85. For more on Joanna's will, see Part V, Chapter 2. Berengaria herself was also clearly deemed learned enough to be entrusted by Richard with the care and education of the captive young daughter of Isaac of Cyprus, who had travelled with the royal women to the Holy Land, Trindade, *Berengaria*, 54.

sources, and it is this subject, along with the political motivations for their marriages, which forms the basis of Part II of this book.

PART II

Satisfied as to her beauty: Marriage Negotiations and Political Motivations

This section will examine the political motivations behind the dynastic alliances secured for the Angevin dynasty through the marriages of Matilda, Joanna and Leonor. The carefully orchestrated negotiation processes, as well as the status of the ambassadorial personnel involved in helping to arrange and oversee the conclusion of these matches, testifies to their political significance as well as serving to highlight the importance of these women. A comparison with Berengaria of Navarre, the sister-in-law of Matilda, Leonor and Joanna, further demonstrates the intricacies of Angevin marriage policy.

It is only with their respective marriages that Henry and Eleanor's daughters appear, if almost incidentally, in most contemporary Angevin accounts. As noted in Part I, Matilda's marriage to Henry the Lion of Saxony is only briefly referred to in Howden's *Chronica*, erroneously placed under the year 1164.[1] Torigni, Diceto and Gervase of Canterbury variously give details regarding the envoys which arrived at Henry II's court to negotiate the marriage, and on the personnel who accompanied Matilda on her journey to Saxony.[2]

Similarly, Diceto records Leonor's marriage to Alfonso VIII of Castile in a single sentence, almost as an aside, giving the erroneous date of 1169.[3] Howden is also inaccurate, placing the marriage in 1176.[4] Torigni gives the correct date of Leonor's marriage to Alfonso as 1170, although he provides no details on the negotiations, the marriage itself, or the ambassadors who escorted Leonor to Castile.

Torigni also records William II's petition in 1176 for a marriage with Joanna, and further details of the negotiation process and the ambassadors involved in this are provided by Howden.[5] Clearly, the marriages of the king's daughters, and the political alliances these would necessarily generate, were deemed to be of great importance by contemporary chroniclers. What Henry, and perhaps Eleanor, hoped to achieve by way of such dynastic alliances, will now be examined in greater detail.

---

* This section greatly develops and expands on the arguments I previously made in 'Shifting Patterns in Angevin Marriage Policies: The Political Motivations for Joanna Plantagenet's Marriages to William II of Sicily and Raymond VI of Toulouse', in Matin Aurell (ed.), *Les Stratégies Matrimoniales, IXe-XIIIe Siècle* (Brepols, Turnhout, 2013), 155-67.

[1] Howden, *Chronica*, I, 220.

[2] Torigni, 224; Diceto, I, 330; Gervase of Canterbury, *The Chronicle of the Reigns of Stephen, Henry II, and Richard I, by Gervase, the Monk of Canterbury*, in *Opera Historica – The Historical Works of Gervase of Canterbury*, ed. William Stubbs, 2 vols. (Rolls Series, 73.1, London, 1879; hereafter Gervase, I), 204.

[3] Diceto, I, 334. However, as Julio González has pointed out, the marriage was first proposed in November 1169, and the negotiations may have been successfully concluded by the end of the year – which may provide the reason for Diceto's error, *Alfonso VIII*, I, 187.

[4] Howden, *Chronica*, II, 105. Diceto, I, 415-6, 418-20, devotes more space to Henry II's arbitration between the kings of Castile and Navarre in 1177 than to Leonor's birth or marriage. Gervase of Canterbury's *Gesta Regum* contains no references to Leonor, although it does include a brief paragraph recording the arrival in Lent 1177 of the Spanish envoys seeking Henry's mediation, and Henry's decision, given after Easter, Gervase of Canterbury, *Gesta Regum*, in *Opera Historica – The Historical Works of Gervase of Canterbury*, ed. William Stubbs, 2 vols. (Rolls Series, 73.2, London, 1880; hereafter Gervase II), 261. Similarly, in the *Gesta*, I, 138-54, Howden devotes several pages to Henry's arbitration, although Leonor herself is merely mentioned in passing as the daughter of Henry and wife of Alfonso. The later *Chronica* contains slightly more information on Leonor, including the brief reference to her marriage, as well as various references to events in Spain, largely pertaining to Alfonso's efforts against the Moors. The events of 1177 are at *Chronica*, II, 120-31; they are largely similar to the account given in the *Gesta*, with both including full transcripts both of the complaints of the Spanish kings, and of Henry's adjudication. Howden also provides a brief history of the kings of Spain, *Chronica*, III, 90-2, as does Diceto, II, 240-1.

[5] Torigni, 271; Howden, *Gesta*, I, 115-7, 119; *Chronica*, II, 94-5.

Chapter One
Matilda and Henry the Lion

Negotiations for Matilda's marriage to Henry the Lion began in 1164, apparently at the instigation of the emperor Frederick I, who was seeking Henry II's support against Pope Alexander III and recognition of his own papal candidate, Pascal III.[1] In April 1165, imperial ambassadors, headed by Reinald Dassel, archbishop of Cologne, arrived at Henry's court at Rouen, and the negotiations were successfully concluded.[2] As well as Matilda's betrothal to Henry the Lion, it was agreed that Henry II's younger daughter Leonor would marry Frederick, the emperor's sole son and heir, thereby cementing the Anglo-Imperial alliance.[3] On his return to Germany, Archbishop Reinald was accompanied by Henry II's ambassadors, who, on Henry's behalf, formally declared against Alexander III at the Diet of Würzburg in May 1165.[4] It would seem, however, that Henry II had never genuinely intended to break with Alexander, and his promise to support Pascal was given solely to give him leverage in the papal curia in an attempt to gain positive influence there with regard to his own quarrels with Becket and the English church.[5]

Henry the Lion was clearly favourable to a dynastic alliance with Henry II, as a union with the powerful Angevin dynasty would bring him greater prestige both within his own lands and in the wider world of western Christendom. Moreover, his betrothed was not just the daughter of a king, but the granddaughter of an empress, a fact which was of further assistance in bolstering Henry's status.[6] Duke Henry's ambassador Gunzelin of Schwerin was immediately dispatched to Henry II's court to confirm the duke's agreement to the union,[7] and in 1167 a further embassy, led by Provost Baldwin of Utrecht, arrived in England to escort Matilda to Saxony.[8]

Matilda sailed from Dover to Normandy around Michaelmas 1167, possibly celebrating Christmas in Normandy before continuing to Germany.[9] According to Gervase of Canterbury, Matilda was accompanied to Saxony by her mother, although Eleanor's subsequent move-

---

[1] Karl Jordan, *Henry the Lion*, trans. P.S. Falla (Clarendon Press, Oxford, 1986), 144.

[2] Torigni, 224; Jordan, *Henry the Lion*, 144. Diceto, I, 318, and Wendover, I, 39, place the embassy in Westminster.

[3] Jordan, *Henry the Lion*, 144. See also Eyton, *Itinerary*, 78; Peter Munz, *Frederick Barbarossa: A Study in Medieval Politics* (Cornell University Press, 1969), 239. Torigni, 244, is the only Angevin chronicler to refer to a German embassy arriving in 1165, although interestingly, he does not mention Leonor by name. The betrothal was broken off some time before 1169, and the young Frederick, always a 'sickly child', died soon thereafter; Jordan, *Henry the Lion*, p. 149. Norgate, 'Matilda, duchess of Saxony', believes it was Henry II who decided not to go ahead with the proposed marriage between Frederick and Leonor.

[4] Jordan, *Henry the Lion*, 144. A short account of this is given by Gervase, I, 206, under the year 1168.

[5] Jordan, *Henry the Lion*, 145. For more on Henry's quarrel with Becket, see Part IV, Chapter 1.

[6] Matilda's royal and imperial heritage is highlighted in the illustrations found in the Gospel Book of Henry the Lion. For more on this work and on Matilda's possible involvement in its production, see Part IV, Chapter 2.

[7] Jordan, *Henry the Lion*, 144. Gervase, II, 78, records the arrival of this embassy, but implies that the proposal of marriage was instigated by Henry the Lion.

[8] Jordan, *Henry the Lion*, 147. Pipe Roll entries for 1167 record the expenses incurred in the ambassadorial visit at PR 13 Hen II, 2-3, 13, 37, 193-4.

[9] Torigni, 234n; Norgate, 'Matilda, duchess of Saxony'. See also PR 13 Hen II, 193-4, which refers to the payment for the crossing.

ments make this unlikely, and it is probable that she accompanied her daughter to Normandy at the furthest.[10] Torigni states that Matilda was escorted to Saxony by the earls of Arundel and Warenne;[11] according to Diceto, her envoys included the earls of Arundel and Striguil.[12]

The Pipe Rolls record that Henry II provided Matilda with a palfrey and a courser for her use in Saxony, as well as various clothes and household items including rich furs, gilded furniture and beautifully-wrought tapestries.[13] It is unclear whether these were gifts, or whether they comprised part of her dowry. Etienne of Rouen remarked that it was impossible to describe the extent and variety of gifts which Matilda brought to Saxony as dowry.[14] Torigni, who was careful to note Henry the Lion's imperial descent, stated that Matilda was conveyed to Germany with 'infinita pecunia et apparatu maximo'.[15] Helmold, a priest at Bosau, noted that the dowry included an undefined amount of gold, silver, and 'great treasures', although he does not mention Matilda by name, nor does she appear anywhere else in his *Cronica Slavorum*.[16] Presumably, the 'great treasures' noted by Helmold refer to the gilded furniture, rich furs, and tapestries mentioned in the Pipe Rolls. The possessions which Matilda took with her to Saxony were so numerous that they filled twenty bags and twenty chests, and it took three ships and thirty-four pack-horses to convey Matilda and her belongings to her new homeland.[17]

The financial element of Matilda's dowry subsequently went some way towards financing Henry the Lion's pilgrimage to the Holy Land in 1172.[18] It might be thought that, in consequence of the rich dowry which Matilda brought to her ducal husband, he in turn would have bestowed upon his wife a comparably rich and sizeable dower. Unfortunately, there is no extant record of this, and with the exceptions of Lüneburg and Hildesheim, no chronicler mentions any lands or religious foundations in which Matilda was visibly active.[19] It cannot therefore be known precisely what Matilda received as her marriage portion. As has been seen, however, Matilda ultimately spent several years of her married life as an exile, and both she and her husband were financially dependant on her natal family.[20]

---

[10] Gervase, I, 204. See also Part I, Chapter 1.

[11] Torigni, 234n.

[12] Diceto, I, 330.

[13] PR 13 Hen II, 2-3, 5; PR 14 Hen II, 15, 34, 50, 60-1, 100, 117, 139, 157, 174, 192, 208; PR 13 Hen II, 193-4.

[14] Etienne of Rouen, *Draco Normannicus*, in *Chronicles of the the Reigns of Stephen, Henry II, and Richard I*, ed. Richard Howlett (*RS*, 82.2, 1885), 719.

[15] Torigni, 234.

[16] Helmold of Bosau, *Cronica Slavorum*, 209.

[17] See Part I, Chapter 1.

[18] Jordan, *Henry the Lion*, 150. Torigni, 253, records Henry the Lion's pilgrimage to the Holy Land, noting that he distributed alms amongst the poor and made many donations to churches whilst he was there.

[19] For more on Matilda's dower, see Part III, Chapter 1.

[20] For more on Matilda's years in exile, Part III, Chapter 1.

Chapter Two
Leonor and Alfonso VIII of Castile

As noted in the previous chapter, Leonor had initially been betrothed to a son of the Emperor Frederick I, with negotiations beginning in 1165, at the same time as those for the future marriage between her elder sister Matilda and Henry the Lion of Saxony. However, this union failed to proceed beyond the negotiation process, for reasons which are unclear, and in 1169 – the year of the crucial dynastic settlement at Montmirail, whereby Henry attempted to ensure the survival of his vast domains after his death by instituting a redistribution of family power[1] - negotiations began for the eight-year-old Leonor's marriage to the fourteen-year-old Alfonso VIII of Castile.

The Anglo-Castilian alliance was beneficial for both parties, and has been described as a 'diplomatic coup' for Alfonso VIII.[2] Alfonso gained a powerful ally against his greatest rival, the king of Navarre, who had posed various threats to his own kingdom since his accession in 1158.[3] He was also able to avoid any problems of consanguinity by marrying abroad.[4] Furthermore, Aragón, Alfonso's firm ally on the Iberian peninsula, was also allied with England, and indeed, Alfonso II of Aragón was related to Leonor's mother, Eleanor of Aquitaine.[5] An embassy was therefore sent to England in November 1169 to request the hand of Henry's daughter Leonor for the crown of Castile.[6]

Henry II, for his part, gained an important ally against the count of Toulouse, with whom Henry had been contesting that county's lordship since 1159. Henry's claim to Toulouse lay

---

[1] At Montmirail in January 1169, Henry and his eldest sons did homage to Louis for their continental domains: the Young King for Maine and Anjou, and Richard for Aquitaine; Geoffrey later did homage to the younger Henry for Brittany, Kelly, *Eleanor of Aquitaine*, 135. At the same ceremony, Louis' nine-year-old daughter Alice was affianced to Richard and given into Plantagenet custody, with the county of Berry as her dowry; Louis also consented as overlord to the marriage between Geoffrey and Constance of Brittany, Kelly, *Eleanor of Aquitaine*, 136. For more on Henry II paying homage to Louis VII, see John Gillingham, 'Doing Homage to the King of France', in Christopher Harper-Bill and Nicholas Vincent (eds.), *Henry II: New Interpretations* (Boydell, Woodbridge, 2007), 63-84.

[2] Simon Barton, *The Aristocracy in Twelfth-Century León and Castile* (CUP, 1997), 19.

[3] For the years of Alfonso's minority, see *PCG*, 668-70; *Crónica Latina*, 34-5. The *Crónica de España* has little on Alfonso's minority, focusing rather on the reign of Fernando II de León, who is presented in such glowing terms as '*Hic piissimus rex*', 402. By 1170, Alfonso had been reigning for twelve years, and had finally managed to stabilise his kingdom after the turbulent years of his minority. See also Torigni, 193-5, 247.

[4] Marta Van Landingham points to the advantages of exogamous marriages, as a bride would be 'an outsider...displaced from her family...completely separated from any web of alliances of birth and obligation', in short, completely dependant on her husband, 'Royal Portraits: Representations of Queenship in the Thirteenth Century Catalan Chronicles', in *Queenship and Political Power*, 115. These advantages, however, do not seem to apply in the case of Leonor's marriage to Alfonso of Castile.

[5] González, *Alfonso VIII*, I, 187. Eleanor of Aquitaine's father William X was the brother of Agnes of Poitou, who had married Ramiro II of Aragón. Leonor was thus the great-niece of Queen Petronilla of Aragón, González, *Alfonso VIII*, I, 198. Díez, *Alfonso VIII*, 212, suggests that Alfonso's marriage to Leonor also offered new opportunites for facilitating commercial relations with England and elsewhere, but there were surely other means of boosting trade than by means of a dynastic marriage.

[6] González, *Alfonso VIII*, I, 792. According to the later *Tercera Crónica General*, the Cortes at Burgos decided it was time for Alfonso to marry, and chose the twelve year old Leonor because 'she was very beautiful, very elegant, and of all good habits', González, *Alfonso VIII*, I, 187n. González notes that as well as giving Leonor's age as one or two years older than the Angevin sources, the date of the marriage itself is also placed a decade too early, in 1160.

through his wife Eleanor. Eleanor's grandmother, Philippa of Toulouse, had been disinherited in 1096, and Philippa's paternal uncle, Raymond IV of St Gilles, had succeeded in her place. Philippa's husband, William IX of Aquitaine, had tried without success to reclaim the county;[7] their son William X – Eleanor's father – was less so inclined. However, both of Eleanor's husbands subsequently attempted to claim Toulouse through right of their wife, and indeed, as Jane Martindale has pointed out, Eleanor's claim to Toulouse was little different from the successfully implemented claim to Normandy made by Geoffrey of Anjou on behalf of Henry's mother, the Empress Matilda.[8] The ensuing conflict - termed the Forty Years War by William of Newburgh - only ended in 1196, with the second marriage of Henry's youngest daughter, Joanna, to count Raymond VI.[9]

Table 8: Genealogical claims to the county of Toulouse

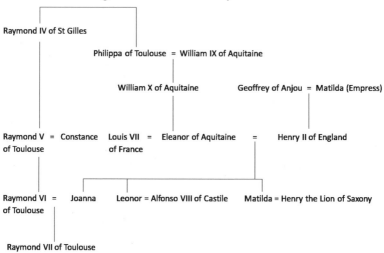

---

[7] First in 1098, and again in 1123. See Jane Martindale, 'An Unfinished Business: Angevin Politics and the Siege of Toulouse, 1159', *Anglo-Norman Studies*, 23 (2001), 147.

[8] Martindale, 'Eleanor of Aquitaine', 28; 'An Unfinished Business', 150-1. Philippa's claim to inherit was unsupported by either Philip I or his successor Louis VI; however, Eleanor's situation two generations later was exactly the same, and was wholeheartedly supported by her husband Louis VII, to the exclusion and disinheritance of her younger sister Petronilla, to ensure his son's accession to the duchy on his marriage to Eleanor. See Martindale, 'Eleanor of Aquitaine', 28-9; 'An Unfinished Business', 143-53.

[9] For a full discussion of the conflict over Toulouse, see Richard Benjamin, 'A Forty Years War: Toulouse and the Plantagenets, 1156-96', *Historical Research*, LXI (1988), 270-85. Jane Martindale has pointed out that as well as dynastic motivations, there were 'probably...underlying economic...aims' behind Henry's claim to Toulouse, as whoever held both Bordeaux and Toulouse would effectively control all trade along the Garonne, 'Eleanor of Aquitaine', 26-7. See also Martindale, 'Succession and Politics in the Romance-Speaking World, c.1000-1140', in Michael Jones and Malcolm Vale (eds.), *England and Her Neighbours, 1066-1453* (Hambledon Press, London, 1989), 34-7. By 1173 Henry had been able to force Raymond VI to recognise some form of overlordship, and to counter the threat of the alliance between Henry and Barcelona, Raymond 'entered into a dangerous agreement with Henry II's dissatisfied son, the Young King, whose death in 1183 irretrievably weakened Raymond's position' (Dunbabin, *France in the Making*, 301). Raymond VII, the son of Raymond VI and Joanna, represented in his person the ultimate solution to the conflict, as he was descended through his father from the counts of St Gilles, and through his mother from the dukes of Aquitaine.

In 1170, however, the struggle for the possession of Toulouse had been ongoing for several years. In 1154, Raymond V of Toulouse had allied himself with Henry's old enemy Louis VII of France, by marrying Louis' sister Constance. Constance had previously been married to Eustace, the son of Henry's predecessor Stephen, so her marriage to the count of Toulouse, backed by the French crown, presented a major threat to Henry. Constance had given Raymond two sons, who were for some time the only male members of the Capetian line.[10] Thus, not only were the sons of Henry's enemy potential heirs to the French throne, but their mother was also the widow of Eustace, the son of Henry's predecessor on the English thone, and the dynastic links thus forged between Toulouse and the French royal house ensured Louis' support of Raymond over Henry.

To counter this threat, in 1159 Henry had allied himself with Count Raymond Berengar IV of Barcelona,[11] who by virtue of marriage was also king of Aragón, and who was also an old enemy of the counts of Toulouse due to struggles over control of Provence.[12] The count's death in 1162, however, left a minor on the throne of Aragón, and Henry bereft of his strongest southern ally.[13] An ally in Castile, therefore, which lay to the south of the contested territory of Toulouse, would prove a considerable advantage for Henry, who unsurprisingly looked favourably on the Castilian embassy which arrived in England seeking a dynastic match for their king with his eldest marriageable daughter. Clearly, the Anglo-Castilian alliance was beneficial both to Henry and to Alfonso. Both kings gained an important ally, and while Henry was in the enviable position of having several daughters to marry off to whomever he chose, Alfonso benefitted greatly from the prestige of being linked to the powerful Angevin dynasty.

In June 1170, a firm peace treaty was concluded at the Castilian town of Sahagún, which established a perpetual alliance between Alfonso VIII and Alfonso II of Aragón, against all other rulers – with the exception of Henry II, "al cual tenemos por padre".[14] Alfonso VIII then returned to Burgos, in order to despatch his ambassadors to Henry's court, and to secure a safe conduct from the king of Navarre. Alfonso's embassy journeyed by sea, embarking either from Castro-Urdiales or Santoña.[15] The following month Alfonso met again with Alfonso of Aragón in Zaragoza, probably with the knowledge that an agreement had been reached regarding his marriage to Leonor.[16] According to the *Tercera Crónica General*, Alfonso's ambassadors had been well received by Henry, and were already returning with their young charge, who had been present when the Castilian ambassadors arrived at Henry's court in Bordeaux

---

[10] Dunbabin, *France in the Making*, 301.

[11] Jane Martindale has suggested that an alliance may have been concluded soon after Christmas 1158, 'An Unfinished Business', 120-21.

[12] The rivalry of the houses of Barcelona and Toulouse had a long history. See Dunbabin, *France in the Making*, 300-3, and 299-305 for Toulouse in general; Martindale, 'An Unfinished Business', 128; Benjamin, 'Forty Years War', 272.

[13] Although Raymond Berengar had named Henry guardian for his son Alfonso II, who was later to continue his father's policy of war with Toulouse and alliance with England, Benjamin, 'Forty Years War', 275.

[14] González, *Alfonso VIII*, I, 794. The treaty effectively ended the incessant warfare that had been a feature of past Castilian-Aragonese relations, with various castles being exchanged as sureties of the peace.

[15] González, *Alfonso VIII*, I, 794. Both are northern sea-ports in modern day Cantabria.

[16] González, *Alfonso VIII*, I, 188. There is a reference to the betrothal in the peace treaty between Castile and Aragón (Zaragoza, July 1170), which confirmed their alliance against the Moors and any Christian ruler, with the exception of Henry II of England, 'a quien el rey de Inglaterra declara tener como padre, sin duda en consideración del ya imminente matrimonio con doña Leonor'; Díez, *Alfonso VIII*, 41, 187; see also González, *Alfonso VIII*, II, nos. 140 & 147.

to seek her hand.[17] Leonor had been brought to Bordeaux from Poitou by her mother, where she had been resident for some years at Eleanor's court, and it was Eleanor who had presided over the council at Bordeaux which settled the terms of Leonor's marriage.[18]

Eleanor had been closely involved in the organisational process of her daughter's marriage to Alfonso of Castile, and the Angevin ambassadors who had travelled with Eleanor and Leonor to Bordeaux were all prelates drawn from Eleanor's own lands in Aquitaine and Poitou. Leonor and Eleanor had been accompanied to Bordeaux by the bishops of Bordeaux, Dax, Poitiers, Angoulême, Saintonge, Perigord and Bazas. Fifteen Norman, Breton and Gascon magnates, including Ralph de Faye, seneschal of Guyenne, Bertram, viscount of Bayonne, and Elias, count of Perigord, also formed part of this important embassy.[19] Similarly, the Castilian envoys chosen by Alfonso VIII were all high-ranking nobles who held important positions at court, and who had proven themselves in various other political engagements and military campaigns.

Leonor's Castilian escorts included Cerebruno, archbishop of Toledo (1167-80), as well as the bishops of Palencia, Burgos, Segovia and Calahorra, and several of the leading magnates of Castile, including Count Nuño Pérez de Lara, who had been regent of Castile during Alfonso VIII's minority.[20] From 1145-1155, Count Nuño had served as Alfonso VII's *alférez*, a primarily military post as leader of the household troops and bearer of the royal standard, the most important position at court after the *mayordomo*.[21] Count Nuño became Alfonso VIII's tutor and was regent from 1164 until Alfonso attained his majority on 11 November 1169, although he retained quasi-regal power until as late as 1176.[22]

---

[17] González, *Alfonso VIII*, I, 188n.

[18] Turner, *Eleanor of Aquitaine*, 194; see also Part I, Chapter 1. Mary Anne Everett Green concluded that in negotiating Leonor's marriage, Eleanor of Aquitaine did not even seek Henry II's consent, a most unlikely proposition, although it does raise the question of Eleanor's attitude to the match, and her role in negotiating it. Furthermore, the alliance with Castile was engineered, according to Green, not for political reasons but because Leonor, Eleanor's beloved daughter and 'constant companion' since the marriage of her eldest daughter Matilda in 1168, would remain geographically close to Eleanor's ancestral lands in Aquitaine, M.A.E. Green, *The Lives of the Princesses of England from the Norman Conquest* (Henry Colburn, London, 1850, 2 Vols.), I, 266. Despite Green's work being coloured by nineteenth century Romanticism, she extensively researched both English and French primary sources, and her study remains useful for chronicling several events of Leonor's life.

[19] The retinue included Eleanor's kinsman Ralph de Faye, seneschal of Guyenne; Elias, count of Perigord; Bertram, viscount of Bayonne; William, viscount of Casteleraldo; Raymond, viscount of Tartas; Rodolfo Martinar, viscount of Castellón and Bedomar; Amanieu of Labrede, viscount of Bézaume; Peter de Mota; and Theobald Chabot, Richard's *magista militum*, González, *Alfonso VIII*, I, 188-9n.

[20] The embassy comprised Count Nuño, Gutierre Fernández, Tello Pérez de Meneses, Count Ponce de Minerva, Gonzalo Ruiz Girón, Pedro and Fernando Ruiz, and García González; González, *Alfonso VIII*, I, 188n; Díez, *Alfonso VIII*, 42.

[21] Barton, *Aristocracy*, 269, 142. The *mayordomo*, or steward, was responsible for the organisation of the household and administration of the royal demesne, and was in 'permanent attendance' on the monarch, Barton, *Aristocracy*, 142, 129. Count Nuño had succeeded his father Count Pedro González in 1162. He married Teresa Fernández, the illegitimate daughter of Count Fernando Pérez de Traba and Teresa Afonso of Portugal. Teresa subsequently married Fernando II of León, Barton, *Aristocracy*, 269.

[22] Barton, *Aristocracy*, 269, 270n. Count Nuño died on 3 August 1177 at the siege of Cuenca, and was buried at his foundation of the Cistercian abbey of Perales, Barton, *Aristocracy*, 269. He had been a prominent patron, both of the Praemonstratensian abbey of Aguilar de Campóo and of the military Order of Calatrava, Barton, *Aristocracy*, 202, 158. He and his wife Teresa also founded a hospital at Puente Itero on the Pisuerga some time before 1174, and were involved with the promotion of the cult of Thomas Becket in Spain, Barton, *Aristocracy*, 199-200; see also Part IV, Chapter 2.

Another of Leonor's escorts, Gutierre Fernández de Castro, was a prominent Castilian magnate who nevertheless never attained the title of count.[23] He had been involved in various political embassies and military campaigns, such as the conquest of Almeria, and had been Alfonso VII's *mayordomo* from 1135 to 1138. He had also been Sancho III's tutor, and had been Sancho's *mayordomo* from 1153-5; he had also been Alfonso VIII's guardian during the years of his minority.[24] Count Tello Pérez de Meneses was another prominent Castilian noble charged with escorting Leonor to Castile. His loyalty to Alfonso VIII was rewarded in 1184 with a grant of some mills on the River Cea near Villanueva.[25] Of Leonor's other escorts, the Catalan Count Ponce de Minerva had served as *alférez* to Alfonso VII from 1140-44; he was Fernando II of León's *mayordomo* from July-October 1167, and Alfonso VIII's from May 1172 to June 1173.[26] Gonzalo Ruiz Girón (or Gonzalo Rodríguez) was Sancho III's *alférez* from 1149-55, and after 1170 he served as Leonor's *mayordomo*, which demonstrates that Leonor was entrusted with the management of her own household.[27] Gonzalo later served Leonor's daughter Berenguella and her son Fernando in the same capacity.[28] After 1175, however, Gonzalo and Alfonso VIII became estranged and Gonzalo moved to the royal court in León.[29]

Alfonso's ambassadors accompanied Leonor overland from Bordeaux via Jaca and Somport in Aragón, thereby bypassing the hostile dominions of the king of Navarre. They reached Tarazona in September 1170, where Alfonso received his bride-to-be, the marriage was celebrated, and the issues of dower and dowry were formally settled.[30]

---

[23] Barton, *Aristocracy*, 33.

[24] *Ibid.*, 32; see also *PCG*, 668-9.

[25] Barton, *Aristocracy*, 107n. Count Tello of Meneses, in the Tierra de Campos, was also a prominent patron of religion. He founded the Cistercian monastery of Matallana in the Tierra de Campos in 1173, the Augustinian abbey of Trianos near Sahagún in c.1185, a hospital at Cuenca for the care of prisoners of war in 1182, and two leper hospitals: one at San Nicolás del Real Camino, near Sahagún, and one at Villamartín, near Carrión, which he granted to the Order of Santiago in 1196. See Barton, *Aristocracy*, 199-200, and 331 for the charter granting the hospital at Villamartín to the Order of Santiago, dated 9 December 1196.

[26] Barton, *Aristocracy*, 286. The sobriquet 'de Minerva' suggests a possible family origin in the Minervois in southern France, at that time under the rule of the counts of Barcelona. Ponce married the Leonese heiress Estefanía Ramírez, daughter of Count Ramiro Froilaz, Barton, *Aristocracy*, 286.

[27] Barton, *Aristocracy*, 260. Gonzalo was the son of Count Rodrigo Gómez and Elvira, daughter of the Infante Ramiro Sánchez of Navarre. He married Sancha Fernández, the illegitimate daughter of Fernando Pérez de Traba and the Infanta Teresa Afonso of Portugal. Sancha had previously been married to, firstly, Álvaro Rodríguez, and secondly to Count Pedro Alfonso, Barton, *Aristocracy*, 260.

[28] Díez, *Alfonso VII*, 214; see also González, *Alfonso VIII*, I, 352-63.

[29] Barton, *Aristocracy*, 260.

[30] González, *Alfonso VIII*, I, 190, 795. Alfonso II of Aragón and his queen Sancha (who was also Alfonso VIII's aunt) were present at the marriage ceremony; Díez, *Alfonso VIII*, 42. In the presence of the Bishop of Bordeaux, Alfonso II of Aragón swore allegiance to Alfonso VIII, and Henry's ambassadors the viscounts of Castellón and Tartas and Pedro de Mota, also did homage to the Castilian king, González, *Alfonso VIII*, I, 189. For Leonor's marriage and dower provisions, see Part III, Chapter 2.

Chapter Three
Continuation of Angevin Marriage Policy:
Richard and Berengaria of Navarre

With the marriage of his daughter Leonor to Alfonso VIII of Castile, Henry II had established a network of dynastic alliance with northern Spain, largely aimed at countering the ambitions of the counts of Toulouse. This in turn sheds important light on Richard I's dynastic alliance with Navarre. As Henry had been aware, a dynastic alliance with the ruler of lands abutting one's own was strategically pragmatic. His son Richard had inherited the wars with Toulouse that had been ongoing since 1159; moreover, when Richard took the cross in 1189, it was 'inevitable' that Raymond VI of Toulouse would attempt to take advantage of Richard's absence on crusade to regain, at the very least, the Quercy, which Richard had taken in 1188.[1] An ally to the south of the most vulnerable part of Richard's kingdom was therefore a matter of crucial importance, and indeed, proved worthwhile, as Sancho VI of Navarre helped suppress revolts in Aquitaine in 1192 and again in 1194, whilst his brother served as hostage for Richard's release from captivity in 1194.[2]

It is interesting that Richard chose Navarre, rather than Aragón, for his dynastic alliance. Alfonso II of Aragón would have been a logical choice of ally, as he had long been in opposition to the counts of Toulouse. Alfonso's kingdom was larger and more powerful than that of Navarre, and Alfonso had repeatedly provided military assistance to Richard. After they had formed an alliance in April 1185, he entrusted Richard to negotiate on his behalf for the return of castles Sancho VI had captured from him, demonstrating that Alfonso believed Richard had a good deal of influence in Navarre.[3] It is possible that, as John Gillingham has suggested, the martial ability of Navarre, despite its small size, may have been one of the 'attractions of the marriage of Berengaria'.[4]

---

[1] John Gillingham, 'Richard I and Berengaria of Navarre', *Bulletin of the Institute of Historical Research*, 53 (1980), 167. Raymond had already, in 1183, joined the Young King against Richard. For the war with Toulouse, see Howden, *Gesta*, I, 345, and II, 34-6; Diceto, II, 43-4, 55.

[2] Gillingham, 'Richard and Berengaria', 167-8. For the 1192 revolt, see Howden, *Chronica*, III, 194; Devizes, 59. For the 1194 revolt, see Howden, *Chronica*, III, 252; Diceto, II, 117.

[3] Gillingham, 'Richard and Berengaria', 158-9.

[4] *Ibid.*, 167n, 168n. Gillingham was, however, mistaken in citing Alfonso's lack of daughters of marriageable age as a potential reason for Richard's alliance with Navarre. Alfonso II did in fact have four living daughters in 1189: Dolça who was a nun at Sigena, and who died later in 1189; Constanza, who subsequently married Aimeric of Hungary; Eleanor, who later married Raymond VI of Toulouse; and Sancha, who later married Raymond VII of Toulouse. For more on Alfonso's familiy, see Martin Aurell, *Les Noces du comte. Mariage et pouvoir en Catalogue (785-1213)* (Publications de la Sorbonne, Paris, 1995); 405-406, 418, 492-493. It is true that Dolça was in holy orders, and both Eleanor and Sancha were perhaps too young in 1189 for marriage, but it is difficult to see any logical reason why Constanza might not have been considered as a choice for Richard's bride. It may be that Richard would have considered such a union to be consanguineous, due to his prior betrothal to Alfonso's sister Dolça. For this betrothal, see Martin Aurell, *The Plantagenet Empire (1154-1224)* (Pearson-Longman, Harlow, 2007), 278 n.

Ultimately, it is not known how and when Richard's marriage to Berengaria was first broached.[5] What is known is that Eleanor of Aquitaine left Bordeaux for Navarre in September 1190.[6] Leaving Navarre with Berengaria, she crossed the Alps in winter, and by 20 January 1191, the two women had reached Lodi, near Milan.[7] They were met in Lombardy by the Emperor Henry VI, who travelled south with them, en route to claiming the Sicilian throne through right of his wife Constance.[8] Eleanor and Berengaria travelled to Sicily via Pisa, Rome and Naples, and Richard welcomed them personally at Reggio.[9] He lavishly entertained them for four days outside the walls of Messina before entrusting Berengaria to Joanna's custody for their onward journey to the Holy Land.[10]

Berengaria herself – much like her sisters-in-law – is not noted in the Angevin sources until her arrival, with her prospective mother-in-law Eleanor, in Italy in the spring of 1191, en route to meet Richard in Sicily.[11] It is not known what Berengaria thought of her impending marriage, nor would her opinions carry any weight, as twelfth-century royal women were seen primarily as useful diplomatic assets. She may well have hoped for some degree of power and influence, as Richard was the ruler of one of the most powerful kingdoms in western

---

[5] For discussions of when Berengaria's betrothal to Richard was first considered, see Gillingham, 'Richard and Berengaria', 158-68; Trindade, *Berengaria*, 43-4, 54, 66-9, 75-6, 82-3; Flori, *Eleanor of Aquitaine*, 133, 144; Turner, *Eleanor of Aquitaine*, 264; Kelly, *Eleanor of Aquitaine*, 263. See also the two crusade chronicles which suggest that Richard had a prior attachment to Berengaria: Ambroise, *Estoire de la Guerre Sainte*, ed. Gaston Paris (Paris, 1897), 31, ll. 1138-52, English trans. M.J. Hubert & J.L. La Monte, *The Crusade of Richard Lion-heart* (New York, 1976), 72; *Itinerarium Peregrinorum et Gesta Regis Ricardi*, ed. W. Stubbs (RS, London, 1864), 175, English trans. by Helen Nicolson, *Chronicle of the Third Crusade* (Aldershot, 1997), 173. A poem by Bertran de Born, probably to be dated c.1188, discusses the rejection of Richard's betrothed, Alice of France, in favour of Berengaria, and alludes to a long-established amity between England and Navarre; see 'S'ieu fos aissi segner ni poderos', in W. Paden, T. Sankovitch & P. Stäblein (eds.), *The Poems of the Troubadour Bertan de Born* (University of California Press, 1986), no. 35, at 380-1.

[6] For arguments favouring Eleanor of Aquitaine's role as initiator of the alliance with Navarre, see Richardson, 'Letters and Charters', 201; Brown, 'Eleanor of Aquitaine', 20-1, 32; W.L. Warren, *King John* (Harmondsworth, 1966), 58. Gillingham, however, has noted the lack of evidence for Eleanor's involvement beyond her journey to Navarre in 1190, and suggests that the alliance was entirely Richard's design, 'Richard and Berengaria', 158-63. Turner has pointed out that Eleanor's role in the negotiation process was still, however, crucial, as she would have had to convince Berengaria's father, Sancho VI, that Richard was serious about rejecting his betrothed, Alice of France, in order to marry Berengaria, *Eleanor of Aquitaine*, 264; see also Trindade, *Berengaria*, 75-6.

[7] Gillingham, 'Richard and Berengaria', 158n.

[8] Cloulas, 'Bérengère', 231. For more on the Sicilian succession, see Part III, Chapter 4.

[9] Trindade, *Berengaria*, 76. Richard heard news that Eleanor and Berengaria, accompanied by Philip of Flanders, had reached Naples in February 1191, and sent ships to convey them to Messina; Gillingham, 'Richard and Berengaria', 164. Gillingham has plausibly suggested that Tancred of Lecce's refusal to allow the ladies to disembark was due to his fear, possibly fostered by Philip of France who wished to save his sister's honour, that Eleanor of Aquitaine had entered into some form of alliance with the German emperor, whom she had met at Lodi in January, and who was en route to claim the Sicilian throne, 'Richard and Berengaria', 164-5. For events in Sicily at this time, including Philip's eventual treaty with Richard in which the betrothal to Alice was finally broken, see also Howden, *Gesta*, II, 157-61; *Chronica*, III, 95-9. For the treaty of Messina, see Landon, *Itinerary*, 229-31.

[10] Kelly, *Eleanor of Aquitaine*, 263-4.

[11] They arrived within hours of Philip Augustus' departure from Sicily on 30 March, having been kept waiting for some time at Messina for Tancred to give permission for them to land. Berengaria later journeyed to the Holy Land with Joanna, stopping off on Cyprus, where she was married to Richard at Limassol. As her dower, Richard granted her lands in Gascony, but she was to hold them only for the duration of Eleanor of Aquitaine's lifetime, as these lands had already been promised to Richard's sister Leonor. For more on Berengaria's dower, see Part III, Chapter 3. Berengaria travelled back from the Holy Land with Joanna via Rome, where they spent some time at the papal court. She hardly saw her husband after this time, and during Richard's captivity in Germany it was his mother Eleanor, rather than his queen, who had direct authority in England.

Europe. We know almost nothing of Berengaria from the sources, however. William of Newburgh calls her 'a lady of beauty and good sense', Richard of Devizes as 'more sensible than attractive'.[12] This is as much comment as Berengaria receives from contemporary Angevin sources. Her marriage to Richard took place in Limassol on Cyprus on 12 May,[13] although – unlike Joanna's marriage, which will be discussed in the following chapter – there is no detailed description of the ceremony.[14]

The union between Richard and Berengaria served important political interests: Richard secured the alliance both of her father, Sancho VI, and of her brother, the future Sancho VII. Both of these men were later instrumental in aiding Richard against Philip Augustus of France.[15] The unusual circumstances surrounding Richard's marriage to Berengaria demonstrate how politically important Richard viewed the union to be. For one thing, Richard had been betrothed to Alice, the daughter of Louis VII, since 1169.[16] For another, for a king to marry whilst on crusade was highly unusual. Richard had had ample time to marry before leaving for the Holy Land, and if, as some historians have suggested, he had indeed wished to delay entering the married state, the crusade would have provided the perfect excuse. Richard's betrothal to Alice had been confirmed as recently as July 1189, when by the treaty of Bonmoulins he had agreed to marry Alice on his return from crusade. For Richard to break this promise would have been diplomatically unwise – unless he viewed a different alliance as more politically profitable.

Richard's alliance with the Iberian kingdom of Navarre, therefore, could be seen as a direct consequence of the alliance made with Castile via his sister Leonor's marriage to Alfonso VIII. Both unions were concluded as part of a policy of aggression against Toulouse. Marital alliances with princesses from the lands bordering the south of the Angevin domains was a practice not confined merely to Henry II, or to Richard – John married Isabella of Angoulême, Henry III married Eleanor of Provence, and Edward I married Eleanor of Castile.[17] The marriage of Henry II's youngest daughter Joanna, however, was concluded as part of a very different strategic policy, which involved a Europe-wide competition for union with the highly desirable William II of Sicily, and which was only realised after the resolution of a complex tangle of negotiations which spanned several years.

---

[12]   William of Newburgh, *Historia Rerum Anglicanum*, in *Chronicles of the Reigns of Stephen, Henry II, and Richard I*, ed. Richard Howlett, 2 vols. (Rolls Series, 82.1; 82.2, London, 1884-5), 346; Richard of Devizes, *De Rebus Gestis Ricardi Primi: The Chronicle of Richard of Devizes*, in *Chronicles of the Reigns of Stephen, Henry II, and Richard I*, ed. Richard Howlett, 4 vols. (Rolls Series, 82.3, London, 1886), 402.

[13]   Trindade has no doubt that Richard intended to marry Berengaria in the Holy Land, as they could not have foreseen the violent storms that would shipwreck the vessel carrying the royal women just off the coast of Cyprus in Easter Week 1191, *Berengaria*, 85. However, Gillingham notes that Philip's presence would have made for an awkward situation if the wedding had in fact taken place in the Holy Land, 'Richard and Berengaria', 165n.

[14]   Howden records that the ceremony was performed by Nicholas the royal chaplain (later dean, then bishop, of Le Mans), and that Berengaria was crowned by John, bishop of Evreux, assisted by the archbishop of Bayonne and the bishops of Auxerre and Apamea, *Gesta*, II, 166-7; *Chronica*, III, 110. See also Nicholson, *Chronicle of the Third Crusade*, 189.

[15]   First in 1192, and again at the siege of Loches in 1194. See Howden, *Chronica*, III, 194, 252-3; Newburgh, 419-20; Devizes, 431.

[16]   Gillingham, 'Richard and Berengaria', 158-9, and 163-6 for the problems between Richard and Philip in Sicily because of this, and of Alice's subsequent fate. Howden, who was in Messina with Richard, stated that a marriage between Philip Augustus and Joanna may have been proposed at this time, *Chronica*, III, 38.

[17]   Gillingham, 'Richard and Berengaria', 157. Although as Nicholas Vincent has pointed out, Angoulême was technically within the Angevin domains, but remained semi-independent, 'John's Jezebel', 166-70.

Chapter Four
Joanna and William II of Sicily

As with her sister Leonor, Joanna first appears in the majority of the Angevin sources when negotiations opened for her marriage to William II of Sicily in 1176. That these negotiations, as well as the marriage itself, are recorded is perhaps an indication of what Howden and other contemporary chroniclers saw as the primary function of royal or aristocratic women. Indeed, the negotiations for Joanna's hand in May 1176 marks her first appearance in the *Gesta*, although this is perhaps because the *Gesta* only begins in 1170, and therefore does not contain references to the births of any of the royal children.[1] Both the *Gesta* and the later *Chronica* record the arrival in London in May 1176 of William's envoys, including Arnulf, bishop of Capua, Elias, elect of Troia, and Florius, count of Camerota, the royal justiciar.[2] The Pipe Rolls contain numerous entries for the expenses incurred for the reception and entertainment of the Sicilian ambassadors.[3]

Howden notes that the Sicilian envoys were accompanied by Rotrou, archbishop of Rouen,[4] and that with the consent of Henry II the ambassadors first travelled to Winchester to see Joanna, who was residing there with her captive mother Eleanor of Aquitaine, before returning to London, to conclude the negotiations.[5] According to John Julius Norwich, this viewing of the potential bride had been stipulated by William, who apparently 'would enter into no formal commitment without some assurance of the physical attractions of his bride'.[6] Norwich, however, does not state where he obtained this information, and Romuald of Salerno does not refer to any insistence on the need for a "bride show" in his brief account of the negotiation process and marriage.[7] It is most likely that Norwich was influenced by Howden's account of the Sicilian envoys travelling to Winchester to see Joanna, from whence they returned, 'satisfied as to her beauty'.[8]

---

[1] Howden, *Gesta*, I, 115-7, 119; *Chronica*, II, 94-5.

[2] The chronicle of Romuald, archbishop of Salerno, corroborates Howden's account of the Sicilian envoys sent to England in 1176, although his version of the embassy, journey to Sicily, and marriage in February 1177 is very brief, Romuald of Salerno, *Chronicon*, 268-9. Muratori noted that Florius, nephew of Alfano, archbishop of Capua, was one of the leading nobles in Calabria, Romuald of Salerno, *Chronicon*, 268n. Gerald of Wales also records the arrival of William's envoys in 1176, one of the few times Joanna is mentioned in his works. He confirms that the bishop of Capua, count Florius, and the elect of Troia were among the Sicilian envoys, Gerald of Wales, *De Principis Instructione Liber*, in *Giraldi Cambrensis: Opera*, ed. G.F. Warner (Rolls Series, 28, 8 Vols., London, 1891), I, 218.

[3] Including a payment of £6.7s.11d. from the bishop of Winchester; PR 22 Hen II, 47, 152, 198; PR 23 Hen II, 18, 105.

[4] The presence of Rotrou of Rouen, a kinsman of William's mother Margaret of Navarre, at the second Council of Winchester in August 1176 was undoubtedly connected to the Sicilian marriage, and is his only known journey to England; see Eyton, *Itinerary*, 205, 205n.

[5] Howden, *Gesta*, I, 115-6; *Chronica*, II, 94. Stubbs notes that Arnulf was in fact bishop of Capaccio, not of Capua, *Chronica*, II, 94n. John Julius Norwich states that the council convened to consider the proposal was merely 'for form's sake', as 'their unanimous agreement was a foregone conclusion', *The Kingdom in the Sun, 1130-1194* (Longman, London, 1970), 309. The Pipe Rolls record the expense of 56 shillings for Eleanor's journey to Winchester in 1176, PR 22 Hen II, 198.

[6] Norwich, *Kingdom in the Sun*, 309.

[7] Romuald, *Chronicon*, 268-9.

[8] *Gesta*, I, 115-6.

Torigni has little to say about Joanna, although his death in 1186 meant that he lived until Joanna, the youngest daughter of Henry and Eleanor, was in her early twenties. He does, however, record William's petition for marriage to Joanna in 1176, stating that 'William, king of Sicily, duke of Apulia, prince of Capua, by honourable legates requested a marriage with Joanna, daughter of Henry, king of England, and the request was granted'.[9] These are styles which William himself employed in his royal correspondence and charters.[10] Torigni may have been emphasising William's high status here to demonstrate the dynastic importance of the union between the royal houses of England and Sicily, although it is more probable that he had seen some of William's letters, such as that sent to Henry in 1173 offering condolences for the rebellions of his sons, or that sent in 1176 wishing to see a speedy conclusion to the marriage negotiations.[11] Diceto provides us with a partial copy of this letter, dated Palermo, 23 August 1176. The letter, in which Joanna is referred to as Henry's 'most noble daughter', ratifies the pledges of William's envoys and urges a speedy completion of the marriage negotiations. It also implies that the original petition for a marriage came from Henry rather than William, although William himself was clearly more than amenable to the idea.[12]

Proceedings were officially concluded in London on 20 May 1176,[13] and at the Council of Westminster on 25 May Henry formally gave his consent to the marriage, and appointed John, bishop of Norwich, Paris, archdeacon of Rochester, Baldwin Buelot (or Beluot), and Richard de Camville as his ambassadors.[14] Henry then visited Joanna at Winchester, presumably to bid farewell to his daughter.[15] With the marriage negotiations finalised, Henry sent his envoys to William in Sicily with Elias of Troia to convey the news that the alliance with his daughter was to proceed.[16] John of Norwich was sent to Sicily to negotiate the settlement of Joanna's dower and dowry. He reached Sicily in August, where he was well received by William, before returning with the Sicilian envoys – including Richard of Syracuse – to collect Joanna, who had left England on 27 August and had been escorted as far as St Gilles by the initial embassy.[17] John of Norwich reached St Gilles in November, and was back in Nottingham by Christmas Eve, Joanna having reached Naples by the same date.[18]

---

[9] Torigni, *Chronica*, 271. William's letter had arrived in England by August, and Eyton suggested that it was probably after this that Henry's ambassador John of Norwich left for St Gilles on the mouth of the Rhone to await Joanna's arrival there, *Itinerary*, 205.

[10] See, for example, his charter of dower settlement, discussed in Part III, Chapter 4.

[11] William's letter of 1173 is reproduced in full in Howden, *Gesta*, I, 55; *Chronica*, II, 48. The letter was clearly sent in response to one he had previously received from Henry, as it commences *In receptione litterarum vestrarum...* It is noteworthy that the only illustration in Howden is a drawing of William II's seal.

[12] See Diceto, I, 413-4. The letter is reproduced in full in Thomas Rymer, *Foedera* (J. Tonson, London, 1727), I, 42. Diceto provides more detail on Joanna's marriage to William than he does for the marriages of either of her sisters, who merit only brief mentions in his chronicle.

[13] Diceto, I, 408. He does not name the envoys who had arrived from Sicily, but notes that the proceedings were witnessed by various high clergy including archbishops, bishops and cardinals.

[14] Eyton, *Itinerary*, 202. Richard de Camville and Baldwin Buelot died before the ambassadors returned from Sicily, Eyton, *Itinerary*, 204n. This was not the same Richard de Camville who accompanied Richard I on the third crusade; see Nicholas Vincent, 'Canville, Richard de (*d.* 1191)', *DNB*. See also Howden, *Gesta*, I, 117; II, 80, 110, 115, 119, 120, 124, 134, 149, 167, 172.

[15] Eyton, *Itinerary*, 204.

[16] Diceto, I, 408. The Hampshire Pipe Roll for Michaelmas 1176 records the ambassadors' departure and the correspondent expenditure of 105 shillings, PR 22 Hen II, 200.

[17] Diceto, I, 414.

[18] Evelyn Jamison, 'Alliance of England and Sicily in the second half of the twelfth century', *Journal of the Warburg and Courtauld Institutes*, 6 (London, 1943), 29. For John of Norwich's journey to Sicily, see Howden, *Gesta*, I,

These various references to Joanna's marriage to William of Sicily in chronicles which otherwise have little to say about the daughters of Henry II and Eleanor of Aquitaine demonstrate the importance of this Anglo-Sicilian dynastic alliance. Gerald of Wales, usually hostile to the Angevins, thought the marriage important enough to be included under 'notable events' in his *De Principis*, which on the whole is critical of the entire Angevin family.[19] So why was this marriage so important, and why was a union between the royal houses of England and Sicily desired at this time?

William II of Sicily was an attractive prospect for any ambitious royal father with marriageable daughters. He had acceded to the wealthy Sicilian kingdom in 1166 on the death of his father William I. As he was a minor, control of the kingdom passed to his mother, Margaret of Navarre, who had been granted powers of regency by her husband on his deathbed. This right was uncontested by the nobles of the realm, and her abilities were such that when William reached his majority and began to rule in his own right in 1171, the kingdom was in a state of peace and prosperity. William's first priority was finding a suitable queen, and the prestige of the Sicilian kingdom meant that he would not find this difficult to accomplish. As John Julius Norwich put it, 'there was not a ruler in Europe who would not have been proud to have the young King as a son-in-law'.[20] Indeed, the Byzantine emperor Manuel Comnenus had already sought William as a husband in 1166-7 for his daughter and sole heir Maria, and although this marriage would have brought the Eastern Empire under Sicilian control, the regency government prevaricated, and when Henry II proposed his daughter Joanna in 1168, an alliance with the Angevin house was deemed much more desirable.[21]

The Byzantine-Norman alliance had been sought by Comnenus as part of his attempt to gain recognition as the legitimate Western emperor. In return, he was willing to agree to the union of the Eastern and Western churches, and to form a coalition with the rulers of France and Sicily against the Holy Roman Emperor, Frederick Barbarossa.[22] Comnenus' 1163 embassy to France proved fruitless; nevertheless, he pursued his interests in Sicily by proposing in 1166 a marriage between his daughter and heir Maria and the new king of Sicily, William II.[23]

115-7, 119-20. For his return to Nottingham, see Diceto, I, 414, 416-7. For Joanna's arrival in Naples, see Romuald, *Chronicon*, 268.

[19] See for example his judgements that the marriage of Henry II and Eleanor of Aquitaine was unlawful and bigamous, 160, 300; that the rebellions of Henry's sons were divine punishment for his sins, 159; and how the whole Angevin dynasty was corrupt, 299-302.

[20] Norwich, *Kingdom in the Sun*, 302.

[21] *Ibid.*, 302-3. See also J.S.R Parker, 'The Attempted Byzantine Alliance with the Norman Kingdom, 1166-7', in *Papers of the British School in Rome*, 24 (1956), 82-93: as the title suggests, he does not discuss the re-opening of negotiations in 1171.

[22] J.M. Hussey, 'The Later Macedonians, the Comneni and the Angeli, 1025-1204', in J.M Hussey (ed.), *Cambridge Medieval History*, 4.1 (CUP, 1966), 230; Munz, *Frederick Barbarossa*, 227n.

[23] Hussey, 'The Later Macedonians', 230. According to Romuald of Salerno, the proposal was made by Comnenus almost immediately after the death of William I, *Chronicon*, 254-5. The 1166-7 negotiations do not appear in either Niketas Choniates or John Kinnamos, the two main Byzantine chronicles for this period. Parker suggests that Comnenus' failure to achieve an alliance with Sicily in 1166-7 may be the reason that the matter does not appear in the Byzantine chronicles: 'unable to report a success, Manuel may well have kept the whole matter quiet...[Kinnamos and Choniates] either knew nothing of the plan to make William the emperor's heir or else considered, for one reason or another, that it was not a matter about which they could write in their histories', 'The Attempted Byzantine Alliance', 92. Romuald of Salerno is the first Western source to mention the attempted Byantine alliance with Sicily, although Kinnamos, 75, does note the failed attempts of Roger II to secure a Byzantine princess for his

To secure papal recognition for his claim over the rights of Barbarossa, Comnenus needed the support of the Sicilian kingdom, the staunchest protectors of the papacy in the 1160s. The death of William I was disastrous news for Alexander III, as William had been his main supporter, and in the autumn of 1166, he had fled to Benevento in the face of Barbarossa's advance on Rome. If Comnenus had been able to secure his position as sole western emperor, both the papacy and the kingdom of Sicily would have been presented with the far greater threat of Byzantine claims to control of southern Italy than they presently were by the schemes of Barbarossa. Nevertheless, Comnenus' proposal for a dynastic alliance between Byzantium and Sicily, the unification of the eastern and western churches, and his desire for imperial coronation was for a time considered by the pope, although Alexander rejected Comnenus' 'radical projects' as soon as the threat from Barbarossa had passed.[24]

The proposal in 1166 for the young William II to marry Comnenus' heir Maria would have guaranteed William's eventual accession to the Byzantine throne, thus bringing the Eastern Empire under Sicilian control.[25] Maria, however, had for the past four years been betrothed to Bela, the heir to the Hungarian throne[26], and the fact that Comnenus was so ready to overturn this betrothal demonstrates how desperate he was for a union with Sicily, particularly in the face of Barbarossa's impending fourth expedition into Italy. Comnenus' proposal, however, was rejected by the regency government, either because of this prior betrothal,[27] or because the union would have made the Byzantine emperor far too powerful in southern Italy, especially if his imperial ambitions were realised.[28] When Henry II proposed a marriage with his daughter Joanna in 1168, therefore, an alliance with the Angevin royal house appeared to be much more attractive to Margaret of Navarre and her council of advisors.[29]

There were many cultural, familial and political links between the Angevin and Sicilian kingdoms. Both royal dynasties were of Norman extraction, and many nobles and prelates in Sicily and in the Angevin domains were of shared kinship. Evelyn Jamison has discussed the 'constant and close' relations between England and Sicily from the time of the Conquest of England to the death of William II of Sicily, which were based on familial as much as political allegiances: members of the same families who journeyed to England in 1066 also travelled to Sicily and southern Italy (as well as to Antioch). There was a 'constant coming and going of relatives and friends between England and Normandy and Apulia and Sicily', and they shared not

---

bride in 1143-4.

[24] Horst Furhmann, *Germany in the High Middle Ages, c. 1050-1200*, trans. Timothy Reuter (CUP, 1986; repr. 1992), 159.

[25] Comnenus' eventual heir, Alexios II, was not born until 1169.

[26] Choniates, 73; Kinnamos, 163; see also Hussey, 'The Later Macedonians', 233. When Alexios was born in 1169, however, the betrothal between Maria and Bela was immediately broken, and Bela was married instead to Comnenus' sister-in-law, Anne, thereby retaining Hungaro-Byzantine links, Choniates, 96; Kinnamos, 214. Bela returned to Hungary in 1172 on the death of King Stephen III, and his daughter Margaret later married the Byzantine emperor Isaac II Angelos, taking the name Maria, Choniates, 203. Almost immediately, Comnenus sought William II of Sicily for his daughter's hand once again. Maria was eventually married to Renier of Montferrat in 1180, and was killed in the terror following Andronicus' usurpation of the Byzantine throne in 1183, Parker, 'The Attempted Byzantine Alliance', 91.

[27] As Parker has proposed, 'The Attempted Byzantine Alliance', 91. He also noted that the withdrawal of Barbarossa's troops in August 1167 removed the immediate threat to Sicily from the emperor, and that this may also have been a deciding factor in the failure of negotiations.

[28] As Hussey helpfully suggests, 'The Later Macedonians', 231. Comnenus' ambitions were, however, unrealistic, and his 1167 embassy to Rome was a failure. Further, after the formation of the Lombard Leagues the pope's position was far stronger than it had been previously.

[29] Especially as, despite the conflict with Thomas Becket, Henry II remained a supporter of Alexander III.

just the same language (French and Latin) but also customs and traditions.[30] There was also a steady stream of cultural and intellectual exchange as well as a consistent flow of officials between the two kingdoms. English scholars who journeyed to Sicily included Adelard of Bath, John of Salisbury, and Robert of Selby, who became chancellor to William I.[31] The ranks of clergy during William II's reign included several English prelates, most notably Richard Palmer, bishop of Syracuse.[32] Palmer had been a scholar at the court of William I, and had replaced Margaret of Navarre's kinsman, Stephen of Perche, as her principal advisor after Stephen's exile in 1168.[33]

Peter of Blois was one of several Frenchmen introduced to the Sicilian court by the regency government after the death of William I.[34] He subsequently became chaplain and secretary to Henry II, acting as ambassador for him on numerous occasions; after Henry's death in 1189, he became Eleanor's secretary and drafted several letters for her, including those to Pope Celestine purporting to be from the grief-stricken Eleanor.[35] Similarly, the Englishman Gervase of Tilbury – who was later to compose the *Otia Imperialia* for Joanna's nephew Otto – spent several years at William's court in the 1180s, presumably after the death of the Young King, in whose household he had previously been employed. Gervase was rewarded for his service with a villa in Nola, but after William's death he lost standing in Sicily, and by 1201 had entered the service of the archbishop of Arles. It is also possible that he either formed part of the embassy accompanying Joanna to Sicily in 1176-7, or was present as a boy, perhaps in the service of one of the ambassadors.[36] Gervase has little to say about Joanna other than that she had been married to William, 'the illustrious king of Sicily', and that she later bore Raymond VII, 'duke of Narbonne, count of Toulouse, and marquis of Provence'.[37] Gervase does, however, praise 'the glorious paps' of all of Henry II's daughters, 'which have brought renown to the most influential parts of the earth by their strengthening milk....'[38]

---

[30] Jamison, 'England and Sicily', 20.

[31] *Ibid.*, p. 21; D.J.A. Matthew, 'Richard [Richard Palmer] (*d.* 1195)', *DNB*.

[32] Another English prelate, Hubert of Middlesex, became archbishop of Conza in Campania, Norwich, *Kingdom in the Sun*, 303. It is no longer believed that Walter, archbishop of Palermo, was of English birth. Walter was tutor to the young William II, and before his election as archbishop in 1168 he had been archdeacon at Cefalù. According to the *Enciclopedia Italiana di Scienze, Lettere ed Arti* (Treves, Treccani, T.V.M. Minelli, 1933), XVIII, 12, Walter had been sent to Sicily by Henry II to become tutor to the intended husband of his daughter Joanna. L.J.A. Loewenthal has argued convincingly against Walter's supposed English nationality, pointing to Peter of Blois' letter to Walter congratulating him on his new position as archbishop of Palermo, in which he describes the character and physical attributes (*formam et mores*) of the father of William's intended bride. As Loewenthal pointed out, if Walter had been at Henry's court he would surely have had no need of such description, 'For the Biography of Walter Ophamil, Archbishop of Palermo', *English Historical Review*, 87 (1972), 79; for the letter, Peter of Blois, *Epistola*, in *Patrologia Latina*, 206, Ep. LXVI, erroneously dated 1077. Further, Walter's support for the proposed match with Maria of Byzantium in 1171 makes it unlikely that he was sent to Sicily by Henry in advance of William's marriage to Joanna. The confusion seems to have arisen from a sixteenth-century work conflating Walter of Palermo with Walter of Coutances, Loewenthal, 'Walter Ophamil', 78-9. Walter was later instrumental in negotiating the marriage between William's aunt Constance and Henry VI, although he was forced to crown Tancred after William's death. His brother Bartholomew became bishop of Agrigento, and succeeded Walter (who died in 1190) as archbishop of Palermo, Loewenthal, 'Walter Ophamil', 81-2. See also D.J.A. Matthew, 'Walter (*d.* 1190)', *DNB*.

[33] Jamison, 'England and Sicily', 23.

[34] For the career of Peter of Blois (1125/30-1212), see R.W. Southern, 'Blois, Peter of (1125x30–1212)', *DNB*; Peter Dronke, 'Peter of Blois and Poetry at the Court of Henry II', *Mediaeval Studies*, 38 (1976), 185-235.

[35] Dronke, 'Peter of Blois', 191. For the letters to Celestine, see Part I, Chapter 2.

[36] Gervase of Tilbury, *Otia Imperialia*, ed. and trans. S.E. Banks & J.W. Binns (OUP, 2002), XXVIII-XXIX; p. xxvi.

[37] *Ibid.*, 489.

[38] *Ibid.*, 489.

The union of England and Sicily thus served important diplomatic interests for both William and Henry. The kingdom of Sicily was a rich and prosperous nation, with an impressive naval force, and it was a centre of academic and scientific excellence renowned throughout Europe. Moreover, Sicily's geographical position made it a convenient, and more importantly, friendly, stop-over point for crusaders and pilgrims to the Holy Land. William had already given his support to the crusade, and had promised to assist the crusaders further in their attempts to defend the Holy Land. The proposal for Henry's daughter Joanna to marry William II of Sicily, then, suggests much about Henry's intention, never fulfilled, to go on crusade himself.[39]

Henry II was in the advantageous position of having three daughters in addition to four sons, enabling him to broker alliances with a variety of important European dynasties. In 1168 he was actively pursuing this policy, and negotiations for the marriages of his two unwed daughters were opened with the kingdom of Castile as well with that of Sicily. For William II, the marriage to Joanna would tie him to a dynasty who were without doubt one of the most powerful ruling families in Western Europe. In 1170, therefore, William sent envoys to Pope Alexander III to discuss the question of his marriage to Henry's daughter Joanna.

One of these envoys, Richard Palmer, recently made bishop of Syracuse, had been on good terms with Thomas Becket, and had received his exiled friends and kinsmen in Sicily.[40] A letter from Becket to Palmer, dated December 1167 and written in response to a now-lost letter he had received from Palmer, thanks him for his 'very persuasive entreaties on our behalf to your friend lord William of Pavia', who had been in Sicily in July or August 1167 before journeying to France.[41] Becket further recommends to Palmer his nephew Gilbert, the bearer of the letter. Becket wrote to Palmer again in late 1169, thanking him for the kindness he had shown to his friends and relatives, and exhorting him to use his influence at court for the reinstatement of Stephen of Perche, Becket's friend and former chancellor of Sicily, who had been driven from the court after the "palace revolution" of 1168. The letter entreats Palmer to 'do your utmost with the king and queen to procure the recall of the venerable Stephen, elect of Palermo...for reasons which we are intentionally keeping secret for the moment'.[42] Palmer was unlikely to acquiesce to this request, as he was hostile to Stephen and had gained his own position at court through Stephen's downfall; moreover, he does not appear to have been on the best of terms with the queen-regent, Margaret of Navarre.[43]

---

[39] William II, having not yet heard the news of Henry's death, had bequeathed to him on his deathbed 'all the treasure accumulated in Sicily for the campaign', which Richard I was later to insist be given to him by William's successor Tancred of Lecce, Jamison, 'England and Sicily', 30. For Richard in Sicily, see Howden, *Gesta*, II, 112-5, 123-9, 132-41, 146, 150-62; and *Chronica*, III, 152-77; see also Ambroise, 13-32. For the treaty between Richard and Tancred (November 1190), in which Richard received the legacy bequeathed to his father, and Joanna received recompense for the loss of her dower lands, see Howden, *Chronica*, III, 57, 62.

[40] In 1176 Palmer was one of the members of the Sicilian embassy who received Joanna at St Gilles and escorted her to Sicily. D.J.A. Matthew suggests that Richard's influence was so great that Henry II attempted to win him over during his quarrel with Becket, to the end that Henry offered him the vacant see of Lincoln as reward for his efforts during the negotiation process for the marriage between Joanna and William, 'Richard [Richard Palmer] (*d.* 1195)', *DNB*. In 1183 Palmer became archbishop of Messina, and it was in this capacity that he negotiated with Richard I in 1190, Matthew, 'Richard [Richard Palmer] (*d.* 1195)', *DNB*.

[41] Anne Duggan, *The Correspondence of Thomas Becket* (Clarendon Press, Oxford, 2000), 2 vols., I, 737.

[42] Duggan, *Correspondence*, II, 973. A letter from Becket to Margaret of Navarre was sent at the same time, thanking her for the clemency she showed in receiving his exiled friends and relatives, and entreating her to favourably receive his friend Thibaud, prior of St-Arnoult de Crépy, and later abbot of Cluny (1179-83), Duggan, *Correspondence*, II, 969.

[43] See Matthew, 'Richard [Richard Palmer] (*d.* 1195)', *DNB*.

Becket would undoubtedly have viewed Palmer's involvement in the 1170 embassy to be a betrayal of their former friendship, although Norwich suggests that Palmer likely viewed his position as mediatory.[44] It would appear in any case that Becket had become disillusioned with Palmer as early as August 1169, as a letter to Hubert, Cardinal Bishop of Ostia, demonstrates. In this letter, Becket accuses Henry II of securing the support of Italian cities through bribes, as also his promise of the bishopric of Lincoln secured the support of Richard Palmer. He states that Palmer, 'corrupted by the hope of gaining the bishopric of Lincoln, supported our persecutors with money, armed them with advice, strengthened them with his power; for, to influence the king of Sicily...for the destruction of the Church and ourselves, they promised the king of England's daughter in marriage'.[45] This view of the motive for Joanna's marriage to William surely represents extreme paranoia on Becket's part.[46]

The other envoy to the papal court in 1170 was Robert, count of Loritello, who had recently returned from exile and been restored to his lands. As William's cousin, he 'gave the mission a status it would otherwise have lacked', and the proposed marriage met with papal approval.[47] However, the murder of Becket on 29 December 1170 brought proceedings to a standstill. England was placed under papal interdict, and the regency government in Sicily understandably viewed a union with an excommunicate kingdom as less than desirable.

Accordingly, in March 1171, negotiations with Byzantium were reopened. Although Comnenus had by this time sired a son to succeed him, meaning that Maria would no longer bring the Byzantine Empire as dowry, her imperial status still made her an attractive proposition. The suggested marriage was fully supported by Walter of Palermo, the most prominent cleric in Sicily,[48] and in 1172 the regency government accepted the Byzantine proposal. Maria was due to arrive in Taranto that spring, and although William went personally to meet his bride-to-be she failed to arrive. Apparently, Comnenus was concurrently considering the son of the Holy Roman Emperor as a better potential husband for his daughter.[49] It appears that when the news of the proposed Siculo-Byzantine alliance reached Barbarossa, he then put forward the proposal that Maria marry his own son, Henry. The emperor's son certainly represented to Comnenus the 'greater prize', and a Byzantine embassy consequently arrived in Cologne in June 1171.[50]

Comnenus' hopes for an alliance between Byzantium and the Holy Roman Empire appear to have been bolstered by Henry II's own son-in-law, Henry the Lion of Saxony. He had arrived in Constantinople en route to Jerusalem, apparently as an unofficial negotiator for Barbarossa, at 'the very moment when a marriage alliance between Byzantium and Sicily was to be concluded', and Peter Munz believes that there is 'almost certain evidence that the Emperor Manuel postponed a final decision in this matter to await the arrival of Henry – for such an alliance would have committed Manuel to a continuation of his old anti-German policy'.[51]

[44] Norwich, *Kingdom in the Sun*, 304.

[45] Duggan, *Correspondence*, II, 945.

[46] Both Becket and Henry II had sought William's intervention during the controversy; Otto Demus suggested that Henry, who had cited both Sicily and Hungary as examples where the Crown had prerogative rights over the Church, first offered Joanna in marriage to William in 1166 'to induce him to embrace the king's cause', but that the murder of Becket in 1170 cooled relations between the two kingdoms, *The Mosaics of Norman Sicily* (London, Routledge & Kegan Paul, 1950), 129-30, at 129.

[47] Norwich, *Kingdom in the Sun*, 304.

[48] Loewenthal, 'Walter Ophamil', 78.

[49] Choniates, 383n; Hussey, 'The Later Macedonians', 231; Munz, *Frederick Barbarossa*, 308.

[50] Hussey, 'The Later Macedonians', 231; Munz, *Frederick Barbarossa*, 308.

[51] Munz, *Frederick Barbarossa*, 308.

Henry the Lion managed to persuade Comnenus to abandon the Sicilian alliance in return for promises of lands in southern Italy, and the Greek chronicler John Kinnamos reports that Henry successfully effected peace between Comnenus and Barbarossa.[52] It is not at all certain how serious Barbarossa was about any of these promises, but he did achieve his aim of preventing a union between the Eastern empire and Sicily.

The hoped-for alliance with the Holy Roman Empire presents the most plausible reason for Maria's non-appearance at Taranto in 1172, although the chronicler Niketas Choniates presents a different reason for the failure of the negotiations with Sicily. He informs us that William had been Comnenus' first choice as husband for Maria, and that 'One envoy after another was sent to him, while he dispatched envoys back again to negotiate the marriage contract; the embassies alternated, and the preliminary wedding deliberations were drawn out in idle chatter. When these oscillated like a scale rising and falling and were frequently altered and modified, the emperor finally changed his mind, deeming a marriage with the king of Sicily to be disadvantageous to the Romans'.[53] In either case, Comnenus neither explained himself nor apologised for his actions, and William harboured a resentful distrust for the Eastern Empire until he died.[54] Comnenus himself must have had cause to regret this course of action when a further embassy to Regensburg in 1174 was refused an audience with the emperor, whose offer of a dynastic alliance does indeed appear to have been not entirely serious.

On the other hand, Henry II's political standing in Europe vastly improved after he received papal absolution for the murder of Thomas Becket at Avranches on 21 May 1172. William of Sicily had by now attained his majority, and was apparently one of the first European monarchs to 're-establish contact, and for the next few years the two Kings maintained a cordial if rather spasmodic correspondence', although the question of marriage to Joanna was not broached again during this time.[55] The resumption of plans for a marital alliance between England and Sicily was eventually proposed by Alexander III, who was seeking support against the Holy Roman Emperor. Barbarossa had himself sought a union between William and one of his own daughters in 1175, but the proposal was rejected on the counsel of William's chancellor, Matthew of Ajello, despite Walter of Palermo's enthusiasm for the match.[56] As Sicily had long been the papacy's strongest supporter, Alexander had understandably been alarmed at the thought of a union between William and his German enemy, and therefore decided to intervene and suggest the re-opening of negotiations for the Anglo-Sicilian union.[57]

---

[52] Henry came to Byzantium for the purpose of effecting peace, and 'After he had achieved what he came for, he departed', Kinnamos, 214. See also Munz, *Frederick Barbarossa*, 308. When Henry the Lion returned to Augsburg in December 1172, Barbarossa welcomed the news he brought regarding the Byzantine embassy; however, this promise to Comnenus was held against him as treasonable by Barbarossa after Henry's fall from favour, Munz, *Frederick Barbarossa*, 308. Nevertheless, by 1174 Barbarossa was also seeking a dynastic alliance with Sicily.

[53] Choniates, 97.

[54] Norwich, *Kingdom in the Sun*, 304-5. When Comnenus himself died in 1180, he entrusted the regency for his eleven year old son Alexios to the boy's mother, Comnenus' second wife Mary of Antioch. This presents an interesting parallel with the regency of Margaret of Navarre for her son William. For Mary's regency, see Hussey, 'The Later Macedonians', 243-4.

[55] Norwich, *Kingdom in the Sun*, 308.

[56] Demus, *Mosaics of Norman Sicily*, 129-30, at 129. The union with Joanna, proposed again in the early 1170s, was supported both by Ajello and by the pope.

[57] Norwich, *Kingdom in the Sun*, 308; Jamison, 'England and Sicily', 29. Alexander was concerned with cementing kingdoms favourable to him in an alliance against Barbarossa. Henry II had much influence in Germany, having

Re-opening of Negotiations

After the prevarications of the preceding years, the negotiations for Joanna's marriage to William now moved at pace. A contingent of English ambassadors arrived in Sicily in early August, requesting that William swear under oath to uphold his pledges to marry Joanna. William refused to do so, stating that this went against the customs of his realm and of his predecessors, even though this was not entirely the case, as William had sworn a similar oath in 1172 to the Byzantine emperor Manuel Comnenus during negotiations to marry his daughter Maria.[58] As has been seen, these negotiations had not only failed spectacularly but had had drastic repercussions for Siculo-Byzantine relations. Léon-Robert Ménager has argued that William's refusal to swear an oath in this instance was due to his desire to present an image of supreme kingship, in much the same manner as the king of France refused to give homage to any other lord.[59] While this is plausible, it is also likely that William's humiliation vis-à-vis the failed Byzantine alliance four years previously played some part in his reluctance to swear an oath in 1176.

Nevertheless, negotiations were finally concluded in May 1176, and Joanna was immediately conveyed to Sicily in the company of an impressive entourage, reflecting both her status as an Angevin princess, and the importance and value of this dynastic alliance. As is often the case, it is the *Gesta* which provides the fullest account of Joanna's journey to her new kingdom.[60] Howden informs us that Joanna was accompanied on her journey to Sicily by Arnulf of Capua and Florius of Camerota, as well as by a large number of Henry's envoys, including the archbishops of Rouen and Canterbury, the bishops of Ely and Evreux, Hugh de Beauchamp, and Hamelin, earl of Warenne, who is referred to as Joanna's uncle (*patruus puellae*).[61]

---

already married his eldest daughter Matilda to Henry the Lion, who was at this time at odds with the emperor. The Anglo-Sicilian alliance proved successful in its object of isolating Barbarossa, who was forced to conclude the Treaty of Venice soon after Joanna's marriage to William. Nevertheless, by 1184 Walter of Palermo had helped to arrange the marriage of Constance, William's aunt and heir, to Barbarossa's son Henry, and in 1185 Henry II had engineered Henry the Lion's reconciliation with the emperor and secured the restitution of his lands. The Hohenstaufens were 'no longer to be isolated...[but] to become the corner-stone of the united effort against Saladin', Jamison, 'England and Sicily', 30. By 1190, however, Henry the Lion was once more in exile. His son Otto, Richard I's 'favourite nephew', was brought up at Richard's court in Poitou, and was, accordingly, 'more of an Angevin than a Welf', Jamison, 'England and Sicily', 31. With the accession in Sicily of Henry VI, the Anglo-Sicilian alliance, which had lasted for some twenty years, was finally broken.

[58] L-R. Ménager, *Hommes et Institutions de l'Italie Normande* (Variorum Reprints, 1981), Part II, 312. The Greek chronicler John Kinnamos does not mention these negotiations, although he does refer to the proposed marriage between Maria and Bela of Hungary, *Deeds of John and Manuel Comnenos*, trans. Charles M. Brand (Columbia University Press, 1976), 163. Niketas Choniates, however, names William as Comnenus' 'first choice' for Maria's husband, *O City of Byzantium, Annals of Niketas Choniates*, trans. Harry J. Magoulias (Wayne State University Press, Detroit, 1984), 97.

[59] Ménager, *Hommes et Institutions*, Part II, 312.

[60] The *Chronica*, II, 95, simply records that once the preparations were finalised, Henry sent his daughter to Sicily, without giving details either of her journey or in whose company she was escorted. The narrative then moves straight to the recording of her arrival in Palermo in February 1177.

[61] Howden, *Gesta*, I, 120. The two Sicilian magnates had remained in England after the conclusion of the marriage negotiations specifically in order to accompany Joanna to Sicily. See Howden, *Gesta*, I, 116-7; *Chronica*, II, 94-5. For more on Hamelin, the natural brother of Henry II, see Thomas K. Keefe, 'Warenne, Hamelin de, earl of Surrey (d. 1202)', *DNB*. He was later one of the many people who received a cure at Becket's shrine, see *Materials for the History of Thomas Becket, archbishop of Canterbury*, ed. J.C. Robertson & J.B. Sheppard, 7 vols. (Rolls Series, 67, London, 1875-85; hereafter *MTB*), I, 452: *De comite Hamelino, cujus alterum oculorum albugo obduxerat*; see also Part IV.

Joanna's journey to Sicily to marry William II marks the first time she appears in the chronicle of Gervase of Canterbury. Although his account is very brief, he does record that in September 1176, Henry sent Richard, archbishop of Canterbury, to accompany Joanna on her journey. Whilst Richard's participation was also noted by Howden, Gervase records only the archbishop by name, along with 'other notable envoys'.[62]

Joanna's outfit and suite were provided by Richard, bishop of Winchester, another highly trusted member of Henry II's curia who also accompanied Joanna to Sicily and was furthermore entrusted with organising the ships which would convey Joanna and her household to Sicily. Richard had held a court at Winchester in mid-August, where the Sicilian ambassadors were 'showered...with presents' before Joanna was formally given over to their care.[63] The Pipe Rolls for Winchester and Southampton record the expenses incurred for Joanna's crossing, including £10 13s for the equipping of seven ships, in addition to £7 10s for the royal *esnecca* in which Joanna herself travelled.[64] Joanna was laden with gifts of cloth, gold, silver, and precious dishes; presumably these were some of the *minutis apparatibus* mentioned in the Pipe Rolls, some of which may have constituted part of her dowry. Furthermore, Henry II provided his daughter with splendid robes which cost a staggering £115 5s 5d, and which were probably intended to be worn at her marriage and coronation.[65] As no land seems to have been granted, it must be presumed that a cash dowry had been agreed. Certainly, Joanna's dowry must have been sufficiently valuable for William to bestow on her a magnificent dower at the time of their marriage, a subject which will be discussed in greater detail in Part III, Chapter 4. According to Diceto, Henry had decreed that worthy men were to accompany Joanna, 'some as far as Toulouse, others as far as the hills of Sicily', and they were not to think of returning before they had witnessed Joanna's marriage and coronation.[66] Joanna was met in Normandy by her eldest brother Henry who escorted her to Poitiers, where she was received with honour by her brother Richard. Richard accompanied her as far as Toulouse - presumably to St Gilles, whence John of Norwich had journeyed in order to receive her - where twenty-five of William's ships were waiting to convey her to Sicily.[67] Joanna was honourably greeted in William's name by Alfano, archbishop of Capua, Richard Palmer, bishop of Syracuse, and Robert de Lauro, count of Caserta.[68] Her reception in Toulouse and the role of Count Raymond VI in Joanna's safe conduct indicates that there were, temporarily, good relations between Henry II and Raymond of Toulouse – indeed, Raymond had formally submitted to Henry at Limoges in 1173, performing homage for Toulouse both to Henry and to his sons, the Young King and Richard, and the peace thereby attained was to prevail until the early 1180s.[69]

---

[62] Gervase, I, 260. Diceto, I, 414, states that Joanna left in late August, not September; his chronology is more accurate, although Eyton has pointed out that as the bishop of Ely, who accompanied Joanna to Sicily, was in England on 29 August, their departure must have occurred at the very end of August. See Eyton, *Itinerary*, 205.

[63] Diceto, I, 414; Eyton, *Itinerary*, 206; Norwich, *Kingdom in the Sun*, 309-10.

[64] PR 22 Hen II, 198-9; Eyton, *Itinerary*, 206. The seven other ships presumably carried the envoys, and perhaps Joanna's baggage.

[65] PR 22 Hen II, 12. Compared to the cost of 42 shillings for Joanna's luxury items, this sum seems astronomical.

[66] Diceto, I, 414.

[67] Howden, *Gesta*, I, 119-20. The account of Joanna being escorted by her brothers does not appear in the *Chronica*; similarly, the return of Henry's envoys is recorded in the *Gesta*, I, 127, 167, but not in the *Chronica*.

[68] Romuald of Salerno, *Chronicon*, 268. The fleet departed from Toulouse on 5 November, Romuald of Salerno, *Chronicon*, 268n. Richard Palmer was an English cleric who was on close terms with Thomas Becket. He had been created bishop of Syracuse in 1169; in 1183 he became archbishop of Messina. Robert of Caserta was grand constable and justiciar for Apulia, Romuald of Salerno, *Chronicon*, 268n.

[69] Benjamin, 'Forty Years War', 274-5. In 1183, Raymond joined the Young King's rebellion, ending the relative

Joanna reached Toulouse by November 1176; John of Norwich had arrived a fortnight previously, having returned from his original embassy to Messina to convey Henry's acceptance of the marriage proposal.[70] He did not accompany Joanna to Sicily, as Diceto records that he returned to England on Christmas Eve 1176.[71] The bishop's journey had been arduous, and a storm at sea in early November had resulted in the loss of ships somewhere between Messina and Toulouse which had been bearing gifts for Henry from William.[72] The fleet conveying Joanna to Sicily therefore took a cautious sea route along the coasts; after six weeks they had reached Naples, at that time part of the kingdom of Sicily, and the decision was made to spend Christmas there, because, according to Romuald of Salerno, Joanna was suffering from terrible sea-sickness.[73] The rest of the journey to Sicily was made by land, through Salerno and Calabria, until Joanna reached Palermo, where she was received with honour by William and his magnates.[74] That the sea-crossing was made at all in November, rather than waiting for the following spring, suggests a sense of urgency in the proceedings, perhaps because of the previous equivocations during the earlier stage of negotiations.

The Royal Ambassadors

Henry was clearly concerned to send his daughters to Saxony, Castile and Sicily in a manner befitting of their rank and status. The marriage of a king's daughter was, usually, a one-off event, and presented an opportunity for display in much the same manner as a royal civic entry. Records of queens' civic entries, coronations and royal progresses are plentiful for the later medieval period, but are not so for the twelfth century.[75] For the daughters of Henry and Eleanor, the lavish arrangements made for their journeys to their new lands provide crucial evidence not just of the political significance of these events, but also for their individual importance to their natal family. Moreover, in the case of Leonor, discussed in Chapter 2, the embassy presented the opportunity to assert a united Aquitanian identity, drawing the dispa-

---

peace that had existed between England and Toulouse for the past decade.

[70] Diceto, I, 415. For the career of John of Oxford, bishop of Norwich (1175-1200), see A. Morey & C.N.L. Brooke (eds.), *The Letters and Charters of Gilbert Foliot* (CUP, 1967), 530; John le Neve, *Fasti Ecclesiae Anglicanae, 1066-1300*, comp. Diana E. Greenway (University of London, Institute of Historical Research, 1971), Vol. II: *Monastic Cathedrals*, 56. He had previously been entrusted to head the 1165 embassy to Germany to negotiate the marriage between Henry's eldest daughter Matilda and Henry the Lion of Saxony, Christopher Harper-Bill, 'Oxford, John of (d. 1200)', *DNB*. Richard of Ilchester had also been one of the ambassadors sent to negotiate the marriage of Matilda to Henry the Lion, and later played an important role in the Young King's coronation. See Charles Duggan, 'Richard of Ilchester, Royal Servant and Bishop', *Transactions of the Royal Historical Society*, 5th ser., Vol. 16 (1966), 1-24; *Letters and Charters of Gilbert Foliot*, 539; *Fasti Ecclesiae Anglicanae, 1066-1300*, II, 85; Eyton, *Itinerary*, 206, 222. His death is recorded in Howden, *Gesta*, II, 58. As with his role in the 1176-7 embassy to Sicily, Richard's participation in this ceremony is not recorded by Howden.

[71] For the account of the bishop of Norwich's journey to Sicily, and his return at Christmas 1176, Diceto, I, 416-7. The archbishop of Canterbury and bishop of Ely also returned to England, arriving later that same month, Eyton, *Itinerary*, 208-9. Joanna continued her journey in the company of the bishops of Evreux and Bayeux, Hugh de Beauchamp, Osbert de Camera and Geoffrey de la Charre, Eyton, *Itinerary*, 208.

[72] Howden, *Gesta*, I, 127.

[73] Romuald of Salerno, *Chronicon*, 268-9.

[74] *Ibid.*

[75] The pageant series devised for Anne Boleyn's coronation in 1533, for example, was recorded by Wynkyn de Worde in his *The Noble and Tryumphaunt Coronacyon of Quene Anne*, ed. Edmund Goldsmid (Edinburgh, 1884). For visual display more generally, see Maurice Keen, 'Introduction', in Peter Coss and Maurice Keen (eds.), *Heraldry, Pageantry and Social Display in Medieval England* (Boydell, Woodbridge, 2002), 1-16.

rate magnates of the south together for perhaps the first time in their history.

The inclusion of such prominent and important members of Henry's court in the embassy to Sicily similarly demonstrates the importance that was attached to the alliance between Joanna and William. Gervase of Canterbury clearly recorded his archbishop's involvement in this important journey as a point of both local interest and of prestige for the see of Canterbury.[76] The role of Joanna's brothers Richard and Henry, and of her uncle Hamelin as escorts suggests that it was thought necessary to have close family members as part of the embassy. It is also worthy of note that Joanna reached Toulouse in November 1176: this is important in light of Henry II's dealings at this time with Count Raymond VI of Toulouse.[77] As shown in Chapter 2, Henry II had married his daughter Leonor to Alfonso of Castile in 1170 as part of a strategic policy against the count of Toulouse. In 1176, however, a tentative peace between Henry and Raymond of Toulouse had been in effect for the past three years.

The descriptions of Joanna's journey, or more specifically, of who accompanied her, are interesting, as the differing accounts of who journeyed with her make it possible to recreate this embassy in some detail. Moreover, the focus in these accounts on different persons of importance demonstrates that Joanna's retinue was both large and comprised some of the most influential members of the English court and clergy, reflecting both her status as an Angevin princess, and the importance and value of this dynastic alliance that Henry intended to impress on the Sicilian court. But who exactly were these men of importance who accompanied Joanna to Sicily, and why were they chosen for this task? And what influenced the various chroniclers in their choice of who they chose to name as being part of this important embassy?

Of the six bishops named as accompanying Joanna on part or all of her journey to Sicily in 1176-7, all were highly involved in the politics of Henry II's reign. They acted as itinerant judges and ambassadors, and attended numerous royal and ecclesiastical councils. Several had found employment in the royal court as clerks or treasurers, and two of them had direct links with Thomas Becket. Rotrou, archbishop of Rouen (1165-83), who accompanied Joanna as far as Toulouse, was the great-uncle of Margaret of Navarre, William II's mother.[78] As archbishop of Rouen, he had conducted the second coronation ceremony at Winchester in 1172 of Henry's son Henry the Young King, when he was crowned with his young wife Margaret. Rotrou was assisted at this ceremony by Giles of Perche, bishop of Evreux (1170-79), who also accompanied Joanna to Sicily and was present at her marriage and coronation.[79] Another of Henry's ambassadors to Sicily was Henry de Beaumont, bishop of Bayeux (1165-1205),

---

[76] It is unclear why Richard, bishop of Winchester was included in Diceto's account but not that given by Howden. Richard had been an opponent of Becket during his quarrel with Henry II, although this is also true of the bishops of Ely and Norwich. Whilst Richard is not mentioned by Howden as being part of the Sicilian embassy, he does record the return of Richard of Canterbury and Geoffrey, bishop of Ely, 'who had accompanied [Joanna] as far as Toulouse', as well as that of John of Norwich, 'who had been sent to King William on behalf of the same daughter of the king', Howden, *Gesta*, I, 127. The reasons for Howden's omission are therefore unclear.

[77] See Part II, Chapter 2.

[78] Rotrou's mother Margaret was the daughter of Geoffrey, Count of Perche, and thus a cousin of Margaret of Navarre. See Romuald of Salerno, *Chronicon*, 268n; and for more on Rotrou's career, see David S. Spear, *The Personnel of the Norman Cathedrals during the Ducal Period, 911-1204* (University of London, Institute for Historical Research, 2006), 134-5, 199; *Letters and Charters of Gilbert Foliot*, 538. His death in 1183 is recorded by Howden, *Gesta*, I, 308.

[79] Howden, *Gesta*, I, 31, 19. For Giles, bishop of Evreux, see *Letters and Charters of Gilbert Foliot*, 533; Spear, *Personnel of Norman Cathedrals*, 135. In 1177 Giles of Evreux, Henry of Bayeux and Richard of Ilchester were witnesses to the peace treaty between Henry II and Louis VII of France at Ivry, see Howden, *Gesta*, I, 194. Giles' death in September 1179 is recorded (under 1180) in Howden, *Gesta*, I, 269.

who had attended the Young King's coronation in 1170, and along with Rotrou of Rouen had witnessed the Young King's formal submission to his father in 1175.[80] Henry is not mentioned in the *Gesta* as being part of the embassy to Sicily, although his return is recorded.

Richard of Dover, archbishop of Canterbury (1173-84), who accompanied Joanna to St Gilles, makes numerous appearances in the *Gesta*.[81] He succeeded Thomas Becket as archbishop of Canterbury and was made papal legate for Canterbury at the same time as his episcopal consecration.[82] As archbishop, he was also responsible for the contentious episcopal consecrations of Richard of Ilchester, bishop of Winchester (1173-88), and Geoffrey Ridel, bishop of Ely (1173-89), who were both part of the 1177 embassy to Sicily.[83] Along with John of Norwich and Geoffrey Ridel, Richard of Dover was also present at the council at London in 1177 where Henry arbitrated between the Spanish kings, finding in favour of his son-in-law, Alfonso VIII.[84] Richard of Ilchester, who made the arrangements for Joanna's journey and 'showered the Sicilian ambassadors with presents' is, strangely, not mentioned in the *Gesta* as being part of the embassy to Sicily: it is only Diceto who records Richard's involvement, which throws up the interesting question of what Howden's relationship was with this key figure. Geoffrey Ridel's friendship with Richard of Ilchester, and their evident hostility towards Becket, may provide an explanation for Howden's dislike of the man; and indeed, Howden's dislike of Ridel is apparent in his work. This however does not explain Howden's inclusion of Ridel and exclusion of Richard of Ilchester as amongst those ambassadors charged with accompanying Joanna on her journey to Sicily. Diceto, the only chronicler to mention Richard of Ilchester, was clearly not mistaken about his involvement, as the Pipe Roll entry for Winchester demonstrates.[85]

Clearly, these men were amongst the most influential and politically active members of the English clergy,[86] and all are mentioned by Howden as being part of the embassy which

---

[80] Howden, *Gesta*, I, 82. Henry later played a role in Richard's coronation, see Sarell Everett Gleason, *An Ecclesiastical Barony of the Middle Ages: The Bishopric of Bayeux, 1066-1204* (Harvard University Press, 1936), 32-3; see also Spear, *Personnel of Norman Cathedrals*, 33; *Letters and Charters of Gilbert Foliot*, 530.

[81] See Howden, *Gesta*, I, 74, 84, 89, 159, 165, 178. He spent Christmas 1182 in Caen with Henry and his family, including his daughter Matilda and her husband Henry the Lion, Howden, *Gesta*, I, 291. See also Charles Duggan, 'Richard (d. 1184)', *DNB*.

[82] This appointment lasted until the death of Pope Alexander III in August 1181; see *Fasti Ecclesiae Anglicanae, 1066-1300*, II, 4. See also *Letters and Charters of Gilbert Foliot*, 531.

[83] For Richard of Ilchester, see above, n. 70. For Geoffrey Ridel, see A.J. Duggan, 'Ridel, Geoffrey (d. 1189)', *DNB*; *Letters and Charters of Gilbert Foliot*, 533, 537, 539; *Fasti Ecclesiae Anglicanae, 1066-1300*, II, 45, 85. Geoffrey had accompanied Joanna to St Gilles, and had returned to England by Christmas 1176. His death in 1189 is recorded in Howden, *Gesta*, II, 78.

[84] Howden, *Gesta*, I, 144, 154; see also Part III, Chapter 2. The arrival of the Spanish envoys in 1177 is briefly recorded by Eyton, *Itinerary*, 211. The Pipe Roll for 1177 (Bosham), lists the expenses as 50 shillings each for the passage of the Navarrese and Castilian embassies, PR 23 Henry II, 188; Eyton, *Itinerary*, 208. A further reference to the Castilian embassy is found in the Pipe Roll for 1188 (*Honor Comitis Gloecestriae*), listing the expenses as £8 6s 8d for the Spanish envoys, and a further £40 7s 1d for two ships and their equipments. 40 shillings were paid for the forty-day stay of the Castilian envoys, named in the Pipe Rolls as Adam and Guncelin, PR 34 Henry II, 14; Eyton, *Itinerary*, 284-5.

[85] See above, n. 64.

[86] In the midst of the negotiation process for Joanna's marriage, Richard of Canterbury and Geoffrey of Ely were entrusted with an embassy to the count of Flanders to persuade him to defer his intention to go on crusade, as Henry feared the count was seeking for himself the crown of Jerusalem, Howden, *Gesta*, I, 116. After the completion of the Sicilian embassy in 1177, Rotrou of Rouen, Geoffrey of Ely, Henry of Bayeux and Richard of Winchester were entrusted with another important mission, that of arguing Henry's case for the Vexin before Louis VII of France, Howden, *Gesta*, I, 168. Richard, Geoffrey Ridel, and John of Oxford also appear as witnesses on a large proportion

accompanied Joanna part or all of the way to Sicily, with the notable exception of Richard of Ilchester, who is only mentioned by Diceto. Indeed, the bishop of Winchester and John, bishop of Norwich are the only ecclesiastics named by Diceto as part of the 1176-7 embassy, whereas Gervase of Canterbury concentrates solely on local politics and records only the participation of his own archbishop. Nevertheless, it is clear that Henry selected the most prominent members of his court to convey Joanna to her new kingdom, highlighting further the importance and significance of this dynastic alliance.

---

of Henry II's charters; in the majority of cases Richard appears as either first or second witness, indicating his prominence and importance, Duggan, 'Richard of Ilchester', 4-5. He was first witness to Henry's will, which was drafted in 1182 at one of Richard's own manors (Bishop's Waltham), Duggan, 'Richard of Ilchester', 5-6. Diceto, I, 381-2, claimed that 'No-one...could speak to the king more intimately, more urgently or more effectively' than Richard, trans. Duggan, 'Richard of Ilchester', 9.

Chapter Five
Love and Marriage in the Twelfth Century

It is not known what Matilda, Leonor or Joanna thought about their impending marriages.[1] Royal and aristocratic daughters were destined – indeed, bred for – dynastic alliances arranged by their families, and their opinions on their parents' choices were rarely, if ever, sought, much less acted upon. In the context of Angevin marriage policy, the daughters of Henry and Eleanor may be seen as little more than pawns in a dynastic game. As royal and aristocratic marriages were, however, arranged for the material, social or political benefit of the family, their experiences were neither unusual nor uncommon, and the care with which the marriages of Henry and Eleanor's daughters were arranged reveals that if they were pawns, they were highly valuable and valued ones.

Historians have debated the existence of romantic love with regards to medieval marriage customs and practices. Jean Flori has stated that love was not a consideration with regard to marriage, and was only apparent in pre- or extra-marital relationships. Although twelfth century Church reforms on marriage placed less weight on parental consent as a necessity for legal marriages, the influence of the family was 'still dominant', and daughters, particularly those of the higher aristocracy, would rarely 'refuse to wed the man her parents had chosen for her'; indeed, as Flori has asserted, the higher a girl's social status, 'the less freedom she was allowed'.[2] Georges Duby has also rejected the idea of love within marriage on the grounds that marriages were arranged, although there are clearly numerous enough cases of arranged marriages from both modern and medieval times which have proved to be felicitous, and as will be seen, Leonor's marriage to Alfonso VIII and her sister Joanna's first marriage to William II are prime examples of this for the twelfth century.[3] Duby has nevertheless viewed contemporary accounts of emotional bonds within marriages, whether positive or negative, as conventional *topoi* and has thus dismissed them as superficial, stating further that excessive love, or

---

[1] The Arabic chronicler Beha ad-Din relates that on hearing the news of Richard's not quite serious proposal that she marry Saladin's brother Saphadin and become joint rulers of Jerusalem, Joanna flew into a fit of anger, and declared that she would 'never suffer the approach of a Muslim', avowing that she would be a traitor to her faith if she consented to such a union, *Suite de la troisieme croisade*, in Joseph Michaud (ed.), *Bibliotheque des Croisades*, (Paris, 1829), IV, 334, 335; see also *The Rare and Excellent History of Saladin*, ed. and trans. D.S. Richards (Ashgate, Hants., 2002), 187-8. The veracity of this vignette may be open to question, but it does show that Beha ad-Din regarded Joanna as a strong woman who was both capable of speaking her mind, and aware of her political (and matrimonial) worth. Richard's proposal to marry Joanna to Saphadin seems to be taken seriously by Amy Kelly, who attributed a rather more proactive role to Joanna in the Holy Land than is truly credible, stating that 'the crusading queen declared that she would not be brought, even for the peace of Christendom, to mount the throne with one of the very paynim she had journeyed to Palestine to defy', *Eleanor of Aquitaine*, 278. In subsequent negotiations Richard said nothing of his sister's furious rejection of the idea, stating merely that he had encountered problems with his clergy over the matter, suggesting papal intervention, and the promise of his niece Eleanor of Brittany instead of Joanna if all else failed, *Rare and Excellent History*, 195-6; Kelly, *Eleanor of Aquitaine*, 278.

[2] Flori, *Eleanor of Aquitaine*, 242; although Elisabeth van Houts has rightly highlighted the fact that royal sons had as little say over their matrimonial destinies as did royal daughters, 'State of Research', 285. For church reforms on marriage, see Duby, *Medieval Marriage*, 15-22; *idem*, *Love and Marriage*, 3-21.

[3] Duby, *Love and Marriage*, 25.

passion, was deemed by the Church to be unfitting within marriage, although it is doubtful how far church rulings on this actually affected practical realities.[4]

John Gillingham, however, has argued that in the twelfth century, the idea of romantic love became much more of a consideration than it had been in previous centuries, a development he attributes to the twin factors of canon law rulings on consent and the indissolubility of marriage, and the rise in number of unwed or widowed heiresses. Such heiresses were always a desirable marriage prospect, as due to favourable changes in inheritance structures they were able, in the absence of male siblings, to become sole heirs not just to vast lands and titles but also to duchies and kingdoms.[5] The unprecedented number of female heirs to the throne of Jerusalem in this period provides some excellent examples, as well as interesting comparisons with the daughters of Henry II.[6] Such women were still status symbols, but the 'real world' of politics was, in Gillingham's words, 'complicated by love and by the expectation of love'.[7] He suggests that the emphasis on the indissolubility of marriage meant that the choice of marriage partner would have been made more carefully, especially when the intended bride was a great heiress with whom marriage would considerably improve a man's wealth and social standing.[8]

Nevertheless, whilst this may hold true for lesser aristocratic men and women, the number of repudiated twelfth and thirteenth century queens, such as Ingebjorg of Denmark, the unfortunate queen of Philip Augustus, proves that this was not necessarily always the case in royal circles.[9] Louis VII did not hesitate to divorce Eleanor of Aquitaine, clearly viewing his need for a male heir as more important than losing his rights over her duchy; Henry II, however, 'could not bring himself' to divorce Eleanor even after her involvement in the rebellion of

---

[4] See *ibid.*, 24, 27-32.

[5] John Gillingham, 'Love, Marriage and Politics in the Twelfth Century', in *Forum for Modern Language Studies*, 25 (1989), 292. Gillingham notes that the marriage of an heiress was 'fundamentally different from the marriage of the heir, and much more important', 'Love, Marriage and Politics', 296. For more on female inheritance in the twelfth century, see the collected articles in J.C. Holt, *Colonial England* (Hambledon Press, London, 1997), especially 'The Heiress and the Alien', 245-69; see also Judith Green, 'Aristocratic Women in Early Twelfth-Century England', in C. Warren Hollister (ed.), *Anglo-Norman Political Culture and the Twelfth-Century Renaissance* (Boydell, Woodbridge, 1997), 59-82. Whilst historians such as Holt and George Garnett argue for a 'revolution' in inheritance practices in England in the aftermath of the Norman Conquest, others, like John Hudson and C. Warren Hollister argue for a more gradual change whose processes began in the reign of Henry I; see Garnett, "Ducal' Succession in Early Normandy', in Garnett and Hudson (eds.), *Law and Government in Medieval England and Normandy* (CUP, 1994), 80-110; Hudson, 'Anglo-Norman Land Law and the Origins of Property', in *ibid.*, 198-222; Hollister, 'Anglo-Norman Political Culture and the Twelfth-Century Renaissance', in *Anglo-Norman Political Culture*, 1-16. What no historian seems to dispute is that there was a fluidity of custom regarding inheritance rights up to and during the twelfth century.

[6] A comparison of this sort remains beyond the scope of this monograph, but would form the basis of a profitable area of research. For a short précis of the fortunes of Queen Sybilla of Jerusalem, whose remarriage to Guy de Lusignan after their enforced separation in 1186 suggests not merely a free choice of partner, but also female initiative in making that choice, see Gillingham, 'Love, Marriage and Politics', 293-4. Queen Melisende was suspected of having an illicit affair with Count Hugh II of Jaffa, yet her husband, Fulk of Anjou, did not seek a divorce, Gillingham, 'Love, Marriage and Politics', 296. Gillingham attributes this to the fact that in obtaining a divorce, Fulk would have been giving up far more than an adulterous wife – better a cuckolded king than a morally vindicated count. See also Gerish, 'Holy War, Royal Wives', 119-44 for a summary of queens-consort in the Holy Land.

[7] Gillingham, 'Love, Marriage and Politics', 294.

[8] *Ibid.*, 296-7.

[9] See Duby, *Medieval Marriage*, 73-80. Philip's repudiation of Ingebjorg provides a clear example of how the upper aristocracy utilised to their advantage Church rulings on consanguinity as the only valid reason for the dissolution of marriages, in order to rid themselves of unwanted wives. According to Duby, it was cases such as that of Philip and Ingebjorg which ultimately led to the revision of these rulings, reducing the degrees of consanguinity from seven to four degrees, *Medieval Marriage*, 80-1.

1173-4.[10] Gillingham attributes Henry's reluctance to the existence of a genuine romantic attachment, noting that whilst (or because) repudiation of unsatisfactory wives was becoming more difficult to attain, love, and a concomitant degree of marital accord on an emotional level, 'may well have become more important...not just as a requisite of marriage but also as a prerequisite'.[11] Marriages, and especially the marriages of royal daughters like Matilda, Leonor and Joanna, were of course still negotiated for political and dynastic reasons, but Gillingham suggests that it would be a 'mistake to think that, in consequence, considerations of emotional compatibility were entirely excluded'.[12]

Whilst this was undoubtedly often difficult to achieve for royalty, who frequently engaged in exogamous marriages, royal ambassadors, such as those sent by William II of Sicily in 1176, and the imperial ambassadors sent to negotiate matches with Henry II's eldest daughters Matilda and Leonor in 1165, attempted to ensure a successful match.[13] The great importance attached to the successful negotiation of a dynastic marriage highlights the need to entrust such missions to the most skilled, able and prominent men of the realm. The ambassadors chosen by Henry the Lion, William of Sicily and Alfonso of Castile demonstrate this. Similarly, the envoys chosen by Henry II and Eleanor of Aquitaine to escort their daughters to their new lands were also chosen with the greatest of care.

The ambassadors of William of Sicily may have been 'mightily pleased' with Joanna's beauty,[14] certain that her charms would appeal to their king, but would Joanna have been similarly pleased with him? In an era before portraiture, would she even have known what to expect? And at the tender ages of, respectively, eleven and nine, would the physical attributes of their future husbands have been the primary concern for either Joanna or Leonor? Perhaps they were merely thankful that, in contrast to their eldest sister Matilda, whose husband was a divorcé more than a quarter of a century older than herself, their husbands-to-be were at least still young men who, despite their relative youth, had both managed to assert control over their respective kingdoms after periods of uncertainty during their minorities. The late twelfth-century kingdoms of Castile and Sicily were both prosperous and wealthy, and their new queens could, theoretically, look forward to substantial wealth and security from the dower portions that their husbands would allocate to them.[15] What these dowers constituted, along with the problems that could arise from the granting of territorial dowers and dowries, will form the basis of Part III.

---

[10] Gillingham, 'Love, Marriage and Politics', 297; see also Duby, *Medieval Marriage*, 54-62.

[11] Gillingham, 'Love, Marriage and Politics', 298-9. Duby viewed the tenth century as having a greater freedom of repudiation, citing as evidence the example of Robert the Pious' three marriages, *Medieval Marriage*, 45-54.

[12] Gillingham, 'Love, Marriage and Politics', 299.

[13] *Ibid.*, 299.

[14] Howden, *Gesta*, I, 116-7, trans. Gillingham, 'Love, Marriage and Politics', 299.

[15] And, by extension, they may also have been able to retain households with ladies of their own choosing, perhaps including some from their natal homelands.

PART III

Bodas muy grandes:
Marriage, Dowry and Dower Settlements

After marriage, most twelfth-century aristocratic women were financially dependent on their husband and his family. The lands or other material goods which a woman brought to a marriage as her dowry, or *maritagium* (French *dot*, Spanish *arras*), whilst technically under the ownership of the wife, usually passed to the control of her husband for the duration of the marriage, although it often reverted to the wife on her husband's death.[1] The size of the dowry could determine the wife's role, status, and power both within the marriage itself and within wider society, as it was indicative of her natal family's wealth and social standing: the higher the bride's status, the larger the dowry, and the larger the dowry, the better the possible alliance.[2] A dowry could provide an opportunity for the bride's natal family to forge strong and lasting alliances, and possibly also to raise or enhance both the bride's and her family's status.[3] Dowries could be used as a tool to control the marriage of daughters, either by tying them to their father in their provision, or by the threat of disinheritance if a marriage was sought or contracted without parental consent.[4] Laws limiting a woman's control over her dowry were 'instituted by men who felt their economic and lineal interests threatened by women's control over property', but a bride endowed with a large dowry could often wield considerable power within the marriage, especially over the marriage of her own daughters.[5]

By the twelfth century, dowries came to be comprised more usually of money or moveable goods rather than landed wealth, in order to limit the division of the patrimony and to prevent its transfer outwith the family.[6] Joanna's dowry seems to have mainly comprised a cash settlement, although Leonor brought to Alfonso VIII the county of Gascony as her dower, a settlement which ultimately led to major conflicts which remained unresolved until well into the thirteenth century.[7]

Conversely, a woman's dower (French *douaire*) was given to her by her husband, and although this was increasingly of lesser value than the dowry she brought to the marriage, it could offer a degree of financial security after her husband's death.[8] It was frequently to be held in usufruct (for the duration of her life only), and would be accessible usually only on the death of her husband.[9] The problems which could arise over conflicting claims to a woman's

---

[1] Marion A. Kaplan, 'Introduction', in Kaplan (ed.), *The Marriage Bargain: Women and Dowries in European History* (Harrington Park Press, New York, 1985), 1; see also Trindade, *Berengaria*, 150. A wife could also demand the return of her dowry if the marriage was dissolved (unless she had been accused of adultery), and if she predeceased her husband, it might revert to her natal family or to any children born of the marriage, Diane Owen Hughes, 'From Brideprice to Dowry in Mediterranean Europe', in Kaplan (ed.), *The Marriage Bargain*, 36-7.

[2] Kaplan, 'Introduction', 2-7; Hughes, 'Brideprice to Dowry', 45.

[3] Kaplan, 'Introduction', 3.

[4] *Ibid.*, 5. Hughes has noted that daughters 'would live all their lives in the light of their fathers' generosity or in the shadow of its absence', 'Brideprice to Dowry', 38, although this should be modified to include those women married by other male kin, such as brothers or uncles.

[5] Kaplan, 'Introduction', 5.

[6] Duby, *Love and Marriage*, 14; Hughes, 'Brideprice to Dowry', 34-5. Although, as Hughes has pointed out, women could still inherit from their natal family if they had no living male siblings, 'Brideprice to Dowry', 32.

[7] Both Joanna's and Leonor's dowry and dower settlements are discussed more fully in Chapters 2 and 4.

[8] The bestowal of a dower is likely a remnant of the older Germanic morning gift, or *morgengabe* (*sponsalicium*, *antefactum*), given to the bride by her husband on the morning after the consummation of their marriage, although dower was usually gifted at the time of the marriage ceremony (but could be revoked if the marriage remained unconsummated). See Duby, *Love and Marriage*, 14; Hughes, 'Brideprice to Dowry', 18-20, 28.

[9] Trindade, *Berengaria*, 150; see also Kimberley A. LoPrete and Theodore Evergates, 'Introduction', in LoPrete and Evergates (eds.), *Aristocratic Women in Medieval France* (University of Pennsylvania Press, 1999), 4.

dower (and particularly in cases of remarriage) invariably led to legal disputes, such as those in which Berengaria of Navarre was embroiled after the death of Richard I.[10]

The systems of bestowing dowries and dowers had origins in older Germanic customs and Roman law, and practices in dowry and dower customs varied over time and place.[11] Lombard law allowed the wife a quarter of her husband's property after his death, and Frankish and Burgundian custom allowed one third, although in Italy this was abolished in 1143 by the Genoese commune, which also limited the amount a bride might receive as dower.[12] By the early thirteenth century, Italian brides were customarily bringing more to the marriage in terms of dowries than they received in terms of dower. Elsewhere, the widow's right to full control of her dower changed to become usufruct only for the duration of her lifetime.[13] Spain, too, followed these patterns of limiting dowers, albeit later than the rest of western Europe.[14]

David Herlihy attributes two reasons for changes in dower portions: firstly, a devaluation of women in the later Middle Ages; secondly, a higher ratio of marriageable women to men at this time, leading to a further, and literal, devaluation of women.[15] These conditions led to a lower age at marriage for women, and a corresponding higher age for men, although Herlihy notes that high-born noblewomen were exceptional in this regard, with lower status women generally marrying later.[16] All of Henry II's daughters were young at the times of their marriages, being just at the threshold of the minimum age for marriage as stipulated by canon law.[17] Diane Owen Hughes has suggested that the 'growing association between dowry and chastity may be one reason why...[fathers] so often married their daughters off at puberty',[18] although in the case of Henry II and other royalty, it was more likely to have been in order to secure or cement a dynastic alliance at the earliest possible opportunity.

---

[10] For Berengaria's dowry and dower portions, see Chapter 3.

[11] Trindade, *Berengaria*, 150. See also Jo Ann McNamara and Suzanne Wemple, 'The Power of Women Through the Family in Medieval Europe, 500-1100', in *Women and Power*, 83-101; and Hughes, 'Brideprice to Dowry', 13-58, for a discussion of the changes in dowry and dower practices from the Classical period to the Middle Ages.

[12] Herlihy, *Medieval Households*, 98-103; Hughes, 'Brideprice to Dowry', 21-2, 50.

[13] Herlihy, *Medieval Households*, 98-103. In the early Middle Ages, the granting of dower to the wife by the husband was a legal necessity in Burgundian, Germanic, and Visigothic law codes, hence the recurrent phrase in early charters which reads "*Nullum sine dote fiat conjugium*", Hughes, 'Brideprice to Dowry', 17. By the twelfth century, the same formula was used to refer to the dowry which the bride brought to the marriage from her natal family, Hughes, 'Brideprice to Dowry', 47-8.

[14] In Spain, Visigothic law stipulated that up to one tenth of the husband's property was to be given as dower, with an optional allowance for further gifts up to the value of 1000 *solidi*. Three quarters of the dower was to be given to any children, but the wife had free disposal of the remaining quarter. If the marriage was childless, however, all of the dower was to return to the husband's possession, or his kin if the husband predeceased the wife. See Barton, *Aristocracy*, 53; Hughes, 'Brideprice to Dowry', 21.

[15] Herlihy, *Medieval Households*, 101-3. See also Duby, *Love and Marriage*, 7-14; *Medieval Marriage*, 4-11.

[16] Herlihy, *Medieval Households*, 103-11. Hughes disagrees with these conclusions, citing changes in inheritance practices as the catalyst for changes in dowry customs, 'Brideprice to Dowry', 40-2.

[17] Twelve years for girls, fourteen for boys, McLaughlin, 'Survivors and Surrogates', 126.

[18] Hughes, 'Brideprice to Dowry', 39.

Chapter One
Matilda, Duchess of Saxony

Henry the Lion met Matilda personally at Minden before their marriage was celebrated at Minden Cathedral on 1 February 1168.[1] The nuptial celebrations were held at Brunswick, the primary ducal residence.[2] Whilst the rich nature of the dowry she brought to the marriage has been attested, there is no extant record of what she received as dower from her husband. Henry the Lion, who was a little more than twenty-five years Matilda's senior, had been previously married to Clementia of Zähringen, but they had divorced in 1162.[3] In this respect, Matilda's marriage was very different from that of her two younger sisters, who both became the first – and only – wives of husbands who were far closer in age to themselves.[4] Similarly, Matilda found herself in a land that was, in contrast with Castile and Sicily, both culturally and politically divergent from the lands of the Angevin realm from whence she had come. Some historians have asserted that it was Matilda's presence in Saxony which brought new, specifically Angevin, literary and artistic influences to her husband's lands.[5] Certainly, her marriage to Henry the Lion effected an Angevin-Welf alliance which was 'long a major factor in the politics of the Western world'.[6] The utility of the alliance for Henry II, however, did not outlast the marriage, and his generosity was to be sorely tested when, a little more than a decade after Matilda left her natal lands for marriage, she was to return, with her husband, as an exile.

Henry the Lion's conflict with the emperor appears to have stemmed from Henry's refusal to answer Frederick's request for aid against the Italian cities in 1175, although the reasons for Henry's refusal are unclear, and chronicle accounts are either confused or contradictory.[7] The most plausible explanation, according to Karl Jordan, is provided by Otto of St Blaise, who states that Henry agreed to assist the emperor on the condition that he receive the advocacy of Goslar.[8] The emperor, viewing such a demand as tantamount to blackmail, denied Henry's request, and the two men were effectively in a stalemate situation. Henry had no feudal obligation to provide military assistance to Frederick, but he did have a moral duty to the man who had protected him so often against the rebellious Saxon princes. On the other hand, if Frederick ceded Goslar, he would be losing the area in northern Germany which offered him the greatest economic support. As Jordan has pointed out, Henry's stance suggests he viewed himself more as an equal than as a vassal, and these events effectively ended the close ties, both personal and political, which had existed between Henry and Barbarossa for the past quarter of a century.[9]

---

[1] Norgate, 'Matilda, duchess of Saxony', *DNB*; Jordan, *Henry the Lion,* 147.
[2] Jordan, *Henry the Lion,* 147. He notes that the church at Brunswick was neither large enough nor sumptuous enough for the marriage ceremony to have taken place there.
[3] Norgate, 'Matilda, duchess of Saxony', *DNB*.
[4] They were also of royal, rather than ducal, descent. For the marriages of Leonor and Joanna, see Chapters 2 and 4.
[5] See, for example, Jordan, *Henry the Lion,* 147; Norgate, 'Matilda, duchess of Saxony', *DNB*. For more on Matilda's patronage, see Part IV.
[6] Jordan, *Henry the Lion,* 147.
[7] *Ibid.,* 161, and 161-4 for the events leading up to Henry the Lion's exile.
[8] *Ibid.,* 162.
[9] *Ibid.,* 163-4. For more on the personal and political relationship between Henry the Lion and Frederick I, see now also Lyon, *Princely Brothers and Sisters,* 89-119.

From 1176-8, whilst Frederick was locked in conflict with the papacy, Henry the Lion was facing problems of his own with the barons and prelates in Saxony.[10] Henry's appeal to the emperor at the Diet of Speyer in November 1178 was unsuccessful; he was summoned to answer charges at the Diet of Worms in January 1179, a summons which Henry ignored.[11] Henry also failed to appear at the subsequent Diet of Magdeburg in June, at which he was accused by the margrave of Lusatia of high treason; a further appeal to the emperor also proved unsuccessful, as Frederick set the price of his mediation at 5,000 silver marks, which Henry refused to pay.[12] At the Diet of Würzburg in January 1180 Henry, who again refused to attend, was formally dispossessed of Saxony and Bavaria, and at the Diet of Regensburg the following June, Henry was declared as an outlaw, and the emperor headed the military campaign against him, forcing him to makes terms of surrender after the capture of Lübeck in August 1181.[13] Henry was allowed to retreat to Lüneburg, which was in Matilda's possession as it was part of her dower, and at the Diet of Erfurt in November 1181 Henry made a formal, unconditional surrender to the emperor and begged for forgiveness.[14] The sentence of outlawry was revoked, and Henry was reinstated with his lands in Saxony, on condition that he leave Germany for a period of three years.[15] He therefore left Saxony in July 1182 for the court of his father-in-law, Henry II, in Normandy, accompanied by his wife Matilda, their daughter Richenza, and their sons Henry and Otto.[16] It is unclear whether Matilda had been ordered to join her husband in exile, or whether she went with him voluntarily.

Henry, Matilda, and their children were met by Henry II at Chinon in August or September,[17] and Pipe Roll evidence indicates that Henry II maintained the ducal couple in lavish style for the duration of their exile.[18] When Duke Henry undertook a pilgrimage to the shrine of St James at Compostela in the autumn of 1182, Matilda remained at her father's court at Argentan, where she met the troubadour Bertran de Born, and where, according to Howden, she gave birth to another son.[19] Duke Henry returned from pilgrimage in time to celebrate Christmas of 1182 with his family at Caen, and they remained in Normandy until 1184.[20] In June, Matilda accompanied her father to England, landing at Dover and travelling first to London, and thence to Winchester, where she was reunited with her mother, and where she gave birth to her last son, William, in July or August.[21] In May 1184, Henry the Lion had returned to Germany, possibly to attend Frederick's great court at Mainz; he returned at the

---

[10] Jordan, *Henry the Lion*, 166-8, 171-2, and 164-5 for the imperial-papal conflict.

[11] *Ibid.*, 168-9.

[12] *Ibid.*, 169-70.

[13] See Jordan, *Henry the Lion*, 170, 175-8.

[14] *Ibid.*, 178.

[15] *Ibid.*, 178.

[16] Diceto, II, 13; Wendover, I, 129; Jordan, *Henry the Lion*, 183. It is unclear why their eldest son, Lothair, remained in Saxony, but it is possible he was left as a hostage to ensure that Henry kept to the terms of his exile.

[17] Jordan, *Henry the Lion*, 183.

[18] See PR 27 Hen II, 157, 160; PR 29 Hen II, 161; PR 30 Hen II, 58, 120, 134-5, 137-8, 144-5, 150; PR 31 Hen II, 9, 21, 171-2, 206, 215, 218; PR 32 Hen II, 168.

[19] Howden, *Gesta*, I, 288; *Chronica*, II, 269-70; Jordan, *Henry the Lion*, 183-4; Norgate, 'Matilda, duchess of Saxony'. No further mention is made of this son, and no other chronicler records his birth. It is probable that the child died either at birth or in very early infancy; Matilda's pregnancy may have been the reason she did not accompany her husband on pilgrimage.

[20] Jordan, *Henry the Lion*, 183-4. For the Christmas court at Caen, see Howden, *Gesta*, I, 291; *Chronica*, II, 273.

[21] Howden, *Gesta*, I, 312; *Chronica*, II, 285; Diceto, II, 21-2; Wendover, I, 130; PR 30 Hen II, xxiv, 134-5; Jordan, *Henry the Lion*, 184; Norgate, 'Matilda, duchess of Saxony'.

end of July, being entertained at Henry II's expense at Dover, Canterbury and London, before joining Matilda at Winchester.[22]

In October 1184, through the successful mediation of Henry II, Henry the Lion was reconciled with the emperor and able to return to his lands in Saxony.[23] The ducal couple nevertheless remained at Henry II's court until the spring of 1185, travelling from Winchester to Berkhampsted and celebrating Christmas 1184 at Windsor with Henry II, Eleanor, and Matilda's brothers, Richard and John.[24] In May 1185 Henry and Matilda, along with their sons Henry and Otto, crossed to Normandy, from whence they returned to Saxony, arriving at Brunswick in the autumn of 1185.[25] Matilda's mother Eleanor appears to have crossed the channel with them, en route to Gascony.[26] Matilda's daughter Richenza and her youngest son William, however, remained in England, for reasons which are unclear, and Pipe Roll evidence shows that they were maintained at Henry II's expense.[27] Efforts were also made to find a suitable husband for Richenza; in 1184, a union with William of Scotland had to be abandoned when papal dispensation was refused.[28] In 1186, Bela of Hungary also sought Richenza's hand, but due to Henry II's prevarications this match also came to nothing, and Richenza was finally married to Geoffrey, heir to the county of Perche, in 1189.[29]

Matilda was not involved in the marriages of any of her children. The marriage of her daughter Richenza was arranged by Henry II, and her sons' marriages all took place after her death.[30] Her eldest son Lothair had, for reasons which are not clear, been left behind in Saxony when the ducal couple departed for their three-year period of exile in 1182, and both Richenza and her youngest son William were brought up at the Angevin court even after her return from exile. Nevertheless, according to Arnold of Lübeck, Matilda undertook to provide her sons with a good grounding in the Scriptures, teaching them 'God's Word from an early age'.[31]

When Henry the Lion faced a second term of exile in 1189, for refusing to either join the emperor on crusade or to forgo certain rights in Saxony and Bavaria, Matilda remained in Saxony and acted as regent in his absence.[32] Her death less than three months later on 28 June,

---

[22] Howden, *Gesta*, I, 316; *Chronica*, II, 285; Wendover, I, 130; PR 30 Hen II, xxv, 134-5, 145; Eyton, *Itinerary*, 256; Jordan, *Henry the Lion*, 184.

[23] See Howden, *Gesta*, I, 287-8, 318-9, 334; Jordan, *Henry the Lion*, 184-5.

[24] Howden, *Gesta*, I, 333-4; *Chronica*, II, 299; PR 30 Hen II, xxv, 134-5.

[25] PR 31 Hen II, 206, 215; Jordan, *Henry the Lion*, 185.

[26] Howden, *Gesta*, I, 337; Gervase, I, 326; PR 31 Hen II, xxiv, 206, 215; Eyton, *Itinerary*, 264.

[27] PR 31 Hen II, 206, 218; PR 32 Hen II, 49, 168; PR 33 Hen II, 194, 203-4, 212; PR 34 Hen II, 171-2.

[28] Howden, *Gesta*, I, 313-4, 322; Jordan, *Henry the Lion*, 185.

[29] PR 33 Hen II, xxii, 203-4; Jordan, *Henry the Lion*, 185; Norgate, 'Matilda, duchess of Saxony (1156-1189)'. Richenza subsequently married Enguerrand III de Coucy; she died before 1210. Bela of Hungary married Margaret, the sister of Philip Augustus and widow of Henry the Young King, in 1186. For more on this marriage, see Chapter 3.

[30] Matilda's eldest son, Lothair, died in 1190, predeceasing his father. Her second son, Henry, became Duke of Saxony on Henry the Lion's death in 1195, and became Count Palatine of the Rhine the following year. His son Henry predeceased him, and he was succeeded on his death in 1227 by two daughters, Irmgard and Agnes. Matilda's third son, Otto, was designated by his uncle, Richard I, as Earl of York in 1190, and as Count of Poitou in 1196. He was elected as Emperor Otto IV in 1198, crowned at Rome in 1209, and deposed and excommunicated in 1210. He died without heirs in 1218. William of Winchester married Helen, daughter of Waldemar I of Denmark. He died in 1213, and his son, Otto, became the sole male heir on the death of his uncle, Count Palatine Henry. See Norgate, 'Matilda, duchess of Saxony (1156-1189)'.

[31] Arnold of Lübeck, *Chronica Slavorum* (*MGH SS*, 14, Hanover, 1868), 12.

[32] *Annales Stederburgenses* (*MGH SS*, 16, Hanover, 1859), 221; see also Jordan, *Henry the Lion*, 187-9. Matilda did not act as regent when Henry the Lion made a pilgrimage to the Holy Land in 1172, possibly due to her age – in 1172, Matilda would have been around fifteen or sixteen. Rather, Henry appointed two *ministeriales*, Henry of

however, means that it is difficult to establish how effective Matilda's regency was.[33] No charters issued in Matilda's name survive, if she had a personal seal, it also has not survived, and she appears on just two of her husband's extant charters, both issued in the early years of their marriage, and both of which concern religious donations.[34] On the first of these, issued at Hertzburg in November 1170, Matilda gives her consent to a donation to the monastery of Northeim.[35] She is only referred to on the second charter, recording the gift Henry made in 1172 of three candles which were to burn in perpetuity in the Holy Sepulchre at Jerusalem for, in Henry's words, 'the sake of the forgiveness of all my sins and those of my famed wife Matilda, daughter of the glorious king of England, and those of my heirs given to me by God as a token of His mercy, and also for [the sake] of my whole lineage'.[36]

The only other extant charter on which Matilda appears is that given by her son Henry in 1223, in which he describes his 'dearest mother of most happy memory' as the donor of the altar dedicated to the Virgin which stands in the church of St Blaise at Brunswick.[37] As there is no record of Matilda as either the founder or the sole patron of any religious establishments during her lieftime – although it may be assumed that, together with her husband, she was a patron of the church at Brunswick and co-donor of the Gmunden Gospels – the mention of Matilda in her son's charter as the sole donor of the altar at Brunswick is of great significance for evidence of Matilda's patronage.

Of even greater interest is a brief inventory from June 1189, which presents us with some highly suggestive evidence for Matilda's religious patronage. This inventory, mentioned in Hildesheim's register of donations and income from the thirteenth century, and published in Karl Jordan's edited collection of Henry the Lion's charters, lists the donations to the church at Hildesheim made by Matilda, 'ducissa ecclesie nostre devotissima *una cum marito suo* Heinrico duce'.[38] The phrasing of this inventory – that Matilda donated gifts *together with her husband* – suggests that the donations were made at Matilda's, rather than at Henry's, behest, and the description of her as *ducissa ecclesie nostre* suggests that the church of Hildesheim may have regarded her as its patron. In light of the fact that the relics of the Anglo-Saxon saint-king Oswald were also housed at Hildesheim, Matilda's patronage of this church is interesting indeed. The implications of such involvement will be discussed more fully in Part IV; before examining the patronage of Matilda and her sisters, however, it is necessary to analyse what resources were available to Leonor and Joanna, and how far they were able to assert authority in their adopted homelands.

Lüneberg and Ekbert of Wolfenbüttel, to look after his young wife, who was already pregnant with their first child, Richenza. See Arnold of Lübeck, 11; see also Jordan, *Henry the Lion*, 150.

[33] Diceto, II, 65, places Matilda's death on 13 July. Her death is not recorded in the *Gesta*, but is briefly mentioned under July 1189 in the *Chronica*, III, 3. The *Gesta Regis Ricardi*, 72, and Wendover, I, 160, also briefly record Matilda's death under July 1189.

[34] Henry the Lion's collected charters have been edited by Karl Jordan, *Die Urkunden Heinrichs des Löwen, Herzogs von Sachsen und Bayern* (MGH, 1941-9; repr. 1957-60).

[35] *Omnia hec acta sunt ex assensu gloriosissime domine Matildis, Bawarie et Saxonie ducisse*, Jordan, *Heinrichs des Löwen*, 123-4, no. 83.

[36] *...pro remissione omnium peccatorum meorum et inclite uxoris mee ducisse Matildis, magnifici Anglorum regis filie*, Jordan, *Heintichs des Löwen*, 143-5, no. 94.

[37] *Ibid.*, 178-9, no. 121. Although the Annals of St Blaise record the donation of the altar as a joint enterprise, *Liber Memoriam Sancti Blasii* (MGH SS, 24, Hanover, 1879), 824.

[38] *Ibid.*, 179, no. 122. My italics.

Chapter Two
Leonor, Queen of Castile

Spanish chronicles are almost as silent about Leonor's marriage as are the Angevin sources. Neither the *Primera Crónica General* nor the *Crónica Latina de los Reyes de Castilla* make any reference to it.[1] The more contemporary *Crónica de España*, composed by Lucas, bishop of Tuy at the behest of Leonor's eldest daughter Berenguella, only briefly records the marriage, before listing Leonor and Alfonso's children.[2] Of the Spanish sources, it is the *Crónica de Veinte Reyes* that provides the fullest account, although it erroneously gives the date of the union as 1167. The *Crónica* refers to Leonor in terms of her prestigious lineage: she was the sister of 'King Richard, who was a very good king, very brave and strong'.[3]

The thirteenth century Flemish chronicler Philippe Mouskes extolled Leonor as one of the most beautiful and accomplished princesses of her age, despite her youth.[4] Spanish sources, on the other hand, stringently avoid all references to the couple's respective ages, affording them 'the same profound respect and...terms as would have been employed, had they both been twenty years older'.[5] Mary Ann Everett Green, whose volumes on the princesses of England, despite the over-romanticised approach, contained the most comprehensive study of Leonor until now, points out further that whilst Angevin sources describe Alfonso as "Parvus" (child), Spanish accounts never refer to his youth and describe him instead as Alfonso "the Good", or "the Noble".[6] Lucas de Tuy frequently compares Alfonso to a 'most strong lion', an epithet more famously associated with his brother-in-law Richard.[7]

It is the later *Crónica General* which first placed Leonor and Alfonso's wedding in Burgos, although Julio González pointed out that this cannot be accurate, despite its acceptance as fact by numerous historians.[8] The *Crónica* states that Alfonso gave privileges to Burgos Cathe-

---

[1] Theodore Babbitt has noted that the *Primera Crónica* follows the chapter heading given in the *Crónica*'s main source, Archbishop Rodrigo de Rada's *De Rebus Hispaniae*, of '*De Rege Aldephonso et persecutione quam infantia tolerauit, et nuptiis eius*', *La Crónica de Veinte Reyes: A Comparison with the Text of the Primera Crónica General and a Study of the Principal Latin Sources* (Yale University Press, 1936), 132-3. However, Pidal's edition, which is that also used by Babbitt, does not contain any reference to the nuptials in the chapter heading, which reads, 'El capitulo de la discordia et desabenencia de los grandes omnes de Castilla sobre la guarda deste rey ninno don Alffonsso, et de como fue leuado a Atiença', *PCG*, Cap. 989.

[2] *Crónica de España*, 406. He then lists the marriages of Berenguella, Blanca, Urraca and Leonor, noting that Constanza took the veil and remained a consecrated virgin.

[3] 'rey Richart, que fue tan buen rrey e tan corajoso e tan esforcado', Babbitt, *Crónica de Veinte Reyes*, 133. My translation. The use of 'rrey' here indicates that the *Crónica* was composed after Richard's accession in 1189.

[4] "Et s'ot III filles, / Bieles et sages et gentiles. / S'en ot li rois d'Espagne l'une, / Ki sage fu, et biele et brune", *Chronique Rimée de Philippe Mouskes*, ed. Le Baron de Reiffenberg (Brussels, 1838), II, 250, ll. 18846-9. Mouskes was first canon and chancellor, and later bishop, at Tournai. He seems to have maintained good relations both with the king of France and with the counts of Flanders until his death in 1282. His metrical chronicle, a history of France and Flanders from the times of the mythical Priam, was begun in 1242. Only one copy of the manuscript survives, held at the Bibliothèque Royal (now the Bibliothèque Nationale) in 1836 [MS 9634]. See Introduction, *Chronique Rimée*, CCVII-CCXXVIII.

[5] Green, *Princesses of England,* I, 267.

[6] *Ibid.*, I, 267.

[7] "leo fortissimus", as at *Crónica de España*, 406, 408.

[8] The *Crónica de Veinte Reyes* also places the wedding in Burgos, noting that Alfonso and Leonor passed through

dral and to its prior Gonzalo Pérez in June 1170, in memory of his wedding; but it also indicates that the celebrations may have been held in September 1170.[9] The royal couple's first joint public act was the issuing of a charter at Soria confirming rights in Burgo de Osma to the church of Osma on 17 September 1170.[10] The diplomatic evidence therefore indicates that the marriage must have been celebrated some time before 17 September 1170, when the first of many joint charters was issued, and that by this date, Alfonso and Leonor had reached Soria.[11]

It is possible that the marriage was solemnised at Burgos, or that further celebrations were conducted there. Burgos was effectively Alfonso's capital, lying in the heart of his secure lands to the north of the central mountains, on the borders of Aragón and Navarre. It had been the traditional capital of the counts of Castile, and was the place where Alfonso attained his majority and was proclaimed king. It is therefore unsurprising that the family spent most of their time there, always returning to this town from their frequent itinerations.[12] Toledo, lying south of these mountains, was essentially a defensive capital against the encroaching Moors. These twin power bases explain Alfonso's title of "king of Castile and Toledo".[13] Burgos was to become much more than just the preferred summer residence of the Castilian royal family, as the monastery of Las Huelgas in Burgos, constructed in 1187, became the favoured royal foundation, and eventual mausoleum of the Castilian dynasty. The establishment of Las Huelgas, which also served as a royal residence as well as a hospital, its status as the royal necropolis, and Leonor's role in its foundation, will be discussed in Part V. Before considering Leonor's role in patronage and dynastic commemoration, however, we must first examine her dowry and dower settlements.

Leonor and Alfonso's nuptial celebrations lasted almost the entire month of September, which was a much longer period of festivity than was the norm for English queens.[14] The Castilian nobles paid homage to their new queen, and Alfonso provided Leonor with a magnificent dower, the like of which had never before been bestowed on a Castilian queen

Soria on 17 September on their journey from Aragón to Castile (i.e. from Tarazona to Burgos); Díez, *Alfonso VIII*, 43. According to Kelly, the betrothal was celebrated in Tarragona and the marriage itself in Burgos, *Eleanor of Aquitaine*, 358. Official documents, however, clearly state that from 1170, Alfonso reigned in Castile 'cum uxore' Leonor, González, *Alfonso VIII*, I, 190n.

[9] González, *Alfonso VIII*, I, 190n.

[10] *Ibid.*, II, no. 148. This charter was almost immediately followed by one issued at Nájera, González, *Alfonso VIII*, I, 190; II, no. 149. Leonor appears on almost all Alfonso's charters as '*uxore mea* [or *nostra*] *Alienor regina* [or *Alionora/Alienorde/Aleonor/Helionor regina*]'; occasionally she is 'la reina doña Leonor mi muger', as at no. 253, but the usual formula is *cum uxore mea Alienor regina*. González states that her name was imperfectly understood to begin with, with royal chancellory scribes writing 'Alienor' or 'Alienord' for several months, sometimes even rendering it as 'Elemburgi', 'Dalihonor', or, referring to her nationality, 'Angrica' or 'Anglica Elionor', *Alfonso VIII*, I, 191. The name Leonor was thus clearly imported to Spain via the Angevin marriage alliance, along with the name Henry (Enrique), given to one of Leonor's sons. For more on the theme of dynastic nomenclature, see Part V.

[11] See González, *Alfonso VIII*, I, 190, 796 for these documents, which are also discussed by Díez, *Alfonso VIII*, 41-2.

[12] Leonor spent most of her time in Burgos when she was not travelling with Alfonso; she was at Burgos when she received the news of Alfonso's victory at Las Navas, and it was at Las Huelgas that several trophies from the battle were deposited, Díez, *Alfonso VIII*, 56. These included a banner captured from the Moorish army, and the tapestry which had hung over the entrance to the caliph's tent, O'Callaghan, *History of Spain*, 248.

[13] Díez, *Alfonso VIII*, 55-6. Burgos only lost its status as capital in the reign of Fernando III, after his conquests of Murcia and Andalucia and the union of Castile with León made it more practicable to use the more central Arlanzón as the king's primary base.

[14] Green, *Princesses of England*, I, 267. Compare the three-day celebration of Richard's marriage to Berengaria, Kelly, *Eleanor of Aquitaine*, 267. The pressing concern of crusade, however, undoubtedly made for a shorter celebration time for these nuptials. See also Howden, *Gesta*, II, 166; *Chronica*, III, 110; *Itinerarium Peregrinorum*, 196.

(see Fig. 1).[15] In addition to the numerous towns, castles and ports Leonor was endowed with, she was also promised half of all lands Alfonso might conquer from the Moors from the time of their marriage; and for the upkeep of her household and expenditure, she was allocated rights over all rents from Burgos, Nájera, and Castrojeriz, in addition to the 5,000 *maravedis* to be paid in rents from Toledo.[16] Unlike her sister Joanna, whose dower provision comprised a single area within the kingdom of Sicily, Leonor's extensive dower lands were widely spread throughout Castile, which is perhaps indicative of the more itinerant nature of the Castilian court.[17]

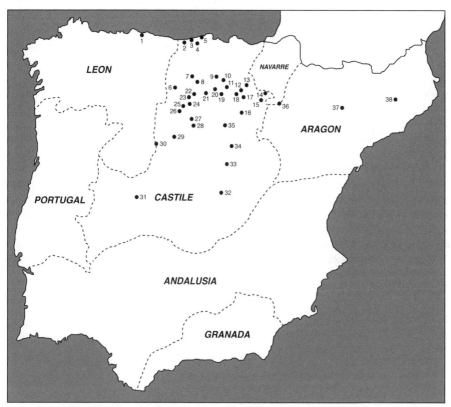

Fig. 1: Leonor's dowerlands.

1. Viesgo **2.** Caviedes **3.** Santillana **4.** Zurita **5.** Santander **6.** Saldaña **7.** Aguilar de Campoo **8.** Amaya **9.** Poza de la Sal **10.** Pancorbo **11.** Grañón **12.** Nájera **13.** Logroño **14.** Calahorra **15.** Amedo **16.** Peña Negra (?) **17.** Viguera **18.** Medrano **19.** Belorado **20.** Monasterio de Rodilla **21.** Burgos **22.** Castrojeriz **23.** Astudillo **24.** Tariego **25.** Dueñas **26.** Cabezón de Pisuerga **27.** Curiel **28.** Peñafiel **29.** Medina del Campo **30.** Villaescusa **31.** Peña Negra (?) **32.** Oreja **33.** Hita **34.** Atienza **35.** Osma **36.** Tudela **37.** Monzón **38.** Avià

[15] Díez, *Alfonso VIII*, 42. For a reproduction of the full charter, see González, *Alfonso VIII*, I, between pp. 192-3. As a point of comparison, Sancha of Aragón received the castles of Daroca, Epila, Uncastillo, Pina, Barbastro, Castro de Esteban, Cervera, Montblanc, and Ciurana as her dowry in May 1187, González, *Alfonso VIII*, I, 825.
[16] Díez, *Alfonso VIII*, 42, 198; see also González, *Alfonso VIII*, I, 189. Compare Leonor's dower with the dowry provided for her daughter Berenguella on her marriage to Alfonso IX of León, discussed below.
[17] For Joanna's dower, see Chapter 4.

109

By the time of his marriage in 1170, Alfonso VIII had already been reigning for twelve years, and had finally managed to stabilise his kingdom after the turbulent years of his minority.[18] Alfonso took full control of the kingdom after his marriage to Leonor, a match which had undoubtedly boosted his prestige in the eyes of both his subjects and his royal contemporaries, as Henry II was without doubt one of the most powerful monarchs in Europe at that time. In 1177, Alfonso sought Henry's aid to arbitrate in the incessant problems with the rival kingdom of Navarre. At the council of Windsor, Henry found in favour of his son-in-law; his letter to the Spanish kings announcing his decision is reproduced in full by Diceto.[19] The fact that Sancho VI of Navarre was also courting Henry's help in this matter demonstrates the high regard Henry was held in by his contemporaries and the wide influence he had as an arbiter in Iberian politics. Henry appears to have remained fair and impartial throughout the negotiations, which are also recorded by Gervase of Canterbury.[20] Howden provides the most detailed account of the proceedings in 1177, recording the summoning of a council to discuss the matter, the pleas of the Castilian and Navarrese ambassadors to Henry at Windsor, and reproducing in full the treaty which Henry helped to negotiate.[21] Leonor, however, does not feature in any of these accounts – indeed, after her marriage, she disappears entirely from Angevin chronicles - and after 1177 Iberian affairs are on the whole absent from Angevin sources.[22] It is therefore necessary to turn to contemporary Spanish chroniclers to glean information on Leonor as queen of Castile.

The *Crónica Latina* states that Leonor was 'of noble lineage, chaste and pure, and very wise'.[23] The *Primera Crónica General*, which barely mentions Leonor, notes that she was 'exquisitely educated, quiet and calm, very beautiful, greatly charitable, very kind to her husband, and honourable in all her dealings with the people of her realm, treating each one according to their estate'.[24] The *Crónica de Veinte Reyes* states that Leonor was 'very sensible and wise, knowledgable, good, and eloquent'.[25] Such effusive praise may be *topoi* used for all queens, but the frequent references to Leonor's wisdom and education in sources from the Iberian peninsula and beyond, coupled with what we know of Leonor's involvement in Castilian politics,

---

[18] For these years, see *PCG*, 668-70; *Crónica Latina*, 34-5.

[19] Diceto, I, 418-20. Henry had previously been asked to adjudicate in the dispute between Toulouse and Aragón, and his successful arbitration resulted in a peace treaty between the king of Aragón and the count of Toulouse in 1173. For a fuller description of these proceedings, see Diceto, I, 36; for the fullest account see Howden, *Gesta*, I, 138-57. Henry was later called on to arbitrate between Philip II of France and the count of Flanders, once more successfully negotiating a peace treaty (in 1181, and again in 1184); he also successfully mediated between his son-in-law Henry the Lion and the emperor Frederick in 1182; see Howden, *Gesta*, I, 277-88, 316-23, 334.

[20] Gervase, I, 261. He makes no mention of Leonor in his chronicle, although he pays more attention to her sisters, Matilda and Joanna. This may be because events in Sicily, Saxony and Toulouse more directly impacted on the Angevin realm than did those on the Iberian peninsula.

[21] Howden, *Gesta*, I, 138-54; *Chronica*, II, 120-31.

[22] With the exception of the marriage of Leonor's daughter Blanca to the future Louis VIII; see below.

[23] *Crónica Latina*, 43.

[24] *PCG*, 683, 709.

[25] 'La dueña salió muy sesuda e mucho entendida e muy buena e muy loçana', cited in Díez, *Alfonso VIII*, 43. Her siblings are also listed in the *Crónica*: 'del rrey don Enrique el Joven, e del rrey Rricharte, que fue tanbién rrey, e tan corajoso e tan esforçado que más non podría; e del conde de Bretaña e del rey Oían Syn Tierra. Esta reyna doña Leonor ouo dos hermanas: la vna fue duquesa de Sansoña [Sajonia], la otra rreyna de Ceçilia [Sicilia]'.

suggest that in this case at least the sources are presenting a genuine depiction of the queen.[26] Further, despite the lack of information in either Spanish or Angevin primary sources concerning the marriage itself, the sources are in agreement that the union was both felicitous and prosperous, a political success and, perhaps, also a true love match. This is certainly how modern Spanish historians – especially Díez and González – have subsequently portrayed it.

The role of the queen, in Spain as in other European kingdoms, was primarily to produce an heir. The queen should also be competent at managing the household, and should patronise religious institutions, preferably retiring to one in widowhood. She might wield influence over her husband, beside whom – in contrast to other contemporary European kingdoms – she would usually be buried in death, quite often in their joint foundation. Great influence and authority could also be available if a queen was widowed with small children – she would often be acknowledged as guardian, and sometimes as regent for the heir.[27] Thus, a Spanish royal woman could expect, through her life cycle, to play several different roles, from daughter to wife and mother, to widow, patron, regent, or *de facto* queen.

Some idea of the roles Leonor was expected to perform can be gained from the earliest known "mirror" for queens, in the thirteenth-century *Siete Partidas* of Alfonso X. The views expressed therein 'likely reflected views generally prevalent not only in Spain, but also throughout Europe'.[28] The *Partidas* rule that royal brides must be of royal blood themselves to avoid diluting or tainting the dynastic line, whilst bastards were a source of shame and should be hidden from public life.[29] As marriages were, theoretically, indissoluble, brides should be both wealthy, to bring riches, honour and prestige; and beautiful, so that they will be easier to love, and will produce in turn attractive offspring.[30] Wives should be cherished and protected, in order that they will in turn cherish and obey their husbands, thereby setting a good example to all. In order to ensure this, virtuous, God-fearing men and women should be employed to attend royal brides, to guard their honour and to teach them proper conduct.[31] Adulterous

---

[26] Similarly, Leonor's daughter Berenguella was always described as 'wise', particularly by Lucas de Tuy, whom she commissioned to compose the *Crónica de España*. De Tuy may simply have desired to gratify his patron, but it seems equally permissible, in light of Berenguella's involvement in political and dynastic affairs, to argue that this was no mere *topos*, and that Berenguella had learnt well from her mother's example.

[27] Joseph F. O'Callaghan, 'The Many Roles of the Medieval Queen: Some Examples from Castile', in *Queenship and Political Power*, 21. Royal women might accede in the absence of male heirs, but 'every effort was made to provide her with a husband who was expected to execute most of the functions attributed to the monarch', O'Callaghan, 'Roles of the Queen', 21.

[28] O'Callaghan, 'Roles of the Queen', 22, and for more on the role of the queen in the *Siete Partidas*, 21-6. O'Callaghan notes that 'most queens...would have acknowledged that the texts summarized fairly well what was expected of them', 'Roles of the Queen', 22. Roughly contemporary with this is the *Llibre dels feits*, the autobiographical work composed by Jaime I of Aragón in the mid to late thirteenth century. In the *Llibre*, Jaime's queen, Violante of Hungary, is portrayed as his co-ruler and principal advisor, as negotiator, intercessor and mediatrix, although at no point is she mentioned by name. Van Landingham has viewed this not as a deliberate attempt to strip Violante of her identity, but as Jaime's intention to depict her as the perfect queen, a model for all future queens: the embodiment and fulfilment of 'all the elements that comprise a model queen. In his work, Violante and the perfect queen are one and the same', 'Royal Portraits: Representations of Queenship in the Thirteenth-Century Catalan Chronicles', in *Queenship and Political Power*, 119. For later medieval queens of Aragon, whose power and authority were 'roughly equivalent to that of kings', see Theresa Earenfight, 'Absent Kings: Queens as Political Partners in the Medieval Crown of Aragon', in *ibid.*, 33-51.

[29] O'Callaghan, 'Roles of the Queen', 23.

[30] *Ibid.*, 23. Good family and good conduct were, however, deemed to be more important, as beauty and riches were 'transitory', O'Callaghan, 'Roles of the Queen', 23.

[31] *Ibid.*, 23-4. Women in the queen's household – her ladies-in-waiting, including relatives, wives and daughters of great magnates and knights, nuns, servants – were under the same protection of their honour as the queen and her

queens throw doubt on the legitimacy of heirs; therefore, an act of adultery with the queen was equated with high treason. Similarly, any offence against the queen was equated with an offence against the king.[32]

What was different in terms of queenship on the Iberian peninsula as opposed to the rest of Western Christendom was the queen's level of authority and degree of political involvement. As well as the usual functions of providing an heir, educating their children, patronising religious institutions and performing charitable deeds, their 'political status as the wife of the king and mother of the heir...permitted a certain measure of autonomy', exemplifying a 'form of queenship that can best be described as a political partnership'.[33] Their status and position enabled them to play a role in politics, and whilst it was not an equal partnership, it was a partnership nonetheless. Moreover, women could – and did – accede in their own right in Castile, León and Aragón when a male heir was lacking, although these were atypical cases.[34] Theresa Earenfight has highlighted the difference between power (force) and authority (influence), noting their centrality to discussions of queenship. Citing the argument that 'influence exercised through the family is indirect power, and therefore not true royal authority', she adds the caveat that 'when the family in question was among the most powerful in Europe, this was indeed real political power'.[35] This was certainly true in the case of Leonor, who had no queenly role model other than her mother: Alfonso VIII's mother had died in childbirth, and he had no known female relatives at court.

The Marriages of Leonor's Daughters

Leonor's youth at the time of her marriage enabled her to integrate more quickly and easily into the kingdom, especially as regards language and culture. Yet it is clear that she did not forget her own heritage, as will be seen in Parts IV and V. She was also instrumental in engineering politically significant marriages for her children, notably her daughters Berenguella, Blanca, and Urraca. Urraca was first betrothed in 1188 at the age of three to the king of León, although this plan was abandoned by 1189.[36] In 1205, she was betrothed to Afonso II of Portugal. The marriage was celebrated in 1208, cementing Castilian-Portuguese relations, and the union produced four surviving children.[37] Urraca died on 2 November 1220, and was buried at Alcobaça. Evidence that Urraca was deeply influenced by her natal family can be found not only in her patronage of this Cistercian monastery, but also in the Castilian ornaments with which she augmented the church of Santa Cruz de Coimbra: a curtain of silk, three silk cloaks, a fine *casulla*, a silver vase, and a cloth of silk.[38]

---

daughters. Any man who ravished any of these women was also punished as traitor, either by execution or by exile and the confiscation of their lands. Wetnurses especially should be chaste, as it was customarily believed that an impure wetnurse's milk was tainted, and could cause serious illness or even death to the nursing infant, O'Callaghan, 'Roles of the Queen', 25-6.

[32] *Ibid.*, 24.

[33] Theresa Earenfight, 'Partners in Politics', in *Queenship and Political Power*, xiii, xiv.

[34] Much later, Isabella of Castile (1451-1504) considered her role as equivalent to, rather than supplementary to, that of a king; she 'saw no political distinction between what she did as queen and what her male ancestors did', Earenfight, 'Partners in Politics', xxv.

[35] *Ibid.*, xxii.

[36] González, *Alfonso VIII*, I, 204.

[37] Sancho II, Afonso III, Leonor, who later became queen of Denmark, and Fernando de Serpa.

[38] González, *Alfonso VIII*, I, 204n.

It is with the marriage of Leonor's eldest daughter Berenguella, however, that Leonor's political and diplomatic astuteness is best demonstrated. Berenguella was first betrothed at the age of eight to Conrad, duke of Rotenburg, son of the Emperor Frederick I, in a solemn ceremony at Carrión in June 1188 at which both Conrad and Alfonso IX of León performed homage to Alfonso VIII.[39] Conrad and Berenguella were to accede to Castile if Alfonso and Leonor had no further male issue. The betrothal to Conrad was an attempt to counter the alliance between Richard of England, Philip Augustus and Alfonso II of Aragón against Henry II of England. In April 1188, the Castilian embassy arrived at the imperial court, and the treaty outlining Berenguella's dower and dowry provisions, as well as her expected rights at her marriage to Conrad, were agreed on 23 April.[40] The betrothal, however, was dissolved the following year by the papal legate, Cardinal Gregory of Sant Angelo, and Gonzalo, Archbishop of Toledo, on grounds of consanguinity.[41] Díez has suggested that the birth of Berenguella's brother Fernando on 29 November 1189 and Berenguella's subsequent loss of the title of heir-apparent provides a further reason for the annulment,[42] although the *Primera Crónica General* seems to suggest that it was Conrad who repudiated Berenguella.[43]

In the autumn of 1197 negotiations began for Berenguella to marry Alfonso IX of León, in an attempt to effect peace between the kingdoms of León and Castile. Leonor was instrumental in achieving this, as she apparently saw that the best chance of a lasting peace would result from the dynastic alliance of her seventeen-year-old daughter Berenguella with the king of León. Alfonso, it seems, was opposed to the marriage as the pair were related in the third degree, but was persuaded by his wife's requests and convinced that this was the best road to achieving the necessary peace.[44] The *Primera Crónica General* attributes the idea solely to Alfonso's magnates,[45] although it does assert that it was Leonor's influence which persuaded Alfonso to agree to the match, and clearly states that she favoured the marriage.[46] She sent nobles to talk with both her husband and with Alfonso of León, and through many efforts was able to effect the union between her daughter and the king of León[47]. Leonor's wise counsel persuaded her husband that, in assuring a lasting peace between Castile and León, the

---

[39] *PCG*, 677; *Crónica Latina*, 37. The *Crónica* states that Alfonso IX was also betrothed at this time to one of Alfonso VIII's daughters, despite the union being 'against the laws of God and against canon law', as the kings of Castile and León were related in the second degree, *CL*, 36. This is clearly a mistake, as Alfonso and Leonor had only one daughter at this time. The author appears to have conflated Alfonso IX's later betrothal to Berenguella with events at Carrión. The illegality of Berenguella's marriage is reiterated at *CL* 42, although the author has erroneously given Fernando II as Berenguella's husband.

[40] González, *Alfonso VIII*, I, 827; and for the charter outlining these terms, II, no. 499. Reference to Berenguella's betrothal to Conrad appears in the end clause on almost all charters after this: of sixty-three remaining charters after this date, reference is made to the match in the *facta* clause forty-nine times; see nos. 506, 508-20, 522-8, 530-3, 535-56, 559-60. The last reference [no. 560] is in the *facta* clause granting Quintana to the monastery of Silos in exchange for the aldea of Nuño Fañez, given at Berlanga, October 1190.

[41] Berenguella and Conrad were both descended from Count William I of Burgundy: his son and successor Stephen I fathered Renaud, father of Beatrice, Conrad's mother; his third son Raymond married Queen Urraca of Castile, González, *Alfonso VIII*, I, 198n.

[42] Díez, *Alfonso VIII*, 47.

[43] *PCG*, 677.

[44] Díez, *Alfonso VIII*, 71, 140.

[45] *PCG*, 677.

[46] *PCG*, 683.

[47] *PCG*, 683. The author of the *Crónica* clearly saw the marriage as a good thing which was divinely favoured: when the two kings met at Valladolid, 'assi quiso alli Nuestro Sennor Dios, que enuio el su spirito en los reyes et en la reyna donna Leonor et en los omnes buenos que andauan y entrellos', 683.

match was 'more an act of mercy than a sin'.[48] The union of Berenguella and Alfonso IX in order to effect peace between Castile and León provides an interesting parallel with Joanna's second marriage to Raymond of Toulouse, which effectively ended the Forty Years' War.[49]

As dowry, Alfonso VIII endowed Berenguella with all the castles he had taken from Alfonso IX; Alfonso IX gave as dower those he had taken from Alfonso VIII. De Tuy states that these thirty castles in León included those of León, Astorga and Valencia.[50] The *Primera Crónica General* describes Berenguella's dower and dowry provisions as 'befitting for such a great lady'.[51] According to the treaty of dower concluded on 23 April 1188, Berenguella's dowry comprised Nájera, Tovia, Pazluengos, Cellorigo y Haro, Pancorbo, Monasterio, Amaya, Orcejón, Urval, Palencia del Conde, Astudillo, Carrión, Frómista, the port of Santander, Villa Curiel, Peñafiel, Magaz and a share of the saltpans at Belinchón.[52]

Berenguella's marriage was celebrated with great pomp and honour, 'as befitting for such great nobles',[53] at Valladolid in early December 1197, despite failing to secure a papal dispensation for the union, and the couple travelled to León later that month.[54] The kings of León and Castile, 'once enemies, were now related, and more than this, they were friends...and the firm peace between them was as between father and son'.[55] The following year, however, Innocent III sent his legate Rainerio to León to order the couple to separate on grounds of consanguinity; Alfonso IX refused, hoping to sire an heir to his kingdom, and wishing to retain the castles that comprised Berenguella's dower and dowry. Innocent accordingly excommunicated Alfonso and placed León under interdict; after a successful Leonese embassy to Rome the interdict was lifted, but Alfonso and Berenguella remained excommunicate whilst they remained married, and Berenguella was ordered to return the thirty castles which comprised her *arras*.[56]

On 8 December 1199, the kings of León and Castile met at Palencia to renew the agreement regarding Berenguella's dower. This comprised extensive territories which Berenguella was to retain until her death, even should she separate from Alfonso.[57] The *Crónica Latina* states that the cause of the kings' former enmity was Alfonso IX's repudiation of Berenguella;

---

[48] *PCG*, 683. The *Crónica* attests to Leonor's wisdom and grasp of politics: 'la reyna donna Leonor...era ella muy sabia et muy entenduda duenna et muy anuisa et entendie los peligros de las cosas', 683. The author of the *Crónica Latina* also considered the marriage to be the best way to effect peace between the two kingdoms, *CL*, 42. Lucas de Tuy similarly refers to the marriage in terms of the peace it would afford, whilst remaining staunchly silent on the matter of the couple's consanguinity, *Crónica de España*, 409. The fact that Berenguella and Alfonso were later forced to separate by papal decree is not mentioned anywhere in de Tuy's chronicle. He does, however, mention that Alfonso IX was free to marry Berenguella as his former marriage to Teresa of Portugal had been dissolved by the pope. Rodrigo de Rada merely noted that Berenguella was free to marry Alfonso of León as her betrothal to Conrad had been annulled by the papal legate, González, *Alfonso VIII*, I, 723.

[49] For more on the Forty Years War and the struggle for the overlordship of Toulouse, see Part II, Chapter 2.

[50] *Crónica de España*, 410.

[51] *PCG*, 683.

[52] González, *Alfonso VIII*, I, 189-90n.

[53] *Ibid.*, I, 683.

[54] Díez, *Alfonso VIII*, 71.

[55] *PCG*, 683.

[56] Díez, *Alfonso VIII*, 72.

[57] *Ibid.*, 72. The lands included San Pelayo de Lodo, Aguilar de Mola, Alba de Bubal, Candrei and Aguilar de Pedrajo (in Galicia); Vega de Ruiponce, Castogonzalo, Valencia de Don Juan, Cabrero, Castro de los Judíos de Mayorga, Villalugán and Castroverde (in Tierra de Campos); Colle, Portilla, Alión and Peñafiel (in las Samozas); Oviedo, Siero, Aguilar, Gozón, Corel, La Isla, Lugaz, Ventosa, Buanga, Miranda de Nieva, Burón, Peñafiel de Aller and Santa Cruz de Tineo (in Asturias).

however, this clearly was not the cause of the discord, as the separation had been enforced by the pope, and had not been observed for several years afterwards.[58]

As queen of León, Berenguella had a 'notable influence'.[59] Lucas de Tuy frequently describes her as 'very wise', and 'most prudent', traits she apparently inherited from her parents.[60] De Tuy states that after she became queen of León, Alfonso amended *fueros*, constructed a palace near the monastery of Santiago, and restored the city walls. Berenguella also augmented Santiago with gold, silver, precious stones and silks, as well as patronising and founding several other religious houses in León.[61] The marriage was finally annulled on grounds of consanguinity in 1204, but the couple had already produced five children: Leonor, who died young; Berenguella, who became queen of Jerusalem through her marriage to John of Brienne; Constanza, who entered holy orders at Las Huelgas; Fernando, later Fernando III of a united Castile-León; and Alfonso de Molina.[62]

Berenguella returned to Castile in 1204, although she retained the title of Queen of León; she lived with her parents, who always defended the rights and expectations of their first-born child to the throne of León, and immersed herself in the upbringing and education of her children, whom she had brought to Castile with her.[63] Alfonso and Leonor took much care to ensure, through treaties, both Berenguella's own rights in León (including her title), and those of her eldest son. Berenguella was frequently in Burgos, intervening in acts concerning Las Huelgas, and she and her sons, especially Fernando, appear specifically together in documents from 1207.[64]

Leonor was considerably less involved in negotiating the marriage of her daughter Blanca to the future Louis VIII of France, but the influence of her mother, Eleanor of Aquitaine, was crucial, and Eleanor's involvement effectively afforded an accord between the English and French kings, who met between Gaillon and Les Andelys on 14 January 1200 to discuss the matter.[65] Negotiations were opened between the English and Spanish ambassadors as part of a peace treaty between King John and Philip II of France.[66] The terms of the treaty, finalised on 18 May, saw Philip's recognition of John as rightful ruler of Normandy, Anjou, Maine, Touraine and Aquitaine, and overlord of Brittany. John performed homage to Philip for these

---

[58] *Crónica Latina*, 44.

[59] González, *Alfonso VIII*, I, 198.

[60] *Fuit praefata Berengaria filia regis Castellae adeo sapientissima, quod patris sapientia ad eam defluxisse videretur*, *Crónica de España*, 411. For further references to Berenguella's wisdom, see 410, 421, 427, 428.

[61] *Crónica de España*, 411.

[62] *Ibid.*, 411. Leonor died in November 1202 and was buried in San Isidoro; for her epitaph in the San Isidoro pantheon, see González, *Alfonso VIII*, I, 199n. Constanza, who died in 1242, was buried at Las Huelgas. The daughter of Berenguella and John of Brienne, Maria, was betrothed to the Byzantine emperor Baldwin. As he was still a minor, Berenguella and John of Brienne were entrusted with the empire by papal decree until Baldwin and Maria came of age, *PCG*, 677; *Crónica de España*, 411.

[63] Díez, *Alfonso VIII*, 47. Berenguella's youngest son Alfonso remained with his brother, while her daughters stayed at Las Huelgas.

[64] González, *Alfonso VIII*, I, 199.

[65] *Ibid.*, I, 855; Kate Norgate, *John Lackland* (MacMillan, London, 1902), 72-3; see also Howden, *Chronica*, IV, 106-7; Ralph of Coggeshall, *Chronicon Anglicanum*, ed. Josephus Stevenson (Rolls Series, 66, London, 1875), 100-1.

[66] The Close Rolls record the arrival of the envoys of 'the king and queen of Castile and Toledo', *Rotuli Litterarum Clausarum* (Close Rolls), I, 1204-1224, ed. Thomas Duffy Hardy (London, 1837), I, 58. Philip's son Louis had been born in 1187, and thus was only a few months older than his bride-to-be, González, *Alfonso VIII*, I, 206. The *Crónica Latina* attributes the engineering of this marriage to Alfonso, p. 45; as it states that Blanca was at that time reigning in France this part of the chronicle must have been composed 1223x1226.

lands, and in addition paid 20,000 silver marks and formally ceded the Vexin, Auvergne, Evreux, Issoudun, Graçay and Bourges.[67]

With the preliminary negotiations completed, Eleanor of Aquitaine journeyed to Castile to collect Blanca, and perhaps also 'to visit her daughter...and meet her grandchildren'.[68] Eleanor stayed in Burgos from January to March 1200, and by April had returned to Aquitaine with her granddaughter.[69] They reached Bordeaux by Easter (9 April), where Eleanor charged Elie de Malmort, archbishop of Bordeaux, with the task of conducting Blanca to Normandy, where John, who had recently returned from Boutavant on the banks of the Seine, was waiting to receive his niece at Chateau-Gaillard.[70] On 22 May John gave Blanca to Louis, together with the holdings of Issoudun and Graçay, with the stipulation that if no heirs were produced, these would return to the English crown.[71] The marriage ceremony was performed on 22 May 1200 by the archbishop of Bordeaux, and on her entry into Paris, her Parisian subjects declared Blanca the most beautiful woman they had ever seen.[72] Despite her numerous achievements as queen of France, Blanca never forgot her family and stayed in regular correspondence with her parents and with her eldest sister (receiving from her, for instance, the news of their father's victory at Las Navas), until her death in 1252.[73]

The political importance of Blanca's marriage to Louis VIII is attested by its being recorded by Angevin chroniclers as well as Spanish and French. Blanca's marriage is treated in detail by Wendover, although he erroneously gives the year of the marriage as 1216.[74] Diceto provides the details of Blanca's dowry, provided by her uncle, King John: she received Berry and the Auvergne, as well as castles and honours in Normandy, Gascony, and 'aliis pluribus locis'.[75] Howden provides the additional information that Eleanor of Aquitaine travelled to Spain to collect her grand-daughter and escort her to France.[76] Nevertheless, whilst Angevin sources stress the role played by Eleanor in the negotiation process, Spanish sources clearly state that the match was engineered by Alfonso. Leonor's involvement in the marriage plans for their

---

[67] Norgate, *John Lackland*, 73-4. Issoudun and Graçay had been ceded to Philip by Richard I in 1189, but had been restored to the English crown by a treaty of 1195. See also Howden, *Chronica*, IV, 115, 148-51; *Foedera*, I, 79-80, 66.

[68] Díez, *Alfonso VIII*, 49; but *cf.* Jane Martindale, 'Eleanor of Aquitaine: The Last Years', in Stephen Church (ed.), *King John: New Interpretations* (Boydell, Woodbridge, 1999), 140-1; 145-6.

[69] González, *Alfonso VIII*, I, 856.

[70] *Ibid.*, I, 206.

[71] *Ibid.*, I, 856.

[72] Díez, *Alfonso VIII*, 49; González, *Alfonso VIII*, I, 207; see also Howden, *Chronica*, IV, 115.

[73] After the battle of Las Navas, Berenguella wrote to her sister Blanca, then married to the heir of France, to 'tell you joyfully that, by the grace of God, from whom all virtue comes, that the king, our lord and father, conquered in a pitched battle Almiramamolin [the Almohad caliph]. We believe that this was an especially notable honor because until now it was unheard of that the king of Morocco would be overcome on the battlefield. Know that a servant of our father's household announced this to me, but I did not wish to believe until I saw our father's own letters', González, *Alfonso VIII*, III, no. 898, trans. O'Callaghan, 'Roles of the Queen', 28.

[74] Wendover, II, 177-80. Wendover later makes a brief reference to Blanca's marriage when he recounts the second baronial objection against King John: the reference pertains to Louis' claim to the English throne through right of his wife Blanca, II, 186-8.

[75] Diceto, II, 168.

[76] Howden, *Chronica*, IV, 114. The marriage itself is discussed at IV, 115, with an earlier reference at IV, 81. William of Newburgh, II, 505-6, also briefly records the marriage. In none of these accounts, however, is Blanca referred to by name.

elder daughter Berenguella, coupled with the assistance of her own mother Eleanor, strongly suggest that she also played some part in arranging Blanca's marriage.

Leonor did not live to see the marriage of her daughter Leonor; it was her eldest daughter Berenguella, as queen of Castile, who arranged her sister's marriage to Jaime I of Aragón.[77] Clearly, Berenguella had learnt well from her parents regarding the importance of diplomatic dynastic alliances. Leonor's marriage was concluded in Ágreda on 6 February 1221, but was annulled in 1229 with papal approval at Jaime's petition, citing the impediment of kinship.[78] It seems that the cause of the annulment was simple incompatibility; Leonor had already given Jaime a son, Alfonso, who died in 1260, predeceasing his father.[79] Leonor and her son returned to Castile where they remained with Berenguella and her son Fernando, from whom Leonor recieved several gifts, for the remainder of her life.[80] In September 1234 Jaime reached an agreement with Fernando in Huerta, that Leonor be granted the town and castle of Ariza for the rest of her life, on condition that she did not remarry.[81] Leonor died in 1244, never having remarried, and was buried at the family mausoleum at Las Huelgas.[82]

Gonzalo Martínez Díez may have been over-romanticising somewhat when he stated that Providence had rewarded Alfonso VIII, bereft of parents since the age of two, with a loving and very fertile wife who was a mere five years younger than himself, but he has rightly highlighted the importance of securing the succession as quickly as possible. With no siblings, the security of Alfonso's kingdom depended on his ability to sire potential heirs.[83] Here, then, was a crucial queenly function which Leonor was able to fulfil exceptionally well, and her years of childbearing – she produced eleven children between 1181-1204, her last child being born when Leonor was forty-two – provide a parallel with her own, equally fertile mother, Eleanor of Aquitaine.

Leonor was clearly educated enough to undertake the education both of her children and her grandchildren.[84] Spanish royal daughters were educated in order to prepare them for possible queenship. They were closely guarded, and 'the task of providing immediate supervision fell principally to the queen'.[85] Loyal, intelligent, honest and virtuous *amas* (nurses) and *ayas* (governesses) were provided as daily companions, protectors, and instructors in manners

---

[77] González, *Alfonso VIII*, I, 211. The *Crónica Latina*, 71-3, asserts that it was also Berenguella who arranged Fernando's marriage to Beatrice, daughter of Philip of Germany and granddaughter of two emperors. The marriage ceremony was performed in Burgos on 30 November 1219, and Berenguella was also responsible for the post-nuptial celebrations. The two emperors referred to were Isaac II Comnenos and Frederick the Great. Berenguella also seems to have engineered the marriage between her own daughter Berenguella and John of Brienne, *Crónica Latina*, 73.

[78] In his autobiographical *Llibre dels faits*, Jaime claimed that he had been too young to be able to "do with her that which men do with their wives", Van Landingham, 'Royal Portraits', 113, although the birth of Alfonso, who remained his legitimate heir even after the marriage was dissolved, proves that he was eventually able to undertake such a task.

[79] Díez, *Alfonso VIII*, 52.

[80] González, *Alfonso VIII*, I, 211.

[81] Díez, *Alfonso VIII*, 52; see also González, *Alfonso VIII*, I, 211n.

[82] For more on the royal burials at Las Huelgas, see Part V.

[83] Díez, *Alfonso VIII*, 41.

[84] *Ibid.*, 46. González definitively established the order in which Leonor's children were born as: Berenguella, Sancho, Urraca, Blanca, Fernando, Mafalda, Leonor, and Enrique, *Alfonso VIII*, I, 195, 195n. This list, however, omits Sancha, who died in infancy, and Constanza, who was a nun at Las Huelgas, and who died in 1243. No chronicle records their births. The list of Alfonso and Leonor's children provided by Lucas de Tuy includes Constanza, but omits Sancho and Mafalda, *Crónica de España*, 406.

[85] O'Callaghan, 'Roles of the Queen', 24.

and good customs, and daughters would be taught to read (especially psalms and the hours), as well as how to dress, speak, eat and drink with refinement.[86] When arranging their marriages, the qualities of attractiveness, wealth, good habits and good family would be sought in their prospective bridegrooms, in the same manner as choosing brides for kings and princes.

The practice of giving royal children to wetnurses was common throughout medieval Europe, and the wetnurses of Leonor and Alfonso's children were rewarded magnanimously.[87] Their daughters as well as their sons were placed under the tutelage of trusted magnates for their education: Sancha was entrusted to Lope Díaz de Haro, Urraca to Pedro García de Lerma, the royal *mayordomo*, and Blanca to Pedro Rodríguez de Castro, nephew of the former regent Gutierre Fernández de Castro.[88] It is likely that the itinerant nature of the Castilian monarchs necessitated the use of personal tutors, and is further evidence of their desire to provide a full, rich, and stable upbringing for their children.[89] Leonor's own learning and talents are frequently referred to in Spanish chronicles; it is therefore highly probable that she understood the benefits a royal education could provide, and wished her children to enjoy the same privileges.

Both Alfonso and Leonor were clearly devoted parents. González refers to numerous testimonies which demonstrate that Alfonso as much as Leonor 'always showed their love to them'.[90] All of Leonor's surviving daughters remained either emotionally or geographically connected with her, and the death of her son Fernando prompted such grief that Leonor expressed the desire to die with him if he could not be saved.[91] When Leonor was not at Alfonso's side, she and her children were kept frequently and fully informed of such matters as the dangers he faced in his wars against the Moors: Berenguella especially was immediately informed of the victories at las Navas de Tolosa in 1212 and at Alcaraz the following year, on which occasion Leonor, Berenguella, and Berenguella's sons Fernando and Alfonso left Burgos for Orgaz, where they were reunited with Alfonso.[92] After the conquest of Alcaraz, which Alfonso entered in state on Ascension Day (February 1213), Leonor, Enrique, Berenguella and her sons celebrated Pentecost with Alfonso in Sant Toreat. The *Primera Crónica* does not state whether Alfonso's family had travelled there to meet him, although it seems to imply that they were already there when Alfonso arrived.[93]

The marriage of Leonor and Alfonso was perhaps the most successful of Henry II's matrimonial alliance policies. The marriage seems to have been a happy one, and it would appear that not only did Leonor commemorate her parents in the naming of two of her many children, she also learned from them the valuable lesson of making important diplomatic marriage alliances for her own daughters.[94] Perhaps she had also learnt that the bestowal of landed

---

[86] *Ibid.*, 24.

[87] González, *Alfonso VIII*, II, nos. 367, 530, 549.

[88] Díez, *Alfonso VIII*, 56-7. Díez has no doubt that these appointments were made because both Alfonso and Leonor led a peripatetic lifestyle.

[89] This raises an interesting parallel with Eleanor of Aquitaine's own itinerant lifestyle.

[90] González, *Alfonso VIII*, I, 194.

[91] See Part I. Eye-witnesses swore that they had never seen such pain as hers when she entered the room where her son lay on his deathbed, González, *Alfonso VIII*, I, 195.

[92] González, *Alfonso VIII*, I, 194, and for this reunion 194-5. Berenguella subsequently wrote to her sister Blanca, queen of France, to inform her of their father's victory. The letter is published in González, *Alfonso VIII*, III, no. 898.

[93] *PCG*, 706.

[94] Berenguella's marriage to Alfonso of León ultimately united the kingdoms of León and Castile, whilst Leonor's marriage to Jaime I temporarily effected an Aragonese alliance. Urraca married Afonso of Portugal, cementing ties with almost all of the Christian kingdoms on the peninsula, whilst Blanca's marriage to Louis VIII of France saw her

dowries could be potentially problematic, as was very much the case with the dowry which she had brought to her own marriage.

Leonor's Dowry

Gascony had been promised as Leonor's dowry at the time of the marriage negotiations, to be attainable on the death of her mother Eleanor of Aquitaine.[95] Henry II would then, through his son-in-law, have a valuable ally in the south whose territories bordered his own. For Alfonso, the region was similarly strategically important, as his possession of the county would mean his lands effectively encircled those of Navarre, whose king Sancho VI was also hoping to attain overlordship of Gascony.[96] The Castilian claims to the county increased Sancho's mistrust of Castile; furthermore, Leonor's endowment of Gascony as dowry was problematic as parts of the county belonged to the viscountess Maria of Béarn (who had paid homage to Alfonso II of Aragón on 30 April 1170 for those parts of the county not belonging to the English crown), whilst others belonged to Leonor's brother Richard.[97] The contentious issue of Gascony marks Leonor's first appearance in the *Crónica Latina*, which states that Gascony had been promised to Alfonso at the time of his marriage to Leonor.[98]

Until 1200, Gascony remained quasi-autonomous, and the problem of the hostile kingdom of Navarre lying between Alfonso's lands in Castile and Gascony, as well as the incessant threats he faced from the Moors, initially prevented Alfonso from attempting to claim Leonor's dowry.[99] In 1200, however, Alfonso reincorporated the castles and surrounding lands of Álava and Guipúzcoa into his realm, with the objective of recovering the old frontier of the kingdom of Castile-León that had been attained by his ancestor Alfonso VI. These lands, gained in Alfonso's winter campaign of 1199-1200, gave Castile a border with Gascony.[100] Díez notes that there were rumours that Alfonso had planned to invade Gascony to assert his rights there in the mid 1190s; once the border lands of Álava and Guipúzcoa were incorporated into the Castilian kingdom, Alfonso had a secure base at Bidasoa from which to launch his campaign.[101] Moreover, he was able to profit from King John's wars with Philip of France, as both England and France attempted to maintain cordial relations with Castile and win Alfonso as an ally.[102] After the death of Eleanor of Aquitaine in April 1204, and Philip's occu-

---

wield enormous power and influence as regent for her saintly son Louis IX.

[95] Gillingham, 'Richard and Berengaria', 161-2; O'Callaghan, *History of Spain*, 236.

[96] González, *Alfonso VIII*, I, 793. The kingdom of Aragón had held political influence in the south of the duchy, notably in Béarn and Bigorre, since about 1120, and although Richard's campaign of 1178 had resulted in the count of Bigorre swearing fealty to him, surrendering two castles as surety, an Aragonese presence remained in the south of Gascony. See Dunbabin, *France in the Making*, 340; 344; see also Howden, *Gesta*, I, 212-3.

[97] González, *Alfonso VIII*, I, 794; 794n.

[98] *Crónica Latina*, 43.

[99] Díez, *Alfonso VIII*, 199. Díez states that Alfonso seemed to have taken little interest in Gascony while Eleanor of Aquitaine was alive, but this does not take into account the fact that Leonor was only to receive her dowry on her mother's death. In 1190, Bertan de Born had composed the poem "Miez sirventes vueilh far dels reis amdos" to inspire Richard I to go to war with Alfonso VIII over Gascony, which Richard had promised to Berengaria as dower. Berengaria was only to hold Gascony until the death of Eleanor of Aquitaine, at which time the duchy was to be Leonor's dowry. In the poem, Alfonso VIII is referred to as 'del valen rei', although the valour of both Alfonso and Richard would be proved to de Born only through battle. See W. Paden, T. Sankovitch & P. Stäblein (eds.), *The Poems of the Troubadour Bertran de Born* (University of California Press, 1986), no. 38.

[100] Díez, *Alfonso VIII*, 200.

[101] *Ibid.*

[102] Prior to this, in October and November 1201, John and Sancho VII of Navarre had exchanged letters of friend-

pation of the former English territories north of the Loire, an alliance with Alfonso would prove of considerable aid to either Philip or John. Philip especially was courting Alfonso's aid in expelling all English from France,[103] eventually succeeding in winning an alliance with Castile in 1205.[104]

Furthermore, many Gascon nobles were themselves seeking Alfonso's support, while others looked to the kingdom of Navarre. At San Sebastian in October 1204, Alfonso was recognised as lord of Gascony by the bishops of Bayonne and Dax and the Gascon nobility, including the count of Armagnac and the viscounts of Béarn, Orthez and Tartas.[105] In 1205 the archbishops of Compostela and Tarragona, acting under papal decree, were able to effect peace between Castile and Navarre, enabling Alfonso to plan an expeditionary force into Gascony, which resulted in an almost total victory: only Bordeaux, La Réole and Bayonne remained loyal to John.[106] Alfonso's lordship over Gascony was reconfirmed by the bishops of Dax, Bayonne and Bazas, and by most Gascon nobles; as Díez has pointed out, it was the support of the Gascon nobility which ultimately determined Alfonso's hold over the county.[107] The siege of Bayonne is recorded in the *Crónica de veinte reyes*, which relates that Alfonso was forced to abandon the siege because of a Moorish invasion at home.[108]

The *Primera Crónica*, however, whilst confirming that Alfonso was able to enforce his lordship over all Gascony save Bordeaux, Reole and Bayonne, makes no mention of a Moorish invasion at this time.[109] Rather, it states that the truce he had made with the Moorish ruler 'Miramomelin' had come to an end, and that Alfonso, suffering still from the humiliation of his defeat at Alarcos, and ready to die for the faith of Christ, turned his attention away from Gascon affairs to concentrate on making war against the Moors.[110] It was, however, the arrival of John in June 1206, and his successful siege of Montauban in August, along with the resist-

---

ship, forming an alliance in February 1202 against Castile and Aragón, Ivan Cloulas, 'Le douaire de Bérengère de Navarre, veuve de Richard Coeur de Lion, et sa retraite au Mans', in Martin Aurell (ed.), *La Cour Plantagenêt 1152-1204* (Poitiers, 2000), 91-2. For the charters of alliance, see *Foedera*, I.1, 85-6. For John's wars with Philip, culminating in the Battle of Bouvines in 1214, see J.W. Baldwin, *The Government of Philip Augustus* (University of California Press, 1989), 94-100, 191-219.

[103] Díez, *Alfonso VIII*, 200-1.

[104] Margaret Wade Labarge, *Gascony, England's First Colony, 1204-1454* (Hamish Hamilton, London, 1980), 14. The French king's position as feudal overlord of all princes of the realm, as Abbot Suger had attempted to demonstrate was the case in his *Life* of Louis VI, technically afforded him the right to intervene in disputes; see Dunbabin, *France in the Making*, 257; and for Suger's 'restoration' of Carolingian-inspired ideas of sacral kingship generally, 256-68; see also 358-65 on twelfth century feudalism. Henry II, for example, had sworn homage to Louis VII for his continental domains in 1158, Dunbabin, *France in the Making*, 262; Gillingham, however, disputes that homage was performed on this occasion, 'Doing Homage', 63-84.

[105] Díez, *Alfonso VIII*, 201; Wade Labarge, *Gascony*, 14.

[106] Díez, *Alfonso VIII*, 201; see also *Crónica Latina*, 43-4. Wade Labarge, however, viewed the expedition as a failure, noting that while Alfonso 'expected an easy victory', Bayonne closed its gates to him, while Elie de Malemort, archbishop of Bordeaux, was able to oppose Alfonso's force and retain the loyalty of La Réole and Bordeaux, with subsidies received from England, forcing the 'discouraged Alfonso' to withdraw, 'and his minor conquests were easily won back', *Gascony*, 14.

[107] Díez, *Alfonso VIII*, 203.

[108] *Crónica de veinte reyes*, 280-1, cited in Díez, *Alfonso VIII*, 202-3, who notes that the *Crónica* is here inaccurate, as there is no evidence of a Moorish assault on Castile in the summer of 1205.

[109] *PCG*, 686.

[110] *PCG*, 686. It is likely that the invasion referred to in the *Crónica de veinte reyes* is that of 1195, immediately preceding the battle of Alarcos.

ance of Bordeaux and the other cities, which ultimately halted Castilian incursions into Gascony and forced Alfonso to return to Spain.[111]

Alfonso resumed his Gascon campaign in 1206, and in a charter issued at Burgos on 22 May 1206 Alfonso is styled 'señor de Gascuña'.[112] Leonor appears to have involved herself personally in the contentious issue of her dowry, although Díez presents it in terms of the queen merely wishing to act as mediator in smoothing relations between her husband and her brother.[113] Apparently, John issued a safe conduct to his sister in 1206 in order that she could travel to England to meet with him; however, there is no evidence to suggest that this journey was undertaken, and there is no mention of it in the Close and Patent Rolls for John's reign.[114]

On 29 October 1207 Alfonso of Aragón helped to negotiate a five year peace treaty between Alfonso of Castile and Sancho of Navarre; by 1208, Alfonso VIII realised that the situation in Gascony was neither sustainable nor resolvable, 'having gained nothing from his campaigns but depleted finances, lost time, and headaches'.[115] Therefore, he renounced his claim to Leonor's dowry, putting an end to the 'costly and futile enterprise', and focused his attentions on marshalling all the Christian kings of Spain to unite together to face the mutual threat posed by the Moors.[116] The *Crónica Latina* blames the poverty of the land and the inconstancy of the Gascon nobles – 'in whom fidelity was a rare thing' - for Alfonso's retreat, noting that although he had undertaken the campaign for love of his wife, the enterprise was like 'ploughing a stone', and, 'seeing that he could gain nothing', he freed the Gascons from their oaths of homage to him.[117]

Alfonso's renunciation of Gascony was neither formal nor definitive; nevertheless, it was not until the reign of Alfonso X that Castile renewed its claim to the county.[118] In May 1253 the premier magnate of Gascony, Gaston of Béarn, a man of dubious trustworthiness whose loyalties changed 'with every breeze, or insubstantial promise of possible gain',[119] came to Seville asking the recently crowned Alfonso to reclaim the duchy after Henry III had transferred authority over Gascony from Simon de Montfort to his young son Edward.[120] To counter the Castilian threat to his southern lands, in February 1254 Henry III of England sent ambassadors to Spain to negotiate a marriage between his son Edward and Alfonso's sister Eleanor.[121] The negotiations were finalised in March: Alfonso promised to renounce all claims to Gascony, and Henry promised in return to provide assistance against Alfonso's struggles

---

[111] Ralph Turner, *King John* (Longman, London & New York, 1994), 130; Norgate, *John Lackland*, 114.

[112] Díez, *Alfonso VIII*, 203.

[113] *Ibid.*, 204.

[114] *Ibid.*, 204.

[115] *Ibid.*, 204.

[116] *Crónica Latina*, 21-2.

[117] *Ibid.*, 44.

[118] Díez, *Alfonso VIII*, 205.

[119] Wade Labarge, *Gascony*, 19. Gaston was also related to Henry III's queen, Eleanor of Provence.

[120] Díez, *Alfonso VIII*, 206; Wade Labarge, *Gascony*, 23. De Montfort was seneschal of Gascony from 1248-53; after being granted Gascony in 1249 in what Michael Prestwich terms an 'empty formality', Edward was formally invested with the duchy in 1253, *Edward I* (Yale University Press, 1988; repr. 1997), 7-8. See also F.M. Powicke, *King Henry III and the Lord Edward* (Clarendon Press, Oxford, 1947), I, 214-36; Maurice Powicke, *The Thirteenth Century, 1216-1307* (Clarendon Press, Oxford, 1962), 110-19.

[121] Díez, *Alfonso VIII*, 206; Wade Labarge noted that negotiations for the marriage were 'well under way' by February 1254, *Gascony*, 25, although Powicke stated that they were 'begun or continued' as early as June 1152, *Thirteenth Century*, 116. See also Powicke, *Henry III*, I, 230-6. Powicke claims that Alfonso never had any intention of invading Gascony to uphold his claim to the county, but that he used this claim in order to engineer a dynastic alliance with England, *Henry III*, I, 232, 235-6.

with the kingdom of Navarre. By the end of April, Alfonso had informed Gaston of his agreement with the English king and instructed him to accept Henry and Edward as overlords of Gascony.[122] Edward arrived in Bordeaux in June, reaching Burgos by November, where he was knighted by Alfonso, and was married to Eleanor at Las Huelgas.[123] As part of the marriage treaty, Alfonso formally renounced to Edward all rights "which we have or almost have or ought to have in Gascony...by reason of the donation which was made or is said to have been made by Henry, then king of England, and his wife Leonor, to their daughter Leonor and Alfonso, king of Castile".[124] It is probable that Gascony was formally ceded as Eleanor's dowry.[125]

The conflicts over Leonor's dowry are comparable to, and indeed intertwined with, the struggles faced by Richard I's widowed queen, Berengaria of Navarre, to receive her own dower. It is to this complex process of negotiations over dower rights that this study will now turn.

---

[122] Wade Labarge, *Gascony*, 25; Powicke, *Thirteenth Century*, 118.

[123] Wade Labarge, *Gascony*, 26; Powicke, *Thirteenth Century*, 118. Edward and Eleanor returned to Gascony at the end of November, where they remained for almost a year, Prestwich, *Edward I*, 10, 14.

[124] González, *Alfonso VIII*, I, 188n. See also *Foedera*, I.i, 310.

[125] Díez, *Alfonso VIII*, 206.

Chapter Three
Competing Queens and Conflicting Claims

Berengaria of Navarre

At the time of their marriage, Richard I had promised to endow Berengaria with 'the traditional dower of English queens', which included lands and castles in England, Normandy, Maine and Touraine, but as this was still held by Eleanor of Aquitaine, Richard bestowed on Berengaria instead a temporary dower comprising the lands he held in Gascony, which was to be hers in the event of his death.[1] The dower granted Berengaria revenues from the Gascon lands, but not the rights of lordship which had been allotted by Henry II as dowry to his daughter Leonor on her marriage to Alfonso VIII.[2] On the death of her mother Eleanor of Aquitaine, Leonor was to recover the entirety of the Gascon inheritance, whilst Berengaria would inherit the 'dower of the Queens of England', in other words, all that Eleanor had held as dowry from Henry II, which were those lands in England, Normandy and Poitou which Richard had confirmed her rights to on his accession.[3] This "traditional dower" comprised Falaise, Domfront, and Bonneville-sur-Touques in Normandy, Loches and Montbazon in Touraine, Château-du-Loir in Maine, Mervent, Jaunay and Oléron in Poitou, and twenty-six towns, castles, manors, honours and fiefs in England, spread over thirteen counties.[4]

When Richard died, however, John withheld Berengaria's dower lands, and bestowed them instead on his own queen, Isabella of Angoulême. On 30 August 1200, John endowed his queen with Saintes, Niort, Saumur, La Flèche, Beaufort, Baugé, Château-du-Loir and Troo.[5] Moreover, he refused to leave to Berengaria her share of the treasure and moveable goods of the late king.[6] To further compound the situation, her brother, Sancho VII of Navarre, was withholding the castles of Rocabruna and Saint-Jean-Pied-de-Port, which had been given to

---

[1] Cloulas, 'Douaire', 89; see also Trindade, *Berengaria*, 143, 151; Gillingham, 'Richard and Berengaria', 161-2; Vincent, 'John's Jezebel', 185-6. As dowry, Berengaria brought to the marriage a mere two castles in the Pyrenees, Saint-Jean-Pied-de-Port and Rocabruna. See Trindade, *Berengaria*, 150.

[2] Cloulas, 'Douaire', 90.

[3] *Ibid.*, 90; Gillingham, 'Richard and Berengaria', 161-2. For the charter, given at Limassol on 12 May 1191, see Edmond Martène and Ursini Durand, *Veterum scriptorum et Monumentorum historicorum, dogmaticorum, moralium, amplissima collectio*, I (Paris, 1724), 995-7.

[4] The manors of Ilchester and Marston in Somerset; the manors of Riseholme, Brascote and North Luffenham in Rutland; the manor of Lambourn in Berkshire; Wilton and Malmesbury in Wiltshire; the honour of Arundel and the town of Chichester in Sussex; the demesne of Stanton in Oxfordshire; Rockingham and the demesne of Northampton in Northamptonshire; the manors of Kenton, Lifton, and Alverdiscott, with the demesnes of Salcombe and Kenn and the town of Exeter in Devon; the manor of *Wiflinton* in Hampshire; the honour of Berkhampsted in Hertfordshire; the manor of Walthamstow in Essex; Queenhithe in London; Grantham and the demesne of Stamford in Lincolnshire; and the honour of Berkeley in Gloucestershire, Cloulas, 'Douaire', 90-1.

[5] Vincent, 'John's Jezebel', 185; Cloulas, 'Douaire', 91. The charter of Isabella's dower settlement is published in *Rotuli Chartarum*, 128. For more on Isabella's dower, and comparisons over her use of her dower resources with that of Eleanor of Aquitaine, Vincent, 'John's Jezebel', 184-93; see also 207-9 for Isabella's efforts to claim her dower rights after John's death.

[6] Cloulas, 'Douaire', 89, 91; Vincent, 'John's Jezebel', 186.

Berengaria as dowry by her father Sancho VI.[7] Berengaria sought refuge for a time with her sister Blanche, who had married Count Theobald of Champagne on 1 July 1199.[8] John's marriage to Isabella, however, gave Berengaria the pretext she needed to recover her rights. On 28 March 1201, John issued Berengaria a safe conduct to journey to England, and with papal support Berengaria obtained recognition of her rights.[9] By way of compensation for her dower, John offered Berengaria lands in Anjou and Normandy along with an annual stipend, and on 2 August 1201 she was granted an annual rent of one thousand silver marks. Approximately 150 livres Angevins was immediately to be taken on the incomes of the prévôté of Segré in Anjou, which was not included in the original charter of dower granted by Richard but was offered by John as recompense for those of her lands which were now held by Philip of France. Half of the remainder would be paid by the exchequer of Caen in the week following Michaelmas, and the other half in the week following Easter.[10]

The terms of the settlement were ratified by and communicated to Berengaria in a letter from Innocent III, dated 1201.[11] Berengaria also received from John the city of Bayeux and two castles in Anjou to hold for the duration of her lifetime.[12] However, it took some twenty years for John's promise of remuneration for Berengaria's dower to be realised.[13] When war between England and France erupted once more in 1202, despite the Treaty of Le Goulet of May 1200, whereby it was agreed that Philip Augustus' son Louis was to marry John's niece (and Berengaria's cousin) Blanca of Castile, John's resources could not stretch to keeping the promises made to Berengaria.[14]

After the death of Eleanor of Aquitaine in 1204, John endowed Isabella with the "traditional dowry" of English queens. The places listed on the charter given at Porchester on 5 May are the same as those enumerated on Richard's charter of dower given at Limassol on his marriage to Berengaria.[15] Berengaria appealed to the pope, and in January 1204 Innocent III accordingly ordered the matter of Berengaria's outstanding payments to be addressed, charging the abbots of Casamari, Marmoutiers and Vierzon to threaten John with ecclesiastical sanctions if he did not uphold his former promises to the widowed queen.[16] However, 'despite a steady stream of papal admonitions, instructions to churchmen entrusted with monitoring the agreements and hypocritical prevarications from John, no money changed hands'.[17] Berengaria should have received the "queens' dower" in March 1204 on the death of Eleanor of Aquitaine, but these lands, with the exception of Domfront and Falaise, were under French control by this time; the rest had already been transferred to Isabella of Angoulême.

---

[7] Cloulas, 'Douaire', 90.

[8] At which marriage Berengaria was present, Cloulas, 'Douaire', 91n; Vincent, 'John's Jezebel', 188n.

[9] Cloulas, 'Douaire', 91.

[10] *Ibid.*, 91; Trindade, *Berengaria*, 151. John's charter is now lost, but his letter to his bankers summarise the terms and is preserved in *Foedera*, I, 84.

[11] Trindade, *Berengaria*, 151.

[12] Howden, *Chronica*, IV, 172-3.

[13] Trindade, *Berengaria*, 145; 150.

[14] Cloulas, 'Douaire', 92.

[15] *Ibid.*; Vincent, 'John's Jezebel', 186-8; see also *Foedera*, I.1, 86, 88; *Rotuli Chartarum*, 213-4.

[16] *RHGF*, XIX, 447; see also Cloulas, 'Douaire', 92.

[17] Trindade, *Berengaria*, 151.

Berengaria accordingly appealed to Philip Augustus for restitution of her rights in Dom-front, Falaise, and Bonneville-sur-Touques, coming to Paris in January 1204.[18] Philip granted her authority over Loches; the following August or September, she concluded a transaction with Philip whereby she exchanged the three castles and towns she held in Normandy for one thousand marks sterling and the town of Le Mans, which granted her lordship over the town and outskirts (which consisted of approximately thirty parishes), from which she was entitled to tithes and rents.[19] Berengaria was able to appoint her own choice of seneschal, although she recognised the French king as her feudal overlord.[20]

Berengaria clearly took her role as Lady of Le Mans seriously, presiding over duels, arbitrating in disputes, and heading major church processions, such as the Palm Sunday procession in 1223.[21] She was a notable benefactor of churches and religious houses in Le Mans, making donations to the cathedral chapter of St Julien, to the abbeys of La Couture and Coëffort, and to the new orders of Franciscans and Dominicans; as well as, notably, to the collegial church of St Pierre.[22] Her authority, however, was not unchallenged. Her attachment to St Pierre led to her embroilment in the near-constant conflicts between the church and St Julien, and the chapter and various bishops of Le Mans made frequent challenges to her authority in the county.[23] Berengaria ceased to use her titles of duchess of Normandy and countess of Anjou from the time she became "Lady of Le Mans", although she continued to style herself as 'most humble former queen of England' (*humilissima regina quondam Anglorum*) in letters and charters until her death.[24]

The exchange of Le Mans for Berengaria's Norman holdings was a politically shrewd move on Philip's part, as it further consolidated his hold over Normandy. The revenues from Le Mans, however, were insufficient for the maintenance of Berengaria's household, and she was left 'virtually penniless'.[25] In 1213, Berengaria's envoys arrived in England to oversee the transfer of funds which John had promised in 1201; however, as a letter from John to Berengaria, dated 1215, testifies, payments had still not been made by this date.[26] In September, John agreed to pay 'two thousand marks including arrears and a further one thousand pounds sterling in two instalments', as well as granting her a safe conduct to his domains; although there is no evidence that she was planning to undertake such a journey, Ann Trindade believes that she 'may have considered passing through those territories in the south still nominally

---

[18] Cloulas, 'Douaire', 92-3. Dunbabin has noted that Philip's aggressive interventionist policies 'seemed a decisive break with earlier Capetian trends. Yet Philip's methods were those of his father and grandfather; and although he had a clearer notion of feudal lordship and a broader canvas on which to exploit that lordship, even here he drew on his predecessors' achievements', *France in the Making*, 267. From his reign onwards began the sovereignty of the French kings over all territorial princes of the realm, see Dunbabin, *France in the Making*, 378-9.
[19] *Veterum Scriptorum*, 1045-7; *Recueil des Actes de Philippe Auguste, Roi de France*, in *Chartes et Diplômes relatifs à l'Histoire de France*, VI, 6 vols., ed. M.H.-François Delaborde (Paris, 1916-79), VI.2, 416, no. 837; see also Cloulas, 'Douaire', 93; Trindade, *Berengaria*, 146; Vincent, 'John's Jezebel', 188.
[20] Her choice of seneshal was Herbert de Tucé, Trindade, *Berengaria*, 146.
[21] Trindade, *Berengaria*, 161, 171.
[22] *Ibid.*, 172.
[23] See *ibid.*, 162-72.
[24] *Ibid.*, 147. Two of Berengaria's letters survive, both of which refer to her lack of compensation for her dower. They are preserved in the Public Record Office in London and have been translated and published by Anne Crawford, *Letters of the Queens of England*, 46-7. In both of these letters, Berengaria styles herself as the 'humble former queen of England'. Berengaria's letter of 1220, to the bishop of Winchester, is one of the earliest original extant letters of an English queen.
[25] Trindade, *Berengaria*, 151-2.
[26] *Ibid.*, 152.

held by England, perhaps on the way to Spain'.[27] Yet in 1216, John wrote to his "dearest sister" Berengaria, explaining that the monies could not be paid as the wars with France had depleted his finances.[28] Thus, despite continued papal support for the payment of her dower monies, the issue was not resolved until the reign of John's son and heir Henry III. In 1218, Innocent's successor Honorius III promised Berengaria his full support in the matter of her outstanding dower monies, and four years later, Henry III finally settled the outstanding debt of four thousand, five hundred pounds sterling, paying in instalments over a five-year period.[29]

At the same time as Berengaria became Lady of Le Mans, John was facing another claim, that of the dowry of his sister Leonor. Alfonso VIII considered that Berengaria, having received compensation, no longer had any rights to the incomes of the Gascon strongholds allotted in dowry to his wife by Henry II, and invaded Gascony; to regulate this dispute, Berengaria and Leonor both decided to go to England in the spring of 1206 and obtained a royal safe conduct with this intention.[30] Ivan Cloulas suggests that the friendship between the two cousins was renewed at this time, and in her later years Berengaria also benefited from the support of Leonor's daughter Blanca, who was Berengaria's niece.[31] Blanca's husband Louis VIII also intervened for Berengaria over the issue of her dower; in a charter of May 1230 he confirmed, at her request, donations made to the Cistercian abbey of La Piété-Dieu [L'Epau], which she had founded near Le Mans, and where she was buried after her death on 23 December 1230.[32]

Margaret of France

The issues of a royal woman's dower and dowry clearly presented problems once the motive for the bestowal of these lands had been rendered redundant. A further example of this from the Angevin family circle is the case of Margaret, daughter of Louis VII of France, who was betrothed as an infant to Henry the Young King in 1158. Thomas Becket had been sent to Paris in the summer of 1158 to confirm the agreement, and the following September Henry II journeyed to Paris to collect both Louis' guarantees and his infant daughter, as stipulated by the betrothal promises.[33] Louis accompanied them as far as Mantes, where the six-month-old Margaret was given to the custody of Robert of Newburgh, steward and justiciar of Nor-

---

[27] *Ibid.*, 152. Berengaria may have planned a trip to her home of Navarre in 1219. In that year, Henry III granted a safe conduct to "Queen Berengaria and all whom she may take with her to travel, if she so wishes, through the territories of Poitou and Gascony to Spain, both departing and returning", although 'No information is given as to the purpose of the request for a safe-conduct, and we do not know whether the journey was ever made', Trindade, *Berengaria*, 178. Trindade suggests that Berengaria may have been seeking the support of her brother, Sancho VII, in the matter of her outstanding dower payments – while this may be a possibility, there is no evidence to support this and Berengaria's motives must remain a matter of speculation, Trindade, *Berengaria*, 178. In 1220, Henry issued a further decree allowing Berengaria's envoys safe passage through his lands to Navarre: "going from her to the king of Navarre her brother and from that king to the queen, with messages, to travel safely through his territory", Trindade, *Berengaria*, 178. See also *Patent Rolls of the Reign of Henry III*, I, 1216-1225 (Public Record Office, London, 1901), I, 189, 228-9.

[28] Trindade, *Berengaria*, 152.

[29] *Ibid.*, 153. For references to Berengaria's dower payments, see *Patent Rolls of Henry III*, I, 73, 179, 243-5, 253-4, 265, 292.

[30] Cloulas, 'Douaire', 93. See also *Foedera*, I.1, 94.

[31] Cloulas, 'Douaire', 93.

[32] *Ibid.*, 93-4.

[33] Lindsay Diggelmann, 'Marriage as a Tactical Response: Henry II and the Royal Wedding of 1160', *English Historical Review* 119 no. 483 (September 2004), 965; see also Torigni, 196; Diceto, I, 303-4.

mandy. Louis' conditions were that the Vexin should not pass to Henry's control until the wedding was realised, and that Margaret should not be placed in Eleanor's household, as would have been customary, but in Normandy near the French border.[34]

Margaret's dower was promised as the city of Lincoln, 1000 pounds, and 300 knights' fees in England, as well as the city of Avranches, two castles, 1000 pounds, and 200 knights' fees in Normandy.[35] Her dowry was to be comprised of the castles of Gisors, Neaufle and Châteauneuf in the Norman Vexin, a long-contested frontier zone between the Angevin and French domains.[36] These lands had been sold by Henry's father, Geoffrey of Anjou, to Louis VII of France, thus for Henry, the restoration of the Vexin to the Angevin domains, as well as the possibility that his heir might one day ascend the throne of France so long as Louis remained without a male heir, was a major coup. For Louis, the marriage served to strengthen the feudal ties binding Henry to his house, establishing what was hoped to be a permanent peace between the two warring kingdoms, and in the event that Louis should sire a son, Henry, as his kin-by-marriage, should be more inclined to support him.[37]

At this stage the proposed union was strategic, in that it represented a mutually beneficial alliance: while Henry would retain all of Margaret's dower for the period of the betrothal, with the promise of the Vexin once the marriage was completed, Louis was guaranteed peace with his more powerful neighbour, as well as providing a 'dynastic safety net'.[38] A number of factors, however, led Henry to speed the marriage to conclusion in 1160, despite the facts that the young Henry and the even younger Margaret had not given their consent to the union, and that they were related within the prohibited seven degrees. Henry's failed siege of Toulouse in 1159 had been vehemently opposed by Louis;[39] nevertheless a truce, followed by a formal peace, was established in May 1160.[40] Louis stipulated that Margaret's marriage should not take place for a minimum of three years, and that if she died within this time he would retain control of the Vexin; Henry was, however, able to add the proviso that if the Church consented to the marriage within this three-year period, the Vexin would be handed over to him immediately.[41]

Lindsay Diggelmann has suggested that as well as Henry's desire to take control of the Norman Vexin, which constituted Margaret's dower, and the pressing issue of Louis' alliance with Blois-Champagne on the death of his second wife Constance of Castile, there was also a short-term strategy behind Henry's sudden rush to marry his five-year-old heir to the three-

---

[34] Kelly, *Eleanor of Aquitaine*, 108. Later that year Louis made a pilgrimage to Mont-Saint-Michel, taking advantage of his time in Normandy to visit his daughter at Newburgh and inspect Avranches, which had been promised as her dower, Kelly, *Eleanor of Aquitaine*, 108.

[35] *RHGF*, XVI, 21-3; *Recueil des Actes de Henri II, Roi d'Angleterre et Duc de Normandie*, in *Chartes et Diplômes relatifs à l'Histoire de France*, IV, 4 vols., ed. Léopold Delisle (Paris, 1916-27 ; hereafter *RHII*), IV.1, 251-3; see also Diggelmann, 'Marriage as a Tactical Response', 956n.

[36] Diggelmann, 'Marriage as a Tactical Response', 956n. Diceto, I, 303-4, mentions only Gisors.

[37] Kelly, *Eleanor of Aquitaine*, 106.

[38] Diggelmann, 'Marriage as a Tactical Response', 956; 956n. Diggelmann defines the difference between dynastic marriages as strategic, implying a long term plan for a mutually beneficial alliance, and tactical, suggesting a reactive and confrontational response to political events, 'undertaken just as much to obstruct or counter the political programme of a rival as it was to promote one's own agenda', 955; see also Gillingham, 'Love, Marriage and Politics in the Twelfth Century', in *Forum for Modern Language Studies*, 25 (1989), 292-303.

[39] Diggelmann, 'Marriage as a Tactical Response', 956; see also Benjamin, 'Forty Years War', 270-85; Martindale, "An Unfinished Business", 115-54.

[40] For the text of this treaty, see *RHII*, IV.1, 251-3.

[41] Diggelmann, 'Marriage as a Tactical Response', 958.

year old Margaret of France.[42] Constance had died in childbirth in September 1160, and within two weeks Louis had announced his decision to marry Adela of Blois-Champagne.[43]

Henry's reaction was swift and decisive: he had Margaret married to his heir at Neubourg in Normandy on 2 November, with the complicity of two cardinal legates who had been assured of Henry's support of the new pope Alexander III, rather than the imperial anti-pope Victor IV. Henry immediately thereafter took control of the castles in the Vexin, held in lieu of the marriage by the Templars, and moved Margaret into his custody to ensure that Louis, who had been neither invited to nor informed of the proceedings, adhered to his end of the bargain.[44]

Papal dispensation had already been secured for the marriage in return for the promise to support Alexander over Victor IV, probably at the council at Beauvais in July 1160.[45] Henry had thus concealed an ace up his sleeve since July, yet did not put it into effect until the following November. In September, he ordered Eleanor to come to him in Normandy, and to bring with her the Young King, who was also in England at this time.[46] In October, the young Henry did homage to Louis for the duchy of Normandy.[47] Louis' intended marriage to Adela of Blois-Champagne seems to have been the catalyst for the hurried marriage of the two children. If Louis was able to sire a son on his new wife, who was the sister of the powerful counts of Blois and Champagne, then Henry's position would be considerably weakened. Moreover, if Margaret died, or if Louis revoked the betrothal, Henry would not regain the Vexin. Digglemann therefore believes it likely that Henry 'bargained for the clause concerning Church approval to be inserted into the agreement of May [1160], with the *deliberate intention* of seeking a dispensation, marrying the children, and regaining the Vexin at an early opportunity'.[48]

There remained, of course, the problem of consanguinity: aside from the fact that Margaret's father Louis and the young Henry's mother Eleanor had once been married to each other, Henry and Margaret were also related in the fifth and sixth degrees.[49] No dispensation had been granted concerning consanguinity, yet senior churchmen gave the match at least tacit approval: Hugh, archbishop of Rouen (who had previously attended the council called to annul the marriage of Louis and Eleanor) either approved or actually presided over the wedding of 1160.[50]

The impediment of consanguinity could still be cited as a reason to annul the match, as had occurred with Louis and Eleanor in 1152, and Digglemann suggests that Louis may have

---

[42] *Ibid.*, 954, 956-9, 961-4.

[43] *Ibid.*, 957. The marriage took place on 13 November 1160.

[44] Kelly, *Eleanor of Aquitaine*, 111; Digglemann, 'Marriage as a Tactical Response', 957. Louis expelled the three Knights Templar whom he had appointed custodians of the Vexin from France for handing the castles over to Henry so quickly, Digglemann, 'Marriage as a Tactical Response', 957n.

[45] Digglemann, 'Marriage as a Tactical Response', 957-8. The legates who granted the dispensation were Henry of Pisa, William of Pavia and Odo, cardinal deacon of S. Nicola. The letter of dispensation is recorded in *RHGF*, XV, 700-1. It makes no allowance for the issue of consanguinity, however.

[46] Digglemann, 'Marriage as a Tactical Response', 959; see also Torigni, 207.

[47] Digglemann, 'Marriage as a Tactical Response', 959.

[48] *Ibid.*, 959. My italics.

[49] The issue of Louis and Eleanor's consanguinity (they were related in the fourth and fifth degrees) was cited as the public reason for their own separation in 1152. Given the high profile of this divorce, the almost identical impediment to the marriage between Margaret and Henry must have been at the forefront of many people's minds. See Digglemann, 'Marriage as a Tactical Response', 960.

[50] Digglemann, 'Marriage as a Tactical Response', 960.

always considered this to be a back-out clause should he wish to use it.[51] His own marriage to Adela of Blois-Champagne, however, was also consanguineous: Louis' brother Philip had apparently been forced to separate from Adela's sister on this account,[52] and moreover, Louis' daughters by Eleanor were betrothed to Adela's brothers, which made Louis 'the brother-in-law of his own sons-in-law-to-be' and thereby, as Diggelmann phrases it, 'sacrificing respect for the principle of *unitas carnis* [the unity of (married) flesh] on the altar of expediency'.[53] By entering into a consanguineous marriage with Adela, Louis had provided Henry with an excuse to marry the children despite their consanguinity, leaving Louis in no position to oppose the union on these grounds.

Thus, whilst an alliance between France and Blois-Champagne made the need to recover the Vexin ever more pressing, it was the issue of consanguinity which was, in the short term, the reason for the speed of the marriage.[54] The betrothal had been strategic, but the marriage itself was tactical, confrontational and reactive;[55] and Henry's 'tactical gamble paid off handsomely'.[56]

When the Young King died in 1183, however, Philip immediately demanded the return of the Vexin as well as the continued payment of revenues from his sister's dower lands in Normandy and Anjou, declaring that Henry had promised these to Margaret in free usufruct should the Young King predecease him without heirs; he also demanded that their sister Alice finally be married to Richard, now Henry's heir. Henry responded that Louis had renounced all future claims to the Vexin when he bestowed it as Margaret's dowry, citing the claim that the Vexin was Norman by ancient hereditary right, while carefully avoiding the twin issues of Alice and of Margaret's dower.[57] At Gisors in December 1183, however, Henry performed homage to Philip in order to retain the crucially strategic Vexin, an act of political expediency similar to John's later performance of homage to Philip at Le Goulet in 1200.[58] Henry also promised to recompense Margaret for the loss of the Vexin with an annual endowment of £2750 Anjou for life,[59] although he claimed that she was not entitled to her Angevin dower as this had been granted to Eleanor of Aquitaine in lieu of her own dower when she handed over control of Poitou to Richard in 1179. It was for this reason that Eleanor was brought out of captivity to make a six months' progress, 'in company with reliable Matilda through the lands of the Angevin dower'.[60] As for Alice, he promised that if she was not married to Rich-

---

[51] *Ibid.*

[52] *Ibid.*, 960n. The sole source to record this is Diceto, I, 303.

[53] Diggelmann, 'Marriage as a Tactical Response', 961.

[54] *Ibid.*, 961.

[55] *Ibid.*, 962-3.

[56] *Ibid.*, 964. The marriages of Louis' daughters to the counts of Blois and Champagne in 1153 can also be viewed as tactical - 'possibly a response to Eleanor's remarriage to Henry II', Diggelmann, 'Marriage as a Tactical Response', 963n – as can those of Henry and Eleanor in 1152, and Henry's mother Matilda and Geoffrey of Anjou in 1128, 'largely a short-term reaction by Henry I of England to William Clito's bid for the contested comital seat of Flanders in 1127', Diggelmann, 'Marriage as a Tactical Response', 963n. The marriages of Henry's daughters can also be regarded as strategic – following the definition given by Diggelmann – in that they all brought short-term advantages to both parties.

[57] Kelly, *Eleanor of Aquitaine*, 227; Howden, *Gesta*, I, 305; *Chronica*, II, 280-1.

[58] See Gillingham, 'Doing Homage', 77-80.

[59] Howden, *Gesta*, I, 306, 343-4; *Chronica*, II, 280-1. For Margaret's charter renouncing her rights to Gisors, in which she styles herself as Margaret, "Dei gratia regina Angl[orum]", see *RHII*, IV.2, 275-7.

[60] Kelly, *Eleanor of Aquitaine*, 229.

ard, she would be married to John, prompting rumours that he intended to disinherit Richard and make his youngest son his heir.[61]

These issues concerning royal women's dowers and dowries highlight the potential problems that could occur when ownership of land was involved. This may be one of the reasons that Henry II seems to have endowed Joanna with moveable goods, rather than lands, as her dowry when she married William II of Sicily.[62] Joanna's marriage, and the contentious issues surrounding her access to her dowerlands after the death of her husband, will form the basis of the following chapter.

---

[61] *Ibid.*; see also Howden, *Chronica*, II, 363; PR 26 Henry II, 135, 206, 215. Alice was twenty-three in 1183 but still not yet married to Richard, which is surprising in light of the fact that her dowry of Bourges and its appurtances in Berry was as essential as the Vexin for securing Henry's borders. Kelly suggests that Henry was planning to divorce Eleanor and marry Alice himself, *Eleanor of Aquitaine*, 192. Alice was still unwed a decade later, having spent twenty-four years at the Plantagenet court. In late summer 1195 she was finally returned to France, where her brother Philip gave her in marriage to his vassal, William of Ponthieu, Kelly, *Eleanor of Aquitaine*, 331-2. Alice was not the only princess of France at the Angevin court to be blighted by salacious rumours. Her sister Margaret was also briefly subject to scandal; *cf.* the gossip that William the Marshal had, or had attempted to, seduce her, which was bruited abroad at the Christmas court at Caen, see Kelly, *Eleanor of Aquitaine*, 209-10.

[62] The lack of physical proximity between Sicily and the Angevin realm provides another possible reason for Joanna's cash dowry.

Chapter Four
Joanna, Queen of Sicily

On the night of 2 February 1177, Joanna arrived in Palermo with the bishop of Evreux and the other envoys who had accompanied her to Sicily. William personally met her at the city gates and escorted her to the palace which had been prepared for her to await her forthcoming marriage and coronation.[1] Howden describes the city as being lit with incomparable illuminations, and relates that Joanna was received with applause by the citizens.[2] His account of Joanna's entry in state, and her procession through the city dressed in royal robes and riding on a fine horse, give nothing away as to the fact that she was a mere girl of eleven years. This is undoubtedly due to the fact that eleven or twelve was a common age for royal and aristocratic daughters to be married and therefore provoked no comment – her sister Matilda was also twelve when she married Henry the Lion of Saxony, and Leonor was eight or nine at the time of her marriage to Alfonso of Castile.

Joanna was married to William in the royal chapel of Palermo Cathedral on 13 February 1177, a little less than a fortnight after her arrival.[3] Unusually for a twelfth-century queen, she was anointed and crowned queen of Sicily at the same ceremony, which was performed in the presence of Walter, archbishop of Palermo, as well as many leading prelates and nobles.[4] Diceto observes that the city was 'resplendent with the marriage celebrations', and that all the clergy, magnates, and people of Sicily hurried to witness the marriage and coronation of the new queen.[5] Howden merely records that the ceremony was also attended by Giles, bishop of Evreux and all the English envoys, as well as the Sicilian clergy and nobles. Having witnessed Joanna's marriage and coronation, Henry, bishop of Bayeux, Hugh de Beauchamp, Osbert, the clerk of the king's chamber, and Geoffrey de la Charre (or Charite) returned to England, arriving at Southampton in June 1177.[6]

---

[1] Norwich supposes this palace to have been the Zisa, *Kingdom in the Sun*, 310.

[2] Howden, *Gesta*, I, 157; *Chronica*, II, 95.

[3] Romuald of Salerno, *Chronicon*, 269; Howden, *Gesta*, I, 158; *Chronica*, II, 95; Diceto, I, 418.

[4] These included the archbishops Alfano of Capua, Rainaldo of Bari, Nicola of Messina, and Ruffo of Cosenza; the bishops Richard of Syracuse, Bartolomew of Agrigento (Walter of Palermo's brother), Theobald abbot of Monreale, Robert of Catania, Guido of Cefalu, Elias elect of Troia (who had been part of the embassy sent to negotiate the marriage), Tustino of Mazzara, Robert of Tricarico, and Giovanni of Potenza; the counts Robert of Caserta, Alfonso of Squillace, Jocelin of Loritello, Hugo of Catanzaro, Riccardo of Fondi, and Robert Malcovenant; and the 'maggiorenti' of the court: Matthew of Ajello, Walter de Moac, Alduin the seneschal, Bernard the constable, Richard the logothete, Rainaldo de Monteforte Master Justiciar, and Perisco and Federico, justiciars of the Magna Regis Curia, Romuald of Salerno, *Chronicon*, 269n.

[5] Diceto, I, 418. The marriage certificate was signed by Theobald, first bishop of Monreale, Demus, *Mosaics of Norman Sicily*, 150-1.

[6] Eyton, *Itinerary*, 215. Osbert the clerk is also found as witness to the Treaty of Falaise concluded between Henry II and William the Lion of Scotland in 1175, Howden, *Gesta*, I, 99. Osbert was the father of William fitz Osbert, to whom he left property in London on his death in 1185/6. William enjoyed the favour of King Richard and attained a governmental post, but in 1196 he led a mob of Londoners protesting over taxes; after his capture he was arrested and hanged. He appears in William of Newburgh, who is hostile to the insurgent, and also in Matthew Paris, who views him as a hero and martyr. See Derek Keene, 'William fitz Osbert, d. 1196', *DNB*.

William and Joanna were both crowned (*se et eam gloriose coronari fecit*) immediately after the marriage ceremony was performed.[7] For William, this was his second coronation, having been crowned king two days after his father's death in May 1166. For Joanna, this ritual set her apart from most of her female contemporaries, as whilst twelfth-century queens were sometimes – but not always – crowned, they were not usually anointed with holy chrism, thereby reflecting their subordinate status to the king. That Joanna was anointed suggests a parity of authority in the Sicilian monarchical regime, although as will be seen, this was illusory, and the ritual was designed and performed to enhance Joanna's status as consort and prospective progenitrix rather than as a co-regnant queen. Nevertheless, this double coronation is the only one we can positively attest to in Sicily under the Norman kings, and an ordo survives from late twelfth-century Palermo outlining a double coronation.[8] The Palermo manuscript outlines two successive ceremonies, and has been attributed to the double coronation of William and Joanna in 1177, although Leon Ménager has noted various similarities with German coronation ordines and therefore attributes it to the double coronation of the Emperor Henry VI and his queen Constance on Christmas Day 1194.[9]

Coronation ordines from eleventh century Sicily and thirteenth century France and England display clear similarities in the style, formulae, prayers, and order of ceremony.[10] It is probable that the coronation ceremony of William and Joanna in 1177 followed a comparable model, where William, as the king, was the main focus of the ritual, and Joanna's part, as consort, came towards the end of the ceremony. This nevertheless does not imply that her participation was a mere afterthought; contrarily her role as queen and provider of future heirs was of the greatest dynastic importance, as stressed in William's settlement of dower.

Moreover, as this was William's second coronation it is feasible that his own part in the ceremony may have been considerably shorter than that prescribed in contemporary French and English and earlier Sicilian ordines, marking less a rite of passage than a reiteration of royal supremacy and a public display of ceremony. The principle of hereditary kingship had been a custom in Norman Sicily since William's grandfather Roger II became the first Norman king and nominated his eldest son as *rex designatus* to ensure smooth transition of the crown.[11] William II's position as sole heir to his father William I meant that he was already expected to succeed to the throne after his father's death; his speedy coronation shortly thereafter, arranged by his mother Margaret of Navarre within days of his father's passing, constituted the true confirmation of his change in status from prince of the realm to king.

---

[7] Romuald of Salerno, *Chronicon*, 269. My italics.

[8] MS. Casatan. 614, Biblioteca Casanatense, Rome, cited in L.-R. Ménager, *Hommes et Institutions de l'Italie Normande* (Variorum Reprints, 1981), Part II, 457. I have not had the opportunity to consult this manuscript. See also Romuald of Salerno, *Chronicon*, 269.

[9] Ménager, *Hommes et Institutions*, Part II, 457. A useful comparison of this ordo with that of the 1130 coronation of Roger II, the first Norman king of Sicily, has been made by Reinhard Elze, 'The Ordo for the Coronation of King Roger II of Sicily: An Example of Dating from Internal Evidence', in János M. Bak (ed.), *Coronations – Medieval and Early Modern Monarchic Ritual* (University of California Press, 1990), 165-78.

[10] For English coronation ordines, Binski, *Westminster Abbey*, 128-38; and for thirteenth century French coronation ordines, see Jean-Claude Bonne, 'The Manuscript of the Ordo of 1250 and Its Illuminations', in *Coronations*, 58-71; Jacques Le Goff, 'A Coronation Program for the Age of Saint Louis: The Ordo of 1250', in *ibid.*, 46-57; and Ralph Giesey, 'Inaugural Aspects of French Royal Ceremonials', in *ibid.*, 35-45.

[11] Roger II designated his son William as the heir apparent on 8 April 1151, in a ceremony at which all the nobles of the realm swore fealty to William. From this date William's name always appeared alongside his father's on royal diplomas, see Chalandon, *Domination Normande*, II, 624.

Joanna, on the other hand, became queen of Sicily only on her marriage to William, and her coronation immediately after the marriage ceremony served to confirm the new status conferred on her by that marriage. In terms of rites of passage, therefore, it is only Joanna who can truly be said to have gone through such a ritual transformation in the double coronation ceremony in 1177. She entered the cathedral of Palermo as an Angevin princess, and left it as the crowned and anointed queen of Sicily.[12]

Joanna's Dower Settlement

William bestowed on his new wife a substantial dower, and we know what this constituted, as Howden recorded William's charter of settlement in full in both the *Gesta* and the *Chronica*. A copy of the charter had arrived in England with the return of Henry II's envoys in June 1177.[13] Howden records that these envoys included Hugh de Beauchamp, Geoffrey of Charre, Osbert the royal clerk, and Henry, bishop of Bayeux, and notes that these men had been present at Joanna's marriage and coronation.[14] Clearly these men had also been part of the embassy that had travelled to Sicily with Joanna, although of these four only Hugh de Beauchamp was mentioned in the account of her journey.

In both the *Gesta* and the *Chronica*, immediately after the account of the marriage and coronation, Howden states that Joanna's dower consisted of the county of Saint Angelo and the towns of Siponto and Vieste, and 'many other places and castles'.[15] The copy of William's charter, dated Palermo, February 1177, appears much later in the *Gesta*, presumably when it was brought to Howden's knowledge with the return of the English ambassadors in June. In the later *Chronica*, the charter is inserted immediately after the account of Joanna's marriage and coronation, and includes a reproduction of William's seal, not found in the *Gesta*. The two reproductions of the charter are almost identical, having only negligible differences in the spelling of some proper names, all of which are easily recognisable despite the variant renderings.[16]

Diceto does not mention Joanna's dower settlement, although it is reproduced by Gervase, with full witness list.[17] The text and witness list are identical to that in Howden, and it is possible that Gervase saw a copy of the charter brought back by Richard, archbishop of Canterbury, who had accompanied Joanna on her journey to Sicily. Her marriage to William, however, is not recorded in his *Chronicle*, and merits merely a sentence in his *Gesta Regum*.[18] Torigni also includes a reproduction of William's charter, placed soon after the record of William's petition of marriage (under the year 1177).[19] The marriage itself, however, is not noted.

---

[12] This 'double coronation' presents an interesting parallel with the crown-wearing of the Young King and coronation of his wife Margaret in 1172.

[13] The full text of William's charter is reprinted in both the *Gesta* and the *Chronica*; however, only the *Chronica* includes a reproduction of William's seal. See Howden, *Gesta*, I, 169-72; *Chronica*, II, 95-8. Romuald of Salerno makes no mention of Joanna's dower whatsoever.

[14] Howden, *Gesta*, I, 167. This does not appear in the *Chronica*.

[15] Howden, *Gesta*, I, 158; *Chronica*, II, 95. It also included 'a golden chair for her use', Jamison, 'England and Sicily', 30. This was one of the items which Richard I later demanded from Tancred of Lecce (see below).

[16] Presumably these variations are the result of slight errors by subsequent copyists; it is likely that Howden simply transcribed the original charter into his updated *Chronica*.

[17] Gervase, I, 263-5.

[18] Gervase, II, 82.

[19] Torigni, 278. Joanna's birth, her marriage to William, and the birth of a son named Bohemond mark her only three appearances in Torigni's chronicle.

Torigni's copy of William's charter is in a much abbreviated form, and does not include a witness list, but it does contain the important information of what Joanna was given as dower.

William's charter of settlement first discusses the holy sacrament of marriage before highlighting Joanna's prestigious lineage – she is 'of excellent royal blood, the most illustrious daughter of Henry, the magnificent king of the English', and as such she is a worthy match for the king of Sicily.[20] What follows in the charter is revealing of what Joanna's role and function as queen of Sicily is expected to be: William hopes for an heir to his kingdom from 'so noble and illustrious an alliance', and it is hoped that 'her fidelity and chaste affection may produce...a royal offspring [who] may, by the gift of God, hereafter succeed us in the kingdom'.[21] This emphasis on providing an heir is reiterated when William states that Joanna's dower is granted under certain conditions, namely, that she 'shall always recognise all the rights of our heirs...and shall do unto our said heirs, fully and unreservedly, all services for the tenements above-written, according as the tenure in fee thereof shall require, and shall always observe her fealty to them'.[22] In other words, the service due from the lands granted as Joanna's dower was to be at William's – rather than Joanna's – use until such time as an heir was provided.

Despite its conditional nature, William bestowed on Joanna, 'our wife, the before-named dearest queen' a dowry befitting her position, comprising the entire county of Mont Sant' Angelo in Apulia, and the cities of Siponto and Vieste, 'with all their rightful holdings and lands pertaining to them'.[23] She was also to hold Lesina, Peschici, Biccari, *Caprile*, and *Filizi*, formerly held by Count Godfrey of Lesina, 'and all other places which the said count is known to possess as of the honour of the said county of Mont Saint Angelo'.[24] Furthermore, she was given Candela, *Saint Clair*, Castelpagano, *Bersenza*, and Cagnano Varano, as well as the monasteries of Saint Mary de Pulsano and Saint John de Lama, 'with all the holdings which those monasteries hold of the honour of the before-named county of Saint Angelo'.[25] Joanna's control over these monasteries is open to question. Lack of any record of Joanna's patronage, in the form of extant charters et cetera, means that it is impossible to ascertain whether she had, for example, the right of appointments, or whether she was considered to be some form of secular abbess. There is no evidence to suggest that she was as active a religious patron as was her mother-in-law, Margaret of Navarre, who had refounded the monastery of Santa Maria di Maniace as a Benedictine abbey in 1173, and who was later involved in her son's establishment of Monreale.[26] Neither is there any evidence that Joanna was considered to be the primary patron of the monasteries in her dowerlands, as her sister Matilda, duchess of Saxony, appears to have been at Hildesheim.[27] It is possible that the restrictive terms under which Joanna held her dower limited her role in such activities, although as I have come across no other cases of

[20] Howden, *Gesta*, I, 170; *Chronica*, II, 96; Gervase, I, 264.

[21] Howden, *Gesta*, I, 170; *Chronica*, II, 96; Gervase, I, 264. Trans. Henry Riley, *The Annals of Roger de Hoveden. Comprising the History of England and of Other Countries of Europe from A.D. 732 to A.D. 1201*, ed. and trans. Henry T. Riley, 2 Vols (H.G. Bohn, London, 1853), I, 414.

[22] Howden, *Gesta*, I, 170; *Chronica*, II, 96; Gervase, I, 264. Trans. Riley, *Annals*, I, 414. Torigni does not include the references to the begetting of heirs nor the conditions under which Joanna was to hold her dower lands in his transcription of William's charter.

[23] Howden, *Gesta*, I, 170; *Chronica*, II, 96; Gervase, I, 263; Torigni, 278.

[24] Howden, *Gesta*, I, 170; *Chronica*, II, 96; Gervase, I, 263-4; Torigni, 278. Trans. Riley, *Annals*, I, 414. See also Romuald, *Chronicon*, 269n.

[25] Howden, *Gesta*, I, 170; *Chronica*, II, 96; Gervase, I, 264; Torigni, 278.

[26] For more on Margaret of Navarre's patronage, see below. For her involvement in the foundation of Monreale, see Part IV.

[27] For more on Matilda's patronage, see Part IV.

queenly dower held in usufruct for their sons in order to make comparisons, this conclusion is naturally a tentative one.

Fig. 2: Joanna's dowerlands. Filizi, Saint Clair, Bersenza and Caprile cannot now be located, although these may have been small holdings even in the twelfth century. Alternatively, they may have been the names of Count Godfrey's manors. As the rest of Joanna's dowerlands were located in Apulia, it is unlikely that Caprile equates to Capriglia, near Naples.

The charter outlining Joanna's dower settlement was drawn up at Palermo on the day of her marriage to William, in the presence of Walter, archbishop of Palermo, the king's vice-chancellor Matthew of Ajello, and Richard Palmer, bishop of Syracuse, who had met Joanna in Toulouse and had accompanied her and her entourage from France to Sicily. The witnesses attesting the charter are all drawn from the Sicilian aristocracy and high clergy, with the archbishop of Palermo heading the list. Elias, elect of Troia, who had been one of William's envoys in 1176 also appears, as does Alfano, archbishop of Capua, another of the men who had greeted Joanna in Toulouse. Of the other members of clergy, the archbishops of Bari, Messina, and Cosenza appear with the bishops of Agrigento, Catania, Cefalu, Mazaren, Tricarico, Galeta, and Potenza. Bishop Theobald, abbot of the newly-created royal monastery of

135

Monreale, appears near the top of the witness list. Count Florius, however, who had been one of the Sicilian envoys in 1176 does not appear, nor do any of the English ambassadors, despite the fact that they were in Palermo to witness Joanna's marriage and coronation. The charter, sealed with William II's royal seal, explicitly stresses the importance of the dynastic alliance between William and Joanna, and emphasises her expected function as progenitrix.[28]

It is, therefore, noteworthy that Joanna's dower lands were located in Apulia, which seems to have been a traditional "apanage" for the eldest son of the Sicilian monarch. The tradition of styling the eldest son as duke of Apulia had been instituted by Roger II, and his successors all followed this practice. From the reign of Roger II onwards, the sons of the king were given royal towns to be held in fief, and were given the title of prince, the eldest being titled Prince of Apulia, and the others princes of Capua or Taranto – if one died, another would receive his title.[29] Roger II had treated his bastards as legitimate children, endowing his natural son Simon as Prince of Taranto, although this custom was revoked by William I who stated that the principalities of Capua and Taranto and the duchy of Apulia were to be reserved solely for legitimate sons of the king.[30] William I, however, did not give the title of Duke of Apulia to his son William after the death of his elder son Roger, although he named William as his heir on his deathbed. William II succeeded without difficulty, and Torigni tells us that a son named Bohemond was born to William and Joanna in c.1181, and was styled Duke of Apulia.[31] It is, therefore, highly significant that all of the dower lands bestowed on Joanna at the time of her marriage seem to have lain in this region, rather than being widely scattered lands which were more commonly allotted to queens elsewhere in Europe, such as the dower portion given to her sister Leonor in Castile.

Joanna's dower was clearly substantial, offering revenues of far greater worth than the dowry she apparently brought to the marriage, which seems to have consisted primarily of money. This suggests that William considered Joanna to be descended from a lineage which not merely equalled but surpassed his own. She was the daughter of the great Henry II, arguably the most powerful monarch in Europe, and as such deserved to be honoured with a dower befitting her rank and status. The lands, however, were bestowed on Joanna conditionally, to be held in usufruct until such time as William's hoped-for heir came of age. The lack of any such heir meant that Joanna's position as queen was one that was entirely dependent on her husband, especially in terms of personal finance.

This marks Joanna's experience as very different from most queen-consorts in Europe, and places her in sharp contrast with her own mother Eleanor, who continued to collect "Queen's Gold" during the reigns of her sons, Richard and John, despite the fact that these dues should rightfully have belonged to their own queens.[32] Joanna's childlessness, then, not only meant

---

[28] For a reproduction of William's seal, Howden, *Chronica*, II, 98.

[29] William I, the third son of Roger II, was created prince of Taranto; on the death of his brother Alfonso he became duke of Naples and prince of Capua.

[30] For the above information, Chalandon, *Domination Normande*, II, 623-4; see also Donald Matthew, *The Norman Kingdom of Sicily* (CUP, 1992), 165-6. The king also had the right to designate ministers in case of minority, as did William I when granting the regency to his queen Margaret, designating ministers to assist with the regency government.

[31] Torigni, 303. Tancred of Lecce continued the tradition of designating his eldest son duke of Apulia, Chalandon, *Domination Normande*, II, 624. For more on Bohemond, see Part V.

[32] For more on Eleanor and Queen's Gold, see Kristen Geaman, "Queen's Gold and Intercession: The Case of Eleanor of Aquitaine" in *Medieval Feminist Forum* 46, no. 2 (2010), 10-33. For Eleanor's continued receipt of Queen's Gold, see also Ralph Turner, 'Eleanor of Aquitaine in the Governments of Her Sons Richard and John', in *Eleanor of Aquitaine: Lord and Lady*, ed. Bonnie Wheeler and John Carmi Parsons (New York: Palgrave MacMillan, 2002),

that she was unable to exert influence through control of her offspring, as her sister Leonor did so ably, it also restricted her power and authority as queen in a very tangible, financial way. If Torigni was correct in stating that a son named Bohemond was born to William and Joanna in or around 1181, this son clearly did not survive infancy, as he does not appear in any other contemporary sources, and when William died unexpectedly in 1189, Joanna was left a vulnerable – and childless – widow, without even the resources of her dowerlands to support her.

The Crisis of 1189 and the Problem of Joanna's Dower

After the accounts of her marriage and dower settlement, Joanna disappears from Howden and the other Angevin chronicles until the arrival in Sicily of Richard I, en route to the Holy Land, in September 1190. When William II died unexpectedly in 1189, the kingdom of Sicily was left facing a succession crisis. With no surviving children of his own, William had designated his aunt Constance as his heir, and the Sicilian magnates had reputedly sworn under oath to recognise her as such.[33] Tancred of Lecce, however, an illegitimate kinsman of William, had usurped the throne in contravention of this oath and had, moreover, taken custody of Joanna as well as of her dower.[34] Immediately upon his arrival on Sicily on 23 September, Richard sent envoys to Tancred demanding his sister's release, which was secured on 25 September. On 28 September Joanna arrived in Messina, where she was reunited with her brother, before being lodged in the hospital of St John.[35] The following day she was visited by Philip Augustus, who rejoiced to see her, and according to Howden may have made a proposal of marriage at this time.[36]

On 1 October Joanna was lodged in Bagnara in Calabria, which Richard had subdued the previous day. He left her with a large number of knights and men before returning to Messina.[37] Whilst no maids are mentioned as having been with Joanna at this time, it is beyond doubt that she would have retained her own ladies, who would also presumably have been

---

78-9; and Lois Huneycutt, 'Alianora Regina Anglorum: Eleanor of Aquitaine and her Anglo-Norman Predecessors as Queens of England', in *ibid.*, 127.

[33] Norwich, *Kingdom in the Sun*, 356; although Donald Matthew doubts that such oaths were in fact made, noting that all sources which report this were written after William's death and may not be reliable on this matter, *Norman Kingdom*, 275, 286. Tancred's election as king was immediately supported by and ratified by Pope Clement III, who feared the prospect of German imperial domains encircling papal territory. See also Walter Frölich, 'The Marriage of Henry VI and Constance of Sicily: Prelude and Consequences', *Anlgo-Norman Studies*, XV (1992), 99-115.

[34] See Howden, *Gesta*, II, 101-2; *Chronica*, III, 29. The author of the *Itinerarium Peregrinorum* also records that Tancred was keeping Joanna in his custody and that he was withholding her dower, but does not refer to any usurpation, noting merely that Tancred succeeded William to the throne, *IP*, 154. Similarly, Diceto, II, 73, notes that William '*absque legitima sobole moriens, Tancredum genere sibi propinquum habuit successorem regni*'. John Julius Norwich has suggested that Joanna was retained in custody because Tancred believed her to be 'a partisan of Constance' and that he feared 'her influence in the kingdom', *Kindgom in the Sun*, 367. If this assessment is correct, it suggests much about the power and influence Joanna may have had as queen, as well as being indicative of her popularity amongst the Sicilian natives. However, the fact that both Joanna and Berengaria visited Sicily on their return from the Holy Land, and were welcomed and suitably entertained by Tancred, suggests that he had not treated her harshly whilst she was his hostage, and that relations between them were at least civil; see Norwich, *Kingdom in the Sun*, 380.

[35] Howden, *Gesta*, II, 126; *Chronica*, III, 55; Diceto, II, 85.

[36] Howden, *Chronica*, III, 56; *Gesta*, II, 126. The *Continuation of William of Tyre* also reports Joanna's great joy at seeing her brother, as well as the joyous family reunion that occurred when Eleanor of Aquitaine arrived with Berengaria, *La Continuation de Guillaume de Tyr (1184-1197)*, ed. and trans. Margaret Ruth Morgan (Paris, 1982), 104, 113.

[37] Howden, *Gesta*, II, 127; *Chronica*, III, 56; Diceto, II, 85.

with her when she was in Tancred's custody. It is unclear how long Joanna was at Bagnara; she is not mentioned as being with Richard at Messina for Christmas 1190, although it is probable that she was with her brother at this time.[38]

It might be expected that, once Joanna's release had been secured, she would then have gained full access to her dower and its associated revenue. Indeed, much of Howden's account of Richard's exploits on Sicily concerns his negotiations and eventual treaty with Tancred regarding Joanna's dower, and these wrangles demonstrate how vast Joanna's holdings were in terms of wealth.[39] Tancred had clearly been withholding Joanna's dowerlands because they provided the crown with a valuable income, and he continued to hold these lands and their associated revenues after Joanna's release. Richard would have had access to the full terms of Joanna's dower provision from a copy of William's charter of settlement, and it is probable that he had a copy of this charter when he confronted Tancred in October 1190. Furthermore, Tancred had refused to uphold William II's promise to provide financial support for the crusade. Richard therefore made demands both for this agreement to be ratified, and for full restitution of his sister's dower rights.[40]

Richard's demands were extensive, including not only the county of Mont Sant' Angelo, but also a golden chair, a golden table with golden trestles, a large silk tent, twenty-four silver cups and twenty-four silver dishes, 60,000 measures each of corn, barley, and wine, and one hundred armed ships replete with provisions for the crusading army for two years.[41] After seeking the counsel of 'wise men', Tancred's initial belligerence gave way to an agreement to pay 20,000 ounces of gold in satisfaction of Joanna's dower, and a further 20,000 in satisfaction of the rest of Richard's demands. Tancred also negotiated a marriage alliance between his daughter and Richard's nephew, Arthur of Brittany, whom Richard had pledged to recognise as his heir in the event that he died without issue.[42]

The text of Richard's agreement with Tancred, dated November 1190, wherein he accepts the payment of 40,000 ounces of gold, agrees to the marriage proposal, and officially names Arthur as his heir, is reproduced by Howden in both the *Gesta* and the *Chronica*, as is the oath sworn by Richard's representatives to uphold the treaty, as well as Richard's subsequent letter to Pope Clement III informing him of the proceedings.[43] Both chronicles record that Tancred paid Richard a further 20,000 ounces of gold in addition to the sum of 40,000 already paid

---

[38] Howden, *Chronica*, III, 92; see also *Itinerarium Peregrinorum*, 172-3 for a more detailed description of this Christmas feast.

[39] The *Itinerarium Peregrinorum*, 154-77, contains by far the most detailed account of Richard's time on Sicily, as would be expected from an eyewitness account. Diceto's account is the shortest of the Angevin chroniclers, and contains very little information about Joanna, Diceto, II, 73. The details of Joanna's experiences are more fully related by Howden, especially with regards to her movements following her release from Tancred's custody.

[40] Howden, *Gesta*, II, 132-3; *Chronica*, III, 61. Both Diceto and the *Itinerarium* relate Richard's negotiations with Tancred, although the accounts here are far shorter, and do not contain the letters reproduced by the royal clerk Howden. See *IP*, 165-6, 169-71; Diceto, II, 85-6.

[41] Howden, *Gesta*, II, 132-3; *Chronica*, III, 61; Devizes, 395-6.

[42] Howden, *Gesta*, II, 133; *Chronica*, III, 61; Diceto, II, 85-6. The payment of 40,000 ounces of gold as well as the proposed marriage between Arthur and Tancred's daughter is also recorded in the *Itinerarium*, 169-71, although no mention is made of Arthur being nominated as Richard's heir. The author does not mention either Richard's vast demands or Tancred's initial hostility, but states that the treaty afforded amity between the two kings thereafter. The marriage agreement was probably a face-saving exercise for Tancred's benefit, for making over such a large payment to Richard, who in all probability was as serious about the proposed match as he was later to be regarding the proposed alliance between Joanna and Saphadin; see Part II, Chapter 5.

[43] Howden, *Gesta*, II, 133-8; *Chronica*, III, 61-6.

to him in restitution of his sister's dower.[44] In none of these accounts is Joanna mentioned by name, however, and furthermore, Richard used all of the money to finance the third crusade – the nobility and piety of such an act was presumably thought to make sufficient amends for the fact that Joanna herself saw none of the recompense for the dower that should rightfully have been hers as the widowed queen of Sicily.[45]

With the exception of Tancred of Lecce, who had already married Sibylla of Acerra before his election to the throne, the Norman rulers of Sicily all married foreign brides. The queens of Norman Sicily all received considerable dowers but in general did not play an important role in government, and in this regard Joanna was unexceptional. Regency, however, could provide a pathway to power and influence, as it had done for Countess Adelaide, Margaret of Navarre, and Sibylla of Acerra, and it is probable that Joanna would have acted in this capacity after Willliam II's death had their son Bohemond survived.[46] Not only would Joanna have controlled her dowerlands and their associated revenue on her son's behalf until he came of age, but she would also have been able to wield substantial power and authority as regent, as her queenly predecessor and mother-in-law Margaret of Navarre had done.

Ultimately, however, Joanna seems to have played an extremely limited role during her brief term as queen of Sicily. Her control over her dowerlands was severely restricted, she does not seem to have issued any charters in her own name, and neither does she appear on any of William II's extant charters.[47] Further, any evidence of Joanna's patronage, either religious or artistic, is limited. It is possible that, as queen, she was somewhat eclipsed by her mother-in-law, Margaret of Navarre, who lived for the first eight years of Joanna's twelve-year marriage, and who was still being styled as *regina* until her death in 1183. Margaret's continued use of this title suggests much about the balance of queenly power at William's court, and presents an interesting parallel with Joanna's mother Eleanor of Aquitaine, who was similarly styling herself as *regina Anglorum* in the reign of Richard I.[48]

Margaret appears more frequently than Joanna in primary sources, not least because she became regent for her young son on her husband's death in 1166. Despite being implicated in the political intrigues of the early 1160s, which ultimately led to the "palace revolution" and the death of her eldest son Roger, she had nevertheless been a strong influence on her husband and her energy and abilities were rewarded when William I named her as regent for their young son on his deathbed.[49] In the presence of the Sicilian magnates and the archbish-

---

[44] Howden, *Gesta*, II, 136; *Chronica*, III, 65.

[45] The author of the *Continuation of William of Tyre*, 104, suggests that Joanna agreed to give Richard her dower monies after he promised that this would be restored to her on their return to England, and that he would also then find for her a suitable second husband. The *Continuation* is, however, the only source to make such a claim.

[46] Countess Adelaide, mother of the future Roger II, and Margaret of Navarre, Joanna's mother-in-law, had both exercised regency powers. For Adelaide, see Chalandon, *Domination Normande*, II, 625; Norwich, *Kingdom in the Sun*, 124-6. For Margaret, see Chalandon, *Domination Normande*, II, 176-7; Ménager, *Hommes et Institutions*, Part II, 449; Falcandus, 137. Sibylla of Acerra was also nominated as regent by her husband Tancred, and held out for some time against Henry VI, the husband of William's designated heir Constance, before she was forced to renounce both her crown and her son's claim to the throne, although Chalandon has stated that this was an insufficient time for her qualities as queen-regent to be truly judged, *Domination Normande*, II, 625; see also Norwich, *Kingdom in the Sun*, 382-8.

[47] I am grateful to Professor Graham Loud for providing me with a pre-publication copy of his forthcoming *Calendar of Extant Charters of William II*. For more on Joanna's patronage, see Part IV.

[48] See Martindale, 'Eleanor of Aquitaine', 17.

[49] Chalandon, *Domination Normande*, II, 177; Falcandus, 137. How far Margaret was involved in the plot to over-

ops of Salerno and Reggio, he designated William as his successor and arranged that Margaret would exercise *totius regni curam et administrationem, que vulgo balium appellatur*.[50] This designation was uncontested by the nobles, and Margaret acted as regent for the next six years, supported by the great magnates of the kingdom, until William attained his majority in 1178. She remained prominent in governmental affairs throughout the period of her regency, and the designation of her as *regina* even after this time suggests that she continued to wield influence in the kingdom even after William's marriage to Joanna.

There is also evidence of Margaret as an active patron. She re-founded the monastery of Santa Maria di Maniace as a Benedictine abbey in 1173, and the marble figure on the altar, adjacent to a portrait of the Virgin, may represent the dowager queen.[51] Margaret was also involved in the foundation of Monreale, the great abbey founded by her son William II in the late 1170s.[52] Whilst it is apparent that Margaret remained influential in her son's life after his marriage, it is uncertain how far Joanna was influenced by her mother-in-law, nor is it possible to ascertain what relations were like between the two queens at the Sicilian court. In comparison, Alfonso VIII's mother Blanca had died more than a decade before his marriage to Leonor, who therefore had no living elder female at her court either to emulate or contend with. Similarly, Matilda was bereft of the influence of an older female at her husband's court in Saxony, although she may have been able to benefit from her mother's advice during her years of exile at her parents' court. What emerges from an examination of the patronage and commemorative programmes of Joanna and Leonor, and of their elder sister Matilda, is that the greatest influence appears to have been that of their natal family. With the exception of Joanna, whose access to her dowerlands was so limited, the lands and their associated revenues with which Henry and Eleanor's daughters were endowed at the times of their marriages undoubtedly provided, at least in part, the financial means to support such projects. The choices that these women made in terms of patronage and commemoration, as well as their motivations for such choices, will be the focus of the final two sections of this study.

---

throw her husband depends on the viewpoint of the chronicler recording it. According to Falcandus, 81, Margaret was rumoured to have been the lover of William I's favourite Maio de Bari, who was assassinated in 1161. For more on the "palace revolution", see Falcandus, 98-126. See also Chalandon, *Domination Normande*, II, 176-7; Norwich, *Kingdom in the Sun*, 216-35; Matthew, *Norman Kingdom*, 213-7.

[50] Ménager, *Hommes et Institutions*, Part II, 449. See also Chalandon, *Domination Normande*, II, 176-7.

[51] Norwich, *Kingdom in the Sun*, 300n.

[52] The establishment of Monreale is discussed in detail in Part IV.

PART IV

The Sins of the Father:
Endowment, Benefaction, and
the Dissemination of the Cult of Thomas Becket

This section focuses on the religious patronage of Matilda, Leonor, and Joanna. Evidence of these sisters' patronage is frequently difficult to establish, with various acts, such as the foundation or endowment of religious houses, often being attributed in sources either solely to their husbands or as joint acts of patronage. Some light has been thrown on this problem by examining the early dissemination of the cult of Thomas Becket, the archbishop famously murdered in his own cathedral at Canterbury on 29th December 1170 and formally canonised by Pope Alexander III in 1173.[1] This section will attempt to define what role, if any, Henry's daughters played in the dissemination of Becket's cult, which spread rapidly after his death both in chronological and geographical terms, what their motives were for such involvement, and how they chose to express their devotion to the new saint.

All three of Henry's daughters appear to have been involved, to varying degrees, in fostering devotion to Becket in their adopted homelands of Saxony, Castile and Sicily. Their participation in the dissemination of Becket's cult generates a further question – why would Henry's daughters promote devotion to the man who had caused their father such troubles, whose quarrel with Henry had damaged his international reputation, and more widely, relations between church and crown, and whose death forced Henry to perform public acts of penance? Can their role in the promotion of Becket's cult be viewed as acts of filial disloyalty? Or is there another, more political reason for these acts of patronage? In order to understand the significance of Henry's daughters' participation in the dissemination of Becket's cult, it will be expedient to consider the importance of dynastic saints' cults, as well as to examine Henry's own reaction to Becket's death, and the role which he himself played in fostering the cult of the martyred archbishop, which became one of the most important saints cult both in the medieval West and beyond.

---

[1] Excellent studies of Becket's life and career have been undertaken by Frank Barlow, *Thomas Becket* (Weidenfeld & Nicolson, London, 1986) and Anne Duggan, *Thomas Becket* (Arnold Publishers, London, 2004). Michael Staunton's works on the various *Vitae* of Becket are also invaluable: *The Lives of Thomas Becket* (Manchester University Press, 2001); *Thomas Becket and his Biographers* (Boydell Press, Woodbridge, 2006). See also Nicholas Vincent, 'The Murderers of Thomas Becket', in N. Fryde & D. Reitz (eds.), *Bishofsmord im Mittelalter* (Göttingen, 2003), 211-72.

Chapter One
From Denial to Appropriation

Henry II was at Argentan when news of Becket's murder reached him on New Year's Day 1171. Chronicle accounts and even Becket's biographers stress Henry's initial grief, noting that he fasted and shut himself in his rooms.[1] Henry's letter to Pope Alexander (*Ob reverentiam*, dated March 1171), however, presents a very different picture. The letter, which in effect blames Becket for his own death, contains no such suggestions of sorrow, shock, or remorse and was clearly an exercise in damage limitation.[2] Attempts to appeal to the papal curia, however, proved unsuccessful, and after Easter 1171 Henry's continental lands were placed under interdict.[3] Moreover, as the author of the *Lansdowne Anonymous* relates, because of Becket's murder, the English were everywhere vilified, with the nation as a whole being held accountable for the actions of a few, and letters from such prominent men as Louis VII blamed Henry for not punishing the men who had committed the crime.[4] Nevertheless, Henry was at this point still maintaining that he had neither approved nor had foreknowledge of the murder, and was attempting to suppress the nascent cult by forbidding pilgrimages to Becket's tomb. By 1172, however, Henry was beginning to take a very different stance, as stories of miracles and suggestions of Becket's sanctity grew in scope. Henry therefore began to make arrangements for a public reconciliation with the pope.[5]

---

[1] According to Herbert of Bosham, after Becket's death Henry II 'retired for forty days of penance and fasting, refusing to leave his apartments at Argentan', *MTB*, III, 542; trans. Nicholas Vincent, 'The Pilgrimages of the Angevin Kings of England, 1154-1272', in C. Morris & P. Roberts (eds.), *Pilgrimage: The English Experience from Becket to Bunyan* (CUP, 2002), 23. The author of the *Lansdowne Anonymous* blamed Henry for the incitement, although not the authorisation, of Becket's murder, and relates that Henry grieved and fasted because Thomas had been his friend, although the mourning lasted a short time: "he hardly sorrowed, or not at all, or else he hid his sorrow completely", *MTB*, IV, 159; trans. Staunton, *Lives of Becket*, 212.

[2] Anne Duggan calls the letter 'a masterpiece of distortion and suppression', noting that Henry was 'more concerned for his reputation than for his conscience', 'Diplomacy, Status, and Conscience: Henry II's Penance for Becket's Murder', in Anne Duggan, *Thomas Becket: Friends, Networks, Texts and Cult* (Ashgate Variorum, Hants., 2007), VII, 267-8. The letter was copied into a twelfth-century decretal from Mont-Saint-Michel, and is now held at the Bibliothèque de la Ville, Avranches, MS 149, foot of fol. 87v.

[3] Duggan has described this as a 'masterstroke of [papal] diplomacy. The king was effectively interdicted *ab ingressu ecclesie*, but he was not excommunicated nor were his English territories subject to interdict', 'Diplomacy', 271.

[4] The author of the *Lansdowne Anonymous* records that "now with threats, now with insistent warnings they instructed him either to purge himself of this charge or make appropriate satisfaction to the Catholic Church, and if he refused, he would have them as adversaries and common enemies forever", *MTB*, IV, 159; trans. Staunton, *Lives of Becket*, 213. The author suggests that Henry may have been lenient with Becket's murderers because "he understood that these attendants had done what they had done out of love or fear of him", *MTB*, IV, 159; trans. Staunton, *Lives of Becket*, 212.

[5] Several preliminary negotiations preceded Henry's public reconciliation at Avranches: Gorron on 16 May, Savigny on 17 May, and Avranches on 19 May. The ceremony at Avranches on 21 May was followed by a larger one at Caen on 30 May, although the reconciliation was not formally confirmed by the pope until 2 September.

On 21 May 1172, Henry engineered a public display of repentance and reconciliation at Avranches.[6] His insistence on the public nature of this reconciliation suggests that he was aware of the general view, prevalent in much of western Europe, of his culpability in Becket's murder. The absolute eradication of all doubt that Henry was guiltless in Becket's murder was paramount for the restoration of Henry's international standing. Royal appropriation of the burgeoning cult was also essential; thus, two years after Avranches, Henry undertook a further act of public display, by making a penitential pilgrimage, on 12 July 1174, to Becket's tomb at Canterbury.[7]

After this first, penitential visit to Becket's tomb in 1174, Henry made at least nine further visits – every year when he was in England – as well as accompanying Louis VII in 1179 when the French king came to pray for the health of his young son Philip.[8] This visit demonstrates that by the late 1170s, Henry's attitude to Becket's cult had changed drastically from (or was a different form of) his initial policy of "damage limitation", which was apparent in his reaction to the news of the murder and his carefully publicised actions at Avranches in May 1172. It also suggests that Becket's cult had the potential to be a common spiritual uniting factor, a sort of extended "family" tradition, over and above the political differences which existed between Henry and Louis.[9]

Henry's pilgrimage to Becket's tomb was a voluntary act of penance, as it had not been mandated by the pope. It is possible that Henry's penance was a public and 'conscious acknowledgement of guilt', as Anne Duggan has suggested, although it is more likely that Henry was driven by political considerations.[10] Henry's standing at this time, both on a national and international level, was greatly reduced due to the conflict with, and subsequent murder of, Thomas Becket. Moreover, Henry was facing the impending invasion of the Young King and his allies, the king of Scots and the count of Flanders. Henry's visit to Becket's tomb was the first act he undertook on coming to England to deal with this threat, and was undoubtedly

---

[6] For accounts of the proceedings at Avranches, see *MTB*, IV, 173-4; *MTB*, VII, 516, no. 772, 518, no. 773, and 520, no. 774; Howden, *Gesta*, I, 32; *Chronica*, II, 35-7; Diceto, I, 352. For the official record of the proceedings, see Anne Duggan, '*Ne in dubium*: The Official Record of Henry II's Reconciliation at Avranches, 21 May 1172', in Duggan, *Friends, Networks, Texts and Cult*, VIII, 643-58. See also Staunton, *Lives of Becket*, 216-7; Duggan, 'Diplomacy', 277-8.

[7] William of Canterbury's *Miracula* (1174) has the fullest account and is the earliest source, *MTB*, I, 173-546; see also the account given by Edward Grim, *MTB*, II, 445-7. Henry, who was accompanied to Canterbury by Eleanor of Aquitaine and Margaret, the wife of Henry the Young King, promised both monetary gifts to Becket's shrine, and the building of a monastery in Becket's honour. See Duggan, 'Diplomacy', 279-81; Vincent, 'Pilgrimages', 30; Staunton, *Lives of Becket*, 217-19. For the payment of these gifts, see PR 19 Hen II, 80-1.

[8] Duggan, 'Diplomacy', 283; see also Eyton, *Itinerary*, 190, 213-4, 223, 228, 241, 256, 257, 259, 268, 276. Philip of Flanders made no less than three trips to Becket's tomb. When Louis VII visited the shrine in 1179, he donated a huge ruby and promised an annual shipment of wine. He described Becket as "the martyr of Canterbury" and noted the miracles performed at his tomb, Duggan, *Thomas Becket*, 226. Similarly, Henry's half-brother Hamelin, Earl of Warenne, visited Becket's tomb at Canterbury, and was there cured of a film over the eye, *MTB*, I, 452. Richard I prayed at Becket's shrine before departing on crusade; John visited the shrine at least three times and was re-crowned at Canterbury in 1202 before leaving for Normandy; see Anne Duggan, 'The Cult of St Thomas Becket in the Thirteenth Century', in *Friends, Networks, Texts and Cult*, 31, 31n.

[9] Continued royal devotion to St Thomas must, however, be considered in the context of the plurality of saints venerated in England – and elsewhere – at this time. Richard's donations on his return from crusade to the shrine of St Edmund, rather than to that of Becket, reveal where his true interests in the patronage of saints' cults lay. For Richard's visit to Bury St Edmunds in 1194, *Itinerarium Peregrinorum*, 446; Coggeshall, 63. Howden, *Gesta*, II, 164, and *Chronica*, III, 108, records Richard's intention to donate the imperial standard of Emperor Isaac of Cyprus to the shrine of St Edmund immediately after the emperor's defeat.

[10] Duggan, 'Diplomacy', 266.

made in order to align the new martyr-saint with the monarchy, and thus prevent the rebels from appropriating the cult for themselves.

Henry had accidentally created a saint of his former political opponent. To prevent this cult becoming a focus for rebellion and a rallying point for his enemies, Henry had needed to act quickly in order to neutralise the potential threat that Becket's cult represented. As examples of later medieval "political saints" demonstrate, in the vast majority of cases, without royal endorsement such cults ultimately tended to vanish within a few short years.[11] Sometimes, as with the case of Simon de Montfort (d. 1265), such cults disappeared as a result of direct royal suppression.[12] Conversely, the cult of Thomas, Earl of Lancaster (d. 1322), and that of Richard Scrope (d. 1405), endured because of royal support.[13]

The intercessory power of saints and their perceived ability to intervene in daily life was one of their crucial attributes. Saint Thomas certainly seemed to have intervened to save Henry's kingdom in 1174 – or at least, that was the way Henry wished to present things, and his contemporaries seem agreed on this.[14] As most chroniclers observed, Henry's fortunes improved dramatically after his penitential visit to the new saint's tomb; most notably, the capture of William the Lion of Scotland at Alnwick, which occurred at the very moment that Henry was praying at Becket's shrine.[15] Jordan Fantosme's verse, written for Henry in 1174-5 to celebrate his victories over his enemies, not only has Henry commend the protection of his realm to the saint, but he also appears to admit a degree of responsibility for Becket's death: "Saint Thomas', dist li reis, 'guardez-mei mun reaume. A vus me rent cupable dunt li autre unt le blasme".[16] Henry later thanks God, St Thomas and all the saints for his victory over the Scots

---

[11] Simon Walker, 'Political Saints in Later Medieval England', in R.H. Britnell & A.J. Pollard (eds.), *The McFarlane Legacy: Studies in Late Medieval Politics and Society* (Sutton Publishing, Stroud, 1995), 77-106, 81-2. See also Evans, *Death of Kings*, 175-205. Henry the Young King was briefly venerated as a saint, and his mother Eleanor of Aquitaine was among those who believed this to be true (or, who promoted this as such), Vincent, 'Pilgrimages', 40-1; see also Thomas Agnellus, 'Sermo de morte et sepultura Henrici Regis iunioris', in Joseph Stevenson (ed.), *Chronicles and Memorials of Great Britain and Ireland during the Middle Ages* (RS, 66, London, 1875), 265-73, which throughout the text describes the Young King as a '*vir sanctus*' whose relics wrought miraculous cures. Newburgh, I, 234, however, discredited the supposed miracles performed at the Young King's tomb.

[12] For de Montfort's cult, see Claire Valente, *The Theory and Practice of Revolt in Medieval England* (Ashgate, Aldershot, 2003); *eadem*, 'Simon de Montfort, Earl of Leicester, and the Utility of Sanctity in Thirteenth-Century England', *Journal of Medieval History*, 21 (1995), 27-49. For comparisons between de Montfort and Becket, see the early fourteenth-century 'The Lament of Simon de Montfort', in *The Political Songs of England, from the reign of John to that of Edward III*, ed. Thomas Wright (Camden Society, old series, VI, London, 1839), 125-6.

[13] For Scrope's cult, see Walker, 'Political Saints', 84-5; Valente, *Revolt*, 216-21. For the cult of Thomas of Lancaster, see Walker, 'Political Saints', 83-4; Evans, *Death of Kings*, 188-92; Valente, *Revolt*, 30, 47, 123-53; and for comparisons of Lancaster with Becket, see 'The Office of Thomas Lancaster', in *Political Songs*, 268. The efforts to sanctify the last Lancastrian monarch, Henry VI, whose cult eventually superseded that of Becket as the most popular English saint, provides a further example both of attempts to establish a dynastic saint, and of the longevity and success of saint cults which enjoyed royal sponsorship. For Henry's cult, see Evans, *Death of Kings*, 199-205.

[14] During the Third Crusade, in 1190, Archbishop Baldwin led a contingent of men against the Muslims under the banner of St Thomas, which provides later evidence of the saint at war on the Angevin side; see *Itinerarium Peregrinorum*, I, 116.

[15] According to Grim, Henry's pilgrimage had the desired effect: the count of Flanders "suddenly changed his mind and retreated" from his planned invasion of the English coast on the very same day as Henry's penance; the following day [*sic*] William the Lion was captured at Alnwick. Thus, "the humbled king, through the intervention of the venerable martyr, divine favour now restored...subdued the enemy", *MTB*, II, 447-8; trans. Staunton, *Lives of Becket*, 219; see also Howden, *Gesta*, I, 72.

[16] *The Metrical Chronicle of Jordan Fantosme*, in *Chronicles of the Reigns of Stephen, Henry II, and Richard I*, ed. Richard Howlett (*RS*, 83, Vol. III, London, 1886), ll. 1605-6; *Jordan Fantosme's Chronicle*, ed. and trans. R.C. Johnston (Clarendon Press, Oxford, 1981), ll. 1599-1600.

king: 'Dunc dit li reis Henris: 'Deus en seit mercié, / E saint Thomas martyr, e tuz les sainz Dé!'[17] These lines reveal that by 1174-5, Henry was ready to admit some culpability in Becket's death – or at any rate, Fantosme was able to present such sentiments to the king in verse. Moreover, they reveal that by this date, Henry had successfully managed to neutralise the political threat that Becket's cult potentially presented. Instead, Becket was promoted as the guardian of Henry's realm, and as such, as the personal protector of the Angevin dynasty, bestowing honour on Henry and his family by way of association with the Canterbury martyr.

Thus, cults that originated as protests 'against the actions of royal government' could sometimes ultimately be sustained by 'direct royal sponsorship'.[18] This is clearly what we see happening with Henry and Becket's cult, although the rebellion of 1173-4 and the capture of William the Lion as proof of Henry's reconciliation with Becket seem to have been crucial catalysts, without which it is doubtful whether Henry would have felt the need for such appropriation. Significantly, William the Lion of Scotland established an abbey in honour of Becket a mere four years after his defeat and capture by Henry II in 1174. Arbroath Abbey, founded in August 1178, was one of three major royal monasteries north of the Tay, and was lavishly patronised by William.[19] The Tironensian (reformed Benedictine) abbey was the only Scottish monastery (although not the only church) to be 'under the special patronage and protection' of Becket, and the feast of Becket's *Regressio de exilio* (2 December) was celebrated only at Arbroath and at Canterbury.[20] Keith Stringer has asserted that William had always intended Arbroath to be his mausoleum, and that the dedication of the abbey to Becket was a 'very clear message that his kingship was inseparably linked with St Thomas and his cult'.[21]

Ultimately, William's motives for founding Arbroath Abbey in honour of Becket seem to have been little different from Henry's desire to promote the saint. Both kings wished to utilise the cult of the martyr to promote, strengthen, and stabilise their dynasties, their kingdoms, and their right to rule them. As Miri Rubin has rightly noted, the cults attached to the veneration of martyrs "lend legitimation to whoever may claim them. So martyrdom…is always open to appropriation, to competition, to contestation".[22] Nevertheless, Arbroath could never rival Canterbury as a centre for Becket devotion, and the abbey fell into a period of decline after William's death.[23] It is likely that Becket's popularity as a 'protector-saint' of the

---

[17] 'Then says King Henry: 'Thanks be to God, and to St Thomas the Martyr, and to all the saints of God!'', Howlett, ll. 2017-18; Johnston, ll. 2011-12. The connection between the capture of William the Lion and Henry's visit to Becket's tomb is also made explicit: 'the king of England had landed while these events were in train and made his peace with St Thomas on that very morning when the King of Scots was made prisoner and led away', Johnston, ll. 1905-7. Fantosme also makes clear that Henry's penance was both humble and genuine: 'The king was truly reconciled with St Thomas the Martyr and to him he confessed his guilt and his sin and his sorrow, and he underwent the penance imposed on him', Johnston, ll. 1912-14.

[18] Walker, 'Political Saints', 85.

[19] The others being Scone and Coupar Angus, Keith Stringer, 'Arbroath Abbey in Context, 1178-1320', in Geoffrey Barrow (ed.), *The Declaration of Arbroath: History, Significance, Setting* (Society of Antiquaries of Scotland, Edinburgh, 2003), 129. For William's generous patronage of Arbroath, see Stringer, Arbroath, 125, 130.

[20] Stringer, 'Arbroath', 116. The abbey's thirteenth-century seal depicts Becket's murder on the obverse. For images of this seal, see Stringer, *Arbroath*, 118; Tancred Borenius, *St. Thomas Becket in Art* (Methuen & Co. Ltd., London, 1932), 75; *eadem*, 'The Iconography of St. Thomas of Canterbury', *Archaeologia*, 79 (1929), pl. XVI, fig. 9. The headless statue discovered in the north-western tower in the nineteenth century (and now placed alongside the south wall of the sacristy) is, according to Borenius, of fifteenth century origin, *Becket in Art*, 26.

[21] Stringer, 'Arbroath', 119. William was buried before the high altar in the abbey when he died in 1214.

[22] Miri Rubin, 'Choosing death? Experiences of martyrdom in late medieval Europe', in Diana Wood (ed.), *Martyrs and Martyrologies* (Studies in Church History, Blackwell, Oxford, 1993), 153.

[23] Although Scots of all classes, including members of the nobility and the royal dynasty itself, continued to pay

Scottish royal dynasty began to wane after the reign of William I precisely because of the effectiveness with which Henry II had appropriated (or in Stringer's words, 'usurped and hijacked') the cult as personal to the Angevin dynasty.[24]

The capture of the Scots king, the defeat or submission of the rest of the rebels, and the subsequent end of the Great Rebellion was Henry's "reward" for his penance; it also provided public evidence that Saint Thomas, once the thorn in Henry's side, was now very much a firm supporter of the Angevin cause. Henry, it seemed, had managed not only to appease the martyr-saint, but had successfully won him over to his side. Nicholas Vincent has noted that it was only after the spring of 1172 – i.e. after Avranches – that Henry began to use the title of king *Dei gratia*, 'reflecting the King's desire to broadcast a new image of himself in the aftermath of the Becket conflict'.[25] This new image, of the king ruling by the grace of god *and* with the support of a powerful saint, was promulgated not merely by Henry himself, it seems, but also by his daughters in Sicily, Saxony and Castile.

---

visits to Becket's shrine at Canterbury. See Stringer, 'Arbroath', 131-2.

[24] Stringer, 'Arbroath', 121; adding that Alexander III 'appears to have taken hardly any interest in Arbroath at all', 130.

[25] Vincent, 'Pilgrimages', 38.

Chapter Two
The Role of Henry's Daughters

When discussing the dissemination of his cult, the many monographs of Becket's life and career focus largely on the various *Vitae* written after his death. Whilst acknowledging that this dissemination was both widespread and rapid, historians of Becket have largely disregarded the possible role of Henry's daughters. Yet it is clear that Becket's cult reached Sicily, Saxony and Castile noticeably quickly. How far can this be attributed to direct dissemination by Henry's daughters? What were their motives for such involvement, and how did they choose to express their devotion to the new saint? And what did the promotion of Becket's cult mean to the respective spouses of these women?

The evidence suggests that all three of Henry's daughters, as well as his daughter-in-law, Margaret, who married the Young King in 1160, were involved in fostering devotion to Becket in their adopted homelands. Anne Duggan sees some paradox in the fact that Henry's daughters chose to promote the cult of his 'chief ecclesiastical adversary'.[1] But was their patronage of Becket an act of filial disobedience, or even betrayal? Or was it rather an act of filial devotion, motivated by political considerations? Were they trying to atone for the sins of the father, or were they, like Henry II and William the Lion, following their own political agendas? In fostering devotion to St Thomas in terms of a dynastic cult, were they also promoting the prestige of their own natal family, and appropriating the cult for, rather than against, the Angevins?

Henry's daughters had clear political motivations for venerating Becket. They were, as Kay Slocum has pointed out, 'determined to demonstrate to the world that the Archbishop had forgiven his old enemy Henry II, and they wished to proclaim that their family was now firmly under the protection of the Canterbury martyr'.[2] By fostering Becket's cult in their respective homelands, they hoped to promote and further the prestige of their lineage, by demonstrating that Becket was 'once again a supporter and protector of the Angevin dynasty'.[3] The patronage of Joanna, Matilda and Leonor provides some of the earliest surviving examples of Becket veneration in Sicily, Saxony and Castile, but how exactly did they choose to demonstrate their devotion? Did they select the same forms or media? And can it be proved that they were, indeed, primarily responsible for such dissemination? It will be necessary to take each daughter in turn, in order to establish firstly, whether a link to the cult of Becket can be made in each case, and secondly, how Becket's cult was promoted in each of their respective territories.

---

[1] Duggan, 'Cult of Becket', 25-6.
[2] Kay Brainerd Slocum, 'Angevin Marriage Diplomacy and the Early Dissemination of the Cult of Thomas Becket', *Medieval Perspectives*, 14 (Richmond, Kentucky, 1999), 217.
[3] Slocum, 'Angevin Marriage Diplomacy', 223.

Joanna and Sicily

Concrete evidence of Joanna's patronage has proved difficult to establish, although some light has been thrown on this problem by examining the early dissemination of the cult of Becket in Sicily. Becket's cult had already reached northern Italy before 1177, when Joanna married William II of Sicily, and William's mother, Margaret of Navarre, had received various exiled friends and kinsmen of Becket at her court.[4] Moreover, Sicily had functioned as a mediator in the controversy, and Jamison has described the Becket controversy as being played out 'not only at the Curia but also at the court of Palermo'.[5] As noted in Part II, Richard Palmer, Margaret's most trusted advisor, had been in correspondence with Becket himself. Initially his relations with Becket were cordial: in a letter of 1168 Becket commended his nephew Gilbert to Palmer, and thanked him for the assistance given to his exiled friends and kinsmen. By 1169, however, Becket was accusing Palmer of deserting his cause and submitting to corruption, by conspiring towards a dynastic alliance between William II and one of Henry II's daughters, in return for the see of Lincoln. Nevertheless, any breach between Palmer and Becket appears to have been healed by the end of that year, as further letters to Palmer and to Margaret of Navarre reiterate his gratitude for the sheltering of his friends and kinsmen.[6] As has been seen, however, whilst the exiled family and friends of Becket were welcomed in Sicily, plans for a formal, dynastic alliance between England and Sicily were already being considered in the late 1160s.

The successful conclusion of the marriage of Joanna and William in 1177 may suggest that Henry had, after all, persuaded William of the just nature of his cause. Moreover, Henry had already done penance at Becket's tomb and been reconciled with the pope. Perhaps by the late 1170s William also felt some sympathy for Henry's position with regard to troublesome clergy, owing to the conflict he had personally experienced with his own metropolitan prelate, Walter of Palermo. Walter had been elected archbishop in 1168, and Margaret of Navarre had apparently sent Alexander III 700 ounces of gold to induce him to oppose this election. Her attempts failed, the gold was returned, and in 1169 Margaret was forced to concede to Walter's election.[7] According to Ferdinand Chalandon, it had been the influence of Margaret of Navarre which induced William II to establish the cathedral of Monreale in opposition to Palermo; William's own relations with the Palermitan archbishop, however, deteriorated steadily throughout his reign, making it unlikely that William would have needed much persuasion either from his chancellor Matthew of Ajello, who was also in opposition to Walter, or from his mother.[8]

---

[4] Several churches in Sicily were subsequently dedicated to Becket, including the Augustinian priory of St Thomas at Raia, founded in January 1179 by William, Count of Morisco, and the conversion of the mosque at Catania, rededicated to Becket by Robert, Bishop of Catania in January 1179. Evelyn Jamison suggests that these are amongst the earliest monuments dedicated to the new saint, 'England and Sicily', 24. A further church dedicated to the martyr, possibly with the purpose of providing shelter for pilgrims to the Holy Land, was established near Bari some time before 1197, Jamison, 'England and Sicily', 24.

[5] Jamison, 'England and Sicily', 22-3.

[6] *Ibid.*, 23. For the letters, see *MTB*, VI, no. CCCCV: Becket to Palmer (1168 – given as c.1167 by Anne Duggan, *The Correspondence of Thomas Becket, Archbishop of Canterbury 1162-1170*, 2 Vols., Clarendon Press, Oxford, 2000), I, no. 159). *MTB*, VII, no. DXXXVIII; Duggan, *Correspondence*, no. 216: Becket to Hubald, bishop of Ostia (August 1169). *MTB*, VII, no. DXCV; Duggan, *Correspondence*, no. 221: Becket to Margaret (1169). *MTB*, VII, no. DXCVI; Duggan, *Correspondence*, no. 222: Becket to Palmer (1169).

[7] He was consecrated in September 1169, and was appointed as William's tutor after the departure of Peter of Blois.

[8] Chalandon, *Domination Normande*, II, 387; Loewenthal, 'Walter Ophamil', 77-8. According to Otto Demus, it

A further connection with Becket's cult and Sicily can be dated to 1177, when Margaret of Navarre was presented with a pendant locket containing "Canterbury Water" (Becket's blood and brains, diluted with water to make the miracle-working substance stretch farther). The contents of the gold and crystal pendant are inscribed around the outer rim, and claim to include relics "from the blood of St. Thomas the Martyr; from his vestments, stained with his blood".[9] The locket is enamelled with a miniature of Becket on one side, and has a relief portraying Margaret and the episcopal donor of the gift on the reverse, with the legend ISTVD REGINE MARGARETE SICVLOR/ TRĀSMITTIT PRESVL RAINAVD/ BATONIOR/ inscribed around the outer edge.

Whilst the pendant may have been presented to Margaret in recognition of the assistance she had given to Becket's exiled friends and kinsmen, the donor of the gift as well as the date of presentation suggests a further link with Joanna's Angevin family. Commissioned by Reginald FitzJocelin, bishop of Bath and Wells and former member of Becket's household, it was presented to Margaret on the day of William's marriage to Joanna.[10] It is therefore very likely that this was a diplomatic gift to the queen from Henry II's court. There is also the possibility that his marriage to Joanna may have influenced William's decision to include Becket in the iconographic programme at Monreale.

Construction of Monreale as a rival to the episcopal see of Palermo had begun in the early 1170s, and the building work must have been completed by the time the foundation charter was issued on 15 August 1176, as Benedictine monks from the abbey of Holy Trinity in Cava had already been installed by this date.[11] The charter grants the abbey extensive privileges and possessions, several of which had formerly been in the possession of the see of Palermo, and which were grudgingly ceded by Archbishop Walter in a charter dated March 1177.[12]

---

was Matthew of Ajello who persuaded William to establish Monreale in direct opposition to Palermo, *Mosaics of Norman Sicily*, 96.

[9] 'de sanguine s<an>c<t>i Thome mart<y>ris; de vestibu<s> suis sanguine suo tinctus', Anne Duggan, 'Aspects of Anglo-Portuguese Relations in the Twelfth Century. Manuscripts, Relics, Decretals and the Cult of St Thomas Becket at Lorvao, Alcobaca and Tomar', *Portuguese Studies*, 14 (London, 1998), 12. John of Salisbury also owned a phial of Becket's blood, and similar relics were housed at the abbeys of Reading and Colchester by 1199.

[10] For the career of Reginald, who also accompanied Leonor to Castile in 1170, see Charles Duggan, 'Reginald fitz Jocelin (c. 1140-1191)', *DNB*. Becket is also depicted on an enamelled book cover, possibly given to Capua Cathedral by Alfano, the archbishop of Capua (d. 1183) who had been one of the envoys sent to collect Joanna from Toulouse in 1176 and who also presented William with relics of St Castrensis on the occasion of his marriage; see Ernst Kitzinger, *The Mosaics of Monreale* (S.F. Flaccovio, Palermo, 1960), 19. The book was presented to Capua Cathedral no later than 1182, and Gameson has noted the possible Palermitan manufacture of the book, which might suggest royal influence, 'Early Imagery', 51. One wonders if there is a common provenance for this book and the equally finely enamelled pendant given to Margaret of Navarre – Limoges, perhaps, which enjoyed a roaring trade in enamelled chasses, and lay within the bounds of the Angevin domains.

[11] Jamison, 'England and Sicily', 27; Demus, *Mosaics of Norman Sicily*, 92-3, 100. The foundation had received papal approval, as well as extensive privileges, by the end of 1174. The final papal privilege, confirming Monreale's rights, was issued by Clement III in April 1188, *Regesta Pontificum Romanorum*, ed. Philippus Jaffé (2 Vols., Leipzig, 1885-8 ; repr. Graz, 1956 ; hereafter *RPR*), II, 543. For the foundation charter and other documents relating to the foundation, see C.A. Garufi, 'Catalogo illustrato del Tabulario di Sta. Maria Nuova in Monreale', in *Documenti per servire alla Storia di Sicilia*, I. Serie, Diplomatica, vols. XVIII & XIX (Palermo, 1902).

[12] Demus, *Mosaics of Norman Sicily*, 92. The charter refers to the building in the past tense, and William states that construction had commenced at the start of his reign, indicating that the work may have begun as early as 1172-3; see Demus, *Mosaics of Norman Sicily*, 100. For the foundation charter, see Garufi, 'Catalogo', no. 15, and no. 27 for Walter's charter. Further grants to Monreale by William were made in 1178, 1182, 1183, 1184, 1185 and 1186. For these grants, see Garufi, 'Catalogo', nos. 24, 28, 33, 35, 36, 37, 47, 50, 51, 53, 54. Joanna does not appear on any of these documents.

Monreale is first referred to in a charter issued by Nicola, archbishop of Messina on 1 March 1174, in which he transfers episcopal jurisdiction to the new abbey, as well as granting it the possessions of the monastery of Santa Maria de Maniace, founded by William's mother Margaret of Navarre. The charter was confirmed by Pope Alexander III on 29 December 1174.[13] On 30 December, a further bull expressed Alexander's 'pleasure at the news of the foundation (which has reached him both through the king's letters and by rumour)', confirmed that Monreale would be subject to papal authority alone, and granted William the status of hereditary papal legate.[14]

Pope Lucius III's bull of 5 February 1183 confirming Monreale's metropolitan status commends the speed of the build and refers to the construction in the past tense, indicating that the building work, at least on the main building, had indeed been completed by that time.[15] Tancred Borenius viewed the bull as evidence that both the construction of the cathedral and that of the mosaics were completed by 1182, and that, therefore, the mosaic of Thomas Becket which appears in the main apse of the cathedral is the 'very earliest posthumous representation' of the saint.[16] Ernst Kitzinger, however, while suggesting that the mosaic work was probably 'well under way' by the time Lucius' bull was issued, believes completion of the mosaic work may be dated to as late as the early 1190s, after which time Monreale had fallen into decline under Hohenstaufen rule.[17] Based on stylistic similarities between the mosaics in the apse and those in the central square, the nave, the transepts and the aisles, Otto Demus viewed the iconographic programme as a homogeneous whole, 'executed by a number of artists and workmen under a uniform direction'.[18] He asserted that the mosaics in the main apse and central presbytery were completed first, followed by those in the central square, nave and aisles, the side apses and, finally, the transepts, with the entire scheme being executed and completed in the mid to late 1180s.[19]

Kay Slocum has proposed – although without substantiating evidence – the even earlier date of 1178 for the execution of the mosaic of Becket, which if true would fit well chronologically with the rapidly growing cult of the murdered archbishop, as well as being significantly just one year after Joanna's marriage to William.[20] If completion of Monreale, including the mosaic work, can be taken as the early date of 1182, as Borenius understood, then the Monreale mosaic of Becket appeared within twelve years of the archbishop's death.[21] If the mosaic work was completed later, however, – the early 1190s, as Kitzinger has suggested – then the assertions of Demus, Borenius, and Slocum that the mosaic of Becket at Monreale constitutes the earliest known representation of the new saint are in need of revision.[22]

---

[13] Demus, *Mosaics of Norman Sicily*, 91. For the charter, see Garufi, 'Catalogo', no. 8.

[14] This bull was subsequently confirmed on 14 January 1176, Demus, *Mosaics of Norman Sicily*, 91-2. For the papal bulls, see *RPR*, II, 278, 296; Garufi, 'Catalogo', nos. 9, 10, 12-14.

[15] *RPR*, II, 452; Garufi, 'Catalogo', nos. 40-44; Demus, *Mosaics of Monreale*, 93, 100. A second bull of the same date confirms William's foundation charter. Lucius' bulls were later confirmed by Clement III in 1188; see Garufi, 'Catalogo', nos. 60-63.

[16] Borenius, 'Iconography', 30. He used an identical argument in his later *Becket in Art*, but gave the definitive date of 1180 for the Becket mosaic in his 'Some Further Aspects of the Iconography of St. Thomas of Canterbury', *Archaeologia*, 83 (1933), 172.

[17] Kitzinger, *Mosaics of Monreale*, 17; see also Demus, *Mosaics of Norman Sicily*, 94, 99.

[18] See Demus, *Mosaics of Norman Sicily*, 130-5; at 134.

[19] *Ibid.*, 123, 126-8, 147-8, 171n.

[20] Slocum, 'Angevin Marriage Diplomacy', 220-1.

[21] Borenius, *Becket in Art*, 13.

[22] For English representations of Becket which post-date 1178, see Borenius, *Becket in Art*, 18-9.

Evelyn Jamison has disagreed both with Borenius' dating of the Monreale mosaics and with his assertion that Becket was included in the iconographical programme at Monreale because of William's marriage to Joanna. According to Jamison, Becket was considered to be 'the latest protagonist of the Church in its age-long struggle with the secular power', and his inclusion in the programme of saints should therefore be considered as 'part of an iconographic scheme, designed to proclaim the dominion of Christ and his Saints over the world and its rulers'.[23] Jamison bases his conclusion on the fact that all of the saints occupying the third tier alongside Becket were noted for their staunch support of the church over secular tyranny; this viewpoint, however, is difficult to reconcile with William's known hostility to his own troublesome archbishop, Walter of Palermo.

Monreale had been established in direct opposition to Palermo and its archbishop.[24] The papal bull of 1176 was 'clearly aimed at eliminating Walter's influence and checking his real or anticipated resistance', and this is reinforced by the emphasis on ecclesiastical harmony and unity, as well as the assertion in the later bull of 1183 that two episcopal sees so close to one another would harm no-one.[25] The continual references to Monreale being founded on the ancient site of the Greek metropolitan see of Sancta Kyriaka denote that a metropolitan status for Monreale was envisaged from its inception, as well as serving to reinforce the idea that Monreale was the 'real and traditional metropolis of Palermo'.[26] This, for Demus, presented the true motivation both for the speed with which Monreale was constructed, and for the lavish scale of the decoration: although he did not entirely discount genuine pious motivations, he believed that Monreale was 'intended to present a *fait accompli* to the enemies of the scheme' – in other words, to Walter of Palermo.[27] William's continual troubles with his archbishop – which present something of a parallel to Henry's conflict with Becket - make the inclusion of another troublesome archbishop in William's dynastic pantheon all the more interesting.

The iconographic programme at Monreale includes more saints than anywhere else in Sicily, and depicts saints both male and female, Eastern and Latin. The choice of saints in the main apse, arranged in pairs, suggest themes both of martyrdom and of resistance to temporal power. Becket appears in a row with Peter of Alexandria, Clement I, Silvester I and Saints Stephen and Lawrence.[28] His immediate neighbours are Pope Silvester I and St Lawrence, the martyred deacon of ancient Rome who faced persecution in the time of Valerian.[29] The pro-

---

[23] Jamison, 'England and Sicily', 25; see also 25-7 for a discussion of the other martyr-saints in the Monreale programme. While Borenius dated the mosaic work to 1173x1182, and Demus to 1183x1189, Jamison has proposed the later date of 1188x1194, with a date of c.1188-9 for the Becket mosaic – for his reasons, based largely on the inclusion of the mosaic of Clement I, and on the fact that neither Ibn Jubayr, who visited Sicily in 1184, nor 'Hugo Falcandus', in a letter dated to 1190, mention the mosaics, despite giving full descriptions of those at Santa Maria dell'Ammiraglio and the Capella Palatina, see 'England and Sicily', 27-9.

[24] Not, as Ryccardo of San Germano suggested, to remedy William's lack of heirs by Joanna, *Chronica*, in L. Muratori (ed.), *R.I.S.S.*, VII.2 (Bologna, 1725), 4-5. For more on William's relations with Walter of Palermo, see Part II; see also Demus, *Mosaics of Norman Sicily*, 95-9.

[25] Demus, *Mosaics of Norman Sicily*, 97-8, at 97.

[26] *Ibid.*, 91, 98.

[27] *Ibid.*, 98. Clearly, the Canterbury monks understood this to be William's motivation also, as the *Allegationes Conventus Cantuariensis contra praecedentia Capitula* (1198) makes clear: the monks feared that Henry II might establish an archbishopric at Lambeth to rival Canterbury, as William had done with Monreale, *Epistolae Cantuariensis*, in *Chronicles and Memorials of the Reign of Richard I*, ed. William Stubbs (*RS*, 38, Vol. II), 532-8, at 536-7.

[28] Richard Gameson, 'The Early Imagery of Thomas Becket', in Colin Morris & Peter Roberts (eds.), *Pilgrimage: The English Experience from Becket to Bunyan* (CUP, 2002), 80; see also Demus, *Mosaics of Norman Sicily*, 128-9.

[29] Not St Stephen, as Jamison stated, 'England and Sicily', 25-6. Demus and Gameson both state that Becket is

tomartyr Stephen, to whom Becket was especially devoted, follows next in the sequence.[30] Both saints had links with Becket: he deliberately identified himself with St Stephen during the conflict with Henry II, and he received relics of St Lawrence shortly before his death.[31]

The mosaic of Becket on the apsidal wall in the chancel depicts the archbishop in his archiepiscopal vestments, his pallium decorated with black crosses, although he does not wear a mitre. He holds a book in his left hand, and gives benediction with his right. Becket appears in the company of the Virgin and archangels; the seven-metre-high representation of Christ Pantokrator stands above, dominating the scene from the conch of the apse. Becket therefore appears in very exclusive company. Of the various saints and martyrs at Monreale, either male or female, 'only a few select ones found a place in the immediate entourage of the Pantokrator in the central apse', with the majority of full-length representations of saints being found in the transept.[32] As with all the Monreale mosaics, the representation of Becket is simple and stylised, although it is a matter of conjecture whether his depiction as a young, saintly archbishop rather than as a martyr is of some significance. Demus has noted that there is 'nothing in the representation...to affront her [Joanna's] filial sentiments',[33] and the lack of any allusion to Becket's brutal murder is perhaps indicative of appropriation of the image of the saint.

Given Margaret of Navarre's involvement with Becket's circle prior to his death, and her possession of a Becket reliquary, there is a possibility that it was she who influenced William's decision to include a portrait of the saint at Monreale. Margaret lived until 1183, by which time the mosaic of Becket may have been completed. Could she perhaps have acted in concert with her daughter-in-law to ensure Becket's place amongst the saints in William's foundation? There is no evidence from diplomatics, as Joanna does not appear on any of the fifty-six charters catalogued by Garufi relating to Monreale in the reign of William II, twelve of which were issued by William himself.[34] Given the extent of Joanna's dower lands, discussed in Part III, her lack of appearance in these documents is striking. The evidence here must remain inconclusive, however, as there must have been many more charters originally in existence than the fifty-six charters Garufi was able to locate.[35] Nevertheless, this small sample suggests that unlike their Spanish counterparts, Sicilian queens did not routinely appear on their husbands' charters.[36] Borenius has nonetheless stressed the importance of the marriages of all of Henry's

---

paired with Peter of Alexandria, who was also exiled and martyred on his return to his see; however, the mosaic inscription clearly identifies Becket's other immediate neighbour as Silvester.

[30] Becket had kept the feast of St Stephen two days before his death, and Jamison notes that his devotion to the martyr provides the reason for their being frequently represented together, 'England and Sicily', 26.

[31] Gameson, 'Early Imagery', 80. Demus has stated that the choice of saints represented here 'make sense only as a programmatic declaration...of all that Monreale stood for at the time of its foundation, and only at that time', and that this is 'especially true' of the mosaic of Becket, *Mosaics of Norman Sicily*, 129. For a reproduction of the mosaic of Becket, see Borenius, 'Iconography', pl. IX, fig. 1.

[32] Kitzinger, *Mosaics of Monreale*, 14.

[33] Demus, *Mosaics of Norman Sicily*, 130, 172n.

[34] G. Millunzi noted that it was not until the fourteenth century that the documents relating to Monreale began to be archived properly, 'Il Tesoro, la Biblioteca ed il Tabulario della Chiesa di Sta. Maria Nuova in Monreale', *Archivio Storico Siciliano*, 28 (1903), 250n. Following a fire in the dome of Monreale on 11 November 1181, the documents were transferred by Domenico Balsamo to the sacristy of S. Castrenze, although they had been returned to Monreale by the time Garufi compiled his Catalogue, 'Catalogo', xii, v-vi.

[35] For a discussion of the poor survival rate of the charters of all the Norman kings of Sicily, see Graham Loud, 'The Chancery and Charters of the Norman Kings of Sicily (1130-1212)', in *English Historical Review*, 124: 509 (2009), 779-810.

[36] In this respect, Sicilian diplomatics conforms to the norm, marking Spain – at least Castile – as different from the rest of Western Europe in this regard.

daughters in the diffusion of Becket's cult, and has insisted that the Monreale mosaic is 'directly to be accounted for' by Joanna's marriage to William II.[37] For Demus, however, the inclusion of Becket at Monreale 'can be explained only by the close rapprochement between William and the Pope' in the late 1170s to early 1180s.[38] It was neither a 'gibe' against Henry II nor a compliment to Joanna, although Demus has noted – without substantiating evidence – that Joanna did seem to be 'genuinely devoted' to St Thomas.[39] As ever with Joanna, what little evidence there is for her patronage proves to be problematic and equivocal. With her eldest sister Matilda, however, evidence for the direct participation of Henry's daughters in the dissemination of Becket's cult is more persuasive.

Matilda and Saxony

Henry's eldest daughter Matilda married Henry the Lion of Saxony and Bavaria in 1168, and it is clear that Saxony in particular became a centre of Becket devotion. Later medieval altar-pieces depict his life in four different cities in the north of the duchy.[40] By far the most compelling piece of evidence for Matilda's influence in promoting the cult of Becket, however, is to be found in the Gmunden Gospels, otherwise known as the Gospel Book of Henry the Lion, in which both Henry and Matilda are prominently portrayed as patrons who receive the crown of eternal life as a reward for their piety. The Gospels, known to have been commissioned by Duke Henry in the 1170s, contain scenes from the Old Testament and provide the earliest known example of St Thomas in Germany. The work was produced for the ducal couple at Helmarshausen monastery, a leading centre of German manuscript illumination, between the mid 1170s and late 1180s.[41]

Whilst the date of composition of the Gospel Book is debated, Otto Gerhard Oexle has convincingly suggested the later date of 1188, based on a comparison of the coronation image in the book with a reliquary found inside the capital of the central column of the altar at Brunswick, which is inscribed with the same date.[42] The inscription, which notes that the altar was dedicated to the honour of the Virgin – specifically, to Mary, Mother of God – by Henry and 'his most pious consort Matilda, daughter of Henry, King of England, son of the Empress Matilda',[43] specifically states that the altar was donated jointly by the ducal couple, emphasis-

---

[37] Tancred Borenius, 'Addenda to the Iconography of St Thomas Becket', *Archaeologia*, 81 (1931), 20; see also Borenius, 'Iconography', 30; *idem, Becket in Art*, 13.

[38] Demus, *Mosaics of Norman Sicily*, 130.

[39] *Ibid.*, 130, 172n.

[40] At St Jürgen in Wismar, where he appears with St Thomas the disciple and Thomas Aquinas; at Tettens in Oldenburg, which parallels his life with St Martin of Tours; at St Nicholas in Stralsund; and at Hamburg Cathedral; see Borenius, *Becket in Art*, 58, 62, 67-9, with images at 62-3 and 69; 'Iconography', 40-3, and pl. XIV, figs. 1-3, pl. XV, figs. 1-2; 'Further Aspects', 178-80, and pl. XLVII, figs. 1-4; 'Addenda', 24-5, and pl. XXI, fig. 1.

[41] Jordan, *Henry the Lion*, 157, and 206-7 for more on the scriptorium at Helmarshausen. Gameson however dates the Gospels to c. 1185-8, 'Early Imagery', 52. See also Otto Gerhard Oexle, 'Lignage et parenté, politique et religion dans la noblesse du XIIe siècle : l'évangéliaire de Henri le Leon', *Cahiers de Civilisation Medievale* (1993) Vol. 36 (4), 339-54.

[42] Oexle, 'Lignage et parenté', 347. The coronation image would therefore signify a reassertion of Henry the Lion's ducal power after his return from exile in September 1185, 'Lignage et parenté', 348.

[43] + ANNO DOMINI MCLXXXVIII DEDICATVM EST HOC ALTARE IN HONORE BEATE DEI GENETRICIS MARIE + AB ADELOGO VENERABILI EPISCOPO HILDELSEMENSI FVNDANTE AC PROMOVENTE ILLVSTRI DUCE HENRICO + FILIO FILIE LOTHARII INPERATORIS ET RELIG-IOSISSIMA EVIS CONSORTE MATHILDI + FILIA HENRICI SECVNDI REGIS ANGLORVM FILII MATHILDIS IMPERATRICIS ROMANORVM; Bertau, *Deutsche Literatur*, I, 460. Oexle points out that this

ing their imperial lineages: Henry is descended from 'the daughter of the Emperor Lothair', whilst Matilda is a descendant of 'Matilda, Empress of the Romans'.[44] As discussed previously, however, a later charter of Matilda's son Henry names Matilda alone as the sole donor of the altar.[45]

The Gospel Book's dedicatory poem, along with the accompanying miniature, the coronation image, and the image of *Majestas Domini* which immediately follows it, similarly highlights the dynastic and political purposes of the work.[46] The dedication, which offers the book to Christ in the hope of attaining eternal life and a place amongst the righteous, identifies Henry as the patron and highlights both his and Matilda's noble ancestry: Matilda is of *stirps regalis*, Henry is of *stirps imperialis* and furthermore is a descendant of Charlemagne (*nepos Karoli*).[47] Henry the Lion was the first Welf to claim such ancestry, and his alleged descent from Charlemagne serves to demonstrate his worthiness of a match with the Angevin royal house.[48] Henry's position in Saxony was 'quasi-regal', and he 'laid much stress on the status conferred by his marriage to Matilda', whose royal ancestry – she was not only the daughter of a king, but the granddaughter of an empress – was frequently referred to.[49]

Although the dedication in the Gospels does not refer to any joint patronage, the accompanying miniature shows both Henry and Matilda being recommended to the Virgin. Henry presents a gilt-bound book, presumably the Gospel Book, to St Blaise; Matilda stands beside him offering a jewelled pendant and holding the hand of St Giles, the patron saint of the Ägidienkloster in Brunswick, suggesting that the donation was made jointly by the ducal couple.[50] Moreover, the inclusion of the newly canonised Becket in the series of illuminations could possibly be attributed to Matilda's influence, strengthened perhaps by her and Henry's exile at the Angevin court in France and England. Matilda and Henry were exiled from Germany from 1182-5, during which time Becket's cult was thriving; it is likely that these years

---

is word for word exactly the same as the inscription on the coronation picture in the Gospel Book, concluding that both therefore date to the late 1180s, 'Lignage et parenté', 347.

[44] Jordan, *Henry the Lion*, 202.

[45] Jordan, *Heinrichs des Löwen*, 178-9, no. 121; see also Part III.

[46] Oexle , 'Lignage et parenté', 340, 350.

[47] Oexle, 'Lignage et parenté', 349-50; Jordan, *Henry the Lion*, 157-8. The *Majestas Domini* image, united with the coronation image, depicts the enthroned Christ holding the Book of Life, which contains the names of the just; and is an allusion to Henry the Lion's Gospel Book, Oexle, 'Lignage et parenté', 353.

[48] *Ibid.*, 349-50. Henry's mother Gertrude and grandmother Richenza were descended from the Brunonides of Brunswick, one of whom, Gisele, married the Salien emperor Conrad II, and was the mother of Emperor Henry III. It seems to have been Gisele who first claimed descent from Charlemagne – she is described in sources as *de stirpe Caroli Magni* – and thus formed the basis of both Salien and Staufen (through the Salien Agnes) claims to descent from Charlemagne, Oexle, 'Lignage et parenté', 351. Henry the Lion's statement of lineage and ancestry appeared at the time when he was on the verge of losing his Welf patrimony in Suabia, given to the Staufens by the heirless Welf VI in 1178; the genealogy thus serves to demonstrate Henry's hereditary right to Suabia, Oexle, 'Lignage et parenté', 351.

[49] Kate Norgate, 'Matilda, duchess of Saxony (1156-1189)', *DNB*.

[50] Jordan, *Henry the Lion*, 206; see also Oexle, 'Lignage et parenté', 348-9, who notes the similarities between this image and the dedicatory image in Henry III's evangeliary of c.1050, which depicts the donors presenting the book to the two patron saints of the church. Oexle suggests a possible English provenance for this imagery, citing the eleventh century *Liber memorialis*, the memorial book of Newminster Abbey (Winchester, *c*.1031-2), wherein the names of all the donors and benefactors are inscribed, and which was placed on the altar there. It depicts Cnut and Emma donating a cross to the altar, with Christ and the patron saints of the abbey above. Winchester was one of the main royal residences; moreover, Henry and Matilda had spent the winter of 1184-5 there, their son William being born there at this time. Oexle believes that either Henry or one of his entourage would have seen this image at Winchester, from whence the idea was transported to Brunswick, 'Lignage et parenté', 349.

spent in the Angevin realm served to strengthen their attachment to Becket's cult, and Pipe Roll evidence shows that in 1184, Duke Henry visited Becket's shrine at Canterbury.[51]

Becket appears in the illumination depicting the coronation of Henry and Matilda at the hands of Christ. The coronation image shows Henry kneeling, dressed in robes decorated with crosses. Behind him stand his father Henry the Proud, his mother Gertrude, daughter of the emperor Lothair III, and his grandparents, Lothair and his consort Richenza.[52] Opposite Henry stands Matilda, and behind her, her father Henry II, her grandmother the empress Matilda, and an unnamed figure of indeterminate sex, perhaps the empress' first husband Henry V. The exclusion of Matilda's mother Eleanor from the Gospel illuminations suggested to Elisabeth van Houts that 'something clearly went wrong between Eleanor…and her daughter'.[53] She believes that Eleanor was either deliberately excluded as an act of '*damnatio memoriae*', or was 'disguised as an insignificant lay woman on the instructions of Matilda herself'.[54]

However, whilst it is plausible that Eleanor's role in the great rebellion of 1173-4 and her position in 1188 as Henry's prisoner provides a reason for her absence, the 'strong pro-mother sentiment on Duke Henry's side' which van Houts has highlighted seems to stem more from the fact that Henry had inherited his lands from these rich heiresses.[55] Moreover, all of the terrestrial figures depicted in the illumination are those who were entitled to wear royal or even imperial crowns, and the impression given is very much that it is the imperial dynastic connection which is being stressed. Karl Bertau has noted the 'extraordinary and unique' nature of a German duke being depicted in art in imperial fashion, and Oexle has pointed out that whilst coronation by the hands of God was a common image in Carolingian, Ottonian, and Salien iconography, this form of image was traditionally reserved for kings and emperors.[56]

In terms of celestial figures, Christ Pantokrator sits in the upper register of the coronation image with various saints and angels. The saints ranged with Christ are those of special importance for Duke Henry, such as St Blaise, as well as for England, such as Thomas Becket, who appears directly above Matilda's namesake the Empress, indicating the special relationship the saint was deemed to share with Matilda's natal family. Becket's position immediately above Matilda's ancestors clearly indicates 'his recently renewed protection and support of the Angevin rulers'.[57] It seems likely that Matilda had some influence over the inclusion of Becket in the Gospel Book. As has been noted, it is not unusual to find joint acts of patronage being attributed to the husband alone, but it is certain that the Gospel Book was presented to the church of St Blaise's by both Henry and Matilda, presumably in a symbolically charged ceremony, where it was probably destined to be placed on the newly-constructed altar.[58]

It has been suggested that Henry the Lion was seeking the Imperial throne for himself.[59] Other than Henry the Lion's parents and the unidentified figure at Matilda's extreme right,

---

[51] PR 30 Hen II, 145. Gervase, I, 311 records that Henry the Lion visited Becket's shrine at Canterbury on his arrival in England, before journeying to London.

[52] Karl Bertau, *Deutsche Literatur im europäischen Mittelalter* (2 vols, Munich, 1972-3), I, 459, and II, pl. 64 for an image of this illustration.

[53] Van Houts, *Memory and Gender*, 96.

[54] Ibid., 97.

[55] Ibid., 97.

[56] Bertau, *Deutsche Literatur*, I, 460; Oexle, 'Lignage et parenté', 342-3.

[57] Slocum, 'Angevin Marriage Diplomacy', 218.

[58] Jordan, *Henry the Lion*, 157; Oexle, 'Lignage et parenté', 348. For more on Brunswick and the collegiate church of St Blaise, see below.

[59] Jordan, *Henry the Lion*, 158; Slocum, 'Angevin Marriage Diplomacy'.

who are shown uncrowned, the ancestors which are depicted in the coronation image are those who were entitled to wear either royal or imperial crowns. The crowns on these figures are depicted as identical to those being bestowed on the ducal couple, and although the crown of eternal life is expressly referred to at each of the corners of the miniature, these earthly crowns have been taken as an indication that Henry was attempting to assert regal power in Saxony and Bavaria.[60] No other contemporary source suggests that Henry was considering such a move, however, and Henry's motivations are therefore unclear.[61] The inclusion of Becket in the coronation image could designate the saint's support of the duke's alleged ambitions. More pertinently for my argument, it demonstrates the appropriation of the saint by the Angevin family.

Matilda clearly had a strong sense of family identity: her devotion to her Anglo-Saxon ancestors included the worship of seven Anglo-Saxon royal saints.[62] These appear on a head-reliquary held at Hildesheim Cathedral in Saxony, which was said to contain a fragment of the skull of the royal saint Oswald, the king of Northumbria who died in battle in 642 against the heathen king Penda of Mercia. Both the workmanship of the artefact and the inclusion of six other saintly Anglo-Saxon kings on the panel-work suggest an English provenance, which has led some historians to conclude that Matilda and her husband Henry were responsible both for the donation of the reliquary to Hildesheim, and for the reintroduction of Oswald's cult in Saxony.[63] The extant inventory from Hildesheim, discussed in Part III, provides further evidence of Matilda's association with Hildesheim.

Dagmar Ó Riain-Raedel has argued that there exists a connection between the growth of Welf power and that of the cult of Oswald, and believes that the arrival of the reliquary must have occurred after Henry the Lion had consolidated his power in the north-east of the duchy, and therefore after his marriage to Matilda. Despite the fact that Oswald was not of the Wessex line of Anglo-Saxon kings, the suggestion that Matilda would have counted these saintly kings amongst her ancestors seems plausible in light of the political clout that was associated with blood relationships to powerful saints. Moreover, the inclusion of so many Anglo-Saxon royal saints would have served the useful political purpose of furthering Welf claims to legitimate authority over Saxony, through Henry's dynastic marriage to Matilda.[64] Their appropriation of Becket, as evidenced in the Gmunden Gospels, would have served the same political ends.

The evidence suggests that Matilda was more involved as a religious patron than has heretofore been accepted. Specifically centred around Hildesheim, which may or may not have

---

[60] Jordan, *Henry the Lion*, 158. Such ambitions were not without precedent. In 1158, Frederick I had granted Duke Vladislav II of Bohemia royal status at the Diet of Regensburg. See Jordan, *Henry the Lion*, 159.

[61] It is difficult to agree with Jordan's assessment, based solely on the evidence of the coronation image in the Gospel Book, that the seeds of Henry's conflict with the emperor were germinating in the early 1170s, as such an argument assumes that Henry played a greater and more direct role in the production of the manuscript and its illuminations than is likely to have been the case. See Jordan, *Henry the Lion*, 159.

[62] Vincent, 'Pilgrimages', 40n. See also William A. Chaney, *The Cult of Kingship in Anglo-Saxon England* (Manchester University Press, 1970), 78, 81-2; David Rollason, *Saints and Relics in Anglo-Saxon England* (Blackwell, Oxford, 1989), 137-63.

[63] Dagmar Ó Riain-Raedel, 'Edith, Judith, Matilda: The Role of Royal Ladies in the Propagation of the Continental Cult', in Clare Stancliffe & Eric Cambridge (eds.), *Oswald: Northumbrian King to European Saint* (Paul Watkins, Stamford, Lincolnshire, 1995), 223.

[64] Whilst these hypotheses remain speculative, the extant inventory from Hildesheim Cathedral which names Matilda as its patron serves to support this argument, and provides further evidence both of Matilda's religious patronage, and of her association with Hildesheim overall.

formed part of her dowerlands, Matilda's religious patronage seems to demonstrate a strong sense of her royal lineage and dynastic connections. She seems to have felt an especial affinity towards Anglo-Saxon saint-kings whom she may have perceived as her ancestors, and she may also have been partially responsible for the reintroduction of the cult of St Oswald in Saxony. Some historians have asserted that it was also Matilda's presence in Saxony which brought new, specifically Angevin, literary and artistic influences to her husband's lands, thereby casting Matilda in the role of literary and artistic patron, as well as a patron of religion.[65]

Henry the Lion was certainly a wealthy and lavish patron of literature and the arts, and, according to Karl Jordan, his connection to the Angevin dynasty, through his marriage to Matilda, 'gave a decisive impulse to intellectual and artistic life in the ducal entourage'.[66] As well as the Gmunden Gospels, Henry the Lion is the probable patron of two illuminated psalters which were also produced at Helmarshausen, and which are now housed at the Baltimore Museum and the British Museum.[67] Certainly the London Psalter, of which only fragments remain, contains an illuminated miniature of the ducal couple kneeling before the crucified Christ, and may have been produced to commemorate their marriage in 1168.[68] Similarly, Jordan believes that the so-called reliquary of Emperor Henry II, which features effigies both of the emperor and of various kings with ties to the English royal dynasty, was commissioned by Henry the Lion soon after his marriage to Matilda.[69]

Matilda herself, according to Kate Norgate, was highly involved in her husband's rebuilding programme at Brunswick, and she has also been credited with introducing a new, specifically French, style of poetry to the Saxon ducal court.[70] Several German romance poems had begun to appear following the canonisation of Charlemagne in 1165, and two epics in particular, the *Rolandslied* and *Tristant und Isalde*, are thought to have been composed as a direct result of Matilda's influence.[71] The German translation of the *Chanson de Roland*, or *Rolandslied*, was produced by Conrad, a cleric at Regensburg, who apparently procured his source material from England at Matilda's behest.[72] In his epilogue, Conrad states that the work was composed at the request of the 'noble spouse' of 'Duke Henry', who was herself the daughter of a 'mighty king'.[73] Evidence from the text itself, such as the conversion of pagan peoples and references to the relics of St Blaise, suggest that the Duke Henry in question was Henry the Lion, and that it was his 'noble spouse' Matilda, daughter of the mighty Henry II, who had requested a German translation of the *Chanson de Roland*.[74] As there is no mention of Matilda's death in the work, it must have been composed before 1189, and Karl Jordan has proposed a date of 1168x1172, as Henry the Lion's journey to the Holy Land is also not referred

---

[65] See, for example, Jordan, *Henry the Lion*, 147; Norgate, 'Matilda, duchess of Saxony'.

[66] Jordan, *Henry the Lion*, 200.

[67] *Ibid.*, 205.

[68] *Ibid.*, 206.

[69] *Ibid.*, 208. This reliquary is now held at the Louvre. For the many other gold and silver reliquaries commissioned by Henry the Lion (the so-called 'Welf Treasury'), see Jordan, *Henry the Lion*, 207-8. The stylistic similarities between the St Lawrence reliquary, now in the Cleveland Museum, and the St Oswald reliquary, now in the Hildesheim cathedral treasury, suggest that they were made by the same craftsman, and the probability that both were produced at Hildesheim presents a further link with the ducal court of Henry the Lion. See Jordan, *Henry the Lion*, 208.

[70] Norgate, 'Matilda, duchess of Saxony (1156-1189)', *DNB*.

[71] Jordan, *Henry the Lion*, 200, and 209-12 for more on these works.

[72] Ó Riain-Raedel, 'Edith, Judith, Matilda', 224. For the poem, *Das Rolandslied des Pfaffen Konrad*, ed. C. Wesle (Tübingen, 1967).

[73] *Rolandslied*, ll. 9017-9025. My thanks to Jitske Jasperse for help with the translation.

[74] Jordan, *Henry the Lion*, 209.

to in the text.[75] The *Rolandslied* is the earliest extant German rendering of the *Chanson de Roland*.[76] Like the images in the Gospel Book, it is suffused with genealogical references, and the epilogue further expresses the hope that both Henry and Matilda will attain paradise.[77]

The author of *Tristant und Isalde* has been identified persuasively by Jordan as the same Eilhart of Oberg who appears as witness on several charters issued by Henry the Lion's sons Henry, Count Palatine, and Otto IV.[78] He would therefore have had close ties to the ducal household, and although the date of composition is unknown, Jordan estimates it to have been completed some time in the 1170s, probably at around the same time as the *Rolandslied*, and therefore before Matilda's death.[79] If the tale of Tristan and Isolde was indeed brought to Saxony via Henry the Lion's marriage to Matilda, then, as with the *Rolandslied*, it is likely that they were the patrons of this work. Eilhart's later associations with Henry and Matilda's sons may have been in recognition of his earlier service to their parents, which may also suggest that this work, along with the *Rolandslied*, was well-known not just at the ducal court, but within the household of their immediate family, perhaps forming part of Henry and Matilda's children's literary education.

Another German epic, *König Rother*, written at Regensburg *c.*1160-70, has many parallels with the German romance legend version of *Oswald* written in the late twelfth century.[80] Both poems are infused with the twelfth century zeal for crusading, and both can be 'reinterpreted to the glory of the Welfs'.[81] The German version of *Roland* in particular could be seen as analogous to Henry the Lion's campaigns both against the east Germans and in the Holy Land.[82]

Matilda herself was commemorated in verse as the lady Elena, or Lana (variants of Helen), by the troubadour poet Bertran de Born, whom she met at Argentan in 1182 whilst in exile in Normandy.[83] De Born addressed two poems to Matilda, which express that the dullness and vulgarity of the court at Argentan was lifted only by Matilda's beauty and 'sweet conversation'.[84] Both poems are overtly erotic, even going so far as to suggest how much more beautiful Matilda would be were she unclothed.[85] In "Casutz sui de mal en pena", de Born laments

---

[75] *Ibid.*, 209.

[76] *Ibid.*, 209-10.

[77] 'des gerte di edele herzoginne, / aines rîchen küniges barn', *Rolandslied*, ll. 9024-5. My thanks to Jitske Jasperse for help with the translation. See also Bertau, *Deutsche Literatur*, I, 460.

[78] Jordan, *Henry the Lion*, 210-11.

[79] *Ibid.*, 211.

[80] *König Rother*, in *Göppinger Arbeiten zur Germanistik*, 168: *Alt = Deutsche Epische Gedichte*, I, ed. Uwe Meves (Göppingen, 1979). For a discussion of this interesting poem, see Annemiek Jansen, 'The Development of the St Oswald Legends on the Continent', in *Oswald*, 230-40.

[81] Ó Riain-Raedel, 'Edith, Judith, Matilda', 224

[82] *Ibid.*, 224.

[83] *Bertran de Born*, 117n; Norgate, 'Matilda, duchess of Saxony (1156-1189)', rev. Timothy Reuter, *DNB*. In 1184 Henry II had sent an embassy to Germany in an attempt to negotiate a truce between Henry the Lion and Frederick I. The successful conclusion of these negotiations enabled Henry to return in 1185. By 1186, however, Henry the Lion was once more plotting against the emperor, and when he took the cross in 1188, he gave the duke an ultimatum: either renounce his possessions, journey to the Holy Land in the emperor's entourage, or return to England for three years. Henry chose the latter, and embarked upon his second period of exile, Mayer, 'Henry II and the Holy Land', 731-2. For Henry II's negotiations to restore his son-in-law, see Howden, *Gesta*, I, 323-4; *Chronica*, II, 289.

[84] *Bertran de Born*, nos. 8 and 9. Matilda is the only one of Henry's daughters to be immortalised in verse by de Born. Leonor appears in a work by the Spanish troubadour Ramon Vidal in which he describes her appearance at the Castilian cortes, wearing a beautiful mantle of red and silver silk, embroidered with a golden lion. See Carl Appel, *Provenzalische Chrestomathie* (Leipzig, 1912), no. 5, 27-32, at 27. As González has pointed out, the lion may be representative of the coat of arms of her natal family, *Alfonso VIII*, I, 193.

[85] *Bertran de Born*, no. 8, ll. 37-48.

the fact that the 'frisky, gay Elena' will 'never keep me', will 'never be mine', and hopes only that she will 'favour me with her smile'.[86] Similar sentiments are expressed in "Ges de disnar non for'oimais maitis", which states further that the imperial crown would be 'honoured if it encircles your head'.[87]

Whether or not Matilda can be viewed as a patron of the arts as well as of religion, or be attributed with introducing innovations in contemporary literature to Saxony, her marriage to Henry the Lion certainly effected an Angevin-Welf alliance which continued to affect the course of western European politics for decades. Henry the Lion had had clear reasons for favouring a dynastic alliance with Henry II, as a union with the powerful Angevin dynasty would bring greater prestige for the duke, both in his own lands and in the eyes of the wider world of western Christendom. Moreover, his bride was not merely the daughter of a king, but the granddaughter of an empress, a fact which was of further assistance in bolstering Henry the Lions's status. The utility of the alliance for Henry II, however, did not outlast the marriage, and his generosity was to be sorely tested when, a little more than a decade after Matilda left her natal lands for marriage, she was to return, with her husband, as an exile.

Matilda's exile, whether forced or voluntary, lasted from July 1182 until May 1185, during which time she and her husband, as well as their children, were financially dependent on her natal family. It is likely that Matilda's associations with her natal family were strengthened during this three-year period; certainly it was during this time that she met the troubadour Bertran de Born, and it is possible that her interest in the cults of her Anglo-Saxon ancestors, as well as that in the newly burgeoning cult of Thomas Becket, was also fostered at this time.

Brunswick Cathedral, which lay at the heart of Henry the Lion's patrimony,[88] also houses a series of mid-thirteenth century wall paintings, repainted in the nineteenth century, which depict Becket's life and death on the south wall of the choir, beneath scenes depicting the lives of the other patron saints of the cathedral, John the Baptist and St Blaise.[89] Both Matilda and Henry were buried at Brunswick, although their joint tomb, which stands before the altar and beneath the choir at the entrance of the cathedral, is not strictly contemporary, having been commissioned by their son Henry of Brunswick in c.1235-40. Above the tomb, at the edge of the choir and to the side of the nave, rises a monumental seven-branched candelabra, which was probably commissioned by Henry the Lion.[90] It has been suggested that it was originally intended to stand by Matilda's tomb, and whilst there is no corroborating evidence for this, if true it would be indicative of some emotional bond between the ducal couple.[91] Certainly, on

---

[86] *Ibid.*, no. 8, ll. 7-9, 17-24, 50-65.

[87] *Ibid.*, no. 9, ll. 21-4. Sentiments such as these could not have failed to appeal to the ducal couple, although Amy Kelly has stated that Matilda was 'not amused' by de Born's more amorous verses, *Eleanor of Aquitaine*, 210.

[88] Brunswick, based on the palace at Goslar, became the permanent ducal residence; a unique phenomenon in an itinerant world. Construction began in 1166, and Oexle believes that the famous bronze lion which stands between the palace and the collegiate church may have been inspired by the lion at Este, near Padua, which Henry would have seen when he was negotiating a treaty there in 1154. As Oexle points out, it stands as a symbol both of ducal power and of judicial authority, as well as a representation of Henry 'the Lion' himself, 'Lignage et parenté', 346. The glory of Brunswick as the principal ducal residence and as Henry's ancestral patrimony is celebrated in the dedicatory poem of the Gospel Book, which asserts that Brunswick has been further augmented by Henry and Matilda through their gifts of relics, Oexle, 'Lignage et parenté', 350.

[89] Only the first four scenes are original; the subsequent three being invented to complete the series by the restorer Heinrich Brandes in the late nineteenth century, see Borenius, *Becket in Art*, 52-4, with image at 55; 'Iconography', 39-40, and pl. XIII, fig. 4.

[90] Oexle, 'Lignage et parenté', 346.

[91] Jordan, *Henry the Lion*, 202.

hearing of his wife's death in July 1189, the twice-exiled Henry returned to Saxony immediately, in direct contravention of his oath to the emperor not to return to his lands within three years.[92]

Matilda was buried in the eastern part of Brunswick Cathedral, which had only recently been completed.[93] Her death is recorded erroneously under the year 1188 in the *Liber Memoriam Sancti Blasii*, which also names Matilda, '*domina nostra*', as patron of the church.[94] Matilda's piety and generous almsgiving, as well as her noble lineage, are extolled in eulogistic passages written by Arnold of Lübeck after Matilda's death. She was 'a most religious woman', who performed many good and charitable works, donated alms freely and richly, prayed frequently, and attended Mass devotedly.[95] When Duke Henry died on 6 August 1195, he was buried in Brunswick Cathedral on the right hand side of his wife.[96] The tomb monument and its accompanying effigies was constructed around 1230-40, and as the artist had in all probability never seen either Henry or Matilda the effigies do not present a true likeness of the ducal couple but an idealised image.[97] Henry holds a sword in his left hand and a representation of Brunswick Cathedral in his right; Matilda wears a circlet around her head, and her hands are raised in prayer.[98] Norgate believes that their tomb monument was commissioned by their son Henry 'as part of a larger project for a family memorial'.[99]

Henry of Brunswick was particularly devoted to St Thomas. He established him as patron saint of the duchy, and added him to the original patron saints of Brunswick Cathedral. It was also Henry who oversaw the completion of the reconstruction of the church of St Blaise, begun by Henry the Lion in 1173, and its consecration on the feast of St Thomas, 29 December, 1226.[100] By the mid-thirteenth century, the feast of St Thomas was celebrated throughout Saxony and Bavaria; by the fifteenth century, it was celebrated throughout Germany. Henry the Lion had personally instituted the cult of Becket at Ratzeburg, which has been viewed as a 'direct result' of his marriage to Matilda.[101] Henry was also a collector of relics, which he acquired on his pilgrimages to Jerusalem and Byzantium; he commissioned goldsmiths to fashion containers for these items,[102] including a silver reliquary depicting the three patron saints of St Blaise's, i.e., St Blaise, St John, and St Thomas.[103]

It is the Gmunden Gospels, however, which provide the earliest surviving example of Becket veneration in Saxony, and whilst Matilda's influence is not noted in the dedication, she certainly acted in concert with Henry the Lion in their joint presentation of the books to St Blaise's. The emphasis on Matilda's royal ancestry serves to highlight the prestige of this mar-

---

[92] *Ibid.*, 189, and 19-99 for the years following Henry the Lion's return to Saxony in 1189 until his death in 1195.

[93] Jordan, *Henry the Lion*, 189.

[94] Anno Domini 1188 domina nostra Mechtildis fundatrix obiit, *Liber Memoriam Sancti Blasii* (*MGH SS* 24), 825.

[95] Arnold of Lübeck, *Chronica Slavorum*, 11.

[96] *Ibid.*, 193; *Annales Stederburgenses*, 231; Jordan, *Henry the Lion*, 198.

[97] Jordan, *Henry the Lion*, 214-5.

[98] *Ibid.*, 215.

[99] Norgate, 'Matilda, duchess of Saxony', *DNB*. Norgate, however, states that it was Otto, rather than Henry, who commissioned the tomb monument.

[100] Jordan, *Henry the Lion*, 201.

[101] Slocum, 'Angevin Marriage Diplomacy', 219.

[102] Known as the Welf Treasury, they are now housed in museums in Berlin and in the United States. Henry also ordained that three candles were to burn in the Church of the Holy Sepulchre in Jerusalem eternally, 'for the forgiveness of all my sins and those of my famed wife the Duchess Matilda', Charter of Henry the Lion, 1172, in Jordan, *Heinrichs des Löwen*, no. 94. My thanks to Jitske Jasperse for help with this translation.

[103] Jordan, *Henry the Lion*, 154-5. The reliquary was once housed at Brunswick and is now in the collection at the Cleveland Museum of Art in Ohio.

riage for Henry the Lion; in the context of promoting Becket as a dynastic saint, who better to seek spiritual protection from than the holy supporter of the great Angevin realm? Thus, with Henry's eldest daughter Matilda we have tangible evidence of the dissemination of Becket's cult in Saxony.[104] With Leonor, the evidence for the promotion of Becket's cult is conclusive.

Leonor and Castile

Leonor's marriage to Alfonso VIII of Castile in 1170 directly brought Becket's cult to Castile. It has been claimed that Leonor maintained close links with her natal family and that she brought Anglo-French customs to Castile, but this claim is unsubstantiated.[105] This is not to say that Leonor retained no contact with her natal family; on the contrary, as discussed in Part I, there was some degree of exchange of gifts and of personnel, and as we shall see in Part V, Leonor was a patron of Fonrevrault, her mother's favoured abbey. It is also clear that Leonor's reign not only provides 'direct evidence of queenly patronage of the cult of Thomas Becket', but that her interest in the new saints' cult was passed on to her descendants.[106] Tancred Borenius was convinced that Leonor's marriage to Alfonso was the stimulus for devotion to Becket on the Iberian peninsula, although how far this influence reached outwith the kingdom of Castile is debatable.[107] Moreover, Becket's cult was flourishing in Catalonia in the 1170s.[108] Nevertheless, the first instance of veneration to Becket in Castile can be directly attributed to Leonor.

The best-known foundation of the Castilian monarchs is their dynastic mausoleum of Las Huelgas de Burgos, which will be discussed in more depth in Part V. What is less well known is that in 1179 Leonor established an altar at Toledo Cathedral dedicated to 'the most holy martyr Thomas'.[109] The donation charter, dated April 1179 and issued by Leonor herself, specifies that not only are certain lands to be allocated to support the foundation, but that the chaplain, William – an Englishman by birth – was to be exempt from all taxes. The altar was endowed with the village of Alcabón and all its appurtenances, including vineyards, meadows, orchards, and streams, as well as several houses in Toledo. The charter was granted by Leonor, 'by grace of God queen of Castile, together with my husband, King Alfonso' at Toledo on 30 April 1179, 'the second year after King Alfonso conquered Cuenca'.[110] Leonor confirmed the charter, before sealing it with her own seal, inscribed with the legend SIGNUM ALIENORIS

---

[104] Indeed, Gameson has asserted that there is 'no doubt that Angevin family connections account for the earliest known example [of devotion to Becket's cult] from Germany', 'Early Imagery', 52.

[105] Slocum, 'Angevin Marriage Diplomacy', 219.

[106] Ibid., 219.

[107] Borenius, *Becket in Art*, 48.

[108] There is ample evidence of Becket veneration in Catalonia, testifying to the close links between the northern Spanish kingdoms and the Angevin realm; see Borenius, *Becket in Art*, 48-51; 'Addenda', 20-23. Hugo de Cervello, Archbishop of Tarragona, had been murdered in the 1170s, so there were similarities in Catalonia with the English example; Hugo, however, was not canonised, Gameson, 'Early Imagery', 51.

[109] Borenius stated that this is now the Capilla de Santiago, *Becket in Art*, 48; 'Addenda', 20, although he was erroneous in believing Leonor's foundation to be a chapel, founded in 1174. The charter evidence clearly states that the foundation was not a chapel, but an an altar. See González, *Alfonso VIII*, II, 542-3, no. 324: 'La reina doña Leonor ampara el *altar* de Santo Tomás, de la catedral de Toledo'. My italics.

[110] *Alienor, Dei gratia regina Castelle, una cum coniuge meo rege Aldefonso... Facta carta in Toleto, pridie kalendas Maii, era MᵃCCᵃXVIIᵃ, secundo anno quo serenissimus rex Aldefonsus per uim Concam optinuit.*

REGINA TOLETI, CASTELLE ET EXTREMATURE.[111] The primary witness was Cerebruno, archbishop of Toledo, primate of all Spain.[112] Leonor's chancellor Egidius is the final witness, and is listed as the one responsible for writing up the charter: *Egidius, cancellarius regine, hoc scribere fecit*.

As it was more usual for Spanish charters to be granted by the king, together with his wife, this departure from usual practice is significant, demonstrating that this act was undertaken at Leonor's own direction, rather than as an attestation of her husband's patronage. In fact, Alfonso, 'together with my wife Queen Leonor', confirmed Leonor's charter on 5 January 1181, using identical wording.[113] The charter was granted at Toledo, 'in the fourth year since Alfonso conquered and Christianised the formerly Muslim province of Cuenca'.[114] Alfonso confirms the charter using the same basic formula as Leonor, before signing it with his seal, bearing the legend SIGNVM ALDEFONSI REGIS CASTELLE. The witness list is similar to that attesting Leonor's charter, with the notable exception of the archbishop of Toledo, as well as various nobles appearing on Leonor's charter but not on Alfonso's (and *vice versa*). Similarly, it is Alfonso's notary Master Geraldus who drew up the charter and who appears as the final witness.

Links to Becket's cult can also be found with the most renowned of Leonor and Alfonso's daughters. Blanca, or Blanche, who married Louis VIII of France, jointly founded the Cistercian abbey of Royaumont with her son, Louis IX. A fragment of Becket's skull was reputedly donated to the abbey by Louis, and whilst the veracity of this claim has been doubted, what matters here is that the church felt the need to put forward such a claim in the first place.[115] Indicative of the widespread appeal of Becket's cult – and nowhere more so than in France – it provides yet another significant link with the female descendants of Henry II.

It is, of course, a possibility that Becket's cult was so widespread by the thirteenth century that royal devotion to the saint was considered as the norm. Nevertheless, Leonor's foundation of an altar dedicated to the martyr of Canterbury is clearly inextricably linked to the Angevin dynasty. Devotion to St Thomas of Canterbury certainly seems to have been transplanted to Castile by Leonor, and her foundation of the altar at Toledo is the earliest surviving example of Becket veneration in Castile. Later foundations may well have been inspired by this, although it is feasible that devotion to the saint would eventually have reached Castile, perhaps via León or Catalonia, due to the speed with which Becket's cult was disseminated.[116] That the spread of Becket's cult was both rapid and widespread has already been noted; what is perhaps more surprising is that devotion to Becket was firmly established by the late 1180s as far east as Hungary. Considering that Henry II's former daughter-in-law Margaret of France married Bela III of Hungary in 1186, the question arises of whether the cult of Becket in

---

[111] *Ego Alienor, Dei gratia regina Castelle, propria manu hanc cartam roboro et confirmo*. For a reproduction of Leonor's seal, see González, *Alfonso VIII*, I, 373-4. The original charter is at Toledo.

[112] Other witnesses include the bishops of Avila, Segovia, Palencia and Burgos, as well as various nobles, including Leonor's *mayordomo* Martin González, and Alfonso's *mayordomo* Rodrigo Gutierre.

[113] *una cum uxore mea regine Alienore*. For the full charter, González, *Alfonso VIII*, II, 603-4, no. 355.

[114] *quinto anno quo prefatus rex Aldefonsus Concam ad fidei christiane subiugauit*.

[115] Michel Huglo, 'Les Reliques de Thomas Becket à Royaumont', *Revue Bénédictine*, 115.2 (2005), 430-38. There is no doubt that certain days connected to Becket's cult were celebrated at Royaumont, notably the feast of his martyrdom on 29 December.

[116] Such as the church of San Tomás Cantuariense in Salamanca, founded in the 1180s, and that of the same name in Toro, founded in 1208. See Borenius, *Becket in Art*, 48, 28; 'Iconography', 29.

Hungary can also be attributed to the influence of a royal woman with ties to the Angevin dynasty.

A Different Perspective: Margaret and Hungary

Hungary appears at first sight to be an unlikely centre for Becket devotion. Like Sicily, Hungary had long enjoyed the kinds of autonomous rights over the church that Henry II had insisted on at Clarendon, and which caused such conflict between the king and his archbishop. Roger I of Sicily obtained these rights from Urban II in 1098. In Hungary, the tradition hailed back to the reign of the saint-king Stephen I (1000-1038), whose 'apostolic status' granted the king the right to appoint bishops.[117] When this was pointed out to Thomas Becket by the cardinals Otto of Brescia and William of Pavia, Becket's response had been to denounce both Hungary and Sicily as despotic states.[118]

Becket had, moreover, a staunch supporter in the person of Archbishop Lucas of Esztergom, whose career presents many parallels with Becket's own.[119] Whilst Lucas and Becket never met in person, they were certainly aware of each other, and they shared much common ground. Both were staunch supporters of Alexander III, and both stood defiant in the face of temporal authority.[120] Furthermore, during the pontificate of Alexander III (1159-81), Hungary had formed an alliance with both Sicily and England against the Imperial antipope Victor IV.

Further evidence of Becket devotion with links to the Angevin family comes from Margaret, the daughter of Louis VII who had married Henry II's eldest son and heir, Henry the Young King, in 1160. Becket, as chancellor, had negotiated the marriage between Margaret and Henry, and had escorted her from France to England, so Margaret would have had personal experience in her childhood of the archbishop, who had remained on excellent terms with Margaret's father, Louis, throughout his life. In 1186, the widowed Margaret was married to Bela III of Hungary, and she appears to have transplanted Becket's cult to her new homeland in much the same way as her sisters-in-law had done in Sicily, Saxony and Castile.[121] Whilst it is unlikely in the extreme that Margaret's interest in Becket's cult had anything to do with the promotion of the Angevin family of which she was once briefly a part, it could well have served similar political ends: whilst Margaret may, understandably, have had little affection for her former father-in-law, her own father Louis VII had long been hailed as a devoted friend and supporter of Becket, and had prayed at Becket's shrine in 1179 for the health of his son Philip. Margaret's promotion of Becket's cult, therefore, can also be viewed as an act of filial devotion, although her views on Becket's life and, especially, the circumstances of his death may well have been different from those of Joanna, Matilda and Leonor.[122]

---

[117] György Györffy, 'Thomas à Becket and Hungary', *Hungarian Studies in English*, IV (Kossuth Lajos Tudomány-egyetem Debrecen, 1969), 46.

[118] *Ibid.*, 45. Duggan points out that Györffy erred in attributing the examples of Hungary and Sicily to a papal missive; rather, they were cited by the papal legates William and Otto, *Correspondence*, 709n. For Becket's letter, see *MTB*, VI, no. CCCXXXI; Duggan, *Correspondence*, no. 150: Becket to Alexander III (December 1167).

[119] For the career of Becket's contemporary Lucas, see Györffy, 'Becket and Hungary', 47-8.

[120] Györffy has suggested that Lucas' refusal to crown László in 1162, and Stephen IV in 1163, may have inspired Becket in his own refusal to participate in the coronation of the Young King, and he has wondered further if Becket's death persuaded Stephen III to concede to Lucas' demands in 1171, 'Becket and Hungary', 49.

[121] Slocum asserts that Margaret was 'instrumental in the development of the cult', 'Angevin Marriage Diplomacy', 222.

[122] Duggan states that Margaret's marriage to Bela III 'may well have advanced the cause of Canterbury's saint [in

In honour of Margaret's arrival in Hungary, Bela III constructed a new royal palace on the southern side of Castle Hill in Esztergom, which had been the seat of the Hungarian royal dynasty since the late tenth century.[123] The church of St Thomas the Martyr at Esztergom was established at the end of the twelfth century on the hill behind Castle Hill, which was similarly dedicated to the saint, and named Szent Tamas-hegy: St Thomas' Hill.[124] The church certainly enjoyed royal patronage, and Slocum believes it was 'undoubtedly' the joint foundation of Margaret and Bela.[125] The first recorded mention of the church appears in a lawsuit concerning the donation of King Imre (1196-1206) of half the tax from the Pest Fair to the church. Györffy posits that as this donation must have been granted after the church was dedicated to St Thomas, construction of the church must have been completed in the previous reign, ie, in the reign of Bela and Margaret, and that as the church enjoyed royal patronage, 'they must have been the founders'.[126] Becket's feast day was introduced into the Hungarian liturgy in the late 1170s-80s; Becket may also have been recognised as one of Hungary's patron saints; and a collegiate church of St Thomas was established in Pest, under the direction of Archbishop Lucas.[127] Margaret's devotion to Becket, therefore, was promoted in a kingdom which had both political ties to Becket's native land, and a primate who was sympathetic to his cause.

There also exists a sixteenth-century copy of a possibly much older Hungarian legend which relates that a "Lady Mary", often taken to mean Bela III's queen Margaret, had woven the hair shirt that Becket wore under his archiepiscopal garments. This legend, however, has clearly become confused with the alternative legend of Bela IV's queen Mary weaving a hair-shirt for their saintly daughter, Margaret. This Margaret entered the nunnery built by her father Bela IV on Margaret Island in 1252; many royal family members retired there, and after Margaret's death in 1271 it became a pilgrimage centre. Both the sixteenth-century copy of the Hungarian legend, and a thirteenth-century Bolognese legend, both of which are preserved at the Margaret Island convent, relate that St Margaret's favourite reading was the *Life* of St Thomas, and that he was her inspiration for the wearing of a hairshirt under her clothes.[128] Thus, while the legend may not refer to Margaret, queen of Bela III and former daughter-in-law of Henry II, it does demonstrate that veneration to Becket in Hungary continued long after she brought the cult to her adopted homeland.

Hungary]. The lady certainly had no love for her former father-in-law', 'Cult of Becket', 28.

[123] Györffy, 'Becket and Hungary', 50.

[124] There are many Hungarian villages with the name Szenttamás, although Györffy points out that these may refer to the apostle rather than the martyr-saint; nevertheless, several other Hungarian churches were subsequently dedicated to the Canterbury martyr.

[125] Slocum, 'Angevin Marriage Diplomacy', 222.

[126] Györffy, 'Becket and Hungary', 50. The church was destroyed during the Turkish Wars.

[127] Duggan, 'Cult of Becket', 27-8.

[128] Györffy, 'Becket and Hungary', 50.

Chapter Three
Royal Women and Saints' Cults

The discussion has so far examined the dissemination of saints' cults from a largely political angle. Whilst it is true that religious and political motivations are not separate, nor mutually exclusive, but ineluctably intertwined, to dismiss a degree of genuine piety and devotion to the saint in question would be a gross misrepresentation. Furthermore, this type of patronage was one of the requisite roles expected of queens, and the connection between royal women and saints' cults must now be considered.

Dagmar Ó Riain-Raedel has studied the links between the introduction of and subsequent waves of interest in the cult of St Oswald in Germany, and the English royal women who had married into the Saxon ducal dynasty during the course of the tenth to twelfth centuries.[1] She sees a clear link between the transmission of this cult and the marriages of the Saxon dukes with women of the English royal dynasty. Edith in particular, who married Otto the Great of Saxony in c.930, was said by one contemporary chronicler to be descended from the royal saint,[2] and she also seems to have been promoted as a saint after her death. An entry for July 8 in the twelfth-century *Martyrology* of Hermann the Lame of Reichenau reads as follows: "Apud Parthenopolim [i.e. Magdeburg] civitatem Saxonie *sancta Enid reginae*, uxoris quondam primi Ottonis".[3] This projection of sainthood was not something out of the ordinary for Saxon royal women: Edith's mother-in-law, Matilda, was herself the subject of two *Vitae* composed at the convent of Nordhausen.[4]

---

[1] Ó Riain-Raedel, 'Edith, Judith, Matilda', 210-29. See also Elisabeth van Houts, 'Women and the Writing of History', in *History and Family Traditions*, 53-68.

[2] This was Hrotsvita of Gandersheim, who composed the *Gesta Ottonis* in c.965 at the request of Otto's niece Gerberga, abbess of Gandersheim. For the possibility that Edith was descended from Oswald, or that claims of this affinity were already being promoted by the Anglo-Saxon royal house at the time of Edith's marriage to Otto, Ó Riain-Raedel, 'Edith, Judith, Matilda', 214-5. The *Gesta* records that two of Edward the Elder's daughters were considered for the Saxon marriage alliance, but that Otto preferred Edith to her sister Aelfgifu (who subsequently married the king of Burgundy), Ó Riain-Raedel, 'Edith, Judith, Matilda', 212-3. There are strong echoes here of the later choice of Blanca over Urraca for marriage with Louis VIII of France. The value of the marriage between Otto and Edith, and of Edith's role in helping to give legitimacy to Otto's rule is highlighted: Edith's ancestry is even more impressive than Otto's, and indeed, more impressive than her half-brother Athelstan's, whose mother seems to have been a concubine, Ó Riain-Raedel, 'Edith, Judith, Matilda', 213, 213n.

[3] Ó Riain-Raedel, 'Edith, Judith, Matilda', 213n (my italics). Edith was buried in Magdeburg Cathedral, Edith and Otto's joint foundation. The cathedral was dedicated to St Maurice, and it is possible that it housed relics of the saint which had once belonged to Athelstan, and which were given as a wedding gift to Edith and Otto; Ó Riain-Raedel has suggested that Otto may have presented Athelstan with a gospel-book in return, 'Edith, Judith, Matilda', 215-6. The manuscript (B.L., Cotton MS Tiberius A.II) is dated to c.900, and is inscribed with the names '*Odda Rex*' and '*Mihthild Mater Regis*'.

[4] Van Houts, 'Women and the Writing of History', 59. Otto I's daughter Matilda, abbess of Quedlinburg, was the dedicatee of Widukind of Corvey's *History of the Saxon People*, and commissioned one of her nuns to compose the *Annales Quedlinburgenses*, van Houts, 'Women and the Writing of History', 58. Otto's granddaughter Matilda, abbess of Essen, was responsible for directing Aethelweard to produce the now-fragmentary Latin translation of the *Anglo-Saxon Chronicle*, which highlights the dynastic links between Matilda's family and the Anglo-Saxon royal house, and she may even have introduced Aethelweard to Widukind's *History*, a copy of which was held at Essen, van Houts, 'Women and the Writing of History, 60-8.

Whilst reference to Edith's saintly ancestry may or may not have been accurate, it is certain that Edith's family were responsible for the continued veneration of Oswald in England. The political expedience of this for Athelstan was that promotion of the Northumbrian saint-king was of assistance in his attempts to establish authority over the newly-Christianised kingdom of Northumbria.[5] This early example of royal appropriation of a saint's cult serves to demonstrate that in appropriating the cult of Becket, Henry II was merely following established and well-tried precedents.

Hrotsvita's *Gesta Ottonis* displays an adroit awareness of 'the potential of the king-saint as a means of promoting political ambition', and Ó Riain-Raedel has noted the importance of religious houses with familial connections to the Saxon dynasty in furthering the cult's subsequent diffusion.[6] Matilda's marriage to Henry the Lion in 1168 saw a renewed Anglo-Welf alliance, and with regards to the presentation of the Oswald relic to Hildesheim Cathedral, discussed above, Matilda's political ambitions not only exceeded those of her tenth-century predecessor Edith, but 'may well have represented something of a political statement on Matilda's part, an act of solidarity with her earlier role model'.[7] Thus, just as Henry was following royal precedent in appropriating a saint's cult for the promotion of his own dynasty, so too did his daughter Matilda follow queenly precedents in promoting her lineage through the worship of sainted ancestors.[8]

The cult of Oswald was promoted by those 'well placed genealogically to use his memory to their own advantage', and through dynastic alliances with England, the Saxon ducal house were able to utilise the cult and their association with it to further their own political agendas.[9] Oswald's monarchical as well as saintly status 'lent a special aura to his devotees', and his credentials 'eminently qualified him for inclusion in the category of sainted ancestors, by then so prevalent in continental royal houses'.[10] Oswald became, in effect, the patron saint of the Saxon dynasty, just as Becket was later adopted as the special protector of the Angevin family. In terms of longevity and geographical diffusion, Oswald's cult seems to have been as successful as Becket's was later to be. In terms of family connections, Henry's eldest daughter Matilda was perhaps the most successful in promoting her lineage through her participation in the dissemination of royally-sponsored saints' cults.

In light of all this, the possible participation of Henry's daughters in the dissemination of Becket's cult can hardly be considered surprising. Devotion to Becket had grown quickly, and the Angevin dynasty was clearly 'instrumental in this rapid development of organised veneration'.[11] As Henry had successfully managed to appropriate Becket's cult for his own political

---

[5] As Ó Riain-Raedel has pointed out, 'As the first southern king of this region, Athelstan's efforts to impose his authority could only have benefited from a claim to a relationship with a historical king and martyr of the calibre of Oswald', 'Edith, Judith, Matilda', 216.

[6] Ó Riain-Raedel, 'Edith, Judith, Matilda', 216.

[7] *Ibid.*, 223. The reliquary is now housed at the Dom- und Diözesanmuseum in Hildesheim. Richard Bailey notes that the first reference to this particular reliquary at Hildesheim occurs in 1286, 'St Oswald's Heads', 202. The relic at Hildesheim provides the only evidence of Oswald's cult in Saxony, although the cult had been established in Bavaria long before, possibly through the efforts of a contingent of Irish monks who established themselves at Regensburg in c. 1080, and whose successors appear to have been responsible for a number of German redactions of Oswald's *Life*, see Ó Riain-Raedel, 'Edith, Judith, Matilda', 225-9.

[8] In 1218 Oswald became joint patron, with Wulfstan, of Worcester Cathedral, Binksi, *Westminster Abbey*, 66.

[9] Ó Riain-Raedel, 'Edith, Judith, Matilda', 229.

[10] *Ibid.*, 222.

[11] Slocum, 'Angevin Marriage Diplomacy', 217.

ends, it is unsurprising that there is some evidence of continued veneration of the saint by Henry's daughters. Far from being a paradox, as Duggan has suggested, their involvement in the dissemination of Becket's cult can be viewed positively, as acts of filial devotion. Moreover, the patronage of saints' cults by royal women was not merely an established tradition, but a role which the daughters and wives of kings were expected to fulfil.

As Richard Gameson has pointed out, the dissemination of 'Imposing cult images…provided a forceful reminder that the holy person in heaven was still very much a living presence on earth'.[12] Art was a form of advertising as well as dissemination, and images of saints could be displayed anywhere, from personal jewellery, such as Margaret of Navarre's pendant, to public altars and paintings, like those at Toledo and Monreale. Gameson notes that saints could, via such depictions, be both appropriated and possessed – and it is clear that in their respective chosen methods of venerating Thomas Becket, Henry and his daughters were attempting to do just that.[13]

What is interesting is that what survives of these women's patronage of Becket's cult is in different forms of media: Matilda and Henry's Gospel Book illumination, Leonor's altar, and the mosaic at Monreale.[14] Both the Monreale mosaic and the representation of Becket in the Gmunden Gospels are simple, non-narrative depictions, which focus on Becket's worthiness as a saint rather than on his murder, which is perhaps indicative of their connection to Henry's daughters. Considering the broader visual setting, in other words, who Becket is depicted alongside, almost all representations place him in the context of a 'continuation of salvation history'.[15] For example, he is often depicted alongside Old and New Testament prophets and kings, other notable saints and martyrs, and is even found in the exclusive company of Christ and the Virgin. In particular, in the Gmunden Gospels, Becket follows a series of images of Christ's life, and appears with angels, John the Baptist, John the Evangelist, and Saints Peter, Blaise, George, and Gregory. At Monreale, he appears in the central apse amidst a series of saints and popes (all of which are at least six hundred years older than Becket) and immediately below the Virgin and infant Christ, the apostles and angels, all of which are placed immediately below the dominating image of Christ Pantokrator. Becket's immediate neighbours in the iconographic programme are Bishop Peter of Alexandria (who had also faced exile), Pope Silvester I, and Saints Stephen and Lawrence. All defied temporal power, and all were martyred.

With Joanna and Leonor, we can suggest the moment of transference: in both cases, ambassadors sent either as chaperones on their journeys to their new homelands, or as permanent members of the bride's new household, can be seen transporting Becket's cult as well as their young charges. Thus there is directly dateable evidence for the transmission of Becket's cult to Sicily and to Castile, at the times of Joanna's and Leonor's marriages. Furthermore, these were not isolated incidents but the precedents for a whole wave of churches, altars and so on which were dedicated to the honour of the English saint. It cannot be coincidental that Becket was included in Henry the Lion's Gospel Book so soon after his marriage to Matilda. It is also possible that Joanna had some influence over the inclusion of Becket at Monreale - presumably William would have needed some persuasion, having some experience himself

---

[12] Gameson, 'Early Imagery', 46.

[13] *Ibid.*, 48.

[14] They may, of course, have commissioned works in other media which are now lost.

[15] Gameson, 'Early Imagery', 78.

with troublesome archbishops. It is certain that Leonor established the altar at Toledo herself, as her charter of foundation survives, attested, and later re-confirmed, by her husband Alfonso.

Thus, all three of Henry's daughters are linked to the veneration of Becket in their adopted homelands. Their motives for dissemination were likely to have been a mixture of dynastic, political, and genuinely pious considerations. As has been demonstrated, Henry II, from 1174 onwards, was particularly concerned with the appropriation of Becket's cult, with perhaps varying degrees of political motivation and genuine devotion. In the immediate aftermath of Henry's penitential visit to Becket's tomb, Henry's enemies were defeated, and Henry was triumphant. Becket was clearly on his side, and was emphatically being promoted as defender of the Angevin dynasty.

Becket was in effect becoming a "patron saint" of the Angevin family; in this light, then, it is not at all surprising that Henry's daughters should play a role in the dissemination of Becket's cult. Far from being an act of filial disobedience, it was more a stamp of authority, a continuation by the daughters of their father's appropriation of a potentially dangerous cult – one which came to symbolise far less a stand against tyranny, than the wholehearted support of the powerful Angevin dynasty, made all the more powerful by having such a mighty saint on their side. That these women could have transplanted what was essentially a family tradition in terms of patronage to their marital lands is testament both to the power and prestige of their natal family, and to their consciousness of their dynastic heritage. In much the same way, their choices in dynastic commemoration served to promote their own lineage, as we shall see in the following section.

PART V

For the benefit of our soul: Dynastic Connections, Nomenclature and Commemoration

This section will further explore the inner emotional world of the Angevin family, concentrating on the relationship between Eleanor of Aquitaine and her daughters. In Part I, I demonstrated that both Leonor and Joanna, as well as their elder sister Matilda, spent many of their early years travelling with their itinerant mother, and suggested that a strong emotional bond may have formed as a result. By examining the patronage patterns of these women, it became clear that all three daughters were involved, to varying degrees, with the dissemination of the cult of Thomas Becket. That this involvement was due to their sense of family heritage is unquestionable, although I propose that this consciousness of identity had at least as much to do with the prestige which came from belonging to such a powerful family as it had to do with filial devotion. In the same way, the choices made by the daughters of Henry and Eleanor with regard to burial and dynastic commemoration indicate that they felt a shared sense of family consciousness, this time suggestive of a possible maternal influence. Evidence from nomenclature reveals further the ways in which these women were able to honour and commemorate both the agnatic and cognatic lines of their natal families through the naming of their own children.

Chapter One
Dynastic Nomenclature

It is pertinent here to pose the question of how much influence a royal or noble woman might exert over the naming of her children. In an age before the widespread use of patronymics or toponymics, personal names were the best indicator of membership within a specific group of blood relatives.[1] This was especially true of first-born sons, who frequently were named either for their fathers or paternal grandfathers, and indeed, sometimes more than one son was so named to ensure the continuity of a given name. The perpetuation of names within a family is demonstrative of a conscious desire to commemorate ancestors, and perhaps also of an aspiration that the person named for their forebear might thus be endowed with some of their ancestor's finer qualities. There are numerous instances of this practice within the English royal house. William the Conqueror named two sons for their paternal grandfather and great-grandfather; William Rufus, presumably named for his father, was the Conqueror's third son.[2] Similarly, Henry I named his sons William and Richard, the names of his paternal ancestors. Henry's only daughter was named Matilda, which commemorated both her mother, Matilda of Scotland, and her paternal grandmother, Matilda of Flanders.[3] This theme of dual commemoration is one to which I will shortly return.

These early examples demonstrate the prevalence with which children of the English royal house, especially sons, were named after members of the agnatic line. Does nomenclature then reveal the influence of a strictly patrilinear family structure? Do naming patterns deny the rights of the maternal side, affording the wife at best a peripheral role, as Constance Bouchard has suggested?[4] Bouchard has pointed out that despite the acknowledged existence of an "extended family", a medieval husband would 'only act in concert with, name one's children

---

[1] Although it should be noted that royal families used family names far less frequently than the nobility. For studies on hereditary toponymics and patronymics with regard to family structure and inheritance in the period immediately preceding and following the Norman Conquest, see the collected articles in J.C. Holt, *Colonial England*. Holt's treatment of personal names is limited, and less concerned with the role of women in the naming of family members. Nevertheless, he ably demonstrated that in exceptional circumstances daughters, as heiresses, could pass on or effect a change in family names. For examples, see 'What's in a Name? Family Nomenclature and the Norman Conquest', in *Colonial England*, 194-5.

[2] These were, respectively, Robert, for Robert the Magnificent (also known as Robert the Devil); and Richard, for Richard I of Normandy, the 'ideal prince' of Wace's *Roman de Rou*. See Scott Waugh, 'Histoire, hagiographie et le souverain idéal à la cour des Plantegenêts', in *Plantagenêts et Capetiens*, pp. 429-46, especially 440. Richard has the most lines devoted to him in Benoît's *Chronique* ; see Peter Damian-Grint, 'Benoît de Sainte-Maure et l'idéologie des Plantagenêt', in *ibid.*, 413-27, especially 418.

[3] It is worth considering Scottish dynastic nomenclature in this context. Matilda of Scotland's mother was Margaret, the daughter of the last Anglo-Saxon king, Edward the Confessor, and sister of Edward Atheling. Matilda's name at birth had been the traditional Anglo-Saxon name Edith, the more Norman name of Matilda being adopted after her marriage to Henry I. Her siblings also had very traditional names, but rather than being traditionally Scottish, like Malcolm, they were very firmly Anglo-Saxon: her three elder brothers were named Edward, Edmund, and Aethelred. By choosing such names, and ignoring previous Scottish names for his sons, was Malcolm III attempting to demonstrate his own legitimacy as a candidate for the English throne, through right of his wife? It is interesting that neither Henry I nor Henry II chose Anglo-Saxon names for any of their own children.

[4] Constance Bouchard, 'Family Structure and Family Consciousness among the Aristocracy in the Ninth to Eleventh Centuries', in *Francia*, 14 (1987), 645.

for, or designate as heirs people from a subgroup of the total group of relatives'.[5] This sub-group consisted of a narrow group of relatives – such as parents, grandparents, and uncles – which often ranged back no further than two generations, and which predominantly came from the agnatic line.[6]

Nevertheless, there were occasions when offspring were named for the maternal line, although in such cases this was often because the wife's lineage was deemed superior to the paternal line.[7] In such instances, the father would wish to associate his children, through nomenclature, with the more powerful heritage, thus bestowing prestige on his own dynasty. This is particularly so when the maternal line was descended from royalty, and returning to the English royal dynasty, we can see exactly this happening with King Stephen. Stephen was not a descendant of the Conqueror's male line, being the son of William I's daughter, Adela, and neither did he follow strictly patrilineal nomenclature patterns.[8] Stephen named his eldest son Eustace, which is interesting, as it commemorates the maternal, rather than the paternal grandfather, although Stephen's second son William was probably named for his paternal great-grandfather, William I. Like Henry I, Stephen also named his eldest daughter Matilda. This was an extremely popular name in eleventh and twelfth century Europe, and usefully commemorated both her mother, Matilda of Boulogne, and her maternal great-grand-mother, Matilda of Flanders. Stephen had also had a sister named Matilda who had drowned in the White Ship disaster in 1120, thus the name Matilda was clearly popular on both sides. Stephen's younger daughter, however, appears to have been named exclusively for the mother's side: she was called Mary, after her maternal grandmother.

Stephen clearly perceived the house of Boulogne to be superior to his own lineage, as his eldest son and both of his daughters were given names from the maternal line. There was also a gradual shift in naming patterns in the eleventh and twelfth centuries, with husbands more willing to give their daughters names from their wives' families, thereby identifying their children with the maternal line. Bouchard has viewed this change as being suggestive of a less than absolute structuring of the medieval family along strictly patrilineal lines.[9] Moreover, whilst a wife may have been considered an "outsider" to her husband's natal family, her children would naturally regard her as an integral part of their family.[10] Thus, while names from her own family might not have been considered suitable for the naming of her own children, these children in turn might very well choose to commemorate their mother through the names they gave to their own daughters. This shift in perception, from the wife who married in, to the mother at the heart of the family, with the accompanying migration of names from

---

[5] Bouchard, 'Family Structure', 640-1.

[6] Constance Bouchard, *"Those of My Blood" – Constructing Noble Families in Medieval Francia* (University of Pennsylvania Press, Philadelphia, 2001), 98; 'Family Structure', 648. This was a practice which had roots reaching back as far as Carolingian times. Daughters were almost exclusively given names from the paternal line, with the mother's name only ever used for younger daughters. See Bouchard, 'Family Structure' 645. Similarly, Henry II's eldest daughter was named Matilda, for his mother; their second daughter, however, bore her own mother's name of Eleanor.

[7] For early examples of this, see Bouchard, 'Family Structure', 646-7; *idem*, *"Those of My Blood"*, 93-7.

[8] Stephen himself had been named for his father, the count of Blois, although he was not the eldest son. His older brothers were named Theobald, for the paternal grandfather, and William, the eldest of the three, who was probably named for his maternal grandfather.

[9] Bouchard, *"Those of My Blood"*, 133-4.

[10] *Ibid.*, 3; 'Family Structure', 641. Therefore, as Bouchard has stated, women's names were not "names attached to a certain family", because in every generation the available names for women in a given family were different', *"Those of My Blood"*, 120.

one lineage to another adds another dimension to the various life stages in a royal or aristo-cratic woman's life.

As the examples given above have demonstrated, daughters were occasionally named for their mothers, although in the earlier period, the same name frequently appears to have existed in the father's family as well, usually being the name of the paternal grandmother. In these instances, the names may have been deemed appropriate precisely because they commemo-rated both sides of the family. Occasionally, sons were also named for the maternal line, as with the case of King Stephen, but in these cases such choices were made because the wife's lineage was the more prestigious. The medieval aristocracy were well aware that great lineage could come from either side of the family; as Bouchard has noted, 'The topos 'born of a progenia of great nobility on both sides'...continued to be a commonplace throughout the Middle Ages', revealing 'awareness that there were two sides to one's origins'.[11] Names might therefore come from the mother's side if the maternal line was more powerful, and this is exactly what we see happening in the immediate family of Henry II.

Henry himself appears to have been named for his maternal grandfather, Henry I. There is no evidence of Henry as an Angevin name prior to this; his father and paternal grandfather were named, respectively, Geoffrey and Fulk, which were traditional Angevin names. It would therefore appear that Henry's mother, the Empress Matilda, used her influence over her hus-band, Geoffrey of Anjou, in order to secure the naming rights of their first born son. Geoffrey would presumably have needed little persuasion, as the naming of his children after the mater-nal line served to link the ducal house of Anjou more closely with the English royal dynasty. Geoffrey and Matilda's second son was named Geoffrey, for his father, but their third son bore the name William, for the boy's maternal great-grandfather.

In the naming of his own sons, Henry II appears to have chosen almost all of their names from his mother's side. With the exception of Henry's fourth son Geoffrey, who was clearly named for Henry's father, none of Henry's children received names originating from the agnatic line.[12] This should not be surprising, as Matilda's royal ancestry was far more power-ful and influential than his father's comital descent, hence Henry's title of fitzEmpress. The names given to Henry's sons were therefore highly politically significant. By employing tradi-tional Norman rather than Angevin names Henry was attempting to cement his position as legitimate heir to the English throne, emphasising his descent, through his mother, from William the Conqueror. Indeed, Henry's first-born son was named William, although Torigni states explicitly that the boy was named for his maternal Aquitanian ancestors.[13] Nevertheless, as William I was Henry II's maternal great-grandfather, it is unlikely that Henry would have vetoed this choice; and, as noted above, the occurrence of a name within both sides of the family could be a useful method of dual commemoration.

Henry's second son bore his father's name, but as this was also the name of his paternal grandfather, Henry I, it provides further evidence of nomenclature at work as a legitimising

---

[11] Bouchard, 'Family Structure', 643. Even kings and members of the high nobility in the twelfth century 'seem to have relaxed somewhat their earlier insistence that their daughters be named for their own rather than their wives' relatives', Bouchard, *"Those of My Blood"*, 134.

[12] It is worth noting here that Henry's elder natural son was also named Geoffrey.

[13] Torigni, 235. In Aquitaine, William was by far the most common name for males; in Anjou, Fulk and Geoffrey were the most popular. Ralph Turner has suggested that because of Henry II's absence when William was born, Eleanor had a free choice in naming the boy, *Eleanor of Aquitaine*, 117. Jean Flori, however, believes that the choice of William was prompted by Henry's mother, the Empress, who was with Eleanor in Rouen in August 1153 when William was born, *Eleanor of Aquitaine*, 72.

principle. The third son, Richard, was also named for the maternal line. There are no recorded instances of the name Richard in Anjou; rather, the name comes from the Norman dynasty, and was likely given in commemoration of Duke Richard I, whose deeds and merits are recorded in Wace's *Roman de Rou*.[14] It was not until the birth of Henry's fourth son, Geoffrey, that any reference was made with regards to nomenclature to Henry's paternal ancestry. The name John, given to Henry's fifth and last son, presents some problems, as the name had no precedent in Norman, Angevin or Aquitanian nomenclature. It is probable that he was named for Saint John the Evangelist, whose feast day is close to that of John's birth; it is also a possibility that this was simply a fashionable name of choice in the late twelfth century.[15] What is very interesting is that none of Henry's sons were given the name Fulk, in commemoration of one of Henry's most successful ancestors, Fulk V of Jerusalem. With the exceptions of Geoffrey and John, then, all of Henry II's sons were given names from the maternal line, and the same is true of Henry's daughters.

Matilda, the eldest, was named for her paternal grandmother, the Empress Matilda, whilst Leonor was named for her mother, Eleanor of Aquitaine. The choice of Joanna, however, is most unusual. Clearly, Joanna is the feminine form of John, which might reinforce the idea that John was becoming a popular name in this period. Yet considering the rise in popularity of the Virgin Mary, whose cult was readily patronised by the Plantagenets, it is strange that Joanna was given a name with no obvious connection to her ancestors, rather than being named for the Virgin, to whom her father seems to have shown especial devotion.[16]

Joanna herself provides the least promising evidence of commemorative nomenclature as, despite being twice-married, she had far fewer children than her elder sisters, dying in childbirth in 1199 at the age of just thirty-three. Her first marriage to William II of Sicily produced only one child before William's sudden death in 1189.[17] The boy, whose birth in *c*.1182 is recorded solely by Torigni, was named Bohemond.[18] This was an interesting choice, as there is no record of Bohemond as an Angevin name, and the only Bohemonds in any way connected to the Sicilian dynasty are only very distantly related. The most likely candidate is Bohemond I of Antioch (1058-1111), the son of Robert Guiscard who, as one of the leaders of the First Crusade, won and held Antioch and was lauded as 'a true soldier and martyr of

---

[14] See above, note 2; see also Part I. Henry II also had an illegitimate uncle named Richard, who had died in the White Ship disaster of 1120.

[15] John was born on 24 December 1166, and the feast of the evangelist falls on 27 December. As Henry's youngest son, it is possible that he may have originally been destined for life in the Church, hence the choice of a religious name. The name John (and therefore also Joanna) may perhaps be connected with the monastery of Our Lady and St John the Evangelist at Fontevrault. His epitaph at Fontevrault suggests that he was an oblate of the abbey; see Pavillon, *La Vie du bienheureux Robert d'Arbrissel*, 585, no. 90. My thanks to Stephen Church for this reference.

[16] See Nicholas Vincent, 'King Henry III and the Blessed Virgin Mary', in R.N. Swanson (ed.), *The Church and Mary: Studies in Church History*, 39 (Boydell, Woodbridge, 2004), 129-31. On the subject of names being chosen from outwith family circles, Edith-Matilda's two younger brothers were named Alexander and David. David is a strong, biblical, royal name; Alexander on the other hand is another interesting choice, and it is probable that he was named for Pope Alexander. David himself named his eldest son Henry, the first time this name had appeared in the Scottish dynasty, and he almost certainly named him thus in honour of his brother-in-law, Henry I.

[17] See Part III. Joanna had been eleven at the time of her marriage in 1177. As it is unlikely that the royal couple would have cohabited before Joanna had reached the age of about fifteen, Bohemond could not have been born before *c*.1182.

[18] His disappearance from Torigni's chronicle after his birth, his complete absence from any other Angevin source, and William's lack of a direct heir at the time of his death, suggests that Bohemond must have died very young, probably in infancy.

Christ' by the author of the *Historia Peregrinorum*.[19] Less plausible, but ruling contemporaneously with William II, is Bohemond of Antioch's descendant, Bohemond III of Antioch (1144-1201), who was also the first cousin of Baldwin IV of Jerusalem. These links to the Sicilian dynasty are tentative at best, and knowing William II's admiration for his paternal grandfather, Roger II, the choice of Bohemond for his first born son (and, as it turned out, his only son) is thus even more intriguing.

Joanna's second marriage to Raymond VI of Toulouse produced one surviving son who was named for his father and who succeeded him in the county as Raymond VII.[20] Raymond was an obvious choice, as the name had been favoured by the counts of Toulouse since at least as far back as the ninth century.[21] Joanna died in childbirth in 1199; the child, another boy, died shortly afterwards, and no record of his name exists. It is tempting to believe that he may have been baptised with the name of one of his Angevin ancestors, perhaps Henry or Richard.[22] If Joanna had chosen a name for her offspring before she died – and given that she had fled Toulouse and was at that time separated from her husband, she would certainly have had a freer choice – it seems appropriate that Joanna would choose to commemorate, through nomenclature, her natal family.

Joanna's eldest sister Matilda bore her husband Henry the Lion four sons and one daughter. This daughter, called Matilda by Angevin sources, was in fact named Richenza, and the fact that the name is a feminine form of Richard – the name of Matilda's famous crusading brother – seems to suggest direct maternal influence on Matilda's part. Henry the Lion's maternal grandmother, however, was also called Richenza, and had been married to the Emperor Lothair III. The name, therefore, does not constitute direct evidence of naming patterns being influenced by the maternal line, although it is plausible to suggest that Richenza was deemed an appropriate choice by the ducal couple as it commemorated their respective families at the same time. This contention favourably supports my hypothesis that the daughters of Henry II and Eleanor of Aquitaine felt a strong affinity with their natal family. In the same way, the name Henry, given to their eldest son, served a dual commemorative purpose, being the name both of the boy's father and paternal grandfather, as well as his maternal grandfather Henry II. Matilda's middle sons were given the traditional German names of Lothair and Otto; the youngest, however, born at Winchester during the ducal couple's exile from Saxony, was named William. This was an interesting choice, as the name was not traditionally employed by the ancestors of Henry the Lion. It must, therefore, commemorate Matilda's ancestors – either her paternal grandfather, William the Conqueror or her maternal grandfather and great-grandfather, William X and IX of Aquitaine.

The sheer number of children borne by some royal women may have allowed them the chance to give daughters and younger sons names from their own families, thereby importing new names to a foreign dynasty. This cannot be said for Eleanor of Aquitaine, who bore Henry II at least nine children, the majority of whom were given names from his mother's line. The example of their daughter Leonor, however, certainly seems to uphold this argument. Tomb evidence from Las Huelgas suggests that her marriage to Alfonso VIII of Castile produced at

---

[19] See H.E.J. Cowdrey, 'Martyrdom and the First Crusade', in Cowdrey, *The Crusades and Latin Monasticism, 11th-12th Centuries* (Ashgate Variorum, Aldershot, 1999), 52.
[20] Raymond VI (1156-1222; count of Toulouse 1174-1222) was the son of Raymond V and Constance of France; his maternal grandparents were Louis VI and Adelaide of Maurienne.
[21] Bouchard, 'Family Structure', 651.
[22] King John also named his second son, designated count of Poitou, Richard.

least twelve children, six of whom survived into adulthood.[23] Their eldest son Sancho, who died in infancy,[24] and their second son Fernando, who died in his early twenties,[25] were both given traditional Spanish dynastic names. Sancho had been the name of Alfonso's father; Fernando was the name of Alfonso's paternal uncle, the king of León. Alfonso VIII himself had been named for his own paternal grandfather, Alfonso VII. Nevertheless, Alfonso was not a name chosen by the Castilian monarchs for any of their sons. Their youngest son was named Enrique, which was a novelty in Spanish dynastic nomenclature. Clearly named for Leonor's father, it was Enrique who eventually succeeded to the Castilian throne.[26] The name was not a popular choice for future generations of the Castilian dynasty, with the majority of kings being named with the more traditional Alfonso or Fernando. The choice of Enrique could be indicative of Alfonso's acknowledgement of Henry II's greater prestige; it was also perhaps a diplomatic courtesy. Furthermore, it may also be demonstrative of Leonor's influence over her husband, which we know that she had a great deal of, in securing the right to name one of her sons – albeit the youngest – after her father.

Leonor and Alfonso's many daughters were given names which were almost exclusively Spanish. The eldest was named Berenguella, for her great-grandmother, the Empress of León.[27] The name was a popular choice for Castilian *infantas* and continued to be so through the generations.[28] Three more daughters were given the similarly traditional Spanish names of Sancha, Urraca and Blanca. Sancha, born in March 1182, was clearly named for her aunts, as well as being the feminine form of Sancho, the name of Alfonso's father.[29] Blanca (or to give her the name she is more commonly known by, Blanche), born in 1188, was named for Alfonso's mother, Blanca of Navarre.[30] Urraca was similarly a traditional dynastic name;

---

[23] For more on the tombs at Las Huelgas, see below. It is impossible to state definitively when Leonor and Alfonso first consummated their marriage, although estimates can be made from the year their first recorded child was born. In 1180 – the year most frequently given for the birth of Berenguella – Leonor would have been twenty, and Alfonso twenty-four. It is unlikely that they would have waited so long to secure the succession, which suggests that there may have been other children born before this time, who died in infancy and whose names are unrecorded. For plausible arguments for placing Berenguella's birth at the earlier date of 1179, see Díez, *Alfonso VIII*, p. 54.

[24] Born in April 1181, his obituary at Burgos gives 9 July 1181 as the date of his death, although he continues to appear on charters until 13 July; see González, *Alfonso VIII*, I, 201; II, nos. 336, 364-72; Díez, *Alfonso VIII*, 48. On all but one of the ten charters on which Sancho appears, he is styled as *rege*.

[25] Born in November 1189, he was groomed for kingship from infancy, and began to participate in government and military strategies at an early age, appearing on all but one of his parents' charters until his death. See González, *Alfonso VIII*, II, nos. 537-56; 558-63.

[26] Born in 1204, he succeeded his father in 1214, but died tragically from an accident a mere three years later.

[27] Berenguella first appears on royal documents in May 1181, and after Sancho's death in July 1181 left her as heir-apparent, is styled *regina* in official documents. From 2 March 1186, charter evidence shows that Alfonso and Leonor considered their reign to be jointly with Berenguella; however, she disappears from the charters after the birth of her brother Fernando in November 1189, presumably because his birth meant that she was no longer heir-apparent. See González, *Alfonso VIII*, I, 197; II, nos. 373-4, 377-82, 386-7, 390, 399, 419, 442, 472, 520, 522, 524-36.

[28] Berenguella herself followed standard Spanish practice by naming her two sons Fernando and Alfonso. These names commemorated several members of her own and her husband's family: both her husband and her father were named Alfonso, and both her brother and her husband's father had been called Fernando (the most popular male name in León). Her first child, a daughter who died in infancy, was named Leonor, clearly in honour of Berenguella's mother. Two other daughters, who both survived to adulthood were named Berenguella and Constanza.

[29] Sancha disappears from charters after 3 February 1184, so it is likely that she died soon after this. See González, *Alfonso VIII*, I, 203; II, nos. 386-7, 390, 399, 419; Díez, *Alfonso VIII*, 48.

[30] Blanca married Louis VIII of France, and the names chosen for their children, especially their sons, are, unsurprisingly, overwhelmingly French: Louis, Robert, Philippe, Charles. A daughter, who did not survive infancy, was named Blanche, presumably for her mother; another was named Isabelle for Louis' own mother. What is most interesting is that one son was named John – perhaps commemorating Blanca's uncle, who had been instrumental in

a previous Queen Urraca had ruled over a united Leon-Castile in her own right in 1109.[31] Leonor's youngest surviving daughter was named Constanza, another traditional Spanish name. She entered her parents' foundation of Las Huelgas, eventually becoming abbess there.[32]

Of the five daughters who survived to adulthood, only one, Leonor, was named for the maternal side, successfully commemorating both her mother and her maternal grandmother.[33] The name was unprecedented in Spanish dynastic nomenclature before Leonor's marriage to Alfonso, and constitutes a direct importation from the Angevin house. The name remained a popular family choice, despite the fact it had not been used before Leonor's arrival in Castile. Leonor's grandson, Fernando III, named his own three daughters Leonor, Berenguella and Maria, perhaps a reflection of the three most influential women in his life. Fernando had spent much of his youth in his grandmother's company, whilst the name Maria undoubtedly refers to the Virgin. Sancha and Urraca were traditionally the most popular names for Spanish *infantas*, thus Fernando's choices of names for his own daughters is highly suggestive of the influence of his female relations. That the name Maria was given only to the third daughter indicates that dynastic links were viewed as more powerful even than the most prestigious of saints' names.

The evidence from nomenclature suggests that there was both a sense of family unity and strong female influence within the Angevin dynasty. Beginning with the Empress Matilda, for largely political purposes, maternal influence can be seen at work in dynastic nomenclature. Henry II named most of his own children for his mother's side of the family, acknowledging his cognates as more powerful than his father's ancestors, and utilising nomenclature as a further legitimising principle for his own rule. Whether the reasons were political or personal, or both, the daughters of Henry II and Eleanor of Aquitaine appear to have been able to transport names from their natal family to the dynasties they married into. Leonor, the daughter who lived the longest and who bore the most children, was able to effect the largest change in dynastic naming practices. Despite its virtual extinction from the English ruling dynasty, the name Leonor was set to continue throughout generations on the Iberian peninsula, and was re-imported to England in the thirteenth century, with the marriage of Edward I to Eleanor of Castile.

---

engineering her marriage. Even more interesting is that not one but two sons (one of whom did not survive infancy), was named Alphonse, clearly in recognition of Blanca's father, Alfonso VIII. See González, *Alfonso VIII*, I, 205-7.

[31] Leonor's daughter Urraca, born in 1186, first appears on royal docments in June 1187, giving her consent to a donation to the monastery of Las Huelgas. She is also found, with her parents and elder sister, attesting an important grant to Las Huelgas in October 1207. See González, *Alfonso VIII*, II, nos. 472, 520, 544. Urraca married Afonso II of Portugal; their sons were named Sancho (later Sancho II), Afonso (later Afonso III), and Fernando: traditional names both in Castile and in Portugal; their only surviving daughter was named Leonor. The name Leonor recurred only once in the Portuguese dynasty; the daughter of Urraca and Afonso's great-grandchild Afonso IV. This Leonor later became queen of Aragón. See González, *Alfonso VIII*, I, 204; Díez, *Alfonso VIII*, 48.

[32] An unidentified text published by Núñez de Castro reads as follows: "*Nobilissima infans Constancia, famula Dei et virgo mundissima, monacha Sanctae Mariae Regalis et abbatissa, illustris Alphonsi regis Castellae obiit era MCCLXXXI*", González, *Alfonso VIII*, I, 211n.

[33] Although her birth is recorded in the *Crónica de Veinte Reyes*, the exact date is unknown, Díez, *Alfonso VIII*, 51. Leonor's marriage to Jaime I of Aragón, arranged by her elder sister, Queen Berenguella, produced one son, named Alfonso, before the marriage was annulled in 1229; the boy returned to Castile with his mother, where they remained with Berenguella and Fernando. The name Alfonso usefully commemorated both Leonor's father and Jaime's paternal grandfather. Jaime, Pedro, and Alfonso were the most common names given to male members of the house of Aragón. See González, *Alfonso VIII*, I, 211; Díez, *Alfonso VIII*, 51-2.

Evidently, family ties in the Middle Ages could be as strong or as weak as they are today, and it seems that for the Angevin dynasty, those ties were felt keenly. The choices these women made in the naming of their children – and indeed, the choices do appear to have been theirs on several occasions – demonstrate strong female influence, and indicate that they had a sense of family cohesion and consciousness of heritage. This is highly suggestive of the existence of deep and lasting family ties within the Angevin royal house, in direct contrast to the more well-known feuds between Henry and his sons, or the now outdated notions of Eleanor of Aquitaine as a "bad" mother. The likely participation of Joanna, Leonor and Matilda in the dissemination of the cult of Thomas Becket, discussed in Part IV, indicates a strong sense of loyalty to their father, Henry II. Similarly, their choices in funerary arrangements for themselves and for their immediate family suggests a degree of matrilineal influence, especially as regards links to Fontevrault. These links between Eleanor's daughters and Fontevrault will form the basis of the following chapter.

Chapter Two
Fontevrault, Patronage and Family Ties

It will be useful at this juncture to briefly outline what patronage meant in the twelfth and thirteenth centuries, why it was important, and how queens could use it to their own advantage.[1] Patronage was undoubtedly one of the primary means by which royal and noble women could express power and authority, a public forum in which women could make their voices heard. For queens, patronage was viewed less as a permissible activity than as an expected duty, although contemporary clerics frequently warned against the dangers of prodigality.[2] Forms of patronage could vary from supporting, influencing, or inspiring literary, artistic, religious, or educational projects. The means to support these projects were usually financed by revenues from the queens' assigned dower lands, and both Joanna and Leonor clearly had access to ample sources of revenue from such a source during their reigns as queens of Sicily and Castile, even if, as we have seen, Joanna's access to her dower was restricted by her husband.[3]

There were two primary objectives in acts of female patronage. The first, and most important, was for spiritual ends, to ensure intercessory prayers for the souls of family members, a traditional role for queens. In 1199, soon after the death of her son Richard, Eleanor of Aquitaine made a grant to Fontevrault of one hundred pounds Poitevin to be paid yearly from her revenues from the Ile d'Oléron to fund an annual commemoration for herself and her family after her death. It was to be observed "firm and undisputed in perpetuity...for the health of our soul and the pious commemoration of our revered (*venerabilis*) husband King Henry, and King Henry our son of good memory, and the powerful man King Richard (*potentis viri regis Ricardi*) and our other sons and daughters".[4]

---

[1] For more on female patronage, see Pauline Stafford, 'The Patronage of Royal Women in England, Mid-Tenth to Mid-Twelfth Centuries', in *Medieval Queenship*, 143-67; June Hall McCash (ed.), *Cultural Patronage*, especially McCash, 'The Cultural Patronage of Medieval Women: An Overview', 1-49, and Shadis, 'Piety, Politics, and Power', 202-27; Webb, 'Queen and Patron', in *Queens and Queenship*, 205-21. Old, but still valuable, is W.W. Kibler's edited volume *Eleanor of Aquitaine, Patron and Politician*. For an interesting, although rather overstated, discussion of Eleanor as patron of courtly poetry, and for possible traces of her in German courtly verse, see Peter Volk, 'La reine Aliénor et la poésie courtoise Allemande', in *Plantagenêts et Capétiens*, 194-203. For Eleanor as an essentially mean and 'indifferent' patron, see Vincent, 'Patronage, Politics and Piety', 17-60.

[2] See Erickson, *Medieval Vision*, 181-212. For more on clerical misogyny, see G. Duby & M. Perrot (eds.), *A History of Women in the West: II. Silences of the Middle Ages*, ed. C. Klapisch-Zuber (Harvard University Press, 1992), especially J. Dalarun, 'The Clerical Gaze', 15-42; C. Klapisch-Zuber, 'Enforcing Order', 13-14; C. Thomasset, 'The Nature of Woman', 43-69; C. Frugoni, 'The Imagined Woman', 336-422. C. Casagrande's categories and subcategories of women is a useful study, 'The Protected Woman', 70-104; although P. L'Hermite-Leclerq's views on a 'golden age' for women in the tenth century are now rather outdated, 'The Feudal Order', 202-49.

[3] For Leonor and Joanna's dowers, see Part III. There is no extant record of Matilda's dower settlement.

[4] Martindale, 'Eleanor of Aquitaine', 17-18. For the charter, see J.H. Round, *Calendar of Documents preserved in France, Illustrative of the History of Great Britain and Ireland*, I, 918-1206 (London, HMSO), 391, no. 1101. See also T.S.R. Boase, 'Fontevrault and the Plantagenets', in *Journal of the British Archaeological Association*, 3rd ser., 34 (1971), 1-10; Robert Favreau, 'Aliénor d'Aquitaine et Fontevraud', in Aurell (ed.) *Alienor d'Aquitaine*, 40-5. Other grants from same period suggest 'the same sense of family solidarity', Martindale, 'Eleanor of Aquitaine', 18; see also Part I of this study.

Nine years previously, in June 1190, her daughter Leonor, together with her husband Alfonso VIII, had made a grant to Fontevrault of one hundred gold coins *annualem uno-quoque anno in perpetuum*.[5] The grant was apparently a late fulfilment of a promise made at the time of Leonor's marriage in 1170, as the charter specifies that Leonor and Alfonso, *ab adholescencia nostra, tempore contracti inter nos matrimonii...redditum centum aureorum promisimus nos daturos*. The primary purpose of the donation, however, was for the health of the soul of Leonor's recently deceased father Henry II, 'of most happy remembrance, whose body is buried in this same monastery of Fontevrault', with an accompanying request for prayers for Leonor, Alfonso, and their son and heir Fernando.[6] Nevertheless, as the charter specifies that the grant was made in fulfilment of Leonor's earlier promise, there is no reason to suppose that this was not the case, and that the donation served the dual purpose of benefaction and commemoration.[7]

Joanna also patronised Fontevrault, bequeathing to the abbey in 1199 one thousand shillings from her salt pans from her dowerlands at Agen for the maintenance of the nun's kitchen 'and for no other purpose'.[8] This is outlined in the sole surviving charter issued by Joanna, given at Rouen in September 1199 shortly before her death and witnessed by her mother Eleanor, in which she attests that the grant was made 'for the welfare of her soul and [that] of her dearest brother king Richard, and her father, mother, brothers and sisters'. Joanna's will confirms this grant, as well as providing further donations to the abbey and its associated convents which amount to approximately half of all her testamentary bequests.[9] In addition to the thousand shillings for the nun's kitchen and the money to support her annual commemoration, Joanna bequeathed 300 marks to all of the abbey's convents, a rent of ten marks to its infirmary, and a further rent of ten marks for buying fish yearly in Lent. Two nuns at Fontevrault, Agatha and Alice, were given a rent of six marks for life, and a staggering 900 marks was donated 'to pay the debts of the abbess'.

Joanna also made provision for her loyal servants, such as her chaplain Joscelin, her clerks Geoffrey and Durand, and a woman whose unusual Greek name of Malekakxa suggests she may either have been a maid Joanna retained after leaving Sicily, or one she acquired on Cyprus, perhaps in association with the daughter of Isaac Comnenos, who was placed under Joanna's charge. Joanna's maids Beatrice and Alice were highly favoured, receiving 200 and 140 marks respectively, as well as two of Joanna's coffers and all their contents. Two chaplains at Fontevrault were to receive ten marks for the celebration of an annual service 'for her soul and those of her ancestors', and a further twenty marks was given to the church 'for the anniversary of the king of Sicily and herself'. This is a touching tribute to her former husband which says as much about Joanna's first marriage as it does her second, as Raymond VI, who was still living, received no such mention.

---

[5] For the charter, see González, *Alfonso VIII*, II, no. 551.

[6] *Ibid.*

[7] Furthermore, an annual remembrance was performed for Henry II at the monastery of Las Huelgas on the anniversary of his death (6 June), González, *Alfonso VIII*, I, 191.

[8] For the charter, in which Joanna styles herself 'formerly queen of Sicily, now duchess of the March (*Duc' March*), countess of Thoulouse [*sic*], Marquise (*March*) of Provence', see Round, *Calendar of Documents*, I, 392, no. 1104. The charter was witnessed by Eleanor, '*carissima matre nostra*', as well as the archbishops of Canterbury and Rouen and the abbot of Turpenay. Raymond VI had acquired the Agenais in 1196 as Joanna's dowry, see Thomas Bisson, 'An Early Provincial Assembly: The General Court of Agenais in the Thirteenth Century', in Bisson, *Medieval France and her Pyrenean Neighbours* (Hambledon Press, London, 1989), 4.

[9] For Joanna's will, see Round, *Calendar of Documents*, I, 392-3, no. 1105. The original document has not survived, but the transcript is held at Archives Départementales de Maine-et-Loire, 101.H.55.

From Joanna's will it is clear that Fontevrault was the main beneficiary, although various other churches and convents in Rouen benefited as well, such as the convent at Bonneville, on the outskirts of Rouen, which received forty marks. Joanna bequeathed fifty marks to Rouen Cathedral, where her brother Henry was buried, and she also specified that six marks should go to St Katherine's, and two marks to every other religious house in Rouen. Of religious institutions in her marital lands of Toulouse, only two received testamentary bequests: the cathedral of St Etienne and the church of St Sernin were each bequeathed one of her tapestries.[10]

Joanna's benefactions thus largely favoured religious institutions, in particular Fontevrault, and in the main, her bequests favoured houses for women. Yet despite her position as countess of Toulouse and former queen of Sicily, it is clear that Joanna did not have access to personal financial resources at the time of her death in 1199. All of the money used to provide for Joanna's beneficence came from the three thousand marks owed to her from Richard's appropriation of the dower from her first marriage.[11] She refers to this in her will, stating that 'the king her brother' still owes her this money. This is a reference to John's promise, made 26 August 1199 at the instigation of their mother Eleanor, to honour the debt which Richard owed to Joanna in lieu of her Sicilian dower.[12] The money was to be provided expressly in order for Joanna to make her testamentary bequests; on the same date, John provided Joanna with the further financial assistance of 100 marks, again 'with the advice of his dearest lady and mother' for 'his dearest sister...to bestow for ever on whom she will, for her soul'.[13] This, along with the number of debts referred to in her will, such as the thousand shillings owed to Proteval the Jew, and the undefined amount owed to the burgesses of Agen and Condom, suggest that her experience as countess of Toulouse was poor in all senses of the word.[14]

The heavily pregnant Joanna had fled to Fontevrault after failing to withstand the siege of Les Casses in Toulouse. According to Joseph Vaissete, whose *Histoire Générale de Languedoc*, whilst being a very late source, provides the fullest account of these events, Joanna herself headed the army against the rebels and besieged the castle. She was apparently betrayed by her own people who smuggled weapons and supplies to the rebels and set fire to her camp, forcing her to lift the siege. Joanna fled Toulouse with the intention of seeking aid from her brother Richard. It was not until she was already en route to Richard's court, however, that she learnt of her brother's death, and, 'overcome with sadness', retired to Fontevrault.[15] Jean Flori, however, states that on learning of Richard's death, Joanna fled first to her mother in Niort, and that it was Eleanor who placed her daughter under the care of the nuns at Fontevrault.[16] Turner, on the other hand, states that Joanna first learnt of Richard's death once she was at Niort with Eleanor, suggesting that it was to her mother that Joanna had originally meant to

---

[10] These were the two largest and most important churches in Toulouse, and both served as burial churches of the comital dynasty.

[11] For the problems relating to Joanna's Sicilian dower, Howden, *Gesta*, II, 132-3; *Chronica*, III, 61-5; see also Part III.

[12] For the charter, in which John is keen to point out that once the three thousand marks have been paid, 'he shall be quit of all debts due from king Richard to queen Joan', see Round, *Calendar of Documents*, 391, no. 1103.

[13] *Ibid.*, 391, no. 1102.

[14] This debt was 'for all she has had from their stalls'. Joanna also discusses possible outstanding amounts owed to the tallager of Toulouse which 'shall be repaid, when proved on oath, from the revenues of the land of Agen', Round, *Calendar of Documents*, I, 393, no. 1105.

[15] Vaissete, *Histoire*, III, 247-8. The account given by Vaissete (1685-1756) is neither contemporary nor first-hand, but he did have access to documents which were subsequently destroyed in the French Revolution.

[16] Flori, *Eleanor of Aquitaine*, 190.

flee.[17] In either case, one of Joanna's first actions upon reaching the safety of her mother's court was to visit Richard's tomb at the abbey of Fontevrault.[18] She spent some months there, before journeying to Rouen for a conference with her brother John. It was whilst Joanna was in Rouen that she fell mortally ill, and declared her intention, despite being married and pregnant, to take religious vows and enter Fontevrault Abbey as a consecrated nun.[19]

Joanna first requested a consultation with the abbess Matilda, but realising that the abbess might not arrive in time, she 'begged the Archbishop of Canterbury [Hubert Walter], who was present, to let her take the veil and be consecrated to God'.[20] The archbishop, however, not wishing to act without the abbess' authority, cited the difficulties inherent in her wish; namely, that her husband, Raymond of Toulouse, was still living, and, more pertinently, that she was soon to bear a child, the future of which would be uncertain should she take the veil.[21] Nevertheless, Joanna 'persisted with such zeal and fervour that the archbishop, believing her to be inspired by heaven, consecrated her to God and the order of Fontevrault'.[22] Joanna's consecration was performed in the presence of her mother Eleanor and various members of clergy, including Luke, the abbot of Turpenay, who had previously overseen the funerary services for Joanna's brother Richard.[23]

Joanna died soon after her consecration, on 24 September 1199, and her son, born posthumously, lived only long enough to be baptised before he was buried in the cathedral at Rouen.[24] The selection of this site is significant, as Rouen had also received the body of Joanna's brother, Henry the Young King, as well as, more recently, the heart of her brother Richard. Her son was therefore being laid to rest amongst the dukes of Normandy, and apparently, it was thought fitting that she should be too, as Joanna's body was also initially laid to rest in Rouen Cathedral, although it was subsequently removed for reburial in the nun's cemetery at Fontevrault, probably at the instigation of her mother.[25] It was certainly Eleanor who acted as executor of Joanna's will, taking the original document personally to Raymond of Toulouse to ensure that he honour the terms of its provisions 'as far as he is concerned'.[26]

---

[17] Turner, *Eleanor of Aquitaine*, 286.

[18] *Ibid.*, 286.

[19] Vaissete, *Histoire*, III, 248; Flori, *Eleanor of Aquitaine*, 190; Turner, *Eleanor of Aquitaine*, 286. Joanna's conference with John in Rouen, and her subsequent entry into the abbey of Fontevrault immediately prior to her death, are also briefly related on Joanna's epitaph; see Pavillon, *Vie du bienheureux Robert d'Arbrissel*, 588, no. 96. It was presumably at this time that the arrangements were made regarding her will.

[20] Vaissete, *Histoire*, III, 249; Kelly, *Eleanor of Aquitaine*, 354.

[21] Kelly, *Eleanor of Aquitaine*, 354-5.

[22] Vaissete, *Histoire*, III, 249; Kelly, *Eleanor of Aquitaine*, 355; Flori, *Eleanor of Aquitaine*, 190; Turner, *Eleanor of Aquitaine*, 286. Trindade, however, asserts that Joanna's desire to become a consecrated nun at Fontevrault was not granted until after her death in childbirth, *Berengaria*, 144.

[23] The abbey of Turpenay was favoured both by Eleanor, in a charter given at Fontevrault on 21 April 1199, and by Joanna in her will. See Flori, *Eleanor of Aquitaine*, 184n; Turner, *Eleanor of Aquitaine*, 278.

[24] Vaissete, *Histoire*, III, 249; Pavillon, *Vie du bienheureux Robert d'Arbrissel*, 588, no. 96; Kelly, *Eleanor of Aquitaine*, 355.

[25] Turner, *Eleanor of Aquitaine*, 286; Joanna's epitaph suggests that the it was the prioress of Fontevrault who oversaw Joanna's interment in the main church, beside the body of her brother Richard ; see Pavillon, *Vie du bienheureux Robert d'Arbrissel*, 588, no. 96. See also *Histoire des Ducs de Normandie et des rois d'Angleterre*, ed. Francois Michel (Paris, 1840), 83-4: 'moru-ele à Ruem d'enfant, et fu enfouie el le mere-eglyse de Ruem; mais ele n'i gist ore pas, car ele fu puis desfouie et portée a Frontevraut, ù ses peres et se mere gisent e li rois Richars ses freres. [Cele dame ot à nom Jehane.]'

[26] Round, *Calendar of Documents*, I, 393, no. 1105.

Joanna's will explicitly expresses her intention to be buried and commemorated at what she probably viewed as the family necropolis. Whether she would have been buried at Monreale, had she ended her life as queen of Sicily, is a moot point. Certainly, William II had intended his foundation to be a dynastic necropolis, but previous queens of Sicily had all been interred in separate churches from their royal husbands.[27] Joanna was not buried in the royal crypt at Fontevrault, but *'inter velatas'*, amongst the nuns.[28] As with much other information about Joanna, the effigy which may once have adorned her tomb, along with the tomb itself, has been lost to time. As Joanna was buried in the nun's cemetery, however, she may not even have had an effigy, and her grave may have been identified merely with a simple marker as a sign of humility.[29]

There is therefore documentary evidence of both Eleanor of Aquitaine and two of her daughters patronising Fontevrault, expressed largely in terms of dynastic commemoration, and this suggests that Eleanor of Aquitaine may have influenced her daughters in this respect.[30] Fontevrault had long been Eleanor's preferred religious house, and it is where she retired to in her later years. Some of her children also seem to have spent some time being educated at the abbey in their early childhood, although it is unclear how long they remained there.[31] The abbey, founded by Robert of Arbrissel in 1100 as a double Benedictine house on the border between Poitou and Anjou, fell under the ecclesiastical jurisdiction of the bishop of Poitiers and therefore lay at the heart of Eleanor's ancestral lands.[32] Moreover, the abbey had been controlled by Eleanor's ancestors since the tenth century: her grandfather, William IX, had donated the lands on which the abbey was to be built, and his wife, Philippa of Toulouse, took refuge at Fontevrault after she was repudiated in 1115, dying there in 1118.[33] Eleanor's father, William X, had made a grant to the abbey in 1134, which she confirmed sometime after his death in 1137 in her capacity as countess of Poitou.[34]

---

[27] Elvira, first wife of Roger II, was buried at the chapel of St Mary Magdalene in Palermo, as was his third wife Beatrice; his second wife Sibylla was buried at Cava. See Norwich, *Kingdom in the Sun*, 89; Chalandon, *Domination Normande*, 310; Jamison, 'England and Sicily', 27. Roger himself was interred at Palermo Cathedral, although he seems to have intended Cefalù to be his resting place. Margaret of Navarre was buried at Monreale, but William I's original burial place was the Capella Palatina. His translation to Monreale was overseen by William II, Josef Deér, *The Dynastic Porphyry Tombs of the Norman Period in Sicily* (Harvard University Press, 1959), 15.

[28] Howden, *Chronica*, IV, 96. See also Boase, 'Fontevrault and the Plantagenets', 6; Trindade, *Berengaria*, 144. Vaissete, however, stated that Joanna was buried at the feet of her father Henry and beside her brother Richard, *Histoire*, III, 249-50.

[29] When Eleanor came to commission the effigies for the dynastic tombs at Fontevrault, however, she may well have ordered an effigy for her daughter. For more on the tombs at Fontevrault, and Eleanor's involvement in commissioning them, see the following chapter.

[30] Similarly, the patronage choices of Leonor's own daughters display influence from their natal family; see Shadis, 'Piety, Politics, and Power', 218.

[31] See Part I.

[32] Martindale, 'Eleanor of Aquitaine', 20. The abbey's rule was confirmed in 1106 by Pope Paschal II, and by Arbrissel's death in 1117 the double house had grown rapidly from its humble origins to become a rich, highly organised, and complex institution. Arbrissel, a successful hermit and preacher, has been credited with holding controversially lenient views on the place of women, both in the Church and in society in general. See J. Smith, 'Robert of Arbrissel: *Procurator Mulierum*', in *Medieval Women*, 175-84.

[33] Martindale, 'Eleanor of Aquitaine', 19; Flori, *Eleanor of Aquitaine*, 20. Philippa of Toulouse had founded the sister-priory of Lespinasse, near Toulouse; and Eleanor's maternal grandfather Aimeri, viscount of Châtellerault, was personally acquainted with Robert of Arbrissel. Eleanor's father also patronised the Fontevriste priories of Soussis and Saint-Bibien, making grants in their favour in 1134; see Favreau, 'Aliénor d'Aquitaine ', 41.

[34] Martindale, 'Eleanor of Aquitaine', 20, 20n.

Fontevrault was also linked to the Angevin dynasty: it was patronised both by Henry II's grandfather Fulk V, as well as his father Geoffrey, and Henry's aunt Matilda was abbess there when he was crowned king of England.[35] Fulk V had been close to Fontevrault's founder, Robert of Arbrissel, and offered his protection to the community he established there, continuing to protect and patronise the abbey and approving of its expansion long after Arbrissel departed from the region to continue his life as an itinerant preacher.[36] Indeed, Jean Dunbabin has described Fontevrault as 'the one place that elicited more than merely the conventional pious response from the ruling house of Anjou'.[37] Fulk's mother, Bertrada of Montfort, established the priory of Hautes-Bruyères as a daughter-house of the abbey, and both she and her daughter Matilda retired to Fontevrault in later life.[38] Matilda, who joined the community in 1128 after the death in 1120 of her husband William, the unfortunate son of Henry I who drowned in the White Ship disaster, became abbess of Fontevrault in 1150, and her presence at the abbey heralded the first English royal grant, 'a gift in 1129 from Henry I of one hundred pounds of money of Rouen and fifty English marks to be paid every Michaelmas for the weal of his father, mother, wife, his son William, and himself'.[39] This grant was an important resource for Fontevrault, and was later confirmed by King Stephen, and reconfirmed by Henry II whilst he was still Duke of Normandy and Count of Anjou.[40] Furthermore, the grant 'did much to consolidate Anglo-Angevin support', and the dynastic links with the abbey were the impetus for Eleanor's visit to Fontevrault in 1152.[41]

Henry and Eleanor both revisited the abbey in 1173 to confirm a grant, their last joint action before Eleanor's imprisonment for her part in their sons' rebellion.[42] In 1185 she returned to France, accompanied by her daughter Matilda and Henry the Lion, and made a further grant to Fontevrault of one hundred pounds per annum and revenue from wine tax in Poitiers. This was given with the consent of her husband and sons, and was later confirmed by both Henry and Richard, who continued the Angevin family tradition of patronising Fontevrault.[43]

Thus Fontevrault had many ties with both Eleanor's natal and affinal families from the time of its foundation in 1100, and family ties to the abbey were cemented when first Henry, and then two of their children, were buried at Fontevrault during Eleanor's lifetime. The decision to inter Henry at Fontevrault may well have been circumstantial – he died at nearby

---

[35] Dunbabin, *France in the Making*, 339-40.

[36] *Ibid.*, 367-8. A fifteenth century transcript of a grant to Fontevrault given by Fulk is held at Arch. Dep. 157 H2.

[37] Dunbabin, *France in the Making*, 368.

[38] Martindale, 'Eleanor of Aquitaine', 20, 20n. For other daughter houses established by the Angevins, see Boase, 'Fontevrault and the Plantagenets', 4.

[39] Boase, 'Fontevrault and the Plantagenets', 4; Martindale, 'Eleanor of Aquitaine', 20, 20n; see also *Regesta Regum Anglo-Normannorum, 1066-1154, II: Regesta Henrici Primi, 1100-1135*, ed. C. Johnson and H.A. Cronne (Oxford, 1956), no. 1580.

[40] For Stephen's confirmation grant, *Regesta Regum Anglo-Normannorum, 1066-1154 : III : Regesta Regis Stephani ac Mathildis Imperatricis ac Gaufridi et Henrici Ducum Normannorum, 1135-54*, ed. H.A. Cronne and R.H.C. Davis (Oxford, 1969), 123-4; for Henry's confirmation grant, *ibid.*, 125-6.

[41] Boase, 'Fontevrault and the Plantagenets', 4. Eleanor stated that she was "moved by divine prompting to visit the congregation of the holy virgins of Fontevrault", and 'touched in her heart' she confirmed all the gifts of her father and predecessors, and the grant [fifty shillings of Poitou per annum] made by herself and Louis of France", Boase, 'Fontevrault and the Plantagenets', 4-5; see also Favreau, 'Aliénor d'Aquitaine', 41-2. These grants continued after Matilda's death in 1154.

[42] See *RHII*, III, nos. CCCCLVII and CCCCLVIII.

[43] See *RHII*, Introduction, 550, and no. 465C; and for Henry's confirmation of the now-lost original, III, no. DCLV.

Chinon – but the burials there in 1199 of Richard and Joanna suggest that by this date at least, Eleanor may have begun to view the abbey as a dynastic mausoleum. Her decision to be interred there amongst the other members of her family could therefore be viewed in terms of a conscious and deliberate programme of dynastic commemoration.[44]

Care of the family's souls after death, demonstrated in the grants to Fontevrault made by Eleanor, Leonor and Joanna, was one of the responsibilities of queens, and control over funerary rites, burials and the commissioning of tombs could prove to be a way for royal women to express their power and authority. The establishment of dynastic mausolea were concrete and permanent reminders of family power and influence, and both Eleanor and her daughter Leonor used patronage as a tool so effectively that their memories are enshrined for eternity – or at least, in the case of Fontevrault, until the French Revolution – at their respective mausolea at Fontevrault and Las Huelgas.

Thus we come to a more political motive for patronage: to bolster the prestige of the royal family. Women were often driving forces behind developments in art and literature, using them for political ends, such as the recording of great deeds performed by their ancestors in order to glorify their dynasty. Leonor's daughter Berenguella, for example, commissioned Lucas de Tuy to compose the *Crónica de España*.[45] The education of their children was a role queens were expected to perform, and this presented them with the opportunity to influence their childrens' choices, not least in terms of patronage.[46] But do these acts of *memoria*, like the evidence found through examining dynastic nomenclature, also indicate a personal, emotional attachment to family members? And what might this suggest about the degree of influence that Eleanor may have had over her daughters?

---

[44] Nicholas Vincent has suggested that Eleanor's retirement to and subsequent burial at Fontevrault beside Henry II is indicative of 'some depth of attachment to her late husband', 'Patronage, Politics and Piety', 28-9. Unlikely as this may be, Vincent is undoubtedly right to point out that Eleanor's involvement in the burials of Henry and two of her children at Fontevrault, as well as the possibility that she oversaw arrangements for her own burial there, demonstrate that dynastic commemoration 'appears to have been one of her most abiding concerns', 'Patronage, Politics and Piety', 29, 44. The burial at Fontevrault of Joanna's son Raymond VII of Toulouse marked 'the close of this widespread family cult', Boase, 'Fontevrault and the Plantagenets', 7. See also C.T. Wood, 'Fontevraud, Dynasticism, and Eleanor of Aquitaine', in *Eleanor of Aquitaine: Lord and Lady*, 407-22.

[45] As de Tuy states in his Prologue, *Crónica de España*, 3.

[46] See Part I. David Herlihy has highlighted the importance of the mother as a 'mediator in generational conflicts... [a repository] of sacred wisdom...[and a channel] through which a significant part of the cultural inheritance passed from the old to the young', *Medieval Households*, 129.

Chapter Three
Burial Patterns and Dynastic Mausolea

The establishment of Fontevrault as a royal necropolis marked a change in the way kings of England were buried. Previous kings had chosen personal foundations as their burial places, in order to receive personal intercessory prayers from the monks.[1] Their queens were similarly buried in separate foundations, apart from their husbands. King Stephen's queen Matilda of Boulogne was the first Anglo-Norman queen to be buried with her husband, at his foundation of Faversham, and this set the precedent for joint burials, although the burial of royal spouses together within the same tomb did not become the norm until the end of the fourteenth century.[2] The tombs of Eleanor of Aquitaine and Henry II at Fontevrault, and those of their daughter Matilda and Henry the Lion at Brunswick which date to c.1240, could be seen as the precedents for this, although they were not interred in the same tomb, and possibly were not originally placed next to each other.[3]

Thus the dynastic mausoleum of the Angevins marks a departure from the normal burial practices of English monarchs. So why the change? Were the burials at Fontevrault circumstantial, or did Eleanor intentionally establish a programme of commemoration for the entire family? The Holy Land, which Eleanor visited in the 1140s on cruasde with her husband Louis VII, contained many contemporary examples of joint royal burials and magnificent tombs, as well as a long tradition of burying queens in particular with great honour. Eleanor almost certainly visited the Church of the Holy Sepulchre in Jerusalem with Louis VII, where the bodies of four crusader-kings, including Fulk of Anjou, were interred, albeit without effigies. Byzantine emperors were traditionally buried at the Church of the Holy Apostles in Constantinople, often with their wives, in magnificent tombs, though also without effigies. Furthermore, there was a tradition in Constantinople of burying queens with honour in specially selected sacred sites, such as at the Church of Our Lady.[4]

Eleanor's travels in the East, then, may have inspired her to implement a programme of dynastic commemoration for her own family. Norman Sicily provided another source of inspiration. Eleanor had visited twice, once in 1147 on her return journey from crusade,[5] and once in 1191 to deliver Richard's bride Berengaria.[6] There had been a long tradition of dynastic

---

[1] Elizabeth Hallam has noted that although such churches were ostensibly chosen for their intercessory capabilities, they were usually magnificent and imposing buildings, demonstrating that 'even while ensuring personalised prayers for themselves, [kings] were concerned that they should be buried in suitably honorific churches', 'Royal Burial and the Cult of Kingship in France and England, 1060-1330', *Journal of Medieval History*, 8:4 (London, 1982), 369.

[2] The first time an English king and queen were interred in the same tomb was the joint burial of Henry IV and his second wife Joan of Navarre. See Evans, *Death of Kings*, 210-11. The magnificent funeral and tomb of Eleanor of Castile, beyond the scope of this thesis, are discussed by Parsons, 'Burials of Queens', 317-37. Her tomb at Westminster, which she helped to establish as the new Plantagenet mausoleum, displays both her Castilian and Ponthevin arms. See also Binski, *Westminster Abbey*, 107-12.

[3] Parsons, 'Burials of Queens', 322n. For more on the tombs at Fontevrault, see the following chapter. For the tombs of Matilda and Henry the Lion, see Part IV.

[4] Nolan, 'The Queen's Choice', 387. For Eleanor in Jerusalem and Constantinople, see Flori, *Eleanor of Aquitaine*, 49-50, 54.

[5] Flori, *Eleanor of Aquitaine*, 54.

[6] See Part II.

mausolea in Norman Sicily, culminating with the foundation of Monreale, the creation of Eleanor's son-in-law, William II.[7] The abbey of St Denis in Paris, which ultimately became the dynastic necropolis of the French monarchy, and which was being constructed by Abbot Suger during Eleanor's time as queen of France, may have been another source of inspiration.[8] It seems possible, however, that the inspiration for Fontevrault to become the Angevin family necropolis may have originated with the foundation of Las Huelgas de Burgos in Castile, of which Eleanor must surely have been aware, despite Rose Walker's unlikely contention that mother and daughter had no contact with each other after Leonor's marriage.[9]

Eleanor and Leonor, Fontevrault and Las Huelgas

Both Fontevrault and Las Huelgas ultimately became dynastic mausloea, and whilst it is unclear how far Eleanor intended this to be the case for Fontevrault, it seems certain that Las Huelgas was intended to be the royal burial house from its inception. The *Primera Crónica General* clearly states that the inspiration for the creation of Las Huelgas came from Leonor: 'because of the many requests of the noble queen Leonor, and because of his fondness for his wife, [Alfonso] began to build near Burgos a convent for Cistercian nuns'.[10] As the *Crónica* was commissioned by Leonor's grandson, Fernando III, Rose Walker has implied that this assertion may have been made simply to please Fernando, by honouring his maternal grandmother.[11] Yet the same would have been equally true had the chronicle claimed that it was Alfonso, Fernando's maternal grandfather, who had instigated the construction of the abbey.

Lucas de Tuy, commissioned to write his *Crónica de España* by Leonor's daughter Berenguella, does not mention Leonor's role and attributes the foundation solely to Alfonso, leading Walker to wonder if Leonor's involvement, as recorded in the *Primera Crónica*, is mere literary *topos*.[12] *Topoi*, however, often work precisely because they contain grains of truth, and there exists decisive evidence of Leonor's involvement in the foundation of the abbey. Both Leonor and Alfonso are recognised as the joint founders in Clement III's bull of 1188, which confirms Las Huelgas's status and recognises its independence from episcopal jurisdiction.[13] That the enterprise was conceived of as a joint foundation does not necessarily preclude Leonor's influence: the issuing of joint charters was standard Castilian royal practice; furthermore, joint acts of patronage are all too easily and all too often attributed to the husband alone, often concealing the possible – and sometimes likely – instigation of the wife.

The foundation charter for Las Huelgas, dated June 1187, also describes the abbey as a joint foundation, and the inclusion of Leonor and Alfonso's daughters, Berenguella (at this

---

[7] For more on Monreale, see Part IV. Elizabeth Hallam has pointed out that Monreale presents 'an interesting parallel to [Las Huelgas]...but its model was probably...Fontevrault', 'Royal Burial', 371.

[8] For a comprehensive assessment of Suger and St Denis, see Lindy Grant, *Abbot Suger of St-Denis: Church and State in Early Twelfth-Century France* (Longman, Essex, 1998). For Eleanor's possible involvement in the early stages of the creation of the abbey, see Eleanor S. Greenhill, 'Eleanor, Abbot Suger, and Saint-Denis', in *Eleanor of Aquitaine: Patron and Politician*, 81-113.

[9] Walker, 'Leonor of England', 356. She suggests that 'family precedents' of the necropolises of the counts of Anjou (at St Nicolas in Angers) and of the counts of Aquitaine (at Montierneuf in Poitiers) are also possible sources of inspiration, 'Leonor of England', 364.

[10] *PCG*, 685. The *Crónica Latina*, 72, describes the foundation of the royal monastery as the joint enterprise of Fernando III's grandparents.

[11] Walker, 'Leonor of England', 350.

[12] *Crónica de España*, 409; Walker, 'Leonor of England', 351.

[13] See Walker, 'Leonor of England', 356n.

time the heir-apparent) and Urraca, giving their consent to the charter provides evidence of the family as an emotional community.[14] The charter, which states explicitly that the convent was to observe the Cistercian rule in perpetuity, gives no indication that the abbey was originally intended as a dynastic mausoleum, but if the possible models for the Castilian convent are considered together with the archaeological evidence of tombs, it would seem clear that this was indeed the intent from its inception.[15] This being the case, it is hard to see how the idea of a royal necropolis could have been borrowed from Fontevrault, as Miriam Shadis has suggested, as Las Huelgas had been constructed and dedicated by 1187, two years before the death and burial of Henry II.[16]

The earliest documented evidence of the decision to establish Las Huelgas as a dynastic mausoleum is found in a charter of Alfonso VIII dated December 1199, by which time Henry II, Richard I and Joanna had all been interred at Fontevrault. In the charter, Alfonso promises that he, Leonor and their children will be buried at the abbey.[17] This promise is confirmed in Alfonso's will of 1204, which also confirms that the foundation was a joint enterprise between husband and wife.[18] These documents seem to suggest that the idea of a dynastic mausoleum at Las Huelgas was first conceived of *after* the Angevin burials at Fontevrault. The existence at Las Huelgas of three child-sized tombs, however, one of which is inscribed with the date 1194, strongly suggest that the abbey was designed from the outset to house the remains of the Castilian royal family.[19]

Several of Alfonso and Leonor's children died young, and it is possible that Las Huelgas may have been conceived of as a burial house for the royal offspring. I propose, however, that its original purpose was indeed as a dynastic mausoleum.[20] The late evidence for Alfonso's wish to be interred at Las Huelgas may have been an astute political decision not to offend the Castilian bishops, especially the archbishop of Toledo, who may well have expected to receive the body of the king into his own cathedral, the traditional resting place of the kings of Castile.[21] Both Fontevrault and Las Huelgas thus mark a departure from previous traditions in

---

[14] For the charter, see González, *Alfonso VIII*, II, no. 472. It makes no reference, however, as to why the abbey was constructed as a house for female religious.

[15] For most later kings of Castile, Las Huelgas also served as their coronation church. In 1255 Alfonso X made a gift to the abbey intended "to do good and to show mercy to the abbess and to the convent of this same place and for the souls of the very noble and honourable king Don Alfonso, my grandfather, who built the above named monastery, and of his wife the queen Doña Leonor and of the queen Doña Berenguella my grandmother and of the queen Doña Beatrice my mother, and of the other *of my lineage* who are buried here", Shadis, 'Piety, Politics, and Power', 209. Her italics.

[16] Shadis, 'Piety, Politics, and Power', 205. Shadis may have been misled by the erroneous chronology in both the *PCG* and the *Crónica de España*, both of which place the foundation of Las Huelgas in the late 1190s. The foundation charter, however, makes it clear that the abbey was founded in 1187. See also Xavier Dectot, *Les tombeaux des familles royales de la péninsule ibérique au Moyen Âge* (Brepols, Belgium, 2009), 118-9.

[17] For this charter, see González, *Alfonso VIII*, III, no. 682. The charter continues to state that if Alfonso or Leonor join any religious order, it will be the Cistercian order and no other.

[18] *Item, dono pro meo aniuersario, monasterio Burgensis Sancte Marie Regalis, quod ego et regina uxor mea construximus, ubi corpus meum tumuletur.* See González, *Alfonso VIII*, III, no. 769. For more on Alfonso's will, see the following chapter.

[19] The tombs are similar in style and iconography to that of Alfonso's mother, Blanca of Navarre, at Santa Maria del Real. See Walker, 'Leonor of England', 356. For more on the tombs at Las Huelgas, see the following chapter.

[20] As both Walker, 'Leonor of England', 366-7, and Dectot, *Les tombeaux*, 122, 248, have suggested. Dectot argues further that Las Huelgas also served as the site where the bodies were prepared for burial, *Les tombeaux*, 122-3.

[21] Alfonso VIII's immediate predecessors were buried at Toledo Cathedral, apart from their queens and offspring; see Walker, 'Leonor of England', 350, 367.

burial practices. Fontevrault may not have been either the model for Las Huelgas or the inspiration for a Castilian pantheon, but could Las Huelgas instead have provided the inspiration for Eleanor of Aquitaine to implement a similar programme of commemoration at Fontevrault? The evidence makes it more likely that Las Huelgas inspired Eleanor to establish a dynastic mausoleum at Fontevrault rather than *vice versa*. But what inspired Las Huelgas?

Rose Walker has convincingly dismissed past theories that Fontevrault was the inspiration for Las Huelgas, concluding that the creation of the Castilian abbey was inspired solely by earlier Spanish *infantados* (convents for unmarried royal daughters or sisters, which offered them considerable authority and influence), such as Sigena, San Isidoro, and, especially, Sahagún.[22] Whilst acknowledging that both Fontevrault and Las Huelgas were female houses dedicated to the Virgin, which came about through acts of female patronage, and which ultimately functioned as dynastic mausolea, Walker draws no connection between the two abbeys, seeing Las Huelgas as a 'peculiarly Iberian, even Castilian, institution'.[23]

The model for the dynastic mausoleum at Las Huelgas appears to have come from Spanish royal burial practices. Several family necropolises existed for the monarchs of the various Spanish kingdoms, such as the eleventh-century monasteries of Sahagún and San Isidoro in León, Sigena in Aragón, and Santa Maria del Real at Najera in Navarre. The tenth-century counts of Barcelona also had their own dynastic mausoleum at Ripoll. Of these, San Isidoro, the joint foundation of Fernando I (1037-65) and his queen Sancha (d.1067), has perhaps the most direct correlations with Las Huelgas. Both were joint foundations, and both became the royal pantheons of their founders and their families. According to the anonymous *Historia Silense*, possibly written under the direction of their daughter Urraca, Fernando founded San Isidoro as a dynastic mausoleum at the behest of his wife, Sancha.[24] An inscription at San Isidoro confirms that the abbey was established by both monarchs, and completed by Sancha after Fernando's death.[25] In the same way, the *Primera Crónica* accredits Leonor with persuading Alfonso to build the convent of Las Huelgas.[26]

San Isidoro was created as an *infantado*, and on his deathbed Fernando bequeathed the abbey to his daughters Elvira and Urraca.[27] It was probably Fernando's granddaughter Urraca, who ruled from 1079-1126, who ordered the construction of the Pantheon of Kings, dated

---

[22] See Walker, 'Leonor of England', 346-68, especially 357-61; see also Dectot, *Les tombeaux*, 171-2.

[23] Walker, 'Leonor of England', 346. Walker is wrong, however, in stating that the establishment of Las Huelgas is the only act of patronage definitively attributed to Leonor, as the creation of the Becket altar demonstrates. She is also wrong to state that Leonor only appears on charters issued conjointly with Alfonso, as testified by the charter she issued for the altar; 'Leonor of England', 350. For a discussion of the Becket altar at Toledo and the charter of donation, see Part IV.

[24] Walker, 'Leonor of England', 360. See also Rose Walker, 'Images of royal and aristocratic burial in northern Spain, c. 950-c. 1250', in Elisabeth Van Houts (ed.), *Medieval Memories: Men, Women and the Past, 700-1300* (Longman, Essex, 2001), 151. The monastery was actually a reconstruction of the tenth century double monastery founded by Sancho I (956-66) and his sister Elvira, who was the first abbess. Sancho's wife Teresa was also later abbess after Sancho's death. It was Fernando's original intention to be buried at either of the Castilian pantheons San Pedro de Arlanza or San Salvador de Oña, suggesting an interesting parallel to the burial of Henry II: in both cases their final resting place was chosen ultimately by their wives.

[25] San Isidoro was dedicated in 1063. When Fernando died in 1065, Sancha entered the order there.

[26] See above, n.10.

[27] San Isidoro was finally given to the Augustinians in 1148 by Sancha, the sister of Alfonso VII and Alfonso VIII's great-aunt who is reputed to have been buried in the abbey. It also claims the burial of Sancha's father, Alfonso V (999-1027), her brother, Vermudo III (1027-37) and, tenuously, Sancho the Great. Fernando's son Garcia, the deposed king of Galicia, is also buried there, as well as some women and children of the family. See Walker, 'Royal and aristocratic burial in Spain', 159.

to the 1080s, which depicts Fernando and Sancha kneeling before the Cross, and which also housed a now-lost statue of Urraca.[28] Political motivations for the promotion of the Leonese dynasty over the rival kingdom of Castile aside, San Isidoro was from the start intended to be the Leonese royal necropolis. Fernando and Sancha's son Alfonso VI, however, established his own pantheon at Sahagún, where he was buried with four of his six wives. Sahagún became the greatest Cluniac monastery in Castile, and has been described as 'the Saint-Denis and Cluny of...León and Castile'.[29] The many similarities between San Isidoro and Las Huelgas suggest that Leonor and Alfonso may have tried to emulate their illustrious forebears, not least in terms of patronage. San Isidoro, Sahagún and Las Huelgas all had palaces on the monastery complex. Unlike San Isidoro and Sahagún, however, Las Huelgas was created as an institution for women.

Houses for female religious were an unusual choice for new establishments at this time. Male Cluniac institutions such as Sahagún were much more popular, although female participation in *memoria* was restricted in such establishments. Women were markedly more visible when mausolea were female houses, under the control of an abbess who more often than not was intimately linked to the royal family. The abbey of Fontevrault was one such institution – could it have provided the inspiration for Leonor and Alfonso to found a house for female religious at Las Huelgas?

There were several convents in Spain both prior to and contemporary with Las Huelgas, such as Sigena in Aragón, founded in 1188 by Alfonso VIII's aunt Sancha.[30] There was also a long tradition of *infantados*, of which San Isidoro is one example; another is the abbey of San Salvador, built in the mid tenth century by Ramiro II (931-51) as an *infantado* for his unmarried daughter Elvira.[31] San Salvador was discontinued in the eleventh century and some of its property was given to the new foundation of Las Huelgas. This suggests that Las Huelgas may have originally been created as a new sort of *infantado*; certainly at least one of Leonor and Alfonso's daughters, Constanza, was dedicated to the abbey from childhood. The early child burials of both male and female offspring at Las Huelgas, however, makes it more likely that the abbey served a dual purpose, as both *infantado* and royal pantheon, as was the case at San Isidoro.

The nuns of Las Huelgas were all drawn from the very highest ranks of the aristocracy. The *Primera Crónica* states that from the time of the abbey's completion it was filled with more princesses and noblewomen than any other convent in Spain.[32] Leonor's daughter Constanza appears to have become abbess at Las Huelgas, and two other daughters entered the abbey in 1229: Berenguella ended her days there, and Leonor retired there after the annulment

---

[28] See Walker, 'Royal and aristcoratic burial in Spain', 151, and for more on the patronage of Fernando and, especially, of Sancha, 150-2.

[29] Serafín Moralejo, 'On the Road: The Camino de Santiago', in *The Art of Medieval Spain* (The Metropolitan Museum of Art, New York, 1993), 179.

[30] Alfonso's contemporary, Pedro II of Aragón, was interred at the Aragonese necropolis at Sigena, 'which his mother Sancha had built and established as a convent for the women of the Order of the Hospital of Jerusalem', *The Chronicle of San Juan de la Peña: A Fourteenth Century Official History of the Crown of Aragon*, ed. and trans. L. H. Nelson (University of Pennsylvania Press, Philadelphia, 1991), 60-1.

[31] San Salvador in León was 'The first of the Infantados, monasteries created deliberately for daughters of royal or comital families, and [it] may have been created as a royal pantheon', Roger Collins, 'Queens-Dowager and Queens-Regent in Tenth Century León and Navarre', in *Medieval Queenship*, 80. Ramiro's daughter Elvira later became titular abbess of the abbey; Ramiro himself, as well as his successors Ordoño III (951-6) and Sancho I (956-66) were all buried there.

[32] *PCG*, 685.

of her marriage to Jaime I of Aragon, although neither woman seems to have taken the veil.[33] Berenguella's granddaughter and namesake, the Infanta Berenguella, entered the abbey in 1241, taking the veil in 1246, probably at her grandmother's instigation. She retained her privileged royal position, acting in concert with the abbesses, and in 1255 her brother Alfonso X formally recognised her as head of the abbey.[34]

The importance of maintaining good relations with the abbess of such a powerful, semi-autonomous institution is obvious, hence the election of royal and noble women who would be at once capable of the job, acceptable to the order, and pliable to the royal family's wishes. This would also have been the case at Fontevrault, which would have had more flexibility in this regard, since Las Huelgas was a Cistercian foundation, whereas Fontevrault was itself the head of its order. Las Huelgas, intended from its inception to be a Cistercian convent for women in perpetuity, was to be the head of the order in Spain – and Alfonso and Leonor, as founders and patrons of Las Huelgas, would thus wield much power and influence. Although the Cistercian order dedicated all their churches to the Virgin by a decree of 1134, women had been initially refused entry into the order.[35] The problem of Cistercian nuns may have been the very reason Alfonso and Leonor chose this order for their foundation, as by operating not strictly under the control of Citeaux, they as patrons would retain more influence and control over their foundation than would normally be the case for patrons. In 1187, the General Chapter at Citeaux granted Las Huelgas authority over all other Cistercian houses in Castile and León, with the right to call its own chapters, and in 1188 Pope Clement III granted Las Huelgas exemption from outside control, effectively placing the abbey under the protection of the papal see.[36] Freed from archiepiscopal jurisdiction, Las Huelgas was able to operate semi-independently.

Both Alfonso and Leonor were lifelong patrons of the Cistercian order, and they changed several formerly Benedictine houses to Cistercian ones. This influence extended to their daughters, Berenguella and Blanca, who both also patronised the order. Berenguella was credited with influencing many of the donations made to Las Huelgas, and Blanca's Cistercian foundations for women at Maubisson and Le Lys were also constructed as familial burial places, reflecting the influence of her natal family, especially her mother Leonor and her grandmother Eleanor of Aquitaine.

The above evidence suggests that the choice of an institution for female religious did not come from Fontevrault, but was a native Iberian tradition. Nevertheless, architectural similarities between Las Huelgas and Fontevrault – notably the wide nave, applied arches, external buttressing, and the 'purely Plantagenet' domed vaulting in the transept chapels – does seem to suggest some Angevin influence, and it is possible that Angevin architects were brought to

---

[33] Shadis notes that 'Even before Berenguela's permanent arrival at the monastery, she was credited with influencing much or most of her family's important donations to and decisions regarding Las Huelgas (including her granddaughter's oblation)', 'Piety, Politics, and Power', 209, although her eulogy in the *PCG* is 'a general discussion of her influence and importance, and not in regard to Las Huelgas specifically', 'Piety, Politics, and Power', 222. Berenguella's daughter Constanza also joined the community some time before 1230.

[34] Shadis, 'Piety, Politics, and Power', 208. Papal correspondence also recognised her as such, although she certainly had not attained the position of abbess by 1262. It is possible that Berenguella was elected abbess towards the end of her life, but there is no clear evidence for this. The *PCG* 'says simply that she entered the convent as a virgin and was consecrated to God by her parents (cap 1036)', 'Piety, Politics, and Power', 222.

[35] For more on women and the Cistercians, see S. Thompson, 'The Problem of Cistercian Nuns in the Twelfth and Early Thirteenth Centuries', in *Medieval Women*, 227-52.

[36] The first chapter was held in 1189, but there is no extant documentary evidence for subsequent meetings.

Burgos, either by Leonor or by her daughter Constanza as titular abbess of Las Huelgas.[37] This would cast serious doubts on Walker's assertion that foreign brides had little influence on the culture of their "host countries", and if Leonor was able to summon a master craftsman from the Angevin realm, this provides further evidence of her continued contact with her natal family after the occasion of her marriage.[38]

Leonor, as queen of Castile, was a powerful and influential patron, issuing grants in her own name and being responsible for the establishment of an altar to Becket at Toledo.[39] Her patronage choices do seem to have been influenced to some degree by those of her mother, as her grants to Fontevrault demonstrate. It could be argued, however, that Leonor may have influenced her mother in turn with the founding in 1187 of the family necropolis of Santa Maria Regalis de las Huelgas in Burgos. This suggestion that Leonor's foundation of a royal mausoleum in Castile may have directly influenced the dynastic burials at Fontevrault therefore challenges the idea that inter-generational influence was solely a one-way exchange.

Fontevrault became the final resting place of the Angevins in much the same way, although not in the same manner, as Las Huelgas became the Castilian dynastic necropolis, and it is possible that both Eleanor and Leonor intended to establish dynastic mausolea for their immediate families. It is, however, ultimately impossible to ascertain how far Leonor was influenced by her mother, or to be sure how much influence Leonor had over her husband and how much input she had in the foundation of Las Huelgas. It would be equally difficult to conclusively state that Leonor influenced her mother in turn, but what can be said with certainty is that Leonor's choices in patronage had a direct influence on those of her own daughters. The links with the Cistercian order that originated with Leonor continued with her daughter Urraca's choice of Alcobaça as the Portuguese dynastic mausoleum, and Blanca's foundations of Maubisson and Le Lys.[40] Berenguella, Leonor, and Constanza all entered the convent of Las Huelgas, thereby cementing the family's links with the abbey. Leonor's legacy can be seen most clearly in the patronage of her daughters Berenguella and Blanca, whose patronage of the Cistercian order can surely be seen as 'acts of filial devotion'.[41] Their patronage of an order hostile to women represents an attempt to assert female power within this framework, a legacy certainly passed down to them from their mother Leonor.

---

[37] As suggested by Elizabeth Hallam (ed.), *The Plantagenet Chronicles* (Greenwich Editions, London, 2002), 115. See also Boase, 'Fontevrault and the Plantagenets', 7; Dectot, *Les tombeaux*, 120-1. The cupola over the crossing is very similar to those found at St Martin in Angers, St Hilaire in Poitiers, and St Front in Perigueux, and Boase notes that this style was widespread throughout the Angevin domains, 'Fontevrault and the Plantagenets', 8.

[38] Walker, 'Leonor of England', 347. It should be noted, however, that Cistercian architecture was a type in its own right. See Kenneth John Conant, *Carolingian and Romanesque Architecture: 800-1200* (Penguin, Middlesex, 1959). He cites Fontenay and Alcobaça (the foundation of Leonor's daughter Urraca) as the best surviving examples of Cistercian architecture, Citeaux itself having been destroyed in the French Revolution; *Architecture*, 131-2. Moreover, as J.N. Hillgarth has pointed out, the continued use of Muslim and Mudejar art at Las Huelgas, as well as at other Spanish churches and abbeys, blended with the French Gothic style to mark Spanish architecture as unique, *The Spanish Kingdoms*, 155-203. Islamic motifs and Mudejar design were at the height of popularity in twelfth- and thirteenth-century Spain, as a visual expression of Christian superiority over and appropriation of Muslim culture. For a fuller discussion of Muslim influence on Spanish art and architecture, see Jerrilynn Dodds, 'Islam, Christianity, and the Problem of Religious Art', and David Simon, 'Late Romanesque Art in Spain', in *The Art of Medieval Spain, 500-1200* (The Metropolitan Musuem of Art, New York, 1993), 27-37; 199-204.

[39] See Part IV.

[40] Nolan has suggested that not only did Las Huelgas directly influence the founding of Alcobaça in Portugal, but that it may also have been the inspiration for both Westminster Abbey and Royaumont, 'The Queen's Choice', 399.

[41] Shadis, 'Piety, Politics, and Power', 213.

This chapter has been concerned with where the daughters of Henry II and Eleanor of Aquitaine were buried, and with establishing links between two of the main dynastic mausolea with connections to the Angevin royal house. The final chapter of this study will focus on *how* they were buried, and will comprise an examination of the tomb monuments – and, where, possible, of their contents – which house the remains of various members of the Angevin dynasty both at Fontevrault and at Las Huelgas. What, if anything, can the ways in which Henry, Eleanor, and their daughters were buried tell us about the construction and perception of identities, both in an individual and in a dynastic sense?

Chapter Four
The Tombs at Fontevrault and Las Huelgas

The Tombs at Fontevrault

The tombs at Fontevrault represent a strong statement of dynastic power and authority, both over the abbey itself and over the surrounding area. Charles Wood has even suggested that the Fontevrault tombs were intended to honour not just Eleanor's marital family, but her natal family as well, as 'monuments to her own greatness and that of her ancestral family'.[1] As well as the innovation of joint burials, discussed in the previous chapter, the precedent for marking funerary monuments may also have originated with the tombs at Fontevrault. Before this, the tombs of English queens had not been decorated, and the Angevin tombs represent the first known life-sized effigies of English monarchs.[2] Moreover, Eleanor's effigy is innovative in that it is the earliest surviving medieval sculpture of a laywoman with an open book, a feature that would 'soon become the attribute of queens and high-born ladies, as the sceptre was already that of kings'.[3]

All of the surviving Angevin tombs have recumbent or reclining effigies which were meant to be placed horizontally to represent the figure lying down, as displayed by the way the drapery is arranged.[4] This was more or less the standard style for funerary monuments in northern Europe in the eleventh and twelfth centuries, although the addition of a pillow was a unique idea and was a device not generally used in northern Europe until the thirteenth century.[5] This device was, however, common in Spain, and was used in several of the tombs at Las Huelgas, as will be seen. The style also appears to have been imported to Germany through Matilda's marriage to Henry the Lion of Saxony.[6] Strong family ties are therefore

---

[1] Wood, 'Fontevraud, Dynasticism, and Eleanor of Aquitaine', 416. Matrilineal descent was still sometimes used to justify accessions to counties and even kingdoms, as emphasised by Raymond VII's request to be buried at the feet of his mother, 'Queen Joanna' – Joanna had of course been queen only by virtue of her first marriage to William II of Sicily, thus in making such a request Raymond overlooked his paternal heritage in order to be equated with his mother's royal connections.

[2] Although see the tomb of the Empress Matilda, not strictly a queen of England, at Bec, and the twelfth-century tomb slab of her husband Geoffrey of Anjou at Le Mans. The slab, possibly commissioned by Matilda, has the first known depiction of heraldry on a funerary monument. Erwin Panofsky views the slab more as a memorial portrait than an effigy, and in wielding his sword, Geoffrey is represented as very much still alive. See Panofsky, *Tomb Sculpture* (Phaidon Press, London, 1992), 50, and Fig. 190.

[3] Flori, *Eleanor of Aquitaine*, 203; see also Turner, *Eleanor of Aquitaine*, 296. Berengaria of Navarre's effigy at her foundation of L'Epau similarly depicts her holding a book or reliquary close to her breast. The cover shows a smaller image of the queen in relief, identifying her as the founder and patron of the abbey in which she is buried. Like the Angevin effigies, her head rests on a pillow. For Berengaria's tomb and burial at L'Epau, see Trindade, *Berengaria*, 10-11, 184-9, 195-7.

[4] As opposed to standing figures, which were meant to be viewed vertically even if placed horizontally.

[5] Panofsky, *Tomb Sculpture*, 57.

[6] *Ibid.*, 57, although the effigies at Brunswick rest on a *tumba* supported by consoles, rather than on a *lit de parade* as at Fontevrault. See Panofsky, *Tomb Sculpture*, Appendix for images of the tombs of Henry and Eleanor and of Henry the Lion and Matilda; see also Part IV.

suggested through this repeated pattern in the programme of dynastic commemoration employed by the Angevins.

Dating the tombs at Fontevrault is problematic, as there is no documentary evidence, although the style suggests a date somewhere in the first quarter of the thirteenth century, when the abbesses of Fontevrault all had close connections to the Angevin family.[7] Certainly, the tombs of Henry and Richard are the earliest, likely having been commissioned by Eleanor during her lifetime, and the similarities in style suggest that the work was undertaken by the same craftsman. As well as the construction of the tomb effigies, Eleanor was probably also responsible for their placement in the chancel, an arrangement which demonstrates the authority Eleanor was able to wield at Fontevrault, as the burial of a male in a house for female religious, let alone in the nun's choir, was 'highly irregular'.[8]

Eleanor's own tomb is later and by a different artist, although the style is similar. All three of the painted limestone effigies have open eyes, which was common practice in northern European funerary sculpture in the early Middle Ages; Spanish tomb sculpture generally portrayed their dead with closed eyes. All of the figures are crowned, but the style of headdress worn by Eleanor's effigy resembles a nun's wimple, suggesting that she had taken the veil before she died.[9] Moreover, hers is the only effigy to be depicted as active – i.e. alive: rather than a sceptre, she holds an opened book – probably a psalter – which at once suggests both literacy and piety, or as Flori phrases it, 'the image of a virtuous, courtly, fair and cultured queen. A woman of power and knowledge'.[10]

That Eleanor commissioned her own effigy as well as those of Henry and Richard is generally accepted by historians. But how much input could she have had over the design of her tomb monument? Flori has disputed the idea that the effigy was made some time after Eleanor's death by an artist who had never seen the living queen and who in any case had not intended to reproduce an accurate likeness. Rather, he argues that she may have closely collaborated with the sculptor, in order to produce an effigy that was doubtless enhanced and idealised, but at the same time a recognisable image of herself.[11] It is hard to argue with Flori's logic: if Eleanor played a prominent role in the commissioning of the tombs at Fontevrault, it seems highly unlikely that she would not likewise seek to have some form of artistic control over the representation of her own image.

---

[7] Boase, 'Fontevrault and the Plantagenets', 9. Although the effigy of Isabella of Angoulême is slightly later, most likely dating to 1254 when her son Henry III ordered that her body be moved to join the others in the royal crypt.

[8] Turner, *Eleanor of Aquitaine*, 294; see also Alain Erlande-Brandenburg, 'Le gisant d'Aliénor d'Aquitaine', in *Aliénor d'Aquitaine*, 174-9.

[9] Indeed, Turner states that, like her daughter Joanna, Eleanor had expressed the desire to take the veil at Fontevrault before her death, as well as her wish to be entombed in the chapel; her will, however, does not survive, *Eleanor of Aquitaine*, 295.

[10] Flori, *Eleanor of Aquitaine*, 4; Turner, *Eleanor of Aquitaine*, 296. Erlande-Brandenburg asserts that the lack of regalia on Eleanor's effigy, as with the effigies of Isabella of Angoulême and of Berengaria at L'Epau, provide evidence that these queens had not been anointed, 'Le gisant d'Aliénor d'Aquitaine', 176.

[11] Flori, *Eleanor of Aquitaine*, 31. Flori adds that other available images of Eleanor, such as those on her various seals, that in the stained glass window at Poitiers Cathedral, or the disputed image in the fresco at Sainte-Radegonde in Chinon, offer less reliably accurate representations of the actual queen. For more on the imagery of Eleanor's seals, see Flori, *Eleanor of Aquitaine*, 31, 117. For more on the identity of the disputed figures in the Sainte-Radegonde mural, see Part I. See also Françoise Perrot, 'Le portrait d'Aliénor dans le vitrail de la crucifixion à la cathédrale de Poitiers', in *Aliénor d'Aquitaine*, 180-5; Cécile Voyer, 'Les Plantagenêts et la Chapelle Sainte-Radegonde de Chinon : Une image en débat', in *ibid.*, 186-93.

The tombs at Fontevrault were realigned in 1638 by the abbess of Fontevrault, Jeanne de Bourbon, so that the effigies of Henry, Eleanor, Richard, and Isabella of Angoulême were placed side by side in a baroque-fronted niche, together with effigies of Joanna and her son Raymond VII. Joanna's effigy was placed to the left of the family group; she was depicted kneeling and wearing a small open crown, an indication either of her royal ancestry, or of her former status as queen of Sicily. Despite his status as count of Toulouse, Joanna's son Raymond VII, who was also shown kneeling and was placed directly opposite his mother, was also depicted with a crown.[12] His 'last wish', according to Boase, 'was that he should be buried in the abbey to which his mother was so devoted'.[13]

After the destruction of the abbey during the French Revolution the effigies of Joanna and Raymond were lost, but in 1816 the four remaining effigies were discovered in a cellar by the English antiquary Charles Stothard. The only damage sustained was to the hands and noses, with Isabella's wooden effigy being the best preserved of the four. In 1846 the effigies were removed to Paris, but were back at Fontevrault by 1851 and are now to be found at the east end of the nave, just before the steps to the crossing.[14] Traces have recently been discovered of a painted image of Raymond VII on the northern pillar of the chancel arch, with a tomb and grave beneath which is considered to be his. Unfortunately, only the mailed feet of the image survive.

The effigy of Joanna remains lost. Daniel Power has recently advanced the interesting hypothesis that the effigy ascribed to Isabella of Angoulême may in fact have been made for Joanna, although the stylistic differences between this effigy and those of the other Angevins at Fontevrault suggest that it was made at a later date.[15] Joanna's effigy, however, was almost certainly designed as part of the rearrangement of the Angevin tombs by Abbess Jeanne in 1638, to fit neatly into the niche constructed to house them.

As recumbent effigies dressed in full regalia, the four remaining effigies at Fontevrault combine the imagery of coronation with the imagery of death. Recalling the coronation confirms the legitimacy of the dynasty as anointed rulers, and Kathleen Nolan has stated that 'Eleanor's purpose in ordering funerary monuments with this novel and deliberate iconography was no doubt political'.[16] This 'novelty', however, does not take into account the effigy of Eleanor's first husband, Louis VII, at Barbeaux, of which Eleanor must surely have been aware.[17]

---

[12] See Boase, 'Fontevrault and the Plantagenets', 8. Boase suggests that the paintwork adorning the effigies, which he states is very badly executed, was also undertaken at this time.

[13] Boase, 'Fontevrault and the Plantagenets', 7; and for more on Raymond VII, see Laurent Macé, 'Raymond VII of Toulouse: The Son of Queen Joanna, 'Young Count' and Light of the World', trans. Catherine Léglu, in *The World of Eleanor of Aquitaine*, 137-56. Boase may be stretching Joanna's supposed devotion to the abbey somewhat here; whilst it is clear that she desired to take the veil there when she felt herself close to death, there is no evidence to suggest that Joanna was a patron of the abbey prior to this time.

[14] See Boase, 'Fontevrault and the Plantagenets', 8-9.

[15] Power, 'The Stripping of a Queen: Eleanor of Aquitaine in Thirteenth-Century Norman Tradition', in *The World of Eleanor of Aquitaine*, 115-35. Erlande-Brandenburg, however, has no doubt that the effigy belongs to Isabella, 'Le gisant d'Aliénor d'Aquitaine', 175.

[16] Nolan, 'The Queen's Choice', 393. The tombs at Fontevrault may therefore have been an attempt on Eleanor's part at one-upmanship, Nolan, 'The Queen's Choice', 391.

[17] Louis' effigy, the first sculpted representation of a Capetian monarch, was commissioned by his widow, Adela of Champagne. Turner has stated that Eleanor must have been aware of the French royal tombs, and 'doubtless intended that the tombs of her second husband and her favorite son should surpass in splendor those of their Capetian rivals', *Eleanor of Aquitaine*, 294.

Queens needed to be monumentalised as well as kings in order to emphasise the noble ancestry of the monarchy in both the agnatic and cognatic lines. It is certain, however, that some queens commissioned their own burial monuments, and it is probable that Eleanor of Aquitaine commissioned all the tombs at Fontevrault 'in the tradition of [French] queens controlling burial sites'.[18] Eleanor's mother-in-law Adelaide of Maurienne had been an active patron of the female Benedictine house of St-Pierre-de-Montmartre in Paris, and had commissioned her own tomb-slab, which once depicted her image but is now badly damaged.[19] It is possible that Adelaide was inspired by the tomb-slab of Bertrada de Montfort, the widow of Philip I who had died in 1117. The slab, now destroyed, may once have been engraved with her image.[20] Bertrada was buried at her foundation of Hautes-Bruyeres, a daughter house of Fontevrault, thus a pattern can be discerned amongst French queens of patronage of an order, followed by joining the order, followed by burial in the order. Adelaide was 'directly connected with Eleanor's personal past, and with her sense of identity as a queen', and Nolan concludes that Adelaide provided the inspiration for Eleanor's decisions regarding the burials of herself and of her family.[21] The evidence from the royal mausoleum at Las Huelgas in Burgos, however, suggests that Eleanor may have had a much closer source of inspiration for her choices regarding burial and dynastic commemoration.

The Tombs at Las Huelgas

Leonor, along with her son and heir Enrique and her eldest daughter Berenguella, had been present at the village of Gutierre Muñoz when Alfonso VIII died from a malarial fever at midnight on 5 October 1214.[22] Alfonso's body was taken to Valladolid in a solemn procession led by the archbishop of Toledo. At Valladolid, the body was embalmed and prepared for the journey to Burgos, where he was to be interred at the monastery of Las Huelgas, 'which he had founded at the request of Queen Leonor', and where their children Sancho, Sancha, Leonor, Mafalda, and Fernando had already been interred.[23] Alfonso's funeral service was conducted by the archbishop of Toledo and attended by the bishops of Palencia, Osma, Segovia, Siguenza, Burgos, Cuenca, Calahorra and Ávila.[24] It was his daughter Berenguella who presided over the funeral and acted as head of the family, directing and arranging the diverse details of Alfonso's burial; Leonor was absent from the ceremonials due to having contracted the same virulent fever as her husband.[25]

---

[18] Nolan, 'The Queen's Choice', 377. A comparison of seal imagery with that on tomb effigies, beyond the scope of this study, would be a fruitful area for future research.

[19] See Nolan, 'The Queen's Choice', 391.

[20] See *ibid.*, 391.

[21] *Ibid.*, 389, 391.

[22] *PCG*, 707-8; *Crónica Latina*, 59; González, *Alfonso VIII*, I, 213.

[23] *PCG*, 708; *Crónica Latina*, 60; Díez, *Alfonso VIII*, 243.

[24] *PCG*, 708; González, *Alfonso VIII*, I, 215; Díez, *Alfonso VIII*, 244. He is commemorated on a plaque inscribed with the words: "*Rex obiit et labitur / Castella(e) gloria. / Allefonsus rapitur / ad celi gloria(m). / Fons aret et moritur / donandi copia. / Petit celestia / a cuius manibus / fluxerunt omnibus / largitatis maria.*", González, *Alfonso VIII*, I, 215.

[25] *Crónica Latina*, 59; González, *Alfonso VIII*, I, 215; Díez, *Alfonso VIII*, 244.

Alfonso's last will has not survived, but a confirmation of an earlier will, drafted in December 1204, still exists.[26] The 1204 will names Leonor and their then-heir, the Infante Fernando, as two of the six executors.[27] On his deathbed in 1214, Alfonso also entrusted Leonor with the regency for their eleven-year-old son Enrique, testament to the esteem in which he held her capabilities.[28] Leonor, however, died a mere two weeks later, on 31 October, and her capability, power, and authority as regent cannot therefore be judged.[29] She nevertheless placed as much faith in her daughter Berenguella as Alfonso had placed in her, naming her eldest daughter as regent and guardian of Enrique on her deathbed.[30] Leonor was buried at Las Huelgas at Alfonso's side, in a magnificent joint tomb which displays the arms of both Castile and England.[31]

The dynastic tombs at Las Huelgas have survived in excellent condition, although a survey of their contents, undertaken by Manuel Gómez-Moreno in 1946, revealed that several of the interiors were in disarray, with contents jumbled and some items displaced.[32] In contrast to the tombs at Fontevrault, none of the tombs at Las Huelgas have effigies, as this form of representative sculpture was forbidden by the Cistercian order. The tombs are, however, not without adornment, featuring fierce-looking lions, which Gómez-Moreno thought were symbolic of the vanquished enemy, presumably the Moors, although there is no evidence for this interpretation.[33] Lions traditionally symbolise Christ conquering death; they were also, perhaps not coincidentally, the heraldic effigy of the Plantagenet dynasty, and both Alfonso and Leonor's brother Richard were referred to as lions.[34] The sculptural elements on all of the tombs are traditionally Spanish, with figural and narrative designs such as are also found on the tomb of Alfonso's mother, Blanca, at Santa Maria del Real in Navarre.[35]

Blanca's tomb, like those at Las Huelgas, lacks an effigy, but it does incorporate a depiction of her death and the resulting grief of her husband, Sancho III.[36] Similarly, the joint tomb of Alfonso and Leonor, located in the choir in the central nave at Las Huelgas, displays representative images of the founders of the abbey on the sides of the tomb, along with the heraldic lions of England and the castles Castile.[37] Alfonso is depicted offering Las Huelgas to the

---

[26] González, *Alfonso VIII*, I, 217-18; III, no. 769.

[27] The others being the archbishop of Toledo, the bishop of Segovia, the prior of the Hospitallers, and the Master of the Order of Santiago, Díez, *Alfonso VIII*, 242-3.

[28] Díez, *Alfonso VIII*, 243.

[29] *PCG*, 709. González, *Alfonso VIII*, I, 215-16 and Díez, *Alfonso VIII*, 244-5, claim that Leonor succumbed to the fever in grief at losing Alfonso. They were perhaps influenced in this by the account in the *Crónica Latina*, 60, which states that after Alfonso's burial, Leonor, 'deprived of the solace of so great a man, and wishing to die from her pain and anguish, immediately fell to her sickbed, and died around midnight on the vigil of All Saints'.

[30] *PCG*, 709. Despite being commissioned by Berenguella, Lucas de Tuy's *Chronicon*, 416-7, treats only very briefly the deaths of both Leonor and Alfonso.

[31] Dectot believes that the tombs were carved after the deaths of Alfonso and Leonor, as the sculptural elements are more consistent with mid-thirteenth century carvings; see *Les tombeaux*, 248-9.

[32] Manuel Gómez-Moreno, *El Panteon Real de las Huelgas de Burgos* (Madrid, 1946). See also Dectot, *Les tombeaux* for a more recent overview of Spanish royal burial practices.

[33] Gómez-Moreno, *Panteon*, 16.

[34] The Angevins used one lion until three were adopted by Richard in or after 1194. See also below, n. 39.

[35] See Panofsky, *Tomb Sculpture*, 59-61.

[36] See also the tomb of Fernando I's queen Sancha (d. 1096) at Jaca, which depicts her funeral and includes a sculpted portrait of Sancha with her sisters, all of whom were buried at Santa Cruz de la Seros. For images of Sancha's tomb and that of Alfonso's mother Blanca of Navarre, see Panofsky, *Tomb Sculpture*, Appendix.

[37] Gómez-Moreno, *Panteon*, 9. For images, see Dectot, *Les tombeaux*, figs. 58-60.

Virgin, to whom the abbey is dedicated.[38] Unusually for a donor image, Alfonso is shown enthroned, rather than in the traditional posture of genuflexion, and it is the recipient of the gift who kneels, as his subject, to receive it. Such imagery has led Xavier Dectot to conclude that the female figure is in fact not the Virgin, but a personifaction of religion, and that Alfonso is meant to be seen not as a donor, but an 'institutional being', elected by God as His instrument on earth.[39] The depiction of Leonor, meanwhile, shows her soul ascending to heaven in the form of a crowned woman, pictorially reminiscent of the Virgin herself.[40] Conversely, the tomb of their eldest daughter, Berenguella, which lies adjacent to the joint tomb of her parents in the nave, is plain; she had apparently preferred this to the more elaborate tomb, replete with Marian iconography, which had originally been constructed for her, and which was later used for her granddaughter Berenguella, who died in 1288.[41]

The Castilian royal family were all interred at Las Huelgas in raised table-tombs, where the sarcophagi rest not on solid bases but on supporting feet, carved in the shape of lions. It has been suggested that this was done to counter the problem of lay burial on Cistercian ground – it was not until 1222 that the General Chapter permitted the burial of founders within the sacred spaces of their abbeys, an act which was extended in 1227 by Pope Gregory IX to include other secular patrons.[42] It is surely inconceivable, however, that the royal patrons of Las Huelgas would be dictated to regarding their own foundation. They were powerful and influential enough to be able to deal with Las Huelgas as they wished, and it seems certain that it was their intention to use the abbey as a dynastic mausoleum from its inception.

This is clear from the fact that the earliest tombs at Las Huelgas belong to the children of Alfonso and Leonor who had predeceased them: the small sarcophagus of the Infante Sancho,[43] and the tombs of the Infantas Sancha, Leonor and Mafalda.[44] Fernando, who died of a virulent fever in 1211, was the first adult to be entombed in the abbey, followed by Leonor

---

[38] Walker, 'Royal and aristocratic burial in Spain', 164.

[39] Dectot, *Les tombeaux*, 255-6. He notes that the armrests of Alfonso's throne are carved in the shape of lions, and that the imagery overall is deliberately reminiscent of King Solomon. The foundation of Las Huelgas is therefore, he believes, being equated with the foundation of Solomon's Temple, thereby 'proclaiming, indirectly, a new covenant between God and His representative on earth, the king of Castile', *Les tombeaux*, 256.

[40] Walker, 'Royal and aristocratic burial in Spain', 164. Walker notes that Leonor was viewed by contemporaries as 'an ideal queen with the virtues of the Virgin', and that her religious devotion was notable, although she points out that the tomb itself most likely dates to either the mid-thirteenth or early fourteenth century, 352. Dectot, however, believes it more likely, based on the contents of the tombs at Las Huelgas, that the sarcophagi are contemporary with the deaths of Alfonso and Leonor, but were carved at a later date. See above, n. 31.

[41] Walker, 'Royal and aristocratic burial in Spain', 164, and for a description of Berenguella's tomb, 164-5.

[42] See Shadis, 'Piety, Politics, and Power', 223.

[43] For Sancho's sarcophagus, see Gómez-Moreno, *Panteon*, 24, 46. A plaque at Las Huelgas commemorates Sancho with the following lines: '*Plange, Castella misera / plange pro rege Sancio. / quem terra, pontus, ethera / ploratu plangunt anxia. / Casum tuum considera / patrem plangens in filio, / qui, etate tam tenera, / concusso regni solio / cedes sentit et vulnera.*' See González, *Alfonso VIII*, I, 202; Díez, *Alfonso VIII*, 48.

[44] The *Crónica de Veinte Reyes* is the only source to mention Mafalda, stating that she was born after Fernando but before Leonor; thus, between 1189-1204, and that she died at Salamanca; see Díez, *Alfonso VIII*, 51. An epitaph at Salamanca Cathedral gives the date of Mafalda's death as 1204: 'Aquí yace la ynfanta Mafalda, hija del rey don Alfonso VIII de Castilla y de la reyna Leonor y hermana de la reyna doña Berenguela, muger del rey don Alfonso IX de León, que finó por casar en Salamanca el año de 1204', Díez, *Alfonso VIII*, 51; see also González, *Alfonso VIII*, I, 210-11, who, on the basis of this epitaph, suggests that Mafalda, who would have been aged around 14 in 1204, may have been so far from her parents' lands when she died because she was to marry Fernando, the son (and then-heir) of Alfonso IX of León and his spouse Teresa. The name Mafalda was unprecedented in either Leonese or Castilian dynasties before this time, although it had entered Portuguese dynastic nomenclature with Mafalda, the daughter of Count Amadeus of Savoy, who married Afonso Enríquez, the first king of Portugal, Díez, *Alfonso VIII*, 50-1.

and Alfonso themselves in 1214, and their son and eventual heir Enrique in 1217.[45] Their daughters Constanza (d. 1243), Leonor (d. 1244), and Berenguella (d. 1246), as well as several grandchildren and more remote descendants who died in the sixteenth century, were all later buried in the family mausoleum.[46] Most of the bodies entombed at Las Huelgas are still in a very well preserved state (presumably because of their being embalmed), with the exception of the scattered and largely destroyed bones found in the three tombs corresponding to the three young infantas.[47]

Only the tombs of Leonor, Alfonso and their eldest daughter Berenguella are situated in the central nave at Las Huelgas.[48] Alfonso's sheepskin-lined coffin has a covering of green and blue wool and linen, embroidered with diamonds or rhombuses, which is very well preserved, despite some tears in the fabric. Alfonso's body is mummified, except for the head, and is buried with several items of clothing: a shirt with narrow sleeves and gold, red and white embroidered seams; and a rectangular cloth with a small cord tether, which may have been used as undergarments. His large, dark blue taffeta tunic is decorated with a narrow strip of tapestry bordered with twin stripes of gold, which runs the entire width of the tunic, although all that now remains is the frayed and threadbare upper part. There are also pieces of a cloak, made of the same fabric; loose pieces of heavy yellow taffeta; and a green brocade of Mudejar style, decorated with crimson escutcheons with gold castles. A small cushion of straw-coloured silk with red stripes was also placed in his tomb.[49]

Leonor's 2.02m long, taffeta-lined coffin is covered with three layers of fabric: one of plain white linen; one of white silk imprinted with gold stars and a strip of gold decorated with crimson and yellow hexagons; and one of white silk with Arabic decorations of small squares dotted with gold buttons between interlaced stars and foliage. A wide gold band forms a cross on the outer cover of the coffin.[50] Her body is conserved well, but, in contrast to Alfonso's tomb, no clothing has survived apart from a number of strips of gold, black and white striped muslin with gathered and braided edges, which probably comprised Leonor's veil.[51] A pin, which would have been used to fix the veil in place, has also survived, as have scraps of pointed

---

[45] The *PCG*, 687, describes mass lamentations at Fernando's death: 'fue lloro a la tierra, et lloro al padre'. Similarly, the *Crónica Latina*, 47, relates that everywhere people mourned. Lucas de Tuy noted that these lamentations were well deserved, because of the many good qualities Fernando had possessed, *Crónica de España*, 413. Fernando was also commemorated in a verse by the poet Giraut de Calanson; see González, *Alfonso VIII*, I, 210.

[46] Gómez-Moreno, *Panteon*, 7. Urraca, who married Afonso II of Portugal and who died in 1220, is buried at Alcobaça; see Gómez-Moreno, *Panteon*, 28. For Constanza's coffin, in which are preserved her linen shirt, black woollen habit, and thin-soled shoes, as well as a cushion worked in a complicated design, see Gómez-Moreno, *Panteon*, 29, 74, 79, 29, 88.

[47] See Gómez-Moreno, *Panteon*, 9-10, 24; and for more on the Iberian practice of embalming their dead, especially at Las Huelgas, see Dectot, *Les tombeaux*, 51-4. Sancha's coffin contains a skull and two sets of teeth, suggesting that some dispersal of the remains of these children has occurred at some point; see Gómez-Moreno, *Panteon*, 24. The tomb which Gómez-Moreno has identified as belonging to Mafalda contains a coarse, thickly woven blue cushion; as well as a fine blue and gold taffeta cloak, decorated with stars, medallions, and pairs of griffins; and a colourful striped striped veil, *Panteon*, 56, 48, 72.

[48] Gómez-Moreno, *Panteon*, 9. As Rose Walker has pointed out, burial within a Cistercian church signified extremely high status, as before 1190 it was permitted solely to kings and high ranking clergy, 'Royal and aristocratic burial', 366.

[49] For the above information, see Gómez-Moreno, *Panteon*, 26-7, 57.

[50] *Ibid.*, 27, 57, 47.

[51] *Ibid.*, 27, 69, 72.

shoes lined with worked hemp.[52] Leonor was also buried with an array of exquisite cushions, placed at her feet and beneath her head. They are worked in blue and crimson taffeta and silk, and are embroidered with tapestries depicting geometric shapes, dots, and castles.[53]

The textile items in the tombs at Las Huelgas, such as the robes found in the tombs of Alfonso and his daughters Berenguella and Leonor, and the caps and other clothing items buried with Fernando and Enrique, provide important evidence for the type of clothing worn by members of the Castilian dynasty in the twelfth and thirteenth centuries.[54] Both men and women seem to have worn linen undershirts beneath a floor length tunic and wide-sleeved *pellote*. Luxury fabrics such as silks, taffeta, and exquisitely worked brocades were used for their outer garments, which were frequently embroidered with Moorish geometric designs, sometimes with Christian motifs picked out in Cufic lettering. The men clearly wore hose, held up by points attached to linen undergarments. Young men, such as Fernando and Enrique, sported embroidered caps worked from linen and kidskin. The women, as in most European countries at this time, wore fine veils, often of muslin, which were fastened with decorative metal pins, and the shoes *à la mode* had flat soles and pointed toes.

Thus the members of the Castilian dynasty were 'buried as they had lived...in silks and muslins from North African or Mudejar workshops, occasionally in 'Tartar' silks from China or Central Asia', and the austere Cistercian order to which they entrusted their bodies and their souls were powerless to prevent the magnificence with which they were entombed.[55]

Taken together, the evidence suggests the possibility that Leonor and her foundation of Las Huelgas may have influenced her mother's decision to establish a dynastic programme of burial for her own immediate family at her favoured religious institution of Fontevrault. The abbey of Fontevrault was itself the recipient of patronage from Leonor and Joanna, and in this, their choices appear to have been informed largely by matrilineal influence. Thus, just as with Joanna, Leonor and Matilda's probable involvement in the promotion of the cult of Thomas Becket, discussed in Part IV, their choices in commemoration as well as dynastic nomenclature suggest both consciousness of their dynastic heritage and a degree of emotional attachment to their natal family.

---

[52] *Ibid.*, 28.

[53] *Ibid.*, 27, 68, 87-8. Her daughters Berenguella and Leonor were also buried with several fine embroidered cushions; see Gómez-Moreno, *Panteon*, 30, 52-3, 82-3, 89.

[54] For the clothing found in Berenguella's and Leonor's tombs, see Gómez-Moreno, *Panteon*, 23-4, 30-1, 49. For the clothing found in Fernando's and Enrique's tombs, see *ibid.*, 25-6, 57-8, 68, 81-2, 91. The obvious trepanation that has occurred at the fontanelle of Enrique's skull provides conclusive proof that the skull belongs to Enrique, as well as being important evidence for this type of surgery in the early thirteenth century.

[55] Hillgarth, *The Spanish Kingdoms*, 169.

Conclusion

The aim of this study has been to present a wider and more coherent picture of the daughters of Henry II and Eleanor of Aquitaine, both as individuals in their own right, and as composite parts of the Angevin dynasty as a whole. The monograph therefore presents a comparative study of the experiences of three twelfth-century women in a variety of European locations. I chose to focus on these women in particular precisely because of their status as royal women who were members of one of the most powerful families in twelfth-century Europe. Whilst their experiences cannot be taken as being representative of twelfth-century women as a whole, they provide crucial evidence for the dynamics and functionality of twelfth-century royal and aristocratic families, and the women who were a part of them.

Medieval women at all levels of society were defined by their marital as well as social status in a way that men were not, and chronicle evidence suggests that the central event in the lives of Matilda, Leonor, and Joanna was their marriages. Prior to the dynastic alliances they made, little is recorded about them after their births, which are either referred to in the briefest of notes, or not mentioned at all. The fact that when they are mentioned, they are described with reference to the male members of their family – the daughter of Henry, the sister of Richard or John – may suggest a degree of marginalisation. Further, they may be most visible in the sources as wives and mothers, but this does not mean that the arena of domestic politics, deemed to be suitable and appropriate for women, was an unimportant or insignificant one.[1] Both Matilda and Leonor enjoyed brief periods of regency, and Leonor in particular was highly involved in influencing the politics of her realm, appearing consistently on her husband's charters and issuing some in her own name. Joanna, by contrast, seems to have exercised no power in either of her marriages, and was only able to assert any real degree of independence through the terms of her will. Access to power for these women was not automatic but contingent and intermittent, as indeed had been the experience of their mother.

The training and education which Matilda, Leonor, and Joanna must have received in their childhood served to prepare them for their roles as wives and mothers, as disseminators of family traditions and reputations, as continuators of the dynastic line and educators of their own children, as administrators of their own resources, and as patrons, mediators, advisors, and regents. As has been seen, these women were entrusted with the instruction of their children, as well as being charged with the care of others, as Joanna was with Richard's betrothed, Berengaria of Navarre. As demonstrated in Part I, the Angevin family had a reputation for scholarly learning, and it is hardly conceivable that these royal daughters could have grown up in ignorance of the literary works produced at or for their parents' court. It is probable that all of Henry and Eleanor's daughters were literate. Leonor in particular was frequently lauded for her education and learning by contemporary Spanish chroniclers, and the evidence suggests that this was no mere literary *topos*.

The importance of dynastic alliances, arranged and controlled by the family, served to further material, social or political interests, and the intricacies of Angevin marriage policy

---

[1] Widows form an entirely different category from wives, although Berengaria's status as a childless widow gave her little to no power at all, and she was entirely eclipsed by her mother-in-law Eleanor, who took precedence at Richard I's court.

has been discussed at length in Part II. Royal and aristocratic women may have been bred for marriage in order to create or cement political alliances, but the care with which Matilda, Leonor, and Joanna's marriages appear to have been chosen and implemented demonstrates their importance. Moreover, this common, shared experience amongst royal and aristocratic women meant that they were well-placed – perhaps best placed – to oversee the marital fortunes of their own children. Parental control over the marriages of their children, therefore, could provide women with an arena in which to exercise a real degree of influence, especially where the marriages of their daughters was concerned. Eleanor of Aquitaine was involved to varying degrees in the marriage negotiations for several of her children, notably her second daughter and namesake Leonor, who, as demonstrated in Part III, was similarly highly involved in arranging prestigious matches for her own daughters, overseeing their marriages into the royal houses of León, Aragón, Portugal, and France.[2]

In providing heirs for the dynastic houses they married into, Leonor was the most successful of her sisters, giving birth to at least twelve children, six of whom survived to adulthood. Similarly, Matilda provided her husband with four sons and a daughter, all of whom survived infancy. Joanna, however, failed in her primary function of progenitrix for the Sicilian dynasty, although if the birth of a son named Bohemond, recorded solely by Torigni, is indeed true, then it raises some interesting questions. Joanna was clearly not barren, as her subsequent marriage to Raymond of Toulouse produced at least two children. Thus, if the birth and subsequent death of a son in or around 1182 could be corroborated, it would mean that there was no biological reason to prevent Joanna and William from having children. Why, therefore, did the couple fail to produce any other issue during the next seven years of their marriage, especially when the wording of William's 1177 charter of dower explicitly states that the production of offspring was the primary reason for the marriage? Ultimately, the reasons why Joanna and William failed to produce any children after 1182 cannot be known, but what is certain is that this failure led to a succession crisis which saw competing claims for the Sicilian crown after William's untimely death in 1189, and Joanna deprived both of her position as queen, and of her dower.

As seen in Part III, the bestowal of dowries and dowers were crucial factors in negotiating such diplomatically important marriages. The impressive dowers with which Leonor and Joanna were endowed at the time of their marriages testify to their political significance, and the revenues from their dowerlands would in all probability have provided them with the financial means to engage in the queenly role of patron. The problematic nature of territorial dowries and dowers, however, meant that in some cases, a queen's access to these revenues could be limited, and in Joanna's case, the generous dower she had received from William II was entirely subsumed by her brother Richard in order to finance the third crusade.

Joanna's marriage to William, like her sister Leonor's marriage to Alfonso VIII, suggests that whilst romantic love may have been a minor consideration when engineering a politically significant dynastic match, it was not impossible to achieve. Alfonso of Castile and William of Sicily were both relatively close in age, by twelfth-century standards, to their respective brides, and both marriages seem to have been felicitous, compatible, and, in Leonor's case, blessed with an abundance of healthy children. The many cultural links between the Angevin kingdom and that of Sicily and, to a lesser degree, of Castile, would also have served to provide a less isolating experience for Joanna and Leonor compared to less fortunate exogamous royal

---

[2] Her fifth surviving daughter, Constanza, entered the religious life at the family foundation, and eventual dynastic mausoleum, of Las Huelgas.

brides like their sister Matilda. Whilst chronicle accounts which describe Leonor dying of a broken heart after the death of her husband Alfonso may need to be taken with a pinch of salt, Joanna's deathbed request for prayers for the soul of her deceased husband William – rather than her still-living husband, Raymond VI of Toulouse – imply that these marriages were happy ones.[3] Matilda's husband, by contrast, was more than twice her age, and had already been married and divorced before their marriage. Nevertheless, on hearing of Matilda's premature death, Henry the Lion raced back to Saxony from exile in the Angevin realm in order to mourn at her tomb, which suggests that an affectionate bond had grown between them, perhaps strengthened by their years of political uncertainty in exile.[4] Political considerations aside, Henry and Eleanor appear to have chosen well for their daughters in terms of their marriages.

This, it seems, was not their only legacy. Matilda, Leonor, and Joanna all left their natal family for marriage with more than a dowry and an education. As demonstrated in Part I, emotional bonds were likely forged in their early childhood as a result of the frequent contact between these women and their parents, in particular their mother, with whom they travelled frequently. That all three daughters may have felt an attachment to their natal family is suggested by the choices these women made in terms of patronage and commemoration, as well as in their decisions to turn to their family in times of crisis, as Joanna did in 1199 after the siege of Les Casses, and Matilda did following Henry the Lion's exile from Saxony in 1182. Their potential involvement in the dissemination of the cult of Thomas Becket, discussed in Part IV, indicates a possible degree of patrilineal influence, and in promoting the cult of the martyred archbishop, they were at the same time promoting the prestige of their own lineage. Similarly, their choices in dynastic commemoration, discussed in Part V, suggest possible matrilineal influence, with both Leonor and Joanna making bequests and donations to their mother's favoured abbey of Fontevrault, and Leonor perhaps influencing her mother in turn with the establishment at Las Huelgas of a dynastic mausoleum. Furthermore, the names bestowed on their own children served to commemorate both their marital and their natal families, and the Angevin names Henry and Eleanor were transplanted to Castile as a direct consequence of Leonor's marriage to Alfonso VIII.

Examining Matilda, Leonor, and Joanna's choices in patronage and dynastic commemoration has enabled me to discern patterns and parallels which give an indication of how the Angevin dynasty may have functioned in terms of physical and emotional connectivity. The cumulative evidence presented in this study suggests the possible existence of a stronger emotional bond than historians such as Rose Walker and Ralph Turner have previously allowed for. That Matilda, Leonor and Joanna appear to have been able to transplant names and customs which were so strongly connected with their natal family is undoubtedly a reflection of their political and social standing – the Angevin 'empire' was perhaps the greatest, and certainly the largest, kingdom in Western Christendom at the time. That these women desired to transplant Angevin traditions to their marital lands, however, could be seen as evidential of an enduring emotional bond to their natal family. If such a bond indeed existed, it could only have been forged in their early childhood, before they left their parents' domains for marriage, and contact with their natal family clearly continued after their marriages. This hypothesis, then, challenges recurrent assumptions that Eleanor of Aquitaine was a "bad" or absent mother, as well as theories that twelfth-century royal and aristocratic parents were both

---

[3] See Part V.
[4] See Part IV.

physically and emotionally unavailable to their children. It would appear that the female members of the "Devil's Brood", at least, were raised by their parents with due consideration both for their emotional and physical well-being, and in making provisions for their future destinies.

Bibliography

Primary Sources:

Ambroise, *L'Estoire de la Guerre Sainte*, ed. Gaston Paris (Paris, 1897).

Annales Stederburgenses, in *Monumenta Germaniae Historica Scriptorum*, 16 (Hanover, 1859).

Arnold of Lübeck, *Chronica Slavorum*, in *Monumenta Germaniae Historica Scriptorum,* 14 (Hanover, 1868).

Bohadin, *Suite de la troisieme croisade*, in Joseph Michaud (ed.), *Bibliotheque des Croisades*, IV (Paris, 1829).

Calendar of Documents preserved in France, Illustrative of the History of Great Britain and Ireland, I, 918-1206, ed. J. Horace Round (1899, London, HMSO).

Catalogo Illustrato del Tabulario di S. Maria Nuova in Monreale, ed. C.A. Garufi, in *Documenti per Servire alla Storia di Sicilia*, 1a. Serie, Diplomatica, XIX (Palermo, 1902).

Chronicle of the Third Crusade: A Translation of the Itinerarium Peregrinorum et Gesta Regis Ricardi, ed. H.J. Nicholson (Ashgate, Hants., 1997).

Crónica Latina de los Reyes de Castilla, ed. Luis Charlo Brea (Madrid, 1999).

Chronique Rimée de Philippe Mouskes, II, ed. Le Baron de Reiffenberg (Brussels, 1838).

Crusader Syria in the Thirteenth Century: The Rothelin Continuation of the History of William of Tyre with part of the Eracles or Acre Text, ed. Janet Shirley (Ashgate, Aldershot, 1999).

Curia Regis Rolls of Richard I and John (Public Record Office, London, 1929).

Das Rolandslied des Pfaffen Konrad, ed. C. Wesle (Tübingen, 1967).

Die Urkunden Heinrichs des Löwen - Herzog von Sachsen und Bayern, ed. Karl Jordan, in *Monumenta Germaniae Historica* (Stuttgart, 1957-60).

Documentacion del Monasterio de Las Huelgas de Burgos, ed. José Manuel Lizoain Garrido (Burgos, 1985).

Epistolae Cantuarienses: The Letters of the Prior and Convent of Christchurch, Canterbury, From AD 1187 to AD 1199, in *Chronicles and Memorials of the Reign of Richard I*, ed. William Stubbs, in *Chronicles and Memorials of Great Britain and Ireland During the Middle Ages* (Rolls Series, 38.2, London, 1865).

Etienne of Rouen, *Draco Normannicus*, in *Chronicles of the Reigns of Stephen, Henry II, and Richard I*, ed. Richard Howlett, 4 Vols., in *Chronicles and Memorials of Great Britain and Ireland During the Middle Ages* (Rolls Series, 82.2, London, 1885).

Gerald of Wales, *De Principis Instructione Liber*, in *Giraldi Cambrensis: Opera*, ed. George F. Warner, 8 Vols., in *Chronicles and Memorials of Great Britain and Ireland During the Middle Ages* (Rolls Series, 21.8, London, 1891).

Gerald of Wales, *Itinerarium Kambriae, et Descriptio Kambriae,* in *Giraldi Cambrensis: Opera,* Vol. IV, ed. James F. Dimock, in *Chronicles and Memorials of Great Britain and Ireland During the Middle Ages,* Vol. 21 (Longmans, London, 1868).

Gerald of Wales, *Speculum Ecclesiae. De Vita Galfridi Archiepiscopi Eboracensis: sive certamina Galfridi Eboracensis Archiepiscopi,* in *Giraldi Cambrensis: Opera,* Vol. VI, ed. J.S. Brewer, in *Chronicles and Memorials of Great Britain and Ireland During the Middle Ages,* Vol. 21 (Longmans, London, 1873).

Gerald of Wales, *The Conquest of Ireland,* in *The Historical Works of Giraldus Cambrensis,* ed. Thomas Wright (H.G. Bohn, London, 1863).

Gerald of Wales, *The Itinerary through Wales,* in *The Historical Works of Giraldus Cambrensis,* ed. Thomas Wright (H.G. Bohn, London, 1863).

Gerald of Wales, *The Topography of Ireland,* in *The Historical Works of Giraldus Cambrensis,* ed. Thomas Wright (H.G. Bohn, London, 1863).

Gervase of Canterbury, *The Chronicle of the Reigns of Stephen, Henry II, and Richard I, by Gervase, the Monk of Canterbury,* in *Opera Historica – The Historical Works of Gervase of Canterbury,* in *The Chronicle of the Reigns of Stephen, Henry II, and Richard I,* ed. William Stubbs (Rolls Series, 73.1, London, 1879).

Gervase of Canterbury, *Gesta Regum,* in *Opera Historica – The Historical Works of Gervase of Canterbury,* in *The Chronicle of the Reigns of Stephen, Henry II, and Richard I,* ed. William Stubbs (Rolls Series, 73.2, London, 1880).

Gervase of Tilbury, *Otia Imperialia,* ed. and trans. S.E. Banks & J.W. Binns (OUP, 2002).

Gesta Regis Ricardi, in *The Chronicle of the Reigns of Henry II & Richard I AD 1169-1192; Known Commonly Under the Name of Benedict of Peterborough,* ed. William Stubbs, 2 Vols., in *Chronicles and Memorials of Great Britain and Ireland During the Middle Ages,* (Rolls Series, 49, London, 1867).

Helmold of Bosau, *Cronica Slavorum,* in *Monumenta Germaniae Historica Scriptorum,* 32 (Hanover 1937).

Histoire des Ducs de Normandie et des Rois d'Angleterre, ed. Francois Michel (Paris, J. Renouard, 1840).

Hugo Falcandus, *The History of the Tyrants of Sicily,* ed. and trans. G.A. Loud and T. Wiedemann (Manchester University Press, 1998).

Itinerarium Peregrinorum et Gesta Regis Ricardi; auctore, et videtur, Ricardo, Canonico Sanctae Trinitatis Londoniensis, in *Chronicles and Memorials of the Reign of Richard I,* ed. William Stubbs, in *Chronicles and Memorials of Great Britain and Ireland During the Middle Ages,* (Rolls Series, 38.1, London, 1864).

John Kinnamos, *Deeds of John and Manuel Comnenos,* trans. Charles M. Brand (Columbia University Press, 1976).

John le Neve, *Fasti Ecclesiae Anglicanae, 1066-1300,* comp. Diana E. Greenway, II: *Monastic Cathedrals* (University of London, Institute of Historical Research, 1971).

Jordan Fantosme's Chronicle, ed. and trans. R.C. Johnston (Clarendon Press, Oxford, 1981).

König Rother, in *Göppinger Arbeiten zur Germanistik*, 168: *Alt = Deutsche Epische Gedichte*, I, ed. Uwe Meves (Göppingen, 1979).

La Continuation de Guillaume de Tyr, ed. and trans. Margaret Ruth Morgan (Paris, 1982).

Lestoire des Engles, solum la translacion Maistre Geffrei Gaimar, ed. Thomas Duffy and Charles Trice Martin, 2 Vols. (Rolls Series, 91, London, 1888-9).

Letters of John of Salisbury, II, ed. W.J. Millor & C.N.L. Brooke (Oxford, 1979).

Liber Memoriam Sancti Blasii, in *Monumenta Germaniae Historica Scriptorum*, 24 (Hanover, 1879).

Lucas de Tuy, *Crónica de España*, ed. Julio Puyol (Real Academia de la Historia, Madrid, 1926).

Magna Vita Sancti Hugonis Episcopi Lincolniensis, ed. James F. Dimock (Rolls Series, 37, London, 1864).

Marie de France, *French Medieval Romances from the Lays of Marie de France*, trans. Eugene Mason (J.M. Dent & Sons, London and Toronto, 1911; repr. 1932).

Materials for the History of Thomas Becket, archbishop of Canterbury, ed. J.C. Robertson & J.B. Sheppard, 7 Vols. (Rolls Series, 67, London, 1875-85).

Matthew Paris, *Matthaei Parisiensis, Monachi Sancti Albani, Chronica Majora*, ed. Henry Richards Luard (Longman & Co., London, 1882), VI.

Monasticon Anglicanum, ed. William Dugdale (6 Vols., London; Vol. 2, 1819).

Niketas Choniates, *O City of Byzantium, Annals of Niketas Choniates*, trans. Harry J. Magoulias (Wayne State University Press, Detroit, 1984).

Patent Rolls of the Reign of Henry III, I, 1216-1225 (PRO, London, 1901).

Peter of Blois, *Petri Blesensis Bathoniensis in Anglia Archidiaconi opera omnia*, in *Patrologia Latina*, CCVII (1855).

Primera Crónica de España, ed. Ramón Menéndez Pidal (Nueva Biblioteca de Autores Españoles, Vol. 5, Madrid, 1906).

Ralph of Coggeshall, *Chronicon Anglicanum*, in *Chronicles and Memorials of Great Britain and Ireland in the Middle Ages*, ed. Josephus Stevenson (Rolls Series, 66, London, 1875).

Ralph of Diceto, *Decani Lundoniensis Opuscula*, in *Radulfi Diceto Decani Lundoniensis Opera Historica: The Historical Works of Master Ralph de Diceto, Dean of London*, ed. William Stubbs, 2 Vols., in *Chronicles and Memorials of Great Britain and Ireland During the Middle Ages* (Rolls Series, 68, London, 1876).

Ralph of Diceto, *Ymagines Historiarum*, in *Radulfi Diceto Decani Lundoniensis Opera Historica: The Historical Works of Master Ralph de Diceto, Dean of London*, ed. William Stubbs, 2 Vols., in *Chronicles and Memorials of Great Britain and Ireland During the Middle Ages* (Rolls Series, 68, London, 1876).

Recueil des Actes de Henri II, Roi d'Angleterre et Duc de Normandie, in *Chartes et Diplômes relatifs à l'Histoire de France*, IV, 4 vols., ed. Léopold Delisle (Paris, 1916-27).

Recueil des Actes de Philippe Auguste, Roi de France, in *Chartes et Diplômes relatifs à l'Histoire de France*, VI, 6 vols., ed. M.H.-François Delaborde (Paris, 1916-79).

Recueil des Historiens des Gaules et de la France, ed. Martin Bouquet (Rerum Gallicarum et Franciarum Scriptores, Paris, 1878, Vol. 16).

Regesta Rerum Anglo-Normannorum, 3 Vols., ed. H.W.C. Davis, C. Johnson, H.A. Cronne (Clarendon, Oxford, 1913-69).

Regesta Pontificum Romanorum, ed. Philippus Jaffé (2 Vols., Leipzig, 1885-8; repr. Graz, 1956), Vol. II.

Richard of Devizes, *De Rebus Gestis Ricardi Primi: The Chronicle of Richard of Devizes*, in *Chronicles of the Reigns of Stephen, Henry II, and Richard I*, ed. Richard Howlett, 4 Vols., in *Chronicles and Memorials of Great Britain and Ireland During the Middle Ages* (Rolls Series, 82.3, London, 1886).

Robert of Torigni, *Chronica de Roberti de Torigneio: The Chronicle of Robert of Torigny, Abbot of the Monastery of St. Michael-in-peril-of-the-sea*, in *Chronicles of the Reigns of Stephen, Henry II, and Richard I*, ed. Richard Howlett, 4 Vols., in *Chronicles and Memorials of Great Britain and Ireland During the Middle Ages* (Rolls Series, 82.4, London, 1889).

Roger of Howden, *Chronica Magistri Rogeri de Houedene*, ed. William Stubbs, 4 Vols., in *Chronicles and Memorials of Great Britain and Ireland During the Middle Ages* (Rolls Series, 51, London, 1868-71).

Roger of Howden, *Gesta Regis Henrici Secundi Benedicti Abbatis. The Chronicle of the Reigns of Henry II & Richard I AD 1169-1192; Known Commonly Under the Name of Benedict of Peterborough*, ed. William Stubbs, 2 Vols., in *Chronicles and Memorials of Great Britain and Ireland During the Middle Ages* (Rolls Series, 49, London, 1867).

Roger of Wendover, *Liber Qui Dicitur Flores Historiarum Ab Anno Domini MCLIV. Annoque Henrici Anglorum Regis Secundi Primo. The Flowers of History by Roger de Wendover: From the Year of Our Lord 1154, and the First Year of Henry the Second, King of the English*, ed. Henry G. Hewlett, 3 Vols., in *Chronicles and Memorials of Great Britain and Ireland During the Middle Ages* (Rolls Series, 84, London, 1886-9).

Romuald of Salerno, *Chronicon*, ed. L.A. Muratori, in *Rerum Italicarum Scriptores, Raccolta degli Storici Italiani dal cinquecento al millecinquecento*, VII.1 (Città di Castello, 1725).

Rotuli Chartarum in Turreni Londiniensi Asservati, I, ed. Thomas Duffy Hardy (Record Commission, London, 1831).

Rotuli Litterarum Clausarum (Close Rolls), I, 1204-1216, ed. Thomas Duffy Hardy (London, 1837).

Rotuli Litterarum Patentium (Patent Rolls), I, 1201-1216, ed. Thomas Duffy Hardy (London, 1835).

Ryccardo of San Germano, *Chronica*, ed. L.A. Muratori, in *Rerum Italicarum Scriptores, Raccolta degli Storici Italiani dal cinquecento al millecinquecento*, VII.2 (Bologna, 1725).

The Annals of Roger de Hoveden. Comprising the History of England and of Other Countries of Europe from A.D. 732 to A.D. 1201, ed. and trans. Henry T. Riley, 2 Vols (H.G. Bohn, London, 1853).

The Autobiography of Giraldus Cambrensis, ed. and trans. H.E. Butler (Jonathan Cape, London, 1937).

The Cartulary of the Abbey of Mont-Saint-Michel, ed. K.S.B. Keats-Rohan (Shaun Tyas, Donington, 2006).

The Chronicle of Ernoul and the Continuations of William of Tyre, ed. M.R. Morgan (OUP, 1973).

The Chronicle of Richard Lion-Heart by Ambroise, ed. M.J. Hubert and J.L. la Monte (Octagon, New York, 1976).

The Chronicle of San Juan de la Peña: A Fourteenth Century Official History of the Crown of Aragon, ed. and trans. Lynn H. Nelson (University of Pennsylvania Press, Philadelphia, 1991).

The Gesta Normannorum Ducum of William of Jumièges, Orderic Vitalis, and Robert of Torigni, ed. and trans. Elisabeth M.C. Van Houts (Clarendon Press, Oxford, 1992).

The Historical Works of Giraldus Cambrensis, ed. Thomas Wright (H.G. Bohn, London, 1863).

The History of the Holy War – Ambroise's Estoire de la Guerre Sainte, trans. Marianne Ailes (Boydell, Woodbridge, 2003), 2 Vols.

The History of William of Newburgh, ed. and trans. Joseph Stevenson (London, 1856; repr. Llanerch Publishing, Felinfach, 1996).

The Itinerary of King Richard I, with Studies on Certain Matters of Interest Connected with his Reign, ed. Lionel Landon, (Pipe Roll Society, New Series 13, London, 1935).

The Letters and Charters of Gilbert Foliot, ed. A. Morey and C.N.L. Brooke (CUP, 1967).

The Metrical Chronicle of Jordan Fantosme, ed. Richard Howlett (Rolls Series, 82.3, London, 1886).

The Pipe Rolls of Henry II (38 Vols., Pipe Roll Society, 1884-1925).

The Plantagenet Chronicles, ed. Elizabeth Hallam (Greenwich Editions, London, 2002),

The Poems of the Troubadour Bertran de Born, ed. W. Paden, T. Sankovitch & P. Stäblein (University of California Press, 1986).

The Political Songs of England, from the reign of John to that of Edward III, ed. Thomas Wright (Camden Society, old series, VI, London, 1839).

The Rare and Excellent History of Saladin, ed. and trans. D.S. Richards (Ashgate, Hants., 2002).

Thomas Agnellus, 'Sermo de morte et sepultura Henrici Regis iunioris', in *Chronicles and Memorials of Great Britain and Ireland in the Middle Ages*, ed. Josephus Stevenson (Rolls Series, 66, London, 1875).

Thomas Rymer, *Foedera*, I, (J. Tonson, London, 1727).

Veterum scriptorum et Monumentorum historicorum, dogmaticorum, moralium, amplissima collectio, ed. Edmond Martène and Ursini Durand, I (Paris, 1724).

Walter Map, *De Nugis Curialium: Courtiers' Trifles*, ed. and trans. M. R. James, rev. C.N.L. Brooke & R.A.B. Mynors (Oxford Medeival Texts, Clarendon Press, Oxford, 1983).

William of Newburgh, *Historia Rerum Anglicanum*, in *Chronicles of the Reigns of Stephen, Henry II, and Richard I*, ed. Richard Howlett, 4 Vols., in *Chronicles and Memorials of Great Britain and Ireland During the Middle Ages* (Rolls Series, 82.1; 82.2, London, 1884-5).

Wynkyn de Worde, *The Noble and Tryumphaunt Coronacyon of Quene Anne*, ed. Edmund Goldsmid (Edinburgh, 1884).

Secondary Sources:

Abulafia, D.S.H., 'Joanna [Joan, Joanna of England], countess of Toulouse (1165-1199), queen of Sicily, consort of William II', *Oxford Dictionary of National Biography* (OUP, 2004).

Airlie, S., 'The History of Emotions and Emotional History', in *Early Medieval Europe*, 10:2 (2001), 235-41.

Appel, C., *Provenzalische Chrestomathie* (Leipzig, 1912).

Ariès, P., *Centuries of Childhood*, trans. Robert Baldick (Pimlico, London, 1962; repr. 1996).

Arnold, B., *Medieval Germany, 500-1300: A Political Interpretation* (MacMillan, London, 1997).

Attreed, L.C., 'From *Pearl* Maiden to Tower Princes: Towards a new history of medieval childhood', in *Journal of Medieval History*, 9 (1983), 43-58.

Aurell, M., *Le Chevalier lettré : savoir et conduite de l'aristocratie aux XIIe et XIIIe siècles* (Fayard, Paris, 2011).

------------- *Les Noces du comte. Mariage et pouvoir en Catalogne (785-1213)* (Publications de la Sorbonne, Paris, 1995).

------------- *The Plantagenet Empire* (1154-1224) (Pearson-Longman, Harlow, 2007).

Babbitt, T., *La Crónica de Veinte Reyes: A Comparison with the Text of the Primera Crónica General and a Study of the Principal Latin Sources* (Yale University Press, 1936).

Bailey, R.N., 'St Oswald's Heads', in Clare Stancliffe and Eric Cambridge (eds.), *Oswald: Northumbrian King to European Saint* (Paul Watkins, Stamford, Lincolnshire, 1995), 195-209.

Bak, J.M., 'Introduction: Coronation Studies – Past, Present, and Future', in János M. Bak (ed.), *Coronations – Medieval and Early Modern Monarchic Ritual* (University of California Press, 1990), 1-15.

Baldwin, J.W., *The Government of Philip Augustus: Foundations of French Royal Power in the Middle Ages* (University of California Press, 1986).

Barber, R., 'Eleanor of Aquitaine and the Media', in Marcus Bull and Catherine Léglu (eds.), *The World of Eleanor of Aquitaine, Literature and Society in Southern France Between the Eleventh and Thirteenth Centuries* (Boydell, Woodbridge, 2005), 13-27.

Barlow, F., 'Roger of Howden', in *English Historical Review*, 65 (1950), 352-60.

------------ *Thomas Becket* (Weidenfeld & Nicolson, London, 1986).

Barton, S., *The Aristocracy in Twelfth-Century León and Castile* (CUP, 1997).

Bedos Rezak, B., 'Women, Seals, and Power in Medieval France, 1150-1350', in M. Erler & M. Kowaleski (eds.), *Women and Power in the Middle Ages* (University of Georgia Press, 1988), 61-82.

Benjamin, R., 'A Forty Years War: Toulouse and the Plantagenets, 1156-96', in *Historical Research*, LXI (1988), 270-85.

Bertau, K., *Deutsche Literatur im europäischen Mittelalter* (2 vols., Munich, 1972-3).

Binski, P., *Westminster Abbey and the Plantagenets: Kingship and the Representation of Power, 1200-1400* (Yale University Press, New Haven & London, 1995).

Bisson, T., 'An Early Provincial Assembly: The General Court of Agenais in the Thirteenth Century', in T. Bisson, *Medieval France and her Pyrenean Neighbours* (Hambledon Press, London, 1989), 3-30.

Bitel, L.M., *Women in Early Medieval Europe, 400-1100* (CUP, 2002).

Boase, T.S.R., 'Fontevrault and the Plantagenets', in *Journal of the British Archaeological Association*, 3rd ser., 34 (1971), 1-10.

Bonne, J.-C., 'The Manuscript of the Ordo of 1250 and Its Illuminations', in János M. Bak (ed.), *Coronations – Medieval and Early Modern Monarchic Ritual* (University of California Press, 1990), 58-71.

Borenius, T., 'Addenda to the Iconography of St. Thomas of Canterbury', in *Archaeologia*, 81 (1931), 19-32.

------------- 'Some Further Aspects of the Iconography of St. Thomas of Canterbury', in *Archaeologia*, 83 (1933), 171-86.

------------- *St. Thomas Becket in Art* (Methuen & Co. Ltd., London, 1932).

------------- 'The Iconography of St. Thomas of Canterbury', in *Archaeologia,* 79 (Oxford, 1929), 29-54.

Bouchard, C.B., 'Family Structure and Family Consciousness among the Aristocracy in the Ninth to Eleventh Centuries', in *Francia*, 14 (1987), 639-58.

------------- *"Those of My Blood" – Constructing Noble Families in Medieval Francia* (University of Pennsylvania Press, Philadelphia, 2001).

Bowie, C., 'Shifting Patterns in Angevin Marriage Policies: The Political Motivations for Joanna Plantagenet's Marriages to William II of Sicily and Raymond VI of Toulouse', in Matin Aurell (ed.), *Les Stratégies Matrimoniales, IXe-XIIIe Siècle* (Brepols, Turnhout, 2013), 155-67.

Brooke, C.N.L., 'Both Great and Small Beasts: An Introductory Study', in Derek Baker (ed.) *Medieval Women* (Blackwell, Oxford, 1978), 1-13.

Brown, E.A.R, 'Eleanor of Aquitaine: Parent, Queen, and Duchess', in William W. Kibler (ed.), *Eleanor of Aquitaine: Patron and Politician* (Texas University Press, 1976), 9-34.

Carpenter, D., 'Abbot Ralph of Coggeshall's Account of the Last Years of King Richard and the First Years of King John', in *English Historical Review*, 113 (1998), 1210-30.

Casagrande, C., 'The Protected Woman', in Georges Duby & Michelle Perrot (eds.), *A History of Women in the West: II. Silences of the Middle Ages*, ed. Christiane Klapisch-Zuber (Harvard University Press, 1992), 70-104.

Chalandon, F., *Histoire de la Domination Normande en Italie et en Sicile*, 2 Vols. (Librairie Alphonse Picard et Fils, Libraire des Archives nationales et de la Societé de l'Ecole des Chartres, Paris, 1907).

Chaney, W.A., *The Cult of Kingship in Anglo-Saxon England* (Manchester University Press, 1970).

Chibnall, M., *The Empress Matilda, Queen Consort, Queen Mother and Lady of the English* (Blackwell, Oxford, 1991).

Clanchy, M.T., *The Letters of Abelard and Heloise* (Penguin, 2003).

Cloulas, I., 'Bérengère de Navarre Raconte Aliénor d'Aquitaine', in Martin Aurell (ed.), *Aliénor d'Aquitaine* (Nantes, 2004), 230-33.

-------------- 'Le douaire de Bérengère de Navarre, veuve de Richard Coeur de Lion, et sa retraite au Mans', in Martin Aurell (ed.), *La Cour Plantagenêt 1152-1204* (Poitiers, 2000), 89-94.

Collins, R., 'Queens-Dowager and Queens-Regent in Tenth Century León and Navarre', in John Carmi Parsons (ed.), *Medieval Queenship* (Sutton Publishing, Gloucs., 1994), 79-92.

Conant, K.J., *Carolingian and Romanesque Architecture: 800-1200* (Penguin, Middlesex, 1959).

Corner, D., 'The Earliest Surviving Manuscripts of Roger of Howden's *Chronica*', in *English Historical Review*, 98 (1983), 297-310.

-------------- 'The *Gesta Regis Henrici Secundi* and *Chronica* of Roger, Parson of Howden', in *Bulletin of the Institute of Historical Research*, 56 (London, 1983), 126-44.

Cowdrey, H.E.J., 'Martyrdom and the First Crusade', in Cowdrey, *The Crusades and Latin Monasticism, 11th-12th Centuries* (Ashgate Variorum, Aldershot, 1999), 46-56.

Crawford, A., *Letters of the Queens of England, 1100-1547* (Stroud, 1994).

Cubitt, C., 'The History of Emotions: a debate. Introduction', in *Early Medieval Europe*, 10:2 (2001), 225-7.

Dalarun, J., 'The Clerical Gaze', in Georges Duby & Michelle Perrot (eds.), *A History of Women in the West: II. Silences of the Middle Ages*, ed. Christiane Klapisch-Zuber (Harvard University Press, 1992), 15-42.

Damian-Grint, P., 'Benoît de Sainte-Maure et l'idéologie des Plantagenêt', in Martin Aurell & Noël-Yves Tonnerre (eds.), *Plantagenêts et Capétiens: Confrontations et Héritages* (Brepols, Belgium, 2006), 413-27.

Dectot, Xavier, *Les Tombeaux des Familles Royales de la Péninsule Ibérique au Moyen Âge* (Brepols, Belgium, 2009).

Deér, J., *The Dynastic Porphyry Tombs of the Norman Period in Sicily* (Harvard University Press, 1959).

Demus, O., *The Mosaics of Norman Sicily* (London, Routledge & Kegan Paul, 1950).

Díez, G.M., *Alfonso VIII rey de Castilla y Toledo (1158-1214)* (Gijón, 1995; 2nd edn. 2007).

Diggelmann, L., 'Marriage as a Tactical Response: Henry II and the Royal Wedding of 1160', in *English Historical Review,* 119 no. 483 (2004), 954-64.

Dodds, J., 'Islam, Christianity, and the Problem of Religious Art', in *The Art of Medieval Spain, 500-1200* (The Metropolitan Musuem of Art, New York, 1993), 27-37.

Dronke, P., 'Peter of Blois and Poetry at the Court of Henry II', in *Mediaeval Studies,* 38 (1976), 185-235.

Duby, G., *Love and Marriage in the Middle Ages,* trans. Jane Dunnett (Polity Press, Cambridge, 1994).

------------- *Medieval Marriage: Two Models from Twelfth-Century France,* trans. Elborg Forster (John Hopkins University Press, Baltimore, 1978).

Duggan, A., 'Aspects of Anglo-Portuguese Relations in the Twelfth Century. Manuscripts, Relics, Decretals and the Cult of St Thomas Becket at Lorvao, Alcobaca and Tomar', in *Portuguese Studies,* 14 (London, 1998), 1-19.

------------- 'Diplomacy, Status, and Conscience: Henry II's Penance for Becket's Murder', in Anne Duggan, *Thomas Becket: Friends, Networks, Texts and Cult* (Ashgate Variorum, Hants., 2007), Part 2, VII, 265-90.

------------- 'Introduction', in Anne Duggan (ed.), *Queens and Queenship in Medieval Europe* (Boydell Press, Woodbridge, 1997), xv-xxii.

------------- *'Ne in dubium*: The Official Record of Henry II's Reconciliation at Avranches, 21 May 1172', in Anne Duggan, *Thomas Becket: Friends, Networks, Texts and Cult* (Ashgate Variorum, Hants., 2007), Part 2, VIII, 643-58.

------------- 'On Finding the Voice of Eleanor of Aquitaine', in *Voix des femmes aux moyen âge. Actes du colloque du Centre d'Études Médiévales Anglaises de Paris-Sorbonne* (26–27 mar 2010), ed. L. Carruthers, *Association des Médiévistes Anglicistes de l'Énseignement Supérieur,* 32 (Paris, 2011), 129–58.

------------- 'Ridel, Geoffrey (d. 1189)', *Oxford Dictionary of National Biography* (OUP, 2004).

------------- *The Correspondence of Thomas Becket,* 2 Vols. (Clarendon Press, Oxford, 2000).

------------- 'The Cult of St Thomas Becket in the Thirteenth Century', in Anne Duggan, *Thomas Becket: Friends, Networks, Texts and Cult* (Ashgate Variorum, Hants., 2007), Part IX, 21-44.

------------- *Thomas Becket* (Arnold Publishers, London, 2004).

------------- 'Thomas Becket's Italian Network', in Anne Duggan, *Thomas Becket: Friends, Networks, Texts and Cult* (Ashgate Variorum, Hants., 2007), Part I, 1-21.

Duggan, C., 'Reginald fitz Jocelin (c. 1140-1191)', *Oxford Dictionary of National Biography* (OUP, 2004).

------------- 'Richard of Ilchester, Royal Servant and Bishop', in *Transactions of the Royal Historical Society*, 5th ser., Vol. 16 (1966), 1-24.

------------- 'Richard (d. 1184)', *Oxford Dictionary of National Biography* (OUP, 2004).

Dunbabin, J., *France in the Making, 843-1180* (OUP, 1985; 2nd edn., 2000).

Dutton, K., '*Ad erudiendum tradidit*: The Upbringing of Angevin Comital Children', in *Anglo-Norman Studies*, 32 (2009), 24-39.

Earenfight, T., 'Absent Kings: Queens as Political Partners in the Medieval Crown of Aragon', in Theresa Earenfight (ed.), *Queenship and Political Power in Medieval and Early Modern Spain* (Ashgate, Aldershot, 2005), 33-51.

------------- 'Partners in Politics', in Theresa Earenfight (ed.), *Queenship and Political Power in Medieval and Early Modern Spain* (Ashgate, Aldershot, 2005), xiii-xxviii.

Elze, R., 'The Ordo for the Coronation of King Roger II of Sicily: An Example of Dating from Internal Evidence', in János M. Bak (ed.), *Coronations – Medieval and Early Modern Monarchic Ritual* (University of California Press, 1990), 165-78.

Enciclopedia Italiana di Scienze, Lettere ed Arti (Treves, Treccani, T.V.M. Minelli, 1933), XVIII.

Erickson, C., *The Medieval Vision* (OUP, 1976).

Erlande-Brandenburg, 'Le Gisant d'Aliénor d'Aquitaine', in Martin Aurell (ed.) *Alienor d'Aquitaine* (Nantes, 2004), 174-9.

Erler, M. and Kowaleski, M., 'Introduction', in M. Erler & M. Kowaleski (eds.), *Women and Power in the Middle Ages* (University of Georgia Press, 1988), 1-17.

Evans, M., *The Death of Kings – Royal Deaths in Medieval England* (Hambledon & London, London, 2003).

Eyton, R.W., *Court, Household, and Itinerary of King Henry II, Instancing also the Chief Agents and Adversaries of the King in his Government, Diplomacy, and Strategy* (James Foster, Cornhill, Dorchester, 1878).

Favreau, Robert, 'Aliénor d'Aquitaine et Fontevraud', in Martin Aurell (ed.) *Aliénor d'Aquitaine* (Nantes, 2004), 40-5.

Ferrante, J., 'Public Postures and Private Maneuvers : Roles Medieval Women Play', in M. Erler & M. Kowaleski (eds.), *Women and Power in the Middle Ages* (University of Georgia Press, 1988), 213-29.

Flori, J., *Eleanor of Aquitaine: Queen and Rebel* (Edinburgh University Press, 2004; Eng. trans. by Olive Classe, 2007).

Freed, J.B., 'Artistic and Literary Representations of Family Consciousness', in Gerd Althoff, Johannes Fried and Patrick Geary (eds.), *Medieval Concepts of the Past: Ritual, Memory, Historiography* (CUP, 2002), 233-52.

Frölich, W., 'The Marriage of Henry VI and Constance of Sicily: Prelude and Consequences', *Anglo-Norman Studies*, XV (1992), 99-115.

Frugoni, C., 'The Imagined Woman', in Georges Duby & Michelle Perrot (eds.), *A History of Women in the West: II. Silences of the Middle Ages*, ed. Christiane Klapisch-Zuber (Harvard University Press, 1992), 336-422.

Fuhrmann, H., *Germany in the High Middle Ages, c. 1050-1200*, trans. Timothy Reuter (CUP, 1986; repr. 1992).

Gameson, R., 'The Early Imagery of Thomas Becket', in Colin Morris & Peter Roberts (eds.), *Pilgrimage: The English Experience from Becket to Bunyan* (CUP, 2002), 46-89.

Garnett, G., ''Ducal' Succession in Early Normandy', in George Garnett & John Hudson (eds.), *Law and Government in Medieval England and Normandy, Essays in honour of Sir James Holt* (CUP, 1994), 80-110.

Garrison, M., 'The study of emotions in early medieval history', in *Early Medieval Europe*, 10.2 (2001), 243-50.

Geaman, K., 'Queen's Gold and Intercession: The Case of Eleanor of Aquitaine', in *Medieval Feminist Forum* 46, no. 2 (2010), 10-33.

Gerish, D., 'Holy War, Royal Wives, and Equivocation in Twelfth-Century Jerusalem', in Niall Christie and Maya Yazigi (eds.), *Noble Ideals and Bloody Realities: Warfare in the Middle Ages* (History of Warfare, 37, 2006), 119-44.

Giesey, R., 'Inaugural Aspects of French Royal Ceremonials', in János M. Bak (ed.), *Corona-tions – Medieval and Early Modern Monarchic Ritual* (University of California Press, 1990), 35-45.

Gillingham, J., 'Doing Homage to the King of France', in Christopher Harper-Bill and Nicholas Vincent (eds.), *Henry II: New Interpretations* (Boydell, Woodbridge, 2007), 63-84.

-------------- 'Kingship, Chivalry and Love: Political and Cultural Values in the Earliest History Written in French: Geoffrey Gaimar's *Estoire des Engleis*', in C. Warren Hollister (ed.), *Anglo-Norman Political Culture and the Twelfth Century Renaissance, Proceedings of the Borchard Conference on Anglo-Norman History* (Boydell Press, Woodbridge, 1997), 33-58.

-------------- 'Love, Marriage and Politics in the Twelfth Century', in *Forum for Modern Language Studies*, 25 (1989), 292-303.

-------------- *Richard I* (Yale University Press, London, 2002).

-------------- 'Richard I and Berengaria of Navarre', in *Bulletin of the Institute of Historical Research*, 53 (1980), 157-73.

-------------- *Richard Coeur de Lion: Kingship, Chivalry and War in the Twelfth Century* (Hambledon Press, London, 1994).

-------------- 'Royal Newsletters, Forgeries, and English Historians: Some Links between Court and History in the Reign of Richard I', in Martin Aurell (ed.), *La Cour Plantagenêt, 1154-1204* (Poitiers, 2000), 171-85.

Gleason, S.E., *An Ecclesiastical Barony of the Middle Ages: The Bishopric of Bayeux, 1066-1204* (Harvard University Press, 1936).

Gómez-Moreno, M., *El Panteon Real de las Huelgas de Burgos* (Madrid, 1946).

González, J., *El Reino de Castilla en la Epoca de Alfonso VIII* (3 Vols., Madrid, 1960).

Goody, J, *The Development of the Family and Marriage in Europe* (CUP, 1983).

Gransden, A., *Historical Writing in England, c. 550 to c. 1307* (Routledge & Kegan Paul, London, 1974), I.

Grant, L., *Abbot Suger of St-Denis: Church and State in Early Twelfth-Century France* (Longman, Essex, 1998).

Green, J., 'Aristocratic Women in Early Twelfth-Century England', in C. Warren Hollister (ed.), *Anglo-Norman Political Culture and the Twelfth Century Renaissance, Proceedings of the Borchard Conference on Anglo-Norman History* (Boydell Press, Woodbridge, 1997), 59-82.

Green, M.A.E., *The Lives of the Princesses of England from the Norman Conquest,* 2 Vols., I, (Henry Colburn, London, 1850).

Greenhill, E.S., 'Eleanor, Abbot Suger, and Saint-Denis', in William W. Kibler (ed.) *Eleanor of Aquitaine, Patron and Politician* (University of Texas Press, 1976), 81-113.

Groag Bell, S., 'Medieval Women Book Owners: Arbiters of Lay Piety and Ambassadors of Culture', in M. Erler & M. Kowaleski (eds.), *Women and Power in the Middle Ages* (University of Georgia Press, 1988), 149-87.

Györffy, G., 'Thomas à Becket and Hungary', in *Hungarian Studies in English*, IV (Kossuth Lajos Tudományegyetem Debrecen, 1969), 45-52.

Hallam, E., 'Royal Burial and the Cult of Kingship in France and England, 1060-1330', in *Journal of Medieval History*, 8:4 (1982), 359-81.

Haluska-Rausch, E., 'Unwilling Partners: Conflict and Ambition in the Marriage of Peter II of Aragon and Marie de Montpellier', in Theresa Earenfight (ed.), *Queenship and Political Power in Medieval and Early Modern Spain* (Ashgate, Aldershot, 2005), 3-20.

Hamilton, B., 'Women in the Crusader States: The Queens of Jerusalem 1100-90', in Derek Baker (ed.), *Medieval Women* (Blackwell, Oxford, 1978), 143-74.

Harper-Bill, C., 'Oxford, John of (d. 1200)', *Oxford Dictionary of National Biography* (OUP, 2004).

Herlihy, D., *Medieval Households* (Harvard University Press, 1985).

Heywood, C., *A History of Childhood: Children and Childhood in the West from Medieval to Modern Times* (Polity Press, Cambridge, 2001).

Hillgarth, J.N., *The Spanish Kingdoms, 1250-1516* (Clarendon Press, Oxford, 1976).

Hivergneaux, M., 'Aliénor d'Aquitaine: Le pouvoir d'une femme à la lumière de ses chartes (1152-1204)', in Martin Aurell (ed.), *La Cour Plantagenêt 1152-1204* (Poitiers, 2000), 63-87.

------------ 'Autour d'Aliénor d'Aquitaine: Entourage et pouvoir au prisme des chartes (1137-1289)', in Martin Aurell and Noël-Yves Tonnerre (eds.), *Plantagenêts et Capétiens: Confrontations et Héritages* (Brepols, Belgium, 2006), 61-73.

------------ 'Le pouvoir a l'epreuve des chartes', in Martin Aurell (ed.), *Aliénor d'Aquitaine* (Nantes, 2004), 64-9.

Hollister, C.W., 'Anglo-Norman Political Culture and the Twelfth Century Renaissance', in C. Warren Hollister (ed.), *Anglo-Norman Political Culture and the Twelfth Century Renaissance, Proceedings of the Borchard Conference on Anglo-Norman History* (Boydell Press, Woodbridge, 1997), 1-16.

------------ 'Introduction', in C. Warren Hollister (ed.), *Anglo-Norman Political Culture and the Twelfth Century Renaissance, Proceedings of the Borchard Conference on Anglo-Norman History* (Boydell Press, Woodbridge, 1997), ix-xi.

Holt, J.C., *Colonial England* (Hambledon Press, London, 1997).

Hudson, J., 'Anglo-Norman Land Law and the Origins of Property', in George Garnett & John Hudson (eds.), *Law and Government in Medieval England and Normandy, Essays in honour of Sir James Holt* (CUP, 1994), 198-222.

Hughes, D.O., 'From Brideprice to Dowry in Mediterranean Europe', in Marion A. Kaplan (ed.), *The Marriage Bargain: Women and Dowries in European History* (Harrington Park Press, New York, 1985), 13-58.

Huglo, M., 'Les Reliques de Thomas Becket à Royaumont', in *Revue Bénédictine*, 115.2 (2005), 430-38.

Huneycutt, L., '*Alianora Regina Anglorum*: Eleanor Aquitaine and her Anglo-Norman Predecessors as Queens of England', in B. Wheeler and J.C. Parsons (eds.), *Eleanor of Aquitaine: Lord and Lady* (New York, Palgrave MacMillan, 2002), 115-32.

------------ 'Female Succession and the Language of Power in the Writings of Twelfth Century Churchmen', in John Carmi Parsons (ed.), *Medieval Queenship* (Sutton Publishing, Gloucs., 1994), 189-201.

------------ 'Images of Queenship in the High Middle Ages', in *Haskins Society Journal*, 1 (1989), 61-71.

------------ *Matilda of Scotland: A Study in Medieval Queenship* (Boydell, Woodbridge, 2003).

------------ 'The Idea of a Perfect Princess: The *Life of St Margaret* in the Reign of Matilda II (1100-1118)', in *Anglo-Norman Studies*, XII (1989), 81-97.

Hussey, J.M., 'The Later Macedonians, the Comneni and the Angeli, 1025-1204', in J.M Hussey (ed.), *Cambridge Medieval History*, 4.1 (CUP, 1966), 233-49.

Jamison, E., 'Alliance of England and Sicily in the second half of the twelfth century', in *Journal of the Warburg and Courtauld Institutes*, 6 (London, 1943), 20-32.

Jansen, A., 'The Development of the St Oswald Legends on the Continent', in Clare Stancliffe & Eric Cambridge (eds.), *Oswald: Northumbrian King to European Saint* (Paul Watkins, Stamford, Lincolnshire, 1995), 230-40.

Jaschke, K.-U., 'From Famous Empresses to Unspectacular Queens: The Romano-German Empire to Margaret of Brabant, Countess of Luxemburg and Queen of the Romans (d. 1311)', in Anne Duggan (ed.), *Queens and Queenship in Medieval Europe* (Boydell Press, Woodbridge, 1997), 75-108.

Jasperse, J., 'Het Cultureele patronaat van Mathilde Plantagenet (1156-1189)', in *Millenium: Tijdschrift voor Middeleeuwse Studies*, 21:2 (2007), 89-103.

Johns, S., *Noblewomen, Aristocracy and Power in the Twelfth-Century Anglo-Norman Realm* (Manchester University Press, 2003).

Jordan, E.L., *Women, Power and Religious Patronage in the Middle Ages* (Palgrave MacMillan, New York, 2006).

Jordan, K., *Henry the Lion: A Biography*, trans. P.S. Falla (Clarendon Press, Oxford, 1986).

Kaplan, M.A., 'Introduction', in M. Kaplan (ed.), *The Marriage Bargain: Women and Dowries in European History* (Harrington Park Press, New York, 1985), 1-11.

Keefe, T.K., 'Warenne, Hamelin de, earl of Surrey (d. 1202)', *Oxford Dictionary of National Biography* (OUP, 2004).

Keen, M., 'Introduction', in Peter Coss and Maurice Keen (eds.), *Heraldry, Pageantry and Social Display in Medieval England* (Boydell, Woodbridge, 2002), 1-16.

Keene, D., 'William fitz Osbert, d. 1196', *Oxford Dictionary of National Biography* (OUP, 2004).

Kelly, A., *Eleanor of Aquitaine and the Four Kings* (Harvard University Press, 1958).

Kenaan-Kedar, N., 'Aliénor d'Aquitaine et les arts visuals, de l'art dynastique à l'art courtois', in Martin Aurell (ed.), *Aliénor d'Aquitaine* (Nantes, 2004), 82-91.

Kitzinger, E., *The Mosaics of Monreale* (S.F. Flaccovio, Palermo, 1960).

Klapisch-Zuber, C., 'Family and Social Strategies: The Hidden Power of Women', in Georges Duby & Michelle Perrot (eds.), *A History of Women in the West: II. Silences of the Middle Ages*, ed. Christiane Klapisch-Zuber (Harvard University Press, 1992), 161-8.

-------------- 'Including Women', in Georges Duby & Michelle Perrot (eds.), *A History of Women in the West: II. Silences of the Middle Ages*, ed. Christiane Klapisch-Zuber (Harvard University Press, 1992), 1-10.

-------------- 'Norms of Control: Enforcing Order', in Georges Duby & Michelle Perrot (eds.), *A History of Women in the West: II. Silences of the Middle Ages*, ed. Christiane Klapisch-Zuber (Harvard University Press, 1992), 13-14.

-------------- 'Vestiges and Images of Women: New Appearances', in Georges Duby & Michelle Perrot (eds.), *A History of Women in the West: II. Silences of the Middle Ages*, ed. Christiane Klapisch-Zuber (Harvard University Press, 1992), 321-2.

------------- 'Women's Words: Daring to Speak', in Georges Duby & Michelle Perrot (eds.), *A History of Women in the West: II. Silences of the Middle Ages*, ed. Christiane Klapisch-Zuber (Harvard University Press, 1992), 425.

Klein, S., *Ruling Women: Queenship and Gender in Anglo-Saxon Literature* (2006).

Lambert, S., 'Queen or Consort: Rulership and Politics in the Latin East, 1118-1228', in Anne Duggan (ed.), *Queens and Queenship in Medieval Europe* (Boydell Press, Woodbridge, 1997), 153-69.

Larrington, C., 'The psychology of emotion and the study of the medieval period', in *Early Medieval Europe*, 10.2 (2001), 251-6.

Léglu, C. and Bull, M., 'Introduction', in Marcus Bull and Catherine Léglu (eds.), *The World of Eleanor of Aquitaine, Literature and Society in Southern France Between the Eleventh and Thirteenth Centuries* (Boydell, Woodbridge, 2005), 1-11.

Le Goff, J., 'A Coronation Program for the Age of Saint Louis: The Ordo of 1250', in János M. Bak (ed.), *Coronations – Medieval and Early Modern Monarchic Ritual* (University of California Press, 1990), 46-57.

Leyser, K.J., *Medieval Germany and its Neighbours, 900-1250* (Hambledon Press, London, 1982).

L'Hermite-Leclerq, P., 'The Feudal Order', in Georges Duby & Michelle Perrot (eds.), *A History of Women in the West: II. Silences of the Middle Ages*, ed. Christiane Klapisch-Zuber (Harvard University Press, 1992), 202-49.

Lifshitz, F., 'The Martyr, the Tomb, and the Matron: Constructing the (Masculine) "Past" as a Female Power Base', in Gerd Althoff, Johannes Fried and Patrick Geary (eds.), *Medieval Concepts of the Past: Ritual, Memory, Historiography* (CUP, 2002), 311-41.

Little, C.T., 'The Road to Glory: New Early Images of Thomas Becket's Life', in *Reading Medieval Images: The Art Historian and the Object* (University of Michigan Press, 2002), 201-11.

Livingstone, A, 'Aristocratic Women in the Chartrain', in K.A. LoPrete & T. Evergates (eds.), *Aristocratic Women in Medieval France* (University of Pennsylvania Press, 1999), 44-73.

Loewenthal, L.J.A., 'For the Biography of Walter Ophamil, Archbishop of Palermo', in *English Historical Review*, 87 (1972), 75-82.

LoPrete, K.A., 'Adela of Blois: Familial Alliances and Female Lordship', in K.A. LoPrete & T. Evergates (eds.), *Aristocratic Women in Medieval France* (University of Pennsylvania Press, 1999), 7-43.

LoPrete, K.A. and Evergates, T., 'Introduction', in K.A. LoPrete and T. Evergates (eds.), *Aristocratic Women in Medieval France* (University of Pennsylvania Press, 1999), 1-5.

Loud, G.A., *Calendar of Extant Charters of William II* (forthcoming).

------------ 'The Chancery and Charters of the Norman Kings of Sicily (1130-1212), in *English Historical Review*, 124: 509 (2009), 779-810.

Lyon, J.R., *Princely Brothers and Sisters: The Sibling Bond in German Politics, 1100-1250* (Cornell University Press, 2013).

Macé, L., 'Raymond VII of Toulouse: The Son of Queen Joanna, 'Young Count' and Light of the World', trans. Catherine Léglu, in Marcus Bull and Catherine Léglu (eds.), *The World of Eleanor of Aquitaine: Literature and Society in Southern France Between the Eleventh and Thirteenth Centuries* (Boydell Press, Woodbridge, 2005), 137-56.

Martindale, J., 'An Unfinished Business: Angevin Politics and the Siege of Toulouse, 1159', in *Anglo-Norman Studies*, 23 (Boydell, Woodbridge, 2000), 115-54.

------------- 'Eleanor of Aquitaine', in Jane Martindale, *Status, Authority and Regional Power – Aquitaine and France, 9th to 12th Centuries* (Variorum, Aldershot, 1997; first published in Janet Nelson (ed.), *Richard Coeur de Lion in History and Myth* (King's College, London, 1992).), 17-50.

------------- 'Eleanor of Aquitaine and a "Queenly Court"?', in B. Wheeler and J.C. Parsons (eds.), *Eleanor of Aquitaine: Lord and Lady* (New York, Palgrave MacMillan, 2002), 423-39.

------------- 'Eleanor of Aquitaine: The Last Years', in S.D. Church (ed.), *King John: New Interpretations* (Boydell, Woodbridge, 1999), 137-64.

------------- 'Succession and Politics in the Romance-Speaking World, c. 1000-1140', in Michael Jones and Malcolm Vale (eds.), *England and her Neighbours, 1066-1453, Essays in honour of Pierre Chaplais* (Hambledon Press, London, 1989), 19-41.

Matthew, D., *The Norman Kingdom of Sicily* (CUP, 1992).

Matthew, D.J.A., 'Richard [Richard Palmer] (*d.* 1195)', *Oxford Dictionary of National Biography* (OUP, 2004).

------------- 'Walter (d. 1190)', *Oxford Dictionary of National Biography* (OUP, 2004).

Mause, L. de, 'The Evolution of Childhood', in Lloyd de Mause (ed.), *The History of Childhood* (Jason Aronson Inc., New Jersey, 1974; repr. 1995), 1-73.

Mayer, H., 'Henry II of England and the Holy Land', in *English Historical Review*, 97 (1982), 721-39.

McCash, J.H., 'The Cultural Patronage of Medieval Women: An Overview', in June Hall McCash (ed.), *The Cultural Patronage of Medieval Women* (University of Georgia Press, 1996), 1-49.

McLaughlin, M.M., 'Survivors and Surrogates: Children and Parents from the Ninth to the Thirteenth Centuries', in Lloyd de Mause (ed.), *The History of Childhood* (Jason Aronson Inc., New Jersey, 1974; repr. 1995), 101-181.

McNamara, J. and Wemple, S., 'The Power of Women Through the Family in Medieval Europe, 500-1100', in M. Erler & M. Kowaleski (eds.), *Women and Power in the Middle Ages* (University of Georgia Press, 1988), 83-101.

Ménager, L.-R., *Hommes et Institutions de l'Italie Normande* (Variorum Reprints, London, 1981).

Millunzi, G., 'Il tesoro, la biblioteca ed il tabulario della Chiesa di Santa Maria Nuova in Monreale', in *Archivio Storico Siciliano*, 28 (1903), 249-459.

Milsom, S.F.C., 'The Origin of Prerogative Wardship', in George Garnett & John Hudson (eds.), *Law and Government in Medieval England and Normandy, Essays in honour of Sir James Holt* (CUP, 1994), pp. 223-44.

Moralejo, S., 'On the Road: The Camino de Santiago', in *The Art of Medieval Spain* (The Metropolitan Museum of Art, New York, 1993), 174-83.

Munz, P., *Frederick Barbarossa: A Study in Medieval Politics* (Cornell University Press, 1969).

Nelson, J., 'Early Medieval Rites of Queen-Making and the Shaping of Medieval Queenship', in Anne Duggan (ed.), *Queens and Queenship in Medieval Europe* (Boydell Press, Woodbridge, 1997), 301-15.

------------- 'Gendering courts in the early medieval west', in L. Brubaker and J.M.H. Smith (eds.), *Gender in the Early Medieval World, East and West, 300-900* (CUP, 2005), 185-97.

------------- 'Queens as Jezebels: The Careers of Brunhild and Balthild in Merovingian History', in Lester K. Little and Barbara H. Rosenwein (eds), *Debating the Middle Ages: Issues and Readings* (Blackwell, Oxford, 1998), 219-53.

------------- 'Women at the Court of Charlemagne: A Case of Monstrous Regiment?', in John Carmi Parsons (ed.), *Medieval Queenship* (Sutton Publishing, Gloucs., 1994), 43-61.

Nolan, K., 'The Queen's Choice: Eleanor of Aquitaine and the Tombs at Fontevraud', in Bonnie Wheeler & John Carmi Parsons (eds.), *Eleanor of Aquitaine: Lord and Lady* (Palgrave MacMillan, New York, 2002), 377-406.

Norgate, K., *John Lackland* (MacMillan, London, 1902).

------------- 'Matilda, duchess of Saxony (1156-1189)', rev. Timothy Reuter, *Oxford Dictionary of National Biography* (OUP, 2004).

Norwich, J.J., *The Kingdom in the Sun, 1130-1194* (Longman, London, 1970).

------------- *The Normans in the South* (Longman, London, 1967).

O'Callaghan, J., *A History of Medieval Spain* (Cornell University Press, London, 1975).

------------- 'The Many Roles of the Medieval Queen: Some Examples from Castile', in Theresa Earenfight (ed.), *Queenship and Political Power in Medieval and Early Modern Spain* (Ashgate, Aldershot, 2005), 21-32.

Ó Riain-Raedel, D., 'Edith, Judith, Matilda: The Role of Royal Ladies in the Propagation of the Continental Cult', in Clare Stancliffe and Eric Cambridge (eds.), *Oswald: Northumbrian King to European Saint* (Paul Watkins, Stamford, Lincolnshire, 1995), 210-29.

Oexle, O.G., 'Lignage et parenté, politique et religion dans la noblesse du XIIe siècle: l'évangéliaire de Henri le Leon', *Cahiers de Civilisation Médiévale* (1993), Vol. 36 (4), 339-54.

Pacaut, M., *Frederick Barbarossa*, trans. A.J. Pomerans (Collins, London, 1970).

Painter, S., *The Reign of King John* (John Hopkins Press, Baltimore, 1949).

Panofsky, E., *Tomb Sculpture* (Phaidon Press, London, 1992).

Parker, J.S.R., 'The Attempted Byzantine Alliance with the Norman Kingdom, 1166-7', in *Papers of the British School in Rome*, 24 (1956), 82-93.

Parsons, J.C., 'Family, Sex and Power: The Rhythms of Medieval Queenship', in John Carmi Parsons (ed.), *Medieval Queenship* (Sutton Publishing, Gloucs., 1994), 1-11.

-------------- 'Mothers, Daughters, Marriage, Power: Some Plantagenet Evidence, 1100-1500', in John Carmi Parsons (ed.), *Medieval Queenship* (Sutton Publishing, Gloucs., 1994), 63-78.

-------------- 'Never was a body buried in England with such solemnity and honour: The Burials and Posthumous Commemorations of English Queens to 1500', in Anne Duggan (ed.), *Queens and Queenship in Medieval Europe* (Boydell Press, Woodbridge, 1997), 317-37.

-------------- 'Ritual and Symbol in the English Medieval Queenship to 1500', in Louise Fradenburg (ed.), *Women and Sovereignty* (Edinburgh University Press, 1992), 60-77.

Pavillon, Balthazar, *La Vie du bienheureux Robert d'Arbrissel* (Paris-Saumur, 1666).

Perrot, F., 'Le portrait d'Aliénor dans le vitrail de la *Crucifixion* à la Cathedrale de Poitiers', in Martin Aurell (ed.), *Aliénor d'Aquitaine* (Nantes, 2004), 180-5.

Piponnier, F., 'The World of Women', in Georges Duby & Michelle Perrot (eds.), *A History of Women in the West: II. Silences of the Middle Ages*, ed. Christiane Klapisch-Zuber (Harvard University Press, 1992), 323-35.

Pohl, W., 'Gender and ethnicity in the early Middle Ages', in L. Brubaker and J.M.H. Smith (eds.), *Gender in the Early Medieval World, East and West, 300-900* (CUP, 2005), 23-43.

Poulet, A., 'Capetian Women and the Regency: The Genesis of a Vocation', in John Carmi Parsons (ed.), *Medieval Queenship* (Sutton Publishing, Gloucs., 1994), 93-116.

Power, D., 'The Stripping of a Queen: Eleanor of Aquitaine in Thirteenth-Century Norman Tradition', in Marcus Bull and Catherine Léglu (eds.), *The World of Eleanor of Aquitaine, Literature and Society in Southern France Between the Eleventh and Thirteenth Centuries* (Boydell, Woodbridge, 2005), 115-35.

Powicke, F.M., *King Henry III and the Lord Edward: The Community of the Realm in the Thirteenth Century* (Clarendon Press, Oxford, 1947), Vol. I.

Powicke, M., *The Thirteenth Century, 1216-1307* (2nd edn., Clarendon Press, Oxford, 1962).

Pratt, K., 'The Image of the Queen in Old French Literature', in Anne Duggan (ed.), *Queens and Queenship in Medieval Europe* (Boydell Press, Woodbridge, 1997), 235-59.

Prestwich, M., *Edward I* (Yale University Press, 1988; repr. 1997).

Remensnyder, A.G., 'Topographies of Memory: Center and Periphery in High Medieval France', in Gerd Althoff, Johannes Fried and Patrick Geary (eds.), *Medieval Concepts of the Past: Ritual, Memory, Historiography* (CUP, 2002), 193-214.

Richard, A., *Histoire des Comtes de Poitou, 778-1204* (2 Vols., Paris, 1903), II.

Richardson, H.G., 'Letters and Charters of Eleanor of Aquitaine', in *English Historical Review*, 74 (1959), 193-213.

Rollason, D., *Saints and Relics in Anglo-Saxon England* (Blackwell, Oxford, 1989).

Rosenwein, B., 'Controlling Paradigms', in *Anger's Past: The Social Uses of an Emotion in the Middle Ages* (Ithaca & London, 1998), 233-47.

------------- 'Introduction', in *Anger's Past: The Social Uses of an Emotion in the Middle Ages* (Ithaca & London, 1998), 1-6.

------------- 'Worrying about Emotions', in *American Historical Review*, 107:3 (June 2002), 821-45.

------------- 'Writing Without Fear about Early Medieval Emotions', in *Early Medieval Europe*, 10:2 (2001), 229-34.

Rubin, M., 'Choosing Death? Experiences of Martyrdom in Late Medieval Europe', in Diana Wood (ed.), *Martyrs and Martyrologies* (Blackwell, Oxford, 1993), 153-83.

Schneidmüller, B., 'Constructing the Past by Means of the Present: Historiographical Foundations of Medieval Institutions, Dynasties, Peoples, and Communities', in Gerd Althoff, Johannes Fried and Patrick Geary (eds.), *Medieval Concepts of the Past: Ritual, Memory, Historiography* (CUP, 2002), 167-92.

Shadis, M., 'Piety, Politics, and Power: The Patronage of Leonor of England and her Daughters Berengaria of Leon and Blanche of Castile', in June Hall McCash (ed.), *The Cultural Patronage of Medieval Women* (University of Georgia Press, 1996), 202-27.

Shadis, M. & Berman, C.H., 'A Taste of the Feast: Reconsidering Eleanor of Aquitaine's Female Descendants', in Bonnie Wheeler & John Carmi Parsons (eds.), *Eleanor of Aquitaine, Lord and Lady* (Palgrave MacMillan, New York, 2002), 177-211.

Shahar, S., *Childhood in the Middle Ages* (Routledge, London, 1990; repr. 1992).

------------- *The Fourth Estate: A History of Women in the Middle Ages* (Methuen, London, 1983).

Simon, D., 'Late Romanesque Art in Spain', in *The Art of Medieval Spain, 500-1200* (The Metropolitan Musuem of Art, New York, 1993), 199-204.

Skinner, P., *Family Power in Southern Italy* (CUP, 1995).

------------- *Women in Medieval Italian Society* (Longman, Essex, 2001).

Slocum, K.B., 'Angevin Marriage Diplomacy and the Early Dissemination of the Cult of Thomas Becket', in *Medieval Perspectives*, 14 (Richmond, Kentucky, 1999), 214-28.

Smith, J., 'Robert of Arbrissel: *Procurator Mulierum*', in Derek Baker (ed.), *Medieval Women* (Blackwell, Oxford, 1978), 175-84.

Smith, J.M.H, 'Introduction: Gendering the early medieval world', in L. Brubaker and J.M.H. Smith (eds.), *Gender in the Early Medieval World, East and West, 300-900* (CUP, 2005), 1-19.

Smythe, D.C., 'Behind the Mask: Empresses and Empire in Middle Byzantium', in Anne Duggan (ed.), *Queens and Queenship in Medieval Europe* (Boydell Press, Woodbridge, 1997), 141-52.

Southern, R.W., 'Blois, Peter Peter of (1125x30–1212)', *Oxford Dictionary of National Biography* (OUP, 2004).

Spear, D.S., *The Personnel of the Norman Cathedrals during the Ducal Period, 911-1204* (University of London, Institute for Historical Research, 2006).

Stafford, P., 'La Mutation Familiale: A Suitable Case for Caution', in Joyce Hill and Mary Swan (eds.), *The Community, the Family and the Saint, Patterns of Power in Early Medieval Europe* (Brepols, Belgium, 1998), 103-25.

-------------- 'Parents and Children in the Early Middle Ages', in *Early Medieval Europe*, 10.2 (2001), 257-71.

-------------- *Queens, Concubines and Dowagers: The King's Wife in the Early Middle Ages* (Leicester University Press, 1998).

-------------- 'The Patronage of Royal Women in England, Mid-Tenth to Mid-Twelfth Centuries', in John Carmi Parsons (ed.), *Medieval Queenship* (Sutton Publishing, Gloucs., 1994), 143-67.

Staunton, M., *The Lives of Thomas Becket* (Manchester University Press, 2001).

-------------- *Thomas Becket and his Biographers* (Boydell Press, Woodbridge, 2006).

Stenton, D.M., 'Roger of Howden and Benedict', in *English Historical Review*, 68 (1953), 574-82.

Strickland, M., 'On the Instruction of a Prince: The Upbringing of Henry the Young King', in C. Harper-Bell & N. Vincent (eds.), *Henry II: New Interpretations* (Woodbridge, 2007), 184-214.

Stringer, K., 'Arbroath Abbey in Context, 1178-1320', in Geoffrey Barrow (ed.), *The Declaration of Arbroath: History, Significance, Setting* (Society of Antiquaries of Scotland, Edinburgh, 2003), 116-141.

Stroll, M., 'Maria *Regina*', in Anne Duggan (ed.), *Queens and Queenship in Medieval Europe* (Boydell Press, Woodbridge, 1997), 173-203.

Tanner, H.J., "Queenship: Office, Custom, or Ad Hoc? The Case of Queen Matilda III of England (1135-1152)", in *Eleanor of Aquitaine: Lord and Lady*, ed. B. Wheeler and J.C. Parsons (New York, Palgrave MacMillan, 2002), 133-58.

Tatton-Brown, T., 'Canterbury and the Architecture of Pilgrimage Sites in England', in Colin Morris & Peter Roberts (eds.), *Pilgrimage: The English Experience from Becket to Bunyan* (CUP, 2002), 90-107.

Thomasset, C., 'The Nature of Woman', in Georges Duby & Michelle Perrot (eds.), *A History of Women in the West: II. Silences of the Middle Ages*, ed. Christiane Klapisch-Zuber (Harvard University Press, 1992), 43-69.

Thompson, S., 'The Problem of Cistercian Nuns in the Twelfth and Early Thirteenth Centuries', in Derek Baker (ed.), *Medieval Women* (Blackwell, Oxford, 1978), 227-52.

Tibbetts Schulenburg, J., 'Female Sanctity: Public and Private Roles, ca. 500-1100', in M. Erler & M. Kowaleski (eds.), *Women and Power in the Middle Ages* (University of Georgia Press, 1988), 102-25.

Trindade, A., *Berengaria: In Search of Richard the Lionheart's Queen* (Four Courts Press, Dublin, 1999).

Turner, R.V., *Eleanor of Aquitaine: Queen of France, Queen of England* (Yale University Press, 2009).

------------- 'Eleanor of Aquitaine and her Children: An Enquiry into Medieval Family Attachment', in *Journal of Medieval History*, 14. 4 (1988), 321-35.

------------- 'Eleanor of Aquitaine in the Governments of Her Sons Richard and John', in *Eleanor of Aquitaine: Lord and Lady*, ed. B. Wheeler and J.C. Parsons (New York, Palgrave MacMillan, 2002), 77-95.

------------- *King John* (Longman, London & New York, 1994).

------------- 'The Households of the Sons of Henry II', in Martin Aurell (ed.), *La Cour Plantagenêt 1152-1204* (Poitiers, 2000), 49-62.

Vaissete, J, *Abregé de l'Histoire Générale de Languedoc* (Paris, 1749), III, 247-50.

Valente, C., 'Simon de Montfort, Earl of Leicester, and the utility of sanctity in thirteenth-century England', in *Journal of Medieval History*, 21 (1995), 29-49.

------------- *The Theory and Practice of Revolt in Medieval England* (Ashgate, Aldershot, 2003).

Van Houts, E., 'Le roi et son historien: Henri II Plantagenêt et Robert de Torigni, abbé du Mont-Saint-Michel', in *Cahiers de Civilisation Médiévale*, 37 (1994), 115-18.

------------- 'Les femmes dans le royaume Plantagenêt: Gendre, Politique et Nature', in Martin Aurell & Noël-Yves Tonnerre (eds.), *Plantagenêts et Capétiens: Confrontations et Héritages* (Brepols, Belgium, 2006), 95-112.

------------- 'Local and Regional Chronicles', in *Typologie des Sources du Moyen Âge Occidental*, 74 (Brepols, Belgium, 1995), 13-60.

------------- *Memory and Gender in Medieval Europe, 900-1200* (MacMillan Press, London, 1999).

------------- 'Orality in Norman Hagiography of the XIth and XIIth Centuries: the Value of Female Testimonies', in E.M.C. van Houts, *History and Family Traditions in England and the Continent, 1000-1200* (Ashgate Variorum, Aldershot, 1999; first pub. in *Early Medieval Europe*, 1 (1992)), 1-13.

------------- 'Robert of Torigni as Genealogist', in E.M.C. van Houts, *History and Family Traditions in England and the Continent, 1000-1200* (Ashgate Variorum, Aldershot, 1999; first pub. in *Studies of Medieval History presented to R. Allen Brown*, ed. C. Harper-Bill, C. Holdsworth & J.L. Nelson (Woodbridge, 1989)), 215-33.

------------- 'The Adaptation of the Gesta Normannorum Ducum by Wace and Benoît', in *History and Family Traditions in England and the Continent, 1000-1200* (Ashgate Variorum, Aldershot, 1999; first pub. in *Non Nova, sed Nove: Mélanges de civilisation médiévale dediés à Willelm Noomen*, ed. M. Gosman & J. van Os, Groningen, 1984), 115-24.

------------- 'The State of Research: Women in Medieval History and Literature', in E.M.C van Houts, *History and Family Traditions in England and the Continent, 1000-1200* (Ashgate Variorum, Aldershot, 1999; first published in *Journal of Medieval History*, 20 (1994)), 277-92.

------------- 'Women and the Writing of History in the Early Middle Ages: The case of Abbess Matilda of Essen and Aethelweard', in E.M.C. van Houts, *History and Family Traditions in England and the Continent, 1000-1200* (Ashgate Variorum, Aldershot, 1999; first pub. in *Early Medieval Europe*, 1 (1992)), 53-68.

Van Landingham, M., 'Royal Portraits: Representations of Queenship in the Thirteenth-Century Catalan Chronicles', in Theresa Earenfight (ed.), *Queenship and Political Power in Medieval and Early Modern Spain* (Ashgate, Aldershot, 2005), 109-19.

Vincent, N., 'Canville, Richard de (d. 1191)', *Oxford Dictionary of National Biography* (OUP, 2004).

------------- 'Isabella of Angoulême: John's Jezebel', in S.D. Church (ed.), *King John: New Interpretations* (Boydell, Woodbridge, 1999), 165-219.

------------- 'King Henry III and the Blessed Virgin Mary', in R.N. Swanson (ed.), *The Church and Mary: Studies in Church History*, 39 (Boydell, Woodbridge, 2004), 126-46.

------------- 'Patronage, Politics and Piety in the Charters of Eleanor of Aquitaine', in Martin Aurell & Noël-Yves Tonnerre (eds.), *Plantagenêts et Capétiens: Confrontations et Héritages* (Brepols, Belgium, 2006), 17-60.

------------- 'The Murderers of Thomas Becket', in *Bischofsmord im Mittelalter: Murder of Bishops*, ed. N. Fryde & D. Reitz (Gottingen, 2003), 211-72.

------------- 'The Pilgrimages of the Angevin Kings of England, 1154-1272', in Colin Morris & Peter Roberts (eds.), *Pilgrimage: The English Experience from Becket to Bunyan* (CUP, 2002), 12-45.

Volk, P., 'La reine Aliénor et la poésie courtoise Allemande', in Martin Aurell (ed.), *Aliénor d'Aquitaine* (Nantes, 2004), 194-203.

Vollrath, H., 'Aliénor d'Aquitaine et ses enfants: une relation affective?', in Martin Aurell & Noël-Yves Tonnerre (eds.), *Plantagenêts et Capétiens: Confrontations et Héritages* (Brepols, Belgium, 2006), 113-23.

Voyer, C., 'Les Plantagenêts et la Chapelle Sainte-Radegonde de Chinon : Une image en débat', in Martin Aurell (ed.), *Aliénor d'Aquitaine* (Nantes, 2004), 186-93.

Wade Labarge, M., *Gascony, England's First Colony, 1204-1454* (Hamish Hamilton, London, 1980), 1-28.

------------- *Women in Medieval Life* (Penguin, London, 1986; repr. 2001).

Walker, R., 'Images of royal and aristocratic burial in northern Spain, c. 950-c. 1250', in Elisabeth Van Houts (ed.), *Medieval Memories: Men, Women and the Past, 700-1300* (Longman, Essex, 2001), 150-72.

------------ 'Leonor of England, Plantagenet Queen of King Alfonso VIII of Castile, and her Foundation of the Cistercian Abbey of Las Huelgas. In Imitation of Fontevrault?', in *Journal of Medieval History*, 31:4 (2005), 346-68.

Walker, S., 'Political Saints in Later Medieval England', in R.H. Britnell & A.J. Pollard (eds.), *The McFarlane Legacy: Studies in Late Medieval Politics and Society* (Sutton Publishing, Stroud, 1995), 77-106.

Warren, W.L., *Henry II* (London, 1973).

------------ *King John* (Harmondsworth, 1966).

Waugh, S., 'Histoire, hagiographie et le souverain idéal à la cour des Plantegenêts', in Martin Aurell & Noël-Yves Tonnerre (eds.), *Plantagenêts et Capétiens: Confrontations et Héritages* (Brepols, Belgium, 2006), 429-46.

Webb, D., 'Queen and Patron', in Anne Duggan (ed.), *Queens and Queenship in Medieval Europe* (Boydell Press, Woodbridge, 1997), 205-21.

Wemple, S.F., *Women in Frankish Society: Marriage and the Cloister, 500-900* (University of Pennsylvania Press, 1981).

White, S., 'The Discourse of Inheritance in Twelfth-Century France: Alternative Models of the Fief in *Raoul de Cambrai*', in George Garnett & John Hudson (eds.), *Law and Government in Medieval England and Normandy, Essays in honour of Sir James Holt* (CUP, 1994), 173-97.

Wolf, A., 'Reigning Queens in Medieval Europe: When, Where and Why', in John Carmi Parsons (ed.), *Medieval Queenship* (Sutton Publishing, Gloucs., 1994), 169-88.

Wood, C.T., 'Fontevraud, Dynasticism, and Eleanor of Aquitaine', in Bonnie Wheeler & John Carmi Parsons (eds.), *Eleanor of Aquitaine: Lord and Lady* (Palgrave MacMillan, New York, 2002), 407-22.

Wright, R.M., 'The Virgin in the Sun and in the Tree', in Louise Fradenburg (ed.), *Women and Sovereignty* (Edinburgh University Press, 1992), 36-59.

Index of names

Achard, bishop of Avranches, p .34
Adam, Castilian envoy, p. 93
Adela, Countess of Blois, p. 178
Adela of Blois-Champagne, Queen of France, p. 128-9, 203
Adela of Louvain, Queen of England, p. 62
Adelaide, Countess of Sicily, p. 139
Adelaide of Maurienne, Queen of France, p. 181, 204
Adelard of Bath, p. 58, 59, 85
Aelfgifu of Wessex, Queen of Burgundy, p .169
Aethelred, Prince of Scotland, p. 177
Aethelweard of England, p. 62, 169
Afonso I Enriquez, King of Portugal,p. 206
Afonso II, King of Portugal, p. 112, 118, 183, 207
Afonso III, King of Portugal, p. 112, 183
Afonso IV, King of Portugal, p. 183
Agatha, nun at Fontevrault, p. 186
Agnes of Poitou, Queen of Aragón, p. 71
Agnes of the Palatinate, Duchess of Bavaria, p. 105
Agrigento, bishop of, p. p. 85, 135
Aimeri, Viscount of Châtellerault, p. 189
Aimeric I, King of Hungary, p. 77
Alduin the Seneschal, p. 131
Alexander I, King of Scotland, p. 180
Alexander III, King of Scotland, p. 149
Alexander III, Pope, p. 69, 84, 86, 88, 93, 128, 143, 145, 152, 154, 167, 180
Alexios II, Emperor of Byzantium, p. 84, 88
Alfano, archbishop of Capua, p. 81, 90, 131, 135, 153
Alfonso, Count of Squillace, p. 131
Alfonso, Duke of Naples, Prince of Capua, p. 136
Alfonso, Infante of Aragón, p. 117, 183
Alfonso II, King of Aragón, p. 71, 73, 75, 77, 113, 119, 121
Alfonso VI, King of Castile-León, p. 119, 197
Alfonso VII, 'Emperor' of Castile-León, p. 34, 74, 75, 182, 196
Alfonso VIII, King of Castile, p. 16, 17, 31, 34, 35, 37, 40, 44, 50, 52, 67, 71, 73-5, 77, 79, 92, 93, 95, 97, 101, 107-10, 112, 113-22, 123, 126, 131, 140, 165-6, 172, 181-3, 186, 194-8, 204-8, 210, 211
Alfonso X, King of Castile, p. 111, 121-2, 195, 198
Alfonso V, King of León, p. 196
Alfonso IX, King of León, p. 109, 113-5, 118, 206
Alfonso de Molina, Infante of León, p. 115, 118, 182
Alice, maid to Joanna, p. 186
Alice, nun at Fontevrault, p. 186
Alice of France, Countess of the Vexin, p. 41, 71, 78, 79, 129, 130
Alix, Countess of Blois, p. 45, 57
Almiramamolin, Caliph of the Almohads, p. 116
Alphonse, Count of Toulouse and Poitiers, p. 183
Álvaro Rodríguez, Count of Sarria, p. 75
Amadeus, Count of Savoy, p. 206
Amanieu of Labrede, Viscount of Bézaume, p. 74
Andronicus I, Emperor of Byzantium, p. 84
Angoulême, bishop of, p. 74
Anjou, counts of, p. 58, 194
Anne Boleyn, Queen of England, p. 91
Anne of Antioch, Queen of Hungary, p. 84
Apamea, bishop of, p. 79
Aquitaine, counts of, p. 194
Aragón, kings of, p. 110
Aragón, queens of, p. 111
Arles, archbishop of, p. 85
Armagnac, count of, p. 120
Arnulf, bishop of Capua (Capaccio), p. 81, 89
Arthur, Duke of Brittany, p. 138
Arundel, earl of, p. 39, 70
Athelstan, King of Wessex, King of the English, p. 169, 170
Auxerre, bishop of, p. 79
Avila, bishop of, p. 166, 204

Baldwin, archbishop of Canterbury, p. 147
Baldwin II, Emperor of Constantinople, p. 115
Baldwin IV, King of Jerusalem, p. 181
Baldwin, Provost of Utrecht, p. 69
Baldwin Buelot (or Beluot), p. 82
Barcelona, counts of, p. 75, 196
Bari, archbishop of, p. 135
Bartholomew, bishop of Agrigento, p. 85
Bayeux, bishop of, p. 91
Bayonne, archbishop of, p. 79
Bayonne, bishop of, p. 120
Bazas, bishop of, p. 74, 120
Béarn, Viscount of, p. 120
Beatrice, Countess of Burgundy, Holy Roman Empress, p. 113
Beatrice, maid to Joanna, p. 186
Beatrice, magistra, p. 59
Beatrice of Rethel, Queen of Sicily, p. 189
Beatrice of Hohenstaufen, Queen of Castile, p. 117, 195
Beatrix, Bavarian noblewoman, p. 61
Bela III, King of Hungary, p. 84, 89, 105, 166-8

Bela IV, King of Hungary, p. 168

Benoît of Sainte-Maure, p. 59, 177

Berengaria of Navarre, Queen of England, p. 23, 27, 45, 50, 52, 53, 62, 63, 67, 77-9, 102, 108, 119, 122, 123-6, 137, 193, 201, 202, 209

Berenguella of Castile, Queen of León, p. 16, 17, 22, 75, 107, 109, 111, 113-5, 116, 117, 118, 182, 183, 191, 194, 195, 197, 198, 199, 204, 205, 206, 207, 208

Berenguella of León, Queen of Jerusalem, p. 115, 117, 182

Berenguella, Empress of León, p. 182

Berenguella, Infanta of Castile, nun at Las Huelgas, p. 183, 198, 206

Bernard the Constable, p. 131

Bertrada of Montfort, Countess of Anjou, Queen of France, p. 190, 204

Bertram, Viscount of Bayonne, p. 74

Bertran de Born, p. 78, 104, 119, 162, 163

Bigorre, count of, p. 119

Blanca of Navarre, Queen of Castile, p. 140, 182, 195, 205

Blanca (Blanche) of Castile, Queen of France, p. 17, 19, 52, 107, 110, 112, 115-7, 118, 124, 126, 166, 169, 182, 183, 198, 199

Blanche of Navarre, Countess of Champagne, p. 124

Blanche, Princess of France, p. 182

Blois, count of, p. 128, 129

Bohemond I of Antioch, p. 180, 181

Bohemond III of Antioch, p. 181

Bohemond, son of Joanna, p. 133, 136, 137, 139, 180, 181, 210

Bordeaux, archbishop of, p. 58

Bordeaux, bishop of, p. 74, 75

Brian FitzCount, Lord of Wallingford, p. 62

Burgos, bishop of, p. 74, 166, 204

Burgundy, king of, p. 169

Calahorra, bishop of, p. 74, 204

Canterbury, archbishop of, p. 89, 91, 186

Casamari, abbot of, p. 124

Castile, counts of, p. 108

Castile, king of, p. 67, 113, 195

Catania, bishop of, p. 135

Cefalu, bishop of, p. 135

Celestine III, Pope, p. 17, 44, 50, 51, 85

Cerebruno, archbishop of Toledo, p. 74, 166

Champagne, count of, p. 128, 129

Charlemagne, p. 158, 161

Charles I, King of Sicily, p. 182

Chester, count of, p. 41

Clement I, Pope, p. 155

Clement III, Pope, p. 137, 138, 153, 154, 194, 198

Clementia of Zähringen, Duchess of Saxony and

Bavaria, p. 103

Cnut, King of England, p. 158

Cologne, archbishop of, p. 37, 38

Cologne, elect of, p. 39

Compostela, archbishop of, p. 120

Conrad, cleric at Regensburg, p. 161

Conrad, Duke of Rotenburg, p. 113, 114

Conrad II, Holy Roman Emperor, p. 158

Constance, Countess of Brittany, p. 41, 71

Constance, Queen of Sicily, p. 78, 85, 89, 132, 137, 139

Constance FitzGilbert, p. 61

Constance of Castile, Queen of France, p. 127-8

Constance of France, Countess of Toulouse, p. 73, 181

Constanza of Aragón, Queen of Hungary, Holy Roman Empress, p. 77

Constanza of Castile, abbess of Las Huelgas, p. 107, 115, 117, 183, 197, 199, 207, 210

Constanza of León, nun at Las Huelgas, p. 115, 182, 198

Cosenza, archbishop of, p. 135

Cuenca, bishop of, 204

David I, King of Scotland, p. 180

Dax, bishop of, p. 74, 120

Dolça of Aragón, nun at Sigena, p. 77

Dolça of Aragón, sister of Alfonso II, Queen of Portugal, p. 77

Domenico Balsamo, p. 156

Durand, clerk to Joanna, p. 186

Edith of Wessex, Queen of England, p. 62

Edith of Wessex, Holy Roman Empress, p. 62, 169-70

Edith-Matilda, Queen of England, p. 19, 22, 23, 28, 62, 177, 180

Edward I, King of England, p. 79, 121-2, 183

Edward Atheling, p. 177

Edward the Elder, King of Wessex, p. 169

Edward, Prince of Scotland, p. 177

Edmund, Prince of Scotland, Bishop of Dunkeld, p. 177

Egidius, chancellor to Leonor, p. 166

Eilhart of Oberg, p. 162

Ekbert of Wolfenbüttel, p. 106

Eleanor of Aquitaine, Queen of England, p. 13, 14, 15, 16, 17, 18, 20, 22, 23, 24, 26, 27, 28, 31, 33, 34, 35-42, 43-5, 46, 50-5, 56-9, 61, 63, 67, 69, 71, 72, 74, 78, 81, 82, 83, 85, 91, 95, 96, 97, 105, 115-7, 118, 119, 123, 124, 127, 128, 129, 130, 136, 137, 139, 140, 146, 147, 159, 175, 178, 179, 180, 181, 183, 184, 185, 186, 187-8, 189-91, 193-4, 196, 198, 199, 200, 201-4, 209, 210, 211

Eleanor of Aragón, Couness of Toulouse, p. 77

Eleanor of Brittany, Countess of Richmond, p. 95
Eleanor of Castile, Queen of England, p. 22, 26, 79, 121-2, 183, 193
Eleanor of Provence, Queen of England, p. 79, 121
Elias, Count of Perigord, p. 74
Elias, elect of Troia, p. 81, 82, 131, 135
Elie de Malmort, archbishop of Bordeaux, p. 116, 120
Elvira of Castile, Queen of Sicily, p. 189
Elvira of Toro, Infanta of León, p. 196
Elvira Ramírez of Navarre, p. 75
Elvira Ramírez, Infanta of León, Abbess of San Salvador, p. 196, 197
Ely, bishop of, p. 89, 90, 91, 92
Emma of Normandy, Queen of England, p. 158
England, kings of, p. 193
Enguerrand III de Coucy, p. 105
Enrique I, King of Castile, p. 108, 110, 117, 118, 182, 204-5, 207, 208
Eremburga, Countess of Anjou, p. 59
Estefanía Ramírez of León, p. 75
Eustace, Prince of England, p. 73, 178
Evreux, bishop of, p. 89, 91, 131

Federico, justiciar of the Magna Regis Curia, p. 131
Fernando, Infante of Castile, p. 50, 113, 117, 118, 182, 186, 204, 205, 206, 207, 208
Fernando, Infante of León, p. 206
Fernando III, King of Castile, p. 75, 108, 115, 117, 118, 182, 183, 194
Fernando I, King of León, 196-7, 205
Fernando II, King of León, p. 34, 71, 74, 75, 113, 182
Fernando de Serpa, Infante of Portugal, p. 112, 183
Fernando Pérez de Traba, p. 74, 75
Fernando Ruiz de Castro, p. 74
Flanders, count of, p. 93, 107, 110, 146, 147
Florius, Count of Camerota, p. 81, 89, 136
France, king of, p. 89
Frederick, son of Frederick I, p. 69
Frederick I, Holy Roman Emperor, p. 33, 38, 69, 71, 83, 103-4, 110, 113, 117, 160, 162
Fulk V, Count of Anjou, King of Jerusalem, p. 96, 179, 180, 190, 193

Galeta, bishop of, p. 135
Garcia II, King of Galicia, p. 196
García González, p. 74
Gaston VII, Viscount of Béarn, p. 121-2
Geoffrey, archbishop of Bordeaux, p. 58
Geoffrey, archbishop of York, p. 179
Geoffrey Ridel, bishop of Ely, p. 92, 93
Geoffrey, clerk to Joanna, p. 186
Geoffrey V, Count of Anjou, p. 58, 127, 129, 179, 190, 201

Geoffrey II, Count of Brittany, p. 31, 33, 40, 41, 71, 179, 180
Geoffrey VI, Count of Nantes, p. 179
Geoffrey III, Count of Perche, p. 92, 105
Geoffrey de la Charre, p. 91, 131, 133
Geoffrey of Monmouth, p. 58, 59
Geraldus, notary to Alfonso VIII, p. 166
Gerberga, abbess of Gandersheim, p. 62, 169
Gertrude of Süpplingenburg, p. 158, 159
Gervase of Tilbury, p. 85
Gilbert, nephew of Thomas Becket, p. 86, 152
Gilbert Foliot, bishop of London, p. 62
Giles of Perche, bishop of Evreux, p. 92, 131
Giovanni, bishop of Potenza, p. 131
Gisele of Suabia, Holy Roman Empress, p. 158
Godfrey, Count of Lesina, p. 134, 135
Gonzalo, archbishop of Toledo, p. 113
Gonzalo Pérez, prior of Burgos Cathedral, p. 108
Gonzalo Ruiz Girón, p. 74, 75
Gregory, cardinal of Sant Angelo, p. 113
Gregory IX, Pope, p. 206
Guido, bishop of Cefalú, p. 131
Guncelin, Castilian envoy, p. 93
Gunzelin I, Count of Schwerin, p. 69
Gutierre Fernández de Castro, p. 74, 75, 118
Guy de Lusignan, King of Jerusalem, p. 96

Hamelin de Warenne, Earl of Surrey, p. 89, 92, 146
Helen of Denmark, Duchess of Lüneburg, p. 105
Henry, Earl of Huntingdon, p. 180
Henry, the Lion, Duke of Saxony and Bavaria, p. 15, 16, 17, 31, 33, 37, 38, 39, 52, 67, 69-70, 71, 87-8, 89, 91, 93, 97, 103-6, 110, 131, 157-65, 170, 171, 181, 190, 193, 201, 211
Henry, the Proud, Duke of Saxony and Bavaria, p. 159
Henry, the 'Young King', p. 31, 35, 37, 38, 40, 51, 71, 90, 92, 105, 126-9, 146, 147, 167, 179, 185, 187, 188
Henry II, Holy Roman Emperor, p. 161
Henry III, Holy Roman Emperor, p. 158
Henry V, Holy Roman Emperor, p. 62, 159
Henry VI, Holy Roman Emperor, p. 78, 85, 87, 89, 132, 137, 139
Henry I, King of England, p. 19, 23, 50, 59, 62, 96, 129, 177, 178, 179, 180, 190
Henry II, King of England, p. 13, 14, 15, 16, 17, 23, 24, 27, 28, 31, 33, 34, 35, 36, 37, 38, 39, 40, 41, 45, 49, 50, 51, 52, 57, 58-9, 61, 63, 67, 69, 70, 71, 72-3, 74, 75, 77, 79, 81, 82, 83, 84, 85, 86, 87, 88, 89, 90, 91, 92, 93, 94, 95, 96, 97, 102, 103, 104-5, 110, 113, 118, 119, 120, 123, 126-30, 131, 133, 134, 136, 140, 143, 145-9, 151, 152, 153, 155, 156, 157, 159, 161, 162, 163, 165, 166, 167, 168, 170, 171,

172, 175, 177, 178, 179-80, 181, 182, 183, 184, 185, 186, 189, 190, 191, 193, 195, 196, 200, 201, 202, 203, 209, 211

Henry III, King of England, p. 79, 121-2, 126, 202

Henry IV, King of England, p. 193

Henry VI, King of England, p. 147

Henry V of Brunswick, Duke of Saxony, Count Palatine of the Rhine, p. 104, 105, 106, 158, 162, 163, 164, 181

Henry VI of Brunswick, Count Palatine of the Rhine, p. 105

Henry de Beaumont, bishop of Bayeux, p. 92, 93, 131, 133

Henry of Lüneberg, p. 105-6

Henry of Pisa, cardinal legate, p. 34, 128

Herbert de Tucé, seneschal of Le Mans, p. 125

Honorius III, Pope, p. 126

Hospitallers, prior of, p. 205

Hrotsvita of Gandersheim, p. 63, 169, 170

Hubald, bishop of Ostia, p. 152

Hubert, cardinal Bishop of Ostia, p. 87

Hubert of Middlesex, archbishop of Conza, p. 85

Hubert Walter, archbishop of Canterbury, p. 59, 188

Hugh, archbishop of Rouen, p. 128

Hugh II, Count of Jaffa, p. 96

Hugh de Beauchamp, p. 89, 91, 131, 133

Hugh of Fleury, p. 62

Hugo, Count of Catanzaro, p. 131

Hugo de Cervello, archbishop of Tarragona, p. 165

Ibn Jubayr, p. 155

Imre I, King of Hungary, p. 168

Ingebjorg of Denmark, Queen of France, p. 96

Innocent III, Pope, p. 114, 124, 126

Irmgard of the Palatinate, Margravine of Baden-Baden, p. 105

Isaac II Angelos, Emperor of Byzantium, p. 84

Isaac II Comnenos, Emperor of Cyprus, p. 63, 117, 146, 186

Isabella I, Queen of Castile, p. 112

Isabella of Angoulême, Queen of England, p. 79, 123, 124, 202, 203

Isabelle, Princess of France, p. 182

Jaime I, King of Aragón, p. 25, 111, 117, 118, 183, 198

Jeanne de Bourbon, abbess of Fontevrault, p. 203

Joan of Navarre, Queen of England, p. 193

Joanna Plantagenet, Queen of Sicily, Countess of Toulouse, p. 13, 15, 16, 17, 18, 19, 21, 24, 25, 27, 28, 31, 33, 34, 35, 38-41, 42, 43, 45-7, 53, 57, 61, 62, 63, 67, 72, 78, 79, 81-94, 95, 97, 101, 103, 106, 109, 110, 114, 130, 131-40, 143, 151, 152-7, 167, 171, 175, 180-1, 184, 185, 186-9, 191, 195, 201, 202, 203, 208, 209, 210, 211

Jocelin, Count of Loritello, p. 131

John, bishop of Evreux, p. 79

John, bishop of Norwich, p. 82, 90, 91, 92, 93, 94

John, clerk of Leonor, p. 52

John, King of England, p. 25, 31, 35, 39, 40, 41, 45, 52, 53, 57, 59, 79, 105, 115, 116, 119, 120-1, 123, 124-6, 129, 130, 136, 146, 180, 181, 187-8, 209

John, Prince of France, p. 182

John of Brienne, King of Jerusalem, p. 115, 117

John of Salisbury, p. 44, 85, 153

Joscelin, chaplain to Joanna, p. 186

László II, King of Hungary, p. 167

Leicester, count of, p. 41

León, king of, p. 113, 114, 182

Leonor, Infanta of Castile, p. 183

Leonor, Infanta of León, p. 115, 182

Leonor Plantagenet, Queen of Castile, p. 13, 15, 16, 17, 18, 19, 21, 22, 24, 26, 27, 28, 31, 33-5, 36, 37-40, 41, 42, 43, 44-5, 50, 51, 52, 57, 58, 63, 67, 69, 71-5, 77, 78, 79, 81, 91, 92, 95, 97, 101, 103, 106, 107-22, 123, 126, 131, 136, 137, 140, 143, 151, 153, 162, 165-6, 167, 171, 172, 175, 180, 181-3, 184, 185, 186, 189, 191, 194-9, 204-8, 209, 210, 211

Leonor of Castile, Queen of Aragón, p. 107, 117, 118, 183, 197-8, 199, 204, 206, 207, 208

Leonor of Portugal, Queen of Aragón, p. 183

Leonor of Portugal, Queen of Denmark, p. 112, 183

Lope Díaz de Haro, p. 118

Lothair III, Holy Roman Emperor, p. 158, 159, 181

Lothair of Bavaria, p. 104, 105, 181

Louis VI, King of France, p. 72, 120, 181

Louis VII, King of France, p. 41, 45, 48, 57, 58, 71, 72, 73, 79, 92, 93, 96, 120, 124, 126-9, 145, 146, 167, 190, 193, 203

Louis VIII, King of France, p. 110, 115-6, 118, 126, 166, 169, 182

Louis IX, King of France, p. 19, 119, 166, 182

Lucas, archbishop of Esztergom, 167-8

Lucius III, Pope, p. 154

Luke, abbot of Turpenay, p. 188

Lusatia, margrave of, p. 104

Mafalda, Infanta of Castile, p. p. 117, 204, 206, 207

Mafalda of Savoy, Queen of Portugal, p. 206

Maio de Bari, p. 140

Malcolm III, King of Scotland, p. 177

Malekakxa, maid to Joanna, p. 186

Manuel I Comnenus, Emperor of Byzantium, p. 58, 83-4, 87-8, 89

Margaret of France, Queen of Hungary, p. 27, 37, 41, 92, 105, 126-30, 133, 146, 151, 166, 167-8

Margaret of Hungary, Empress (Maria) of Byzantium, p. 84

Margaret of Navarre, Queen of Sicily, p. 81, 83, 84, 85, 86, 88, 92, 132, 134, 136, 139-40, 152-3, 154, 156, 171, 189

Margaret of Perche, p. 92

Maria, Infanta of Castile, p. 183

Maria, Viscountess of Béarn, p. 119

Maria Comnena, p. 83-4, 85, 87-8, 89

Maria of Brienne, Empress of Constantinople, p. 115

Marie, Countess of Champagne, p. 57

Marie de France, p. 19, 58

Marie de Montpellier, Queen of Aragón, p. 25

Marmoutiers, abbot of, p. 124

Martin González, mayordomo to Leonor, p. 166

Mary, Countess of Boulogne, p. 178

Mary Laskarina, Queen of Hungary, p. 168

Mary of Antioch, Empress of Byzantium, p. 88

Matilda, abbess of Essen, p. 62, 169

Matilda, abbess of Fontevrault, p. 188

Matilda, abbess of Quedlinburg, p. 62, 169

Matilda, Countess of Chester, p. 177

Matilda, Empress, p. 23, 33, 57, 58, 59, 62, 72, 129, 157, 158, 159, 179, 180, 183, 201

Matilda de Beaumont, Countess of Worcester, p. 178

Matilda of Anjou, Abbess of Fontevrault, p. 59, 190

Matilda of Boulogne, Queen of England, p. 178, 193

Matilda of Flanders, Queen of England, p. 62, 177, 178

Matilda of Ringelheim, Holy Roman Empress, p. 62, 169

Matilda Plantagenet, Duchess of Saxony and Bavaria, p. 13, 15, 16, 17, 21, 24, 27, 28, 31, 33, 35-9, 40, 41, 42, 43, 52, 53, 57, 58, 63, 67, 69-70, 71, 74, 89, 91, 93, 95, 97, 103-6, 110, 129, 131, 134, 140, 143, 151, 157-65, 167, 170, 171, 175, 178, 180, 181, 184, 185, 190, 193, 201, 208, 209, 210, 211

Matthew, bishop of Angers, p. 59

Matthew of Ajello, p. 88, 131, 135, 152, 153

Mazaren, bishop of, p. 135

Melisende, Queen of Jerusalem, p. 18, 96

Messina, archbishop of, p. 135

Morocco, king of, p. 116

Navarre, king of, p. 67, 71, 73, 75, 126

Nicholas, bishop of Le Mans, p. 79

Nicola, archbishop of Messina, p. 131, 154

Normandy, dukes of, p. 35, 59, 188

Nuño Fañez, p. 113

Nuño Pérez de Lara, p. 74

Odo, cardinal deacon of S. Nicola, p. 128

Order of Santiago, master of, p. 205

Ordoño III, King of León, p. 197

Orthez, Viscount of, p. 120

Osbert de Camera, p. 91, 131, 133

Osma, bishop of, p. 204

Otto I, Duke of Brunswick-Lüneberg, p. 105

Otto I, the Great, Holy Roman Emperor, p. 62, 169

Otto IV, Holy Roman Emperor, p. 85, 89, 104, 105, 162, 164, 181

Otto of Brescia, cardinal, p. 167

Palencia, bishop of, p. 74, 166, 204

Paris, archdeacon of Rochester, p. 82

Paschal II, Pope, p. 189

Pascal III, Pope, p. 69

Pedro II, King of Aragón, p. 25, 197

Pedro Alfonso, p. 75

Pedro García de Lerma, p. 118

Pedro González de Lara, p. 74

Pedro Rodríguez de Castro, p. 118

Pedro Ruiz de Castro, p. 74

Penda, King of Mercia, p. 160

Perigord, bishop of, p. 74

Perisco, justiciar, p. 131

Peter de Mota, p. 74, 75

Peter, bishop of Alexandria, p. 155, 156, 171

Peter of Blois, p. 44, 85, 152

Peter of Saintes, p. 58

Petronilla, Queen of Aragón, p. 71

Petronilla of Aquitaine, p. 72

Philip, Prince of France, p. 129

Philip I, Count of Flanders, p. 78, 146

Philip I, King of France, p. 72, 204

Philip II Augustus, King of France, p. 48, 78, 79, 96, 105, 110, 113, 115, 116, 119-20, 124-5, 129, 130, 137, 146, 167

Philip of Suabia, King of the Germans, p. 117

Philippa, Countess of Toulouse, p. 72, 189

Philippe, Prince of France, p. 182

Poitiers, bishop of, p. 74, 189

Ponce de Minerva, p. 74, 75

Potenza, bishop of, p. 135

Proteval the Jew, p. 187

Rainaldo, archbishop of Bari, p. 131

Rainaldo de Monteforte, master justiciar, p. 131

Rainerio, papal legate, p. 114

Ralph de Faye, Seneschal of Guyenne, p. 74

Ralph FitzGilbert, p. 61

Ramiro II, King of Aragón, p. 71

Ramiro II, King of León, p. 197

Ramiro Froilaz, p. 75

Ramiro Sánchez, Infante of Navarre, p. 75

Ramon Vidal, p. 162

Ranulf de Glanvill, justiciar of England, p. 52

Raymond of Antioch, p. 20

Raymond, Viscount of Tartas, p. 74

Raymond IV, Count of St Gilles, p. 72

Raymond V, Count of Toulouse, p. 73, 181

Raymond VI, Count of Toulouse, p. 25, 53, 72, 77, 90, 92, 114, 181, 186, 188, 210, 211

Raymond VII, Count of Toulouse, p. 22, 25, 72, 77, 181, 191, 201, 203

Raymond Berengar IV, King of Aragón, Count of Barcelona, p. 73

Raymond of Burgundy, Count of Galicia, p. 113

Reggio, archbishop of, p. 140

Reginald FitzJocelin, bishop of Bath and Wells, p. 153

Reinald Dassel, archbishop of Cologne, p. 69

Renaud III, Count of Burgundy, p. 113

Renier of Montferrat, p. 84

Riccardo, Count of Fondi, p. 131

Richard, Count of Poitou, p. 181

Richard, son of Henry I, p. 177

Richard, illegitimate uncle of Henry II, p. 180

Richard I, Duke of Normandy, p. 177, 180

Richard I, King of England, p. 23, 25, 31, 33, 37, 38, 39, 40, 41, 44, 45, 50, 51, 52, 53, 57, 59, 63, 71, 74, 77-9, 82, 86, 89, 90, 92, 93, 95, 102, 105, 107, 108, 113, 116, 119, 122, 123, 124, 129, 130, 131, 133, 136, 137-9, 146, 180, 185, 186, 187, 188, 189, 190, 191, 193, 195, 202, 203, 205, 209, 210

Richard Animal, p. 58

Richard de Camville, p. 82

Richard of Dover, archbishop of Canterbury, p. 90, 92, 93, 133

Richard of Ilchester, bishop of Winchester, p. 90, 91, 92, 93, 94

Richard Palmer, bishop of Syracuse, archbishop of Messina, p. 82, 85, 86, 87, 90, 131, 135, 152

Richard Scrope, archbishop of York, p. 147

Richard the Logothete, p. 131

Richenza, Countess of Perche, p. 52, 104, 105, 106, 181

Richenza of Northeim, Holy Roman Empress, p. 158, 159, 181

Robert, bishop of Catania, p. 131, 152

Robert, bishop of Tricarico, p. 131

Robert, Earl of Gloucester, p. 58

Robert I, Count of Artois, p. 182

Robert III, Count of Loritello, p. 87

Robert I, Duke of Normandy, p. 177

Robert Cricklade, p. 58

Robert de Lauro, Count of Caserta, p. 90, 131

Robert Guiscard, Duke of Apulia and Calabria, p. 180

Robert Malcovenant, p. 131

Robert of Arbrissel, p. 189-90

Robert of Newburgh, justiciar of Normandy, p. 126

Robert of Selby, p. 85

Rodolfo Martinar, Viscount of Castellon and Bedomar, p. 74

Rodrigo Gómez, p. 75

Rodrigo Gutierre, mayordomo to Alfonso VIII, p. 166

Roger I, Count of Sicily, p. 167

Roger II, King of Sicily, p. 83, 132, 136, 139, 181, 189

Roger IV, Duke of Apulia, p. 136, 139

Rotrou, archbishop of Rouen, p. 81, 92, 93

Rouen, archbishop of, p. 89, 186

Ruffo, archbishop of Cosenza, p. 131

Saintonge, bishop of, p. 74

Saladin, p. 89, 95

Salerno, archbishop of, p. 140

Sancha, Infanta of Aragón, p. 25

Sancha, Infanta of Castile, p. 117, 118, 182, 204, 206, 207

Sancha, Infanta of León, p. 196

Sancha Fernández de Traba, p. 75

Sancha of Aragón, Countess of Toulouse, p. 77

Sancha of Castile, Queen of Aragón, p. 75, 109, 196, 197

Sancha of León, Queen of León, p. 196, 197, 205

Sancho, Infante of Castile, p. 52, 117, 182, 204, 206

Sancho III, King of Castile, p. 34, 75, 182, 205

Sancho I, King of León, p. 196, 197

Sancho III, King of Navarre, p. 196

Sancho VI, King of Navarre, p. 34, 77, 78, 79, 110, 119, 124

Sancho VII, King of Navarre, p. 79, 119, 121, 123, 126

Sancho II, King of Portugal, 112, 183

Saphadin, p. 95, 138

Scots, king of, p. 146, 147, 148, 149

Segovia, bishop of, p. 74, 166, 204, 205

Sibylla, Queen of Jerusalem, p. 96

Sibylla of Acerra, Queen of Sicily, p. 139

Sibylla of Anjou, Countess of Flanders, p. 59

Sibylla of Burgundy, Queen of Sicily, p. 189

Sicily, king of, p. 83, 87, 88, 134, 139, 186

Sicily, queens of, p. 139, 189

Siguenza, bishop of, p. 204

Silvester I, Pope, p. 155, 156, 171

Simon, Prince of Taranto, p. 136

Simon de Montfort, Earl of Leicester, p. 121, 147

St Bernard, Abbot of Clairveaux, p. 18

St Blaise, p. 158, 159, 161, 163, 164, 171

St Castrensis, p. 153

St Edmund the Martyr, p. 146

St Edward the Confessor, King of England, p. 62, 177

St George, p. 171

St Giles, p. 158

St Gilles, counts of, p. 25, 72

St Gregory I, Pope, p. 171
St Hildegard, Abbess of Bingen, p. 21
St Hugh, Bishop of Lincoln, p. 50
St John the Baptist, p. 163, 164, 171
St John the Evangelist, p. 171, 180
St Lawrence of Rome, p. 155, 156, 161, 171
St Margaret, Queen of Scotland, p. 19, 22, 62, 177
St Margaret of Hungary, p. 168
St Martin of Tours, p. 157
St Mary, Virgin Mother of Christ, p. 17, 18, 19, 20, 21, 23, 49, 61, 106, 140, 156, 157, 158, 171, 180, 183, 196, 198, 206
St Maurice, p. 169
St Oswald, King of Northumbria, p. 106, 160, 161, 162, 169, 170
St Peter, p. 171
St Stephen, p.155, 156, 171
St Thomas Aquinas, p. 157
St Thomas Becket, Archbishop of Canterbury, p. 13, 28, 34, 48, 51, 69, 74, 84, 86, 87, 88, 89, 90, 92, 93, 126, 143, 145-9, 151-61, 163-8, 170, 171, 172, 175, 184, 196, 199, 208, 211
St Thomas the Apostle, p.157
St Wulfstan, Bishop of Worcester, p. 170
Stephen, Count of Blois, p. 178
Stephen, King of England,p. 73, 178, 179, 190, 193
Stephen I, Count of Burgundy, p. 113
Stephen I, King of Hungary, p. 167
Stephen III, King of Hungary, p. 84, 167
Stephen IV, King of Hungary, p. 167
Stephen of Perche, p. 85, 86
Striguil, earl of, p. 39, 70
Suger, abbot of St Denis, p. 120, 194

Tancred of Lecce, King of Sicily, p. 78, 85, 86, 133, 136, 137-8, 139
Tarragona, archbishop of, p. 120, 165
Tartas, Viscount of, p. 75, 120
Tello Pérez de Meneses, p. 74
Teresa Ansúrez, Queen of León, p. 196
Teresa Afonso, Infanta of Portugal, p. 74, 75
Teresa Fernández de Traba, Queen of León, p. 74
Teresa of Portugal, Queen of León, p. 114, 206
Theobald, abbot and bishop of Monreale, 131
Theobald, archbishop of Canterbury, p. 33
Theobald II, Count of Blois (Theobald IV of Champagne), p. 178
Theobald III, Count of Champagne, p. 124
Theobald Chabot, p. 74
Thibaud, abbot of Cluny, p. 86
Thomas, Earl of Lancaster, p. 147
Toledo, archbishop of, p. 166, 195, 204, 205
Toulouse, count of, p. 71, 73, 77, 92, 110, 181
Tricarico, bishop of, p. 135

Turgot of Durham, p. 62
Turpenay, abbot of, p. 186
Tustino, bishop of Mazzara, p. 131

Udo, bishop of Hildesheim, p. 61
Urban II, Pope, p. 167
Urraca, Queen of León-Castile, p. 183
Urraca of Castile, Queen of Portugal, p. 107, 112, 117, 118, 169, 182, 183, 195, 199, 207
Urraca of Zamora, Infanta of León, p. 196-7

Valerian, Emperor of Rome, p. 155
Vermudo III, King of León, p. 196
Victor IV, Pope, p. 128, 167
Vierzon, abbot of, p. 124
Violante of Hungary, Queen of Aragón, p. 111
Vladislav II, Duke of Bohemia, p. 160

Wace, p. 59, 63, 177, 180
Waldemar I, King of Denmark, p. 105
Walter, archbishop of Palermo, p. 85, 87, 88, 89, 131, 135, 152, 153, 155
Walter de Moac, p. 131
Walter of Coutances, bishop of Lincoln, archbishop of Rouen, p. 85
Warenne, earl of, p. 70
Welf VI, Margrave of Tuscany, Duke of Spoleto, p. 158
William, chaplain of the altar of St Thomas at Toledo, p. 165
William, Count of Morisco, p. 152
William, Viscount of Casteleraldo, p. 74
William I, Count of Boulogne, p. 178
William I, Count of Burgundy, p. 113
William IX, Count of Poitiers, p. 31, 50, 179
William X, Count of Poitou, p. 179
William IV, Count of Ponthieu, p. 130
William IX, Duke of Aquitaine, p. 58, 72, 181, 189
William X, Duke of Aquitaine, p. 71, 72, 181, 189
William I, King of England, p. 62, 177, 178, 179, 181
William II, King of England, p. 177
William I, the Lion, King of Scotland,p. 105, 131, 147, 148, 149, 151
William I, King of Sicily, p. 83, 84, 85, 132, 136, 139, 140, 189
William II, King of Sicily, p. 16, 17, 18, 25, 31, 41, 57, 67, 79, 81-92, 95, 97, 130, 131-7, 138, 139, 140, 152, 153, 154, 155, 156, 157, 171, 180, 181, 189, 194, 201, 210, 211
William Adelin, son of Henry I, p. 177, 190
William Clito, Count of Flanders, titular duke of Normandy, p. 129
William FitzOsbert, p. 131
William of Blois, Count of Sully, p. 178

William of Conches, p. 58, 59

William of Pavia, cardinal, p. 86, 128, 167

William of Winchester, Lord of Lüneberg, p. 52, 104, 105, 158, 181

William the Marshal, Earl of Pembroke, p. 130

Winchester, bishop of, p. 81, 94, 125

Index of Places

Agen, p. 186, 187
Agenais, p. 186
Ägidienkloster, p. 158
Ágreda, p. 117
Aguilar, p. 114
Aguilar de Campóo, Abbey of, p. 74, 109
Aguilar de Mola, p. 114
Aguilar de Pedrajo, p. 114
Alarcos, p. 34, 120
Álava, p.119
Alba de Bubal, p. 114
Alcabón, p. 165
Alcaraz, p. 118
Alcobaça, Monastery of, p. 112, 199, 207
Alión, p. 114
Almeria, p. 34, 75
Alnwick, p.147
Alverdiscott, p. 123
Amaya, p. 109, 114
Amedo, p. 109
Andalucia, p. 108
Angers, p. 33, 38, 194, 199
Angoulême, p. 79
Anjou, p. 38, 71, 115, 124, 129, 179, 180, 189, 190
Antioch, p. 84, 180
Apulia, p. 84, 90, 134, 135, 136
Aquitaine, p. 35, 39, 71, 74, 77, 115-6, 179
Aragón, p. 34, 71, 73, 75, 77, 108, 110, 112, 119, 120, 183, 196, 197, 210
Arbroath, Abbey of, p. 148, 149
Argentan, p. 39, 104, 145, 162
Ariza, p. 117
Arlanzón, p. 108
Arundel, p. 123
Astorga, p. 114
Astudillo, p. 109, 114
Asturias, p. 114
Atienza, p. 110
Augsburg, p. 88
Auvergne, p. 116
Avià 110
Avranches, p. 88, 127, 145, 146, 149

Bagnara, p. 137, 138
Barbastro, p. 109
Barbeaux, Abbey of, p. 203
Barcelona, p. 72, 73
Bari, p. 152

Baugé, p. 123
Bavaria, p. 104, 105, 160, 164, 170
Bayeux, p. 37, 124
Bayonne, p. 120
Béarn, p. 119
Beaufort, p. 123
Beauvais, p. 128
Bec, Abbey of, p.58, 201
Bedfordshire, p. 39
Belinchón, p. 114
Belorado, p. 109
Benevento, p. 84
Berkeley, p. 123
Berkhampsted, p. 105, 123
Berkshire, p. 36, 37, 38, 123
Berlanga, p. 113
Berry, p. 116, 130
Bersenza, p. 134, 135
Biccari, p. 134
Bidasoa, p. 119
Bigorre, p. 119
Blois-Champagne, p. 127, 129
Bonmoulins, p. 79
Bonneville, Convent of, p. 187
Bonneville-sur-Touques, p. 123, 125
Bordeaux, p. 16, 35, 40, 72, 73, 74, 75, 78, 116, 120, 121, 122
Bourges, p. 116, 130
Boutavant, p. 116
Bouvines, p. 120
Brascote, p. 123
Bristol, p. 58
Brittany, p. 71, 115
Brunswick, p. 103, 105, 106, 158, 159, 161, 163
Brunswick, Cathedral of, p. 28, 157, 163, 164, 193, 201
Buanga, p. 114
Buckinghamshire, p. 39
Burgo de Osma, p. 108
Burgos, p. 71, 73, 107, 108, 109, 115, 116, 117, 118, 121, 122, 182, 194, 199, 204
Burgos, Cathedral of, p. 107
Burón, p. 114
Bury St Edmunds, p. 146
Byzantium, p. 84, 85, 87, 88, 164

Cabezón de Pisuerga, p. 110
Cabrero, p. 114

Caen, p. 33, 39, 93, 104, 124, 130, 145
Cagnano Varano, p. 134
Calabria, p. 81, 91, 137
Calahorra, p. 109
Calatrava, Order of, p. 74
Candela, p. 134
Candrei, p. 114
Cantabria, p. 73
Canterbury, p. 92, 93, 105, 146, 155
Canterbury, Cathedral of, p. 143, 146, 148, 149, 159
Capella Palatina, p. 155, 189
Capilla de Santiago, p. 165
Caprile, p. 134, 135
Capua, p. 136
Capua, Cathedral of, p. 153
Carrión, p. 75, 113, 114
Castelpagano, p. 134
Castile, p. 13, 15, 16, 17, 28, 31, 34, 52, 67, 71, 73, 74, 75, 79, 86, 91, 97, 103, 108, 109, 112, 113, 114, 115, 116, 117, 118, 119, 120, 121, 136, 143, 149, 151, 153, 156, 165, 166, 167, 171, 183, 185, 194, 197, 198, 199, 205, 210, 211
Castogonzalo, p. 114
Castro-Urdiales, p. 73
Castro de Esteban, p. 109
Castro de los Judíos de Mayorga, p. 114
Castrojeriz, p. 109
Castroverde, p. 114
Catalonia, p. 165, 166
Catania, p. 152
Cava, Abbey of, p. 189
Caviedes, p. 109
Cea, river, p. 75
Cefalu, p. 85, 189
Cellorigo y Haro, p. 114
Cervera, p. 109
Châteauneuf, p. 127
Château-du-Loir, p. 123
Chateau-Gaillard, p. 116
Cherbourg, p. 36, 37
Chichester, p. 123
Chinon, p. 40, 41, 104, 191, 202
Citeaux, Abbey of, p. 198, 199
Ciurana, p. 109
Clarendon, p. 167
Cluny, Abbey of, p. 197
Coëffort, Abbey of, p. 125
Colchester, Abbey of, p. 153
Colle, p. 114
Cologne, p. 87
Compostela, p. 104
Condom, p. 187
Constantinople, p. 58, 87, 193
Cordoba, p. 34

Corel, p. 114
Coupar Angus, Church of, p. 148
Cuenca, p. 34, 35, 74, 75, 165, 166
Curiel, p. 110
Cyprus, p. 78, 79, 186

Daroca, p. 109
Devizes, p. 41
Devon, p. 36, 37, 123
Domfront, p. 34, 37, 123, 124
Dover, p. 38, 39, 69, 104, 105
Dueñas, p. 109

England, p. 16, 31, 35, 36, 37, 38, 39, 41, 52, 62, 69, 71, 73, 78, 81, 82, 83, 84, 86, 87, 88, 89, 90, 91, 93, 96, 104, 105, 119, 120, 121, 123, 124, 125, 126, 127, 128, 131, 132, 133, 139, 146, 152, 158, 159, 161, 162, 167, 170, 183, 205
Epila, p. 109
Erfurt, p. 104
Essex, p. 123
Este, p. 163
Esztergom, p. 168
Evreux, p. 116
Exeter, p. 123

Falaise, p. 36, 123, 124, 125
Faversham, Abbey of, p. 193
Filizi, p. 134, 135
Flanders, p. 107
Fontenay, p. 199
Fontevrault, Abbey of, p. 13, 28, 35, 40, 41, 50, 53, 57, 180, 184, 185-91, 193-200, 201-4, 205, 208, 211
France, p. 16, 35, 37, 52, 59, 63, 75, 83, 86, 107, 115, 116, 119, 120, 124, 126, 127, 128, 129, 130, 132, 135, 158, 166, 167, 190, 210
Frómista, p. 114

Gaillon, p. 115
Galicia, p. 114
Garonne, river, p. 72
Gascony, p. 78, 101, 105, 116, 119-22, 123, 126
Germany, p. 50, 69, 70, 78, 88, 91, 103, 104, 157, 158, 162, 164, 165, 169, 201
Gisors, p. 127, 129
Gloucestershire, p. 41, 123
Gorron, p. 145
Goslar, p. 103, 163
Gozón, p. 114
Graçay, p. 116
Grañon, p. 109
Grantham, p. 123
Guipúzcoa, p. 119

Gutierre Muñoz, p. 204

Hamburg, Cathedral of, p. 157
Hampshire, p. 36, 37, 82, 123
Hautes-Bruyères, Priory of, p. 190, 204
Helmarshausen, Monastery of, p. 157, 161
Hertfordshire, p. 123
Hertzburg, p. 106
Hildesheim, p. 61, 70, 106, 134, 160
Hildesheim, Cathedral of, p. 106, 160, 161, 170
Hita, p. 110
Holy Apostles, Church of the, p. 193
Holy Land, the, p. 63, 70, 78, 79, 86, 95, 96, 105, 137, 152, 161, 162, 193
Holy Sepulchre, Church of, p. 106, 164, 193
Holy Trinity, Aldgate, p. 33
Holy Trinity, Cava, p. 153
Huerta, p. 117
Hungary, p. 84, 87, 89, 167-8

Ilchester, p. 123
Ile d'Oléron, p. 185
Isle of Wight, p. 37
Issoudun, p. 116
Italy, p. 78, 84, 88, 102, 152
Ivry, p. 92

Jaca, p. 75, 205
Jaunay, p. 123
Jerusalem, p. 18, 87, 93, 95, 96, 106, 164, 193, 197

Kenn, p. 123
Kenton, p. 123

La Couture, Abbey of, p. 125
La Flèche, p. 123
La Isla, p. 114
La Reole, p. 120
Lambeth, p. 155
Lambourn, p. 123
Las Huelgas de Burgos, Convent of, p. 15, 19, 28, 50, 108, 115, 117, 122, 165, 181, 182, 183, 186, 191, 194-200, 201, 204-8, 210, 211
Las Navas de Tolosa, p. 34, 108, 116, 118
Las Samozas, p. 114
L'Epau, Abbey of, p. 126, 201, 202
Le Goulet, p. 124, 129
Le Lys, Convent of, p. 198, 199
Le Mans, p. 37, 125, 126, 201
León, p. 34, 63, 75, 108, 112, 113, 114, 115, 118, 182, 196, 197, 198, 210
León-Castile, p. 119, 183
Les Andelys, p. 115
Les Casses, p. 187, 211

Lesina, p. 134
Lespinasse, Priory of, p. 189
Lifton, p. 123
Limassol, p. 78, 79, 123, 124
Limoges, p. 39, 40, 153
Lincoln, p. 86, 87, 127, 153
Lincolnshire, p. 123
Lisbon, p. 34
Loches, p. 79, 123, 125
Lodi, p. 78
Logroño, p. 109
Loire, River, p. 120
Lombardy, p. 78
London, p. 36, 38, 81, 82, 93, 104, 105, 123, 131, 159
Lübeck, p. 104
Lugaz, p. 114
Lüneburg, p. 70, 104

Magaz, p. 114
Magdeburg, p. 104, 169
Magdeburg, Cathedral of, p. 169
Maine, p. 38, 71, 115, 123
Mainz, p. 104
Malmesbury, p. 123
Mantes, p. 126
Margaret Island, p. 168
Marston, p. 123
Matallana, Monastery of, p. 75
Maubisson, Abbey of, p. 19, 198, 199
Medina del Campo, p. 110
Medrano, p. 109
Mervent, p. 123
Messina, p. 78, 79, 91, 137, 138
Milan, p. 78
Minden, p. 103
Minden, Cathedral of, p. 103
Minervois, p. 75
Miranda de Nieva, p. 114
Mirebeau, p. 52
Monasterio, p. 114
Monasterio de Rodilla, p. 109
Monzón, p. 110
Monreale, Abbey-Church of, p. 17, 28, 134, 136, 140, 152-7, 171, 189, 194
Mont-Saint-Michel, Abbey of, p. 16, 34, 35, 127, 145
Mont Sant' Angelo, p. 134, 138
Montauban, p. 120
Montbazon, p. 123
Montblanc, p. 109
Montierneuf, Church of, p. 194
Montmirail, p. 39, 71
Murcia, p. 34, 108

Nájera, p. 108, 109, 114

Naples, p. 78, 82, 83, 91, 135
Navarre, p. 34, 77, 78, 79, 108, 110, 119, 120, 122, 126, 196, 205
Neubourg, p. 128
Neaufle, p. 127
Newminster, Abbey of, p. 158
Niort, p. 123, 187
Nola, p. 85
Nordhausen, Convent of, p. 169
Normandy, p. 25, 33, 34, 35, 37, 39, 52, 59, 69, 70, 72, 84, 90, 104, 105, 116, 123, 124, 125, 127, 128, 129, 146, 162
North Luffenham, p. 123
Northampton, p. 123
Northamptonshire, p. 52, 123
Northeim, Monastery of, p. 106
Northumbria, p. 170
Nottingham, p. 83

Oldenburg, p. 157
Oléron, p. 123
Orcejón, p. 114
Oreja, p. 110
Orgaz, p. 118
Osma, p. 110
Osma, Church of, p. 108
Our Lady, Church of, Constantinople, p. 193
Oviedo, p. 114
Oxford, p. 36
Oxfordshire, p. 123

Padua, p. 163
Palencia, p. 114
Palencia del Conde, p. 114
Palermo, p. 41, 82, 89, 91, 131, 132, 135, 136, 152, 153, 155, 189
Palermo, Cathedral of, p. 131, 133
Pancorbo, p. 109, 114
Paris, p. 116, 125, 126, 194, 203, 204
Pazluengos, p. 114
Peña Negra, p. 109, 110
Peñafiel, p. 110, 114
Peñafiel de Aller, p. 114
Perales, Abbey of, p. 74
Peschici, p. 134
Pest, p. 168
Pina, p. 109
Pisa, p. 78
Pisuerga, river, p. 74
Poitiers, p. 58, 90, 190, 194, 199
Poitiers, Cathedral of, p. 202
Poitou, p. 39, 40, 52, 53, 74, 89, 123, 126, 129, 189
Porchester, p. 124
Portilla, p. 114

Portugal, p. 34, 183, 199, 210
Poza de la Sal, p. 109
Provence, p. 73
Puente Itero, p. 74
Pyrenees, p. 123

Queenhithe, p. 123
Quercy, p. 77
Quintana, p. 113

Raia, p. 152
Ratzeburg, p. 164
Reading, Abbey of, p. 50, 153
Regensburg, p. 88, 104, 160, 161, 162, 170
Reggio, p. 78
Rhone, river, p. 82
Ripoll, Monastery of, p. 196
Riseholme, p. 123
Rocabruna, p. 123
Rockingham, p. 123
Rome, p. 18, 78, 84, 105, 114, 155
Rouen, p. 25, 33, 35, 37, 38, 53, 69, 179, 186, 187, 188
Rouen, Cathedral of, p. 187, 188
Royaumont, Abbey of, p. 166, 199
Rutland, p. 23

Sahagún, p. 73, 75, 196, 197
Saint-Bibien, Priory of, p. 189
Saint Clair, p. 134, 135
Saint-Jean-Pied-de-Port, p. 123
Saintes, p. 123
Salamanca, p. 166, 206
Salamanca, Cathedral of, p. 206
Salcombe, p. 150
Saldaña p. 109
Salerno, p. 91
Salisbury, p. 36, 41
San Castrenze, Sacristy of, p. 156
San Isidoro, Monastery Church of, p. 63, 115, 196, 197
San Nicolás del Real Camino, Hospital of, p. 75
San Pedro de Arlanza, p. 196
San Pelayo de Lodo, p. 114
San Salvador de Oña, p. 196, 197
San Sebastian, p. 120
San Tomás Cantuariense de Salamanca, p. 166
San Tomás Cantuariense de Toro, p. 166
Sancta Kyriaka, p. 155
Sant Toreat, p. 118
Santa Cruz de Coimbra, Church of, p. 112
Santa Cruz de la Seros, p. 205
Santa Cruz de Tineo, p. 114
Santa Maria dell'Ammiraglio, p. 155

Santa Maria del Real, Convent of, Najera, p. 195, 196, 205

Santa Maria di Maniace, Abbey of, p. 134, 140, 154

Santander, p. p. 109, 114

Santiago, Monastery of, p. 115

Santiago, Order of, p. 205

Santillana, p. 109

Santoña, p. 73

Saumur, p. 123

Savigny, p. 145

Saxony, p. 13, 15, 16, 28, 31, 38, 39, 52, 53, 62, 67, 69, 70, 91, 103, 104, 105, 110, 140, 143, 149, 151, 157, 158, 160, 161, 162, 163, 164, 165, 167, 170, 181, 211

Scone, Abbey of, p. 148

Segré, 124

Seine, river, p. 116

Seville, p. 121

Sicily, p. 13, 15, 16, 17, 28, 31, 41, 53, 63, 78, 79, 81, 82, 83, 84, 85, 86, 87, 88, 89, 90, 91, 92, 93, 94, 97, 103, 109, 110, 130, 131, 132, 133, 135, 137, 138, 139, 143, 149, 151, 152, 153, 155, 167, 171, 186, 193, 194, 210

Siero, p. 114

Sigena, Convent of, p. 77, 196, 197

Silos, Monastery of, p. 113

Siponto, p. 133, 134

Somerset, p. 123

Somport, p. 75

Soria, p. 108

Soussis, Priory of, p. 189

Southampton, p. 90, 131

Spain, p. 34, 67, 74, 77, 102, 108, 111, 116, 121, 126, 156, 197, 198, 199, 201

Speyer, p. 104

St Albans, Monastery of, p. 41

St Blaise, Church of, p. 103, 106, 159, 164

St Denis, Abbey of, p. 194, 197

St Etienne, Cathedral of, p. 187

St Front, Perigueux, p. 199

St Gilles, p. 82, 86, 90, 93

St Hilaire, Poitiers, p. 199

St Jürgen, Church of, p. 157

St James, Shrine of, p. 104

St John, Hospital of, p. 137

St John de Lama, Monastery of, p. 134

St Julien, Chapter of, p. 125

St Katherine's of Rouen, Church of, p. 187

St Martin, Angers, p. 199

St Mary de Pulsano, Monastery of, p. 134

St Mary Magdalene, Palermo, Chapel of, p. 189

St Nicholas, Church of, p. 157

St Nicolas, Church of, Angers, p. 194

St Pierre, Church of, p. 125

St-Pierre-de-Montmartre, Church of, p. 204

St Radegonde, Chapel of, p. 41, 202

St Sernin, Church of, p. 187

St Thomas, Priory of, p. 152

St Thomas of Pest, Church of, p. 168

St Thomas the Martyr of Esztergom, Church of, p. 168

Stamford, p. 123

Stanton, p. 123

Stralsund, p.157

Suabia, p. 158

Sussex, p. 123

Szent Tamas-hegy, p. 168

Taranto, p. 87, 88, 136

Tarazona, p. 75, 108

Tariego, p. 109

Tarragona, p. 108

Tay, river, p. 148

Tettens, Church of, p. 157

Tierra de Campos, p. 75

Toledo, p. 108, 109, 165, 166, 171, 172, 196, 199

Toledo, Cathedral of, p. 165, 166, 171, 172, 195, 196, 199

Toulouse, p. 13, 15, 53, 71, 72, 73, 77, 79, 90, 91, 92, 110, 114, 127, 135, 153, 181, 187, 189

Touraine, p. 115, 123

Tovia, p. 113, 114

Trianos, Abbey of, p. 75

Troo, p. 123

Tudela, p. 110

Turpenay, Abbey of, p. 188

Uncastillo, p. 109

Urval, p. 114

Valencia, p. 34, 114

Valencia de Don Juan, p. 114

Valladolid, p. 113, 114, 204

Vega de Ruiponce, p. 114

Ventosa, p. 114

Vexin, p. 93, 116, 127, 128, 129, 130

Viesgo, p. 109

Vieste, p. 133, 134

Viguera, p. 109

Villa Curiel, p. 114

Villaescusa, p. 110

Villalugán, p. 114

Villamartín, Hospital of, p. 75

Villanueva, p. 75

Walthamstow, p. 123

Westminster, p. 69, 82

Westminster, Abbey of, p. 193, 199

Wiflinton, p. 123
Wilton, p. 123
Wiltshire, p. 36, 37, 123
Winchester, p. 36, 37, 38, 39, 41, 52, 81, 82, 90, 92, 93, 104, 105, 158, 181
Windsor, p. 105, 110
Wismar, p. 157
Woodstock, p. 36

Worcester, Cathedral of, p. 170
Worms, p. 104
Würzburg, p. 69, 104

Zaragoza, p. 73
Zisa, Palace of, p. 131
Zurita, p. 109